The Culture of Samizdat

Library of Modern Russia

Advisory Board:

Jeffrey Brooks, Professor at Johns Hopkins University, USA
Michael David-Fox, Professor at Georgetown University, USA
Lucien Frary, Associate Professor at Rider University, USA
James Harris, Senior Lecturer at the University of Leeds, UK
Robert Hornsby, Lecturer at the University of Leeds, UK
Ekaterina Pravilova, Professor of History at Princeton University, USA
Geoffrey Swain, Emeritus Professor of Central and East European Studies at the University of Glasgow, UK
Vera Tolz-Zilitinkevic, Sir William Mather Professor of Russian Studies at the University of Manchester, UK
Vladislav Zubok, Professor of International History at the London School of Economics, UK

Building on Bloomsbury Academic's established record of publishing Russian studies titles, the *Library of Modern Russia* will showcase the work of emerging and established writers who are setting new agendas in the field.

At a time when potentially dangerous misconceptions and misunderstandings about Russia abound, titles in the series will shed fresh light and nuance on Russian history. Volumes will take the idea of 'Russia' in its broadest cultural sense and cover the entirety of the multi-ethnic lands that made up imperial Russia and the Soviet Union. Ranging in chronological scope from the Romanovs to today, the books will:

- Re-consider Russia's history from a variety of inter-disciplinary perspectives.
- Explore Russia in its various international contexts, rather than as exceptional or in isolation.
- Examine the complex, divisive and ever-shifting notions of 'Russia'.
- Contribute to a deeper understanding of Russia's rich social and cultural history.
- Critically re-assess the Soviet period and its legacy today.
- Interrogate the traditional periodisations of the post-Stalin Soviet Union.
- Unearth continuities, or otherwise, among the tsarist, Soviet and post-Soviet periods.

- Re-appraise Russia's complex relationship with Eastern Europe, both historically and today.
- Analyse the politics of history and memory in post-Soviet Russia.
- Promote new archival revelations and innovative research methodologies.
- Foster a community of scholars and readers devoted to a sharper understanding of the Russian experience, past and present.

Books in the series will join our list in being marketed globally, including at conferences – such as the BASEES and ASEEES conventions. Each will be subjected to a rigorous peer-review process and will be published in hardback and, simultaneously, as an e-book. We also anticipate a second release in paperback for the general reader and student markets.

For more information, or to submit a proposal for inclusion in the series, please contact:

Rhodri Mogford, Publisher, History (Rhodri.Mogford@bloomsbury.com).

New and forthcoming:
Fascism in Manchuria: The Soviet-China Encounter in the 1930s, Susanne Hohler
The Idea of Russia: The Life and Work of Dmitry Likhachev, Vladislav Zubok
The Tsar's Armenians: A Minority in Late Imperial Russia, Onur Onol
Myth Making in the Soviet Union and Modern Russia: Remembering World War II in Brezhnev's Hero City, Vicky Davis
Building Stalinism: The Moscow Canal and the Creation of Soviet Space, Cynthia Ruder
Russia in the Time of Cholera: Disease and the Environment under Romanovs and Soviets, John Davis
Soviet Americana: A Cultural History of Russian and Ukrainian Americanists, Sergei Zhuk
Stalin's Economic Advisors: The Varga Institute and the Making of Soviet Foreign Policy, Ken Roh
Ideology and the Arts in the Soviet Union: The Establishment of Censorship and Control, Steven Richmond
Nomads and Soviet Rule: Central Asia under Lenin and Stalin, Alun Thomas
The Russian State and the People: Power, Corruption and the Individual in Putin's Russia, edited by Geir Hønneland et al.
The Communist Party in the Russian Civil War: A Political History, Gayle Lonergan

Criminal Subculture in the Gulag: Prisoner Society in the Stalinist Labour Camps, Mark Vincent

Power and Politics in Modern Chechnya: Ramzan Kadyrov and the New Digital Authoritarianism, Karena Avedissian

Russian Pilgrimage to the Holy Land: Piety and Travel from the Middle Ages to the Revolution, Nikolaos Chrissidis

The Fate of the Bolshevik Revolution, edited by Lara Douds, James Harris, and Peter Whitehead

Writing History in Late Imperial Russia, Frances Nethercott

Translating England into Russian, Elena Goodwin

Gender and Survival in Soviet Russia, translated and edited by Elaine MacKinnon

Publishing in Tsarist Russia, edited by Yukiko Tatsumi and Taro Tsurumi

New Drama in Russian: Performance, Politics and Protest, edited by Julie Curtis

The Culture of Samizdat: Literature and Underground Networks in the Late Soviet Union, Josephine von Zitzewitz

The Culture of Samizdat

Literature and Underground Networks in the Late Soviet Union

Josephine von Zitzewitz

BLOOMSBURY ACADEMIC
LONDON • NEW YORK • OXFORD • NEW DELHI • SYDNEY

BLOOMSBURY ACADEMIC
Bloomsbury Publishing Plc
50 Bedford Square, London, WC1B 3DP, UK
1385 Broadway, New York, NY 10018, USA
29 Earlsfort Terrace, Dublin 2, Ireland

BLOOMSBURY, BLOOMSBURY ACADEMIC and the Diana logo
are trademarks of Bloomsbury Publishing Plc

First published in Great Britain 2021
This paperback edition published in 2022

Copyright © Josephine von Zitzewitz, 2021

Josephine von Zitzewitz has asserted her right under the Copyright,
Designs and Patents Act, 1988, to be identified as Author of this work.

Cover design by Tjaša Krivec
Cover image: Historic typewriter from the collection of the Research and
Information Centre 'Memorial', St Petersburg. Photograph by Evgeniya Kulakova

All rights reserved. No part of this publication may be reproduced or transmitted
in any form or by any means, electronic or mechanical, including photocopying,
recording, or any information storage or retrieval system, without prior
permission in writing from the publishers.

Bloomsbury Publishing Plc does not have any control over, or responsibility for,
any third-party websites referred to or in this book. All internet addresses given
in this book were correct at the time of going to press. The author and publisher
regret any inconvenience caused if addresses have changed or sites have
ceased to exist, but can accept no responsibility for any such changes.

Every effort has been made to trace copyright holders and to obtain their
permissions for the use of copyright material. The publisher apologizes for
any errors or omissions and would be grateful if notified of any corrections
that should be incorporated in future reprints or editions of this book.

A catalogue record for this book is available from the British Library.

Library of Congress Cataloging-in-Publication Data
Names: von Zitzewitz, Josephine, author.
Title: The culture of samizdat : literature and underground networks
in the late Soviet Union / Josephine von Zitzewitz.
Description: London ; New York : Bloomsbury Academic, 2020. | Series: Library
of modern Russia | Includes bibliographical references and index.
Identifiers: LCCN 2020029956 | ISBN 9781788313766 (hardback) | ISBN 9781350229310 (paperback) |
ISBN 9781350142633 (ebook) | ISBN 9781350142640 (epub)
Subjects: LCSH: Underground literature–Soviet Union–History and criticism. |
Underground press publications–Soviet Union–History. | Underground
literature–Publishing–Soviet Union–History. | Dissenters–Soviet Union. |
Books and reading–Soviet Union.
Classification: LCC PG3026.U5 V66 2020 | DDC 070.50947–dc23
LC record available at https://lccn.loc.gov/2020029956

ISBN:		
	HB:	978-1-7883-1376-6
	PB:	978-1-3502-2931-0
	ePDF:	978-1-3501-4263-3
	eBook:	978-1-3501-4264-0

Series: Library of Modern Russia

Typeset by Integra Software Services Pvt. Ltd.

To find out more about our authors and books visit www.bloomsbury.com
and sign up for our newsletters.

Contents

List of figures	viii
List of tables	ix
Acknowledgements	x
Note on the text	xii
Introduction	1
1 Samizdat: A culture of readers and networks	5
2 Readers: An online survey for samizdat readers	25
3 Manufacturers: Samizdat typists	65
4 Collectors: Samizdat libraries	93
5 Patrons: Samizdat journal editors	121
6 Institutions: Literary samizdat and official culture	149
Conclusion	173
Notes	177
Bibliography	223
Index	242

Figures

1 The Communication Circuit   15

Tables

1	Decade of birth	27
2	Sex	27
3	City of birth	27
4	Education	28
5	Samizdat texts by genre	34
6	Samizdat texts	36
7	Samizdat texts by genre II	39
8	Readers of samizdat	56
9	Samizdat activities	59
10	Roles in the samizdat process	98

Acknowledgements

The research on which this book is based was made possible thanks to a Leverhulme Trust/British Academy Early Career Fellowship, held at the University of Cambridge in 2014–2017 and generously supplemented by the Isaac Newton Trust. I finished the manuscript during my Marie Skłodowska-Curie Fellowship (Horizon 2020, MSCA-IF) at the Arctic University of Norway in Tromsø, a place that furnished me with ideal working conditions.

Ideas develop best in conversation with a knowledgeable and creative interlocutor. I am most grateful to Irina Flige, who inspired and encouraged me to interview typists and others who manufactured samizdat in Leningrad-St Petersburg and introduced me to many of those whose voices feature in this volume. The idea of surveying samizdat readers belongs to Gennadii Kuzovkin. He developed the reader questionnaire which helped us collect much of the data I have used for this volume and continues to collect more responses.

This is a book about people and social interaction, and it would have been impossible to realize without the hospitality of those I have come to know over many years of researching the unofficial culture of Leningrad-St Petersburg in the 1970s. For many of them, this period forms part of their own biography, and they have been generous with time, stories, knowledge, books, samizdat and additional contacts. I am most grateful. Special thanks to Polina Bezprozvannaia, who tirelessly collected survey responses from among her friends. Many colleagues have supported me at various stages during the research and writing period. Among them are Susan Larsen, who provided very insightful feedback on my initial grant application to the Leverhulme Trust, and Martin Dewhirst, who attentively read a draft of what became Chapter 2. A big thank you also to Kirsty Jane Falconer for her invaluable help with questions of style!

Material that has made its way into the various chapters of this book has appeared in the following publications:

- A previous version of Chapter 2 and parts of Chapter 1 appeared as 'Reading Samizdat', in *Reading Russia: A History of Reading in Modern Russia*, edited by Damiano Rebecchini and Raffaella Vassena (Milan: Ledizioni, 2020).

- 'Vielseitige Persönlichkeit: Befunde über den Leser des Samizdat', *Osteuropa* 1–2 (2019): 149–62.
- 'Self-Canonisation as a Way into the Canon: the Case of the Leningrad Underground', *Australian and East European Studies* 31 (2017): 197–228.
- 'Reader Questionnaires in Samizdat Journals: Who owns Alexander Blok?', in *Dropping out of Socialism,* edited by Juliane Furst and Josie McLellan (Lanham, MD: Lexington, 2016), 107–27.
- 'Introduction', with Ann Komaromi, to the samizdat journal *37* for the Electronic Archive 'Project for the Study of Dissidence and Samizdat', University of Toronto Libraries. Available online: http://samizdatcollections.library.utoronto.ca/islandora/object/samizdat%3A37 (accessed 1 October 2019).

Josephine von Zitzewitz
October 2019

Note on the text

Transliteration from Russian follows Library of Congress standards; however, in the body of the text, I have used the established English transliteration for well-known figures: Mandelshtam rather than Mandel'shtam, Dostoevsky and Bukovsky rather than Dostoevskii and Bukovskii, Joseph Brodsky rather than Iosif Brodskii. I have also anglicized common first names for the sake of readability: Alexander, Tatiana, Olga, Yurii, Ilya rather than Aleksandr, Tat'iana, Ol'ga, Iurii, Il'ia. In the bibliography, however, Library of Congress transliteration is used for all Russian names.

All translations from the Russian, unless indicated otherwise, are my own. Many copies of Russian samizdat journals are not paginated. In cases where I refer to such a copy no page references are given.

Introduction

Samizdat, that is, the production and circulation of texts without the involvement of the state publishing houses and the censor's office, was a mass phenomenon in the later decades of the Soviet Union, during the years under Brezhnev commonly referred to as Stagnation (*Zastoi*). After Stalin's death in 1953 and Khrushchev's denunciation of the Stalinist 'personality cult' at the 20th Party Congress in 1956, the repressions eased and the central bureaucracy released its grip on culture. The resulting resurgence of cultural activity was one of the major phenomena of the period that became known as the Thaw (*Ottepel'*). The state, however, retained its monopoly on publishing the written word. This brief spell of relative openness unleashed forces in society that proved impossible to suppress when the regime returned to a more restrictive stance.

There were many genres of samizdat, and their origins, as well as the driving forces behind them, were heterogeneous. However, it seems fair to say that these driving forces can be divided into three main categories. The first was a hunger for a greater variety of literary and other reading matter, as well as for information. This hunger affected a broad spectrum of educated society, and these people became readers of samizdat. The second was a hunger for platforms for creative self-expression that were not subject to the aesthetic and/or political proscriptions of the state. Those who experienced this hunger became samizdat authors. The third category concerned the awareness that the Soviet government had been violating, and continued to violate, human rights in contravention of its own legislation. Those who felt compelled to engage with this situation, for example by collecting and publicizing relevant information to their fellow citizens, became what we call dissidents. Dissidents made samizdat famous beyond the Soviet Union, but remained a minority among its practitioners. The three categories overlapped significantly; naturally, all of those who belong to the second and third category also form part of the first.

Samizdat was a system of informal networks which, as a bottom line, supplied reading material that could not be obtained through the official channels. This reading material ranged from pre-revolutionary poetry to religious texts; or, at the extreme end of the spectrum, yoga manuals and the *Kama Sutra*. And then there were political texts – often concerned with human rights issues – that could earn the reader a prison sentence if they were found in his or her possession. It is impossible to give a reliable figure for how many people were involved at every stage, from merely reading to creating and disseminating texts. Moreover, this figure varied widely depending on the decade. Overall estimates range from hundreds of thousands to several million people. And while samizdat activity was naturally highest in big cities, especially the capital city of Moscow, it was present across the entire territory of the USSR.

In the three decades since the end of the Soviet Union, much has been written on samizdat and its protagonists – whether texts or people. In the last decade, scholarship has become increasingly diverse in its approaches, involving researchers from a multitude of disciplines. This book studies neither innovative and/or scandalous texts nor courageous individuals and their ideas and struggles. It is not a history of samizdat or of one of its genres, and it uses cultural theory sparingly. It is a book about people. My focus is on the informal networks that gave birth to the samizdat phenomenon and become harder to research with each passing year. While testimonies about samizdat are many, very few focus on the practicalities of reading, producing and distributing texts and specifically on the structures that enabled these activities. Those witness accounts that do exist languish in archives or are published in specialist volumes or across various, often obscure, websites with no obvious link between them.

Samizdat networks, more or less clandestine and with informal structures and transient membership, were driven by personal acquaintance and mutual trust. De facto illegal, they left few if any records. While it is sometimes possible closely to analyse one particular group, especially if it pursued a dedicated aim, for example, the production of a journal, the phenomenon as a whole cannot be analysed systematically, much less quantitatively. All that is left of the multiple overlapping networks is a hole-ridden tapestry, impossible to restore. Human memory is irreplaceable when it comes to exploring the aspects of samizdat that depend on relationships. Memory is random and fallible, and yet eyewitness accounts have two invaluable benefits: they reflect the particular as opposed to the general, and they are narrative. And it is this type of information, if any, that enables those who remain outside the experience not only to accumulate knowledge, but to understand. Moreover, when many eyewitness accounts come together in one place, they achieve something greater than the sum of their parts: they recreate, as far as it is possible, an impression of the atmosphere in which the remembered phenomenon took place. One poignant example of the power of the eyewitness account is Raisa Orlova and Lev Kopelev's testimony to the importance of poetry in the years after Stalin's death. Over six pages, in informal and convoluted style and with the help of many examples and quotations, they explain how it came to be that 'the flood of poetry was attractive in itself, made us happy and was understood by many as a phenomenon of the political spring'.[1] A story such as theirs might enable a present-day reader to comprehend why a new poet such as Evgenii Evtushenko drew crowds large enough to fill a football stadium. Simply stating that, in the early 1960s, the public readings of certain poets attracted tens of thousands of people does not have the same effect.

This book explores thematic clusters while foregrounding the voices of individuals with personal experience of reading, reproducing, editing and circulating samizdat texts. Most of the testimonies have been collected especially for this study via an online survey and a series of narrative interviews. In addition, I have drawn on a number of published interviews and selected memoirs, as well as archival sources. Bringing these testimonies together in one volume fulfils three different functions: to preserve and publicize the newly collected testimonies; to promote rare published sources that are unknown or hard to access; and to provide a robust empirical base that allows us to conceptualize several different types of samizdat networks.

Chapter 1 conceptualizes the samizdat reader in as far as it is possible to define them. Particular attention is paid to the multiplicity of roles the reader fulfilled in a process that was devoid of the middlemen active in print culture, such as printing presses and editors. The chapter also outlines the challenges facing the researcher who sets out to study the samizdat reader, and introduces theoretical ideas about samizdat networks.

Chapter 2 evaluates the responses to an online survey for samizdat readers, gathered in the period 2017–2018. This survey allowed me to test several widespread hypotheses about samizdat, derived from 'common knowledge' and the testimony of a small number of well-known samizdat activists, against empirical data. It also throws into sharp relief the extraordinary role the figure of the reader played in the process of samizdat, this time from a practical angle.

The remaining four chapters investigate ever more specifically defined networks. Chapter 3 is dedicated to a lamentably under-researched group: the typists who produced samizdat on a larger scale. Their commitment was pivotal to the process, especially to the production of periodicals, which became common in the 1970s. This chapter is mainly based on a series of narrative interviews I collected in St Petersburg in 2015.

Throughout the 1970s, samizdat grew both more professional and more stratified. Distinct networks created institutions, such as libraries and journals, as well as literary criticism, conferences and prizes. These structures required a greater degree of organization and commitment; the roles of individuals became more specific.

Chapter 4 examines associations for the targeted exchange of samizdat texts; these associations effectively fulfilled the role of libraries. Their members copied and disseminated texts on a larger scale; some organizers left behind documentation and memoirs, thus providing the researcher with valuable case studies. This chapter is mainly based on published interviews and archival materials. The samizdat librarians studied for this chapter were committed to increasing the number of people who had access to alternative reading material; the libraries were squarely focused on the needs of the reader.

Chapters 5 and 6 are closely related. They comprise a series of case studies followed by a theoretical analysis of overlapping networks that effectively mimicked the regular institutions of print culture. The literary samizdat journals that emerged in Leningrad in the mid-1970s created communities that remained stable for a number of years. The texts published in these journals were devoid of the sensational appeal of a Solzhenitsyn novel, and they reflected a parallel world inside Soviet culture. Journal communities usually left ample documentation, first and foremost in the form of the journals themselves, but also in the memoirs and scholarly work subsequently undertaken by their editors. These chapters are based on narrative interviews with several journal editors, conducted in 2015, as well as a large number of published sources and scholarship. Perhaps the most surprising insight granted by these case studies is that the journals were orientated towards the needs of the unofficial writers rather than the readership. As such, they help us understand how samizdat networks came to create an alternative cultural sphere, fostering an environment in which authors outside the official cultural process could grow as artists. At the same time, the journals emerge as a structure built on, and ultimately specific to, the Soviet system. Studying their internal processes and their relationship to official culture affords a number of theoretical insights which are to some degree applicable to samizdat as a whole.

1

Samizdat: A culture of readers and networks

What was samizdat?

Samizdat developed in the second half of the 1950s on the crest of the poetry boom that saw newly famous poets such as Evgenii Evtushenko perform to full stadiums. Enthusiasm for poetry inspired cultural initiatives that were organized by interested citizens rather than any official structure, such as the weekly gatherings on Mayakovsky Square from 1958 onwards, where large groups of young people would read poetry out loud. In the centrally organized Soviet cultural sphere that had just emerged from Stalinism, such spontaneous initiatives were a novelty.

Poets who came onto the scene after Stalin's death, such as Evtushenko, Andrei Voznesenskii, Bella Akhmadulina, Robert Rozhdestvenskii and others, represented one group that captured the attention of the reading public. Another such group were the poets of the Silver Age who had been popular in the years preceding the 1917 revolution. In many cases their work had not been republished under Soviet rule, and some, notably Anna Akhmatova, Osip Mandelshtam and the returned émigré Marina Tsvetaeva, produced a significant body of work after the revolution that was never available in print. Silver Age texts re-emerged slowly during the late 1950s and 1960s; they had a huge influence on reading tastes and ultimately on the writing techniques of new poets.[1] New official editions notwithstanding – and such editions were always selective – Silver Age poets were not widely published. Readers who had access to their texts – for example because they owned pre-revolutionary editions – would copy out poems, frequently by hand, and share them with their acquaintances. Samizdat was born. This process is described in many written first-hand accounts, and the respondents to our online survey of samizdat readers, discussed in detail in Chapter 2, confirm its basic mechanics. Respondent #22 (b.1976) remembers that 'my first [samizdat] texts were my mum's handwritten copies of Esenin's poetry'.[2] One respondent dutifully recorded the characteristic mixture of old and new poetry: 'A lot of poetry was circulating. People were copying Tsvetaeva, by hand, from the books published in tiny print runs in the 1920s, and [Nikolai] Gumilev, but also [Naum] Korzhavin and [Joseph] Brodsky. I myself copied little, but provided many texts for people to copy.'[3]

The term 'samizdat' became attached to this phenomenon in the 1960s, but it predates the mass practice of circulating texts in this way. Its origin is commonly attributed to Nikolai Glazkov who, as early as the 1940s, would give self-bound typescripts of his prose miniatures to his friends, adorned with the word *samsebiaizdat* ('self-published' or 'self-publishing house') in the place where you would expect to find the name of the publishing house. *Samsebiaizdat* was a pun on the abbreviated names of official publishing houses such as *Litizdat* (Literary Publishing House) or *Gosizdat* (State Publishing House).[4] This means that samizdat was, from the very beginning, also an outlet for contemporary writers who could not, or did not try to, publish their texts in the official press. Some of the best-known Russian writers of the late twentieth century owe all, or most, of their reputation to samizdat. Among them are Alexander Solzhenitsyn (1918–2008) – whose *Arkhipelag Gulag* (*The Gulag Archipelago*, published in Paris in 1973) eclipsed the fame of the earlier, officially published *Odin den' Ivana Denisovicha* (*One Day in the Life of Ivan Denisovich*, 1962) – and the poet Joseph Brodsky (1940–1996). Both are Nobel Prize winners. Others include Venedikt Erofeev (1938–1990), Elena Shvarts (1948–2010) and Dmitrii Alexanderovich Prigov (1940–2007).

From the mid-1960s onwards, samizdat began to include material relating to history, religion, politics, public affairs and other topics. The non-literary texts that made samizdat famous to an international audience were generated by the members of the growing human rights movement (known as 'dissidents') and included letters of protest and news items, including the periodical human rights bulletin *Khronika tekushchikh sobytii* (*Chronicle of Current Events*, 1968–1983). The *Chronicle* was smuggled out to the West and republished in English.[5] Western radio stations, such as the BBC, Voice of America, Deutsche Welle and Radio Liberty (RL)/Radio Free Europe (RFE), the latter founded for the purpose of broadcasting to the Eastern bloc countries, broadcast such materials back to the Soviet Union, hugely increasing the audience for samizdat.[6] Samizdat proper, that is – textual material produced inside the Soviet Union – was increasingly supplemented by texts published abroad and smuggled back into the Soviet Union, a practice known as *tamizdat* (published over there). Many iconic texts, including Solzhenitsyn's novels and Brodsky's poetry, were published abroad, often decades before the first Soviet or Russian editions.

Samizdat texts today

The texts circulated in samizdat have been scrupulously collected and, in many cases, reproduced in print form. By now, lesser-known literary texts and political writings have been collected, too. The following overview of sources is indicative, but does not make a claim to completeness.

Two major sources exist in both book form and online: Viacheslav Igrunov's *Antologiia samizdata* (Anthology of Samizdat) is divided into sections for poetry, prose and social journalism (*publitsistika*).[7] The section on unofficial poetry collected in *Samizdat veka* (The Samizdat of the Century) has been incorporated into the *Russkaia virtual'naia biblioteka* (Russian Virtual Library).[8] The archives and records of Radio Liberty, which broadcast samizdat back to the Soviet Union, are at the Hoover Institution Library and Archives, with additional material held in the Open Society Archive at the Central European University in Budapest; many of the items of samizdat broadcast were made accessible online in 2016.[9] Different branches of the Memorial Society hold extensive samizdat archives, many of them from private collections.[10] The archive of the Forschungsstelle Osteuropa (Research Centre for East European Studies) at the University of Bremen holds a sizeable samizdat collection, sourced from private archives, alongside what might well be the largest existing collection of samizdat periodicals.[11] The University of Toronto's Project for the Study of Samizdat and Dissidence offers a database of Soviet samizdat periodicals, illustrated timelines of dissident movements, interviews with activists, and maps, attempting to render part of the process visible. Of particular value are the digital reproductions of samizdat periodicals, some of which have been made fully searchable.[12] The Keston Center at Baylor University, Texas, now holds the archives of Keston College/the Keston Institute, an organization founded in the UK in 1969 with the aim of researching religion in communist societies; the Institute amassed a large amount of religious samizdat.[13] The Tsentr Andreia Belogo (Andrei Belyi Centre) in St Petersburg is continuing to expand its digital archive of literary samizdat.[14] The ImWerden project, which set itself the ambitious goal of becoming the online library of the RuNet, the Russian internet, maintains a special section for 'Second Literature': namely, texts not officially published in the Soviet Union; the collection is large and texts are downloadable.[15] The now-defunct website of the International Samizdat Association published a list of archives holding samizdat collections.

Thus, if we consider samizdat to be merely a body of texts, the scholar or interested layperson will find plenty of sources. However, this is a reductive interpretation. Indeed, the question 'What was samizdat?' is hotly debated. A roundtable at the Memorial Society in 2014 asked researchers to consider precisely this question – 'Chto takoe samizdat?' (What is samizdat?).[16] Contemporary research has evolved beyond the focus on samizdat as a sociopolitical phenomenon that is often fixated solely on the content transmitted by the texts. In the introduction to the essay collection *Samizdat, Tamizdat and Beyond*, editors Friederike Kind-Kovacs and Jessie Labov invite their contributors to ponder whether samizdat was a publishing practice, a reading practice, a set of texts, or a state of mind; the collection stresses the function of samizdat as a media form.[17] The Russian historian Alexander Daniel calls samizdat a 'mode of existence of the text',[18] while the historian and archivist Elena Strukova discusses its importance as a 'memorial to book culture in the late 20th century'.[19] The Canadian researcher Ann Komaromi, who runs the Project for the Study of Samizdat and Dissidence, asks whether samizdat was a medium, a genre, a corpus of texts, or a textual culture,[20] an approach she developed further in her recent monograph.[21] The Italian scholar Valentina Parisi has produced a richly illustrated volume focusing on the samizdat reader that considers literary and cultural theory alongside the paratextual aspects of samizdat periodicals.[22]

Moreover, there are several dedicated outlets and discussion forums for questions relating to samizdat: the Memorial Society publishes a biannual almanac, *Acta Samizdatica: Zapiski o Samizdate* (Acta Samizdatica: Notes on Samizdat), which includes new research alongside archival publications. There are several bespoke Facebook groups facilitating the exchange of information, including the International Samizdat [Research] Association community and the Samizdat group.[23] This means that there is plenty of material available on the content transmitted by samizdat as well as on the material medium. Yet, surprisingly, little research has been conducted on the process of reading, and even less on the ordinary reader of samizdat. Or perhaps this should not come as a surprise, because the largest group involved in samizdat is notoriously difficult to research.

Samizdat readers

Are samizdat readers dissidents?

The literature – and public opinion, too – commonly understands samizdat as a function of 'dissidence', namely, the many forms in which different groups or individuals protested against the Soviet regime's practices. This is true in one direction only: all dissidents were involved in samizdat, which provided them with alternative social and communication networks. Indeed, reading samizdat was often the first step towards dissidence. To put it differently, reading uncensored texts inspired 'uncensored', independent thought. For a significant minority, the next logical step was the writing and circulation of their own texts, and/or various forms of activism, from the dissemination of texts to the creation of entire samizdat periodicals. Some actions were more or less political, such as the letters intellectuals wrote to protest against the arrest, in 1965, of Andrei Siniavskii and Yulii Daniel for publishing abroad;[24] the demonstration on Red Square on 25 August 1968, by eight people, against the Soviet occupation of Czechoslovakia in 1968;[25] or the foundation of the Moscow Helsinki Group, the oldest human rights group still operating in Russia, in 1977.[26]

One example of how reading forbidden literary texts led to a critical reassessment of Soviet ideology is the story of Sergei Khodorovich, who read Polish author Stanislaw Lem's 1971 collection *The Star Diaries*. His gradual move towards active dissidence saw him becoming one of the managers of the (unofficial and illegal) Public Foundation for Political Prisoners and their Families (Solzhenitsyn Foundation) in 1977, and culminated in arrest and a prison camp sentence.[27] The historian Leonid Zhmud' remembers how samizdat literature formed his political opinion, 'and so my modest role as a distributor of anti-Soviet literature was exceptionally beneficial for my subsequent work as a historian'.[28] The art historian Igor Golomshtok, who did not consider himself an active dissident, also remembers his own disagreement with the regime in the 1960s as being inspired by literature: 'We did not protest against the regime, but against the regime's lies ... This we learned from the songs of [Alexander] Galich and [Bulat] Okudzhava, the poems of [Joseph] Brodsky, the stories and later, the novels of [Vladimir] Voinovich, not to mention the Russian classics from Pushkin to Mandelshtam, Tsvetaeva and [Andrei] Platonov.'[29] Much of Soviet dissent was even more restrained and often did not directly engage with the regime at all. The poet Olga Sedakova remembers the mature cultural underground of the 1970s as follows: 'For us, culture in its broadest historical aspect signified the very freedom and soaring height of spirit denied to us by the Soviet system ... We all emerged from some kind of protest movement, which was not so much political as aesthetic or spiritual resistance.'[30] The degree to which samizdat was persecuted depended on the nature of the texts circulated. Naturally, texts engaging with the political situation and human rights abuses in the Soviet Union past or present, such as

Solzhenitsyn's *The Gulag Archipelago* and the *Chronicle of Current Events*, were more likely to lead to reprisals than 'purely' literary texts.[31]

Samizdat texts and the channels by which they circulated were instrumental to the functioning of informal networks, including those that readers, both Russian and Western, have in mind when they say 'dissidents'. Dissidents are 'all those who actively protested against the regime in one way or another: by signing protest letters, participating in demonstrations, or serving a camp sentence or term of exile'.[32] Most often, dissidents are equated with the Soviet human rights activists (*pravozashchitniki*, literally 'defenders of rights'). The human rights activists acted on a moral imperative but did not have a vision or indeed the desire to fight the system; indeed, their first 'action' was accompanied by an iconic slogan exhorting the authorities to 'Respect the Soviet Constitution'.[33] The activity of most groups that were critical of aspects of the official system was characterized by an emphasis on the provision of information and education via the written word.

It is in this function, as an information channel for dissidents, that veteran human rights activist Liudmila Alekseeva describes samizdat in her seminal survey *Istoriia inakomysliia v SSSR* (*The History of Dissent in the Soviet Union*). Characteristically, the section 'The Birth of Samizdat' is embedded into the chapter on human rights activists, although Alekseeva dutifully mentions the origins of samizdat in the circulation of poetry in the 1950s.[34] The English translation of the book differs in structure and carries additional information; here, the phenomenon of samizdat is described as 'The Core of the Movement' in a chapter dedicated to 'The Communication Network of Dissent'.[35] The tendency to treat samizdat as a function of dissidence can be observed in contemporary research, too: in 2017, the literary scholar and editor Gleb Morev published a book of twenty narrative interviews with Soviet dissidents, who all talk about samizdat as a function of their daily life, while their reading practice is reduced to a footnote.[36] The University of Toronto's Project for the Study of Samizdat and Dissidence implicitly identifies dissent and samizdat in its very title.

However, while all dissidents read samizdat, by no means all readers of samizdat were active dissidents. The dissidents numbered in the hundreds, the readers of samizdat at least in the hundreds of thousands. This is easier to understand when we consider that unofficially reproduced and circulated texts included a large number of works that were neither literary nor in any sense related to current affairs, but rather to everyday life or even leisure. The poet Lev Losev identifies six categories of samizdat texts: literary; political; religious and philosophical; mystical and occult; erotica; and instructions.[37] Elizaveta

Starshinina, a journalist from Irkutsk, remembers the early 1980s: 'Practically everybody had some samizdat at home, depending on their interests and level of education: instructions for yoga and urine therapy, handbooks for herbal remedies, guitar tabs of Beatles songs and even recipes for pickling vegetables at home. All this circulated actively, because there was no other way of obtaining information.'[38]

Samizdat was irrepressible. And it owed much of its vitality to the fact that it lacked any kind of central organization. But now this very guarantor of success constitutes a serious impediment to any attempt to reconstruct how people actually read samizdat and who these people were.

Silent witnesses

For the researcher, the biggest challenge is that samizdat culture resists most attempts at recording it using our usual tools. For a start, the only element of this culture that is easily accessible is the text itself, preserved in a private or public archive. But this text is intriguingly and frustratingly silent. If we are lucky, a preserved archival copy gives away two names: that of the author and that of the last person to read it. Even if other sources confirm that both these people participated in the samizdat chain – and that is not always the case – the preserved fragments are too few and far between to enable us to reconstruct the journey and readership of a given individual text. Samizdat's informal nature is only one reason why this journey is hard to trace. Its de facto illegality compounds the problem, as those involved often concealed their identity. Indeed, it is impossible to imagine a samizdat text accompanied by something like a borrowing sheet listing its readers. Only very few people marked their samizdat texts with their names – after all, an inscription could become incriminating evidence. Moreover, none of the statistics normally used by book historians are available, for example print run, editions, sales figures, reviews and translations. While printed books and journals feature information about editors, publishers and print runs, and libraries have borrowing registers, virtually no similar records exist for samizdat.

During an interview with Natalia Volokhonskaia, a samizdat typist and poet from Leningrad, we discussed the samizdat journal *Kolokol* (The Bell), which circulated in the 1960s and earned its makers lengthy prison camp sentences.[39] A scheme illustrating the circulation of the journal was part of the investigation file discovered in the KGB archive. When I remarked how interesting it was to look at the reconstruction of this small network, she replied: 'To make this possible you needed (a) observation, (b) interrogations and (c) people telling the truth during these interrogations. That's possible for *Kolokol,* for one copy, or for a couple of issues. But all the rest?'[40] Volokhonskaia's remark is instructive, locating samizdat reading firmly within the field of activities which people routinely concealed from those around them. By contrast, generalized accounts of the workings of samizdat networks are easy to find. This one is by Liudmila Alekseeva:

> The mechanism of samizdat was like this: the author would print their text in the way that was most accessible to a private individual under Soviet conditions – i.e. on the typewriter, in a few copies – and give these copies to his acquaintances. If one of them considered the text interesting, they would make copies from the copy they had got and give them to their acquaintances, and so on. The more successful a work the more quickly and widely it would be disseminated.[41]

This is a generic story lacking individual detail, but more importantly, its focus is – and this is typical – on the process of textual production at the expense of the process of reading. It is of course an exaggeration to say that the reading of samizdat left no traces at all. We find such traces, for example, in private diaries held in archives, as well as in published memoirs.[42] But, as a rule, these reminiscences make no attempt to establish or analyse the way in which reading networks functioned. In some isolated cases, specific networks were documented out of necessity. To give an example, Yurii Avrutskii, the organizer of what he called a 'club' for reading samizdat, decided to begin a register of texts and readers but encrypted the entries for fear of incriminating his friends should the register be found. The register has survived and can be seen among the papers of Avrutskii's private archive, held by the Memorial Society in Moscow. The papers are a valuable source precisely because Avrutskii has commented on them. However, without the owner's explanatory comments, records of this kind are of limited use to the researcher.[43]

Sources that focus explicitly on samizdat reading exist but are limited in scope for various reasons. One is a series of interviews conducted by Raisa Orlova, the philologist and wife of the well-known dissident Lev Kopelev, in Germany and other Western European countries in the early 1980s. In collaboration with the newly founded Research Centre for East European Studies at the University of Bremen, Orlova interviewed recent émigrés from the Soviet Union about their experience with samizdat. Her sample was small, however, and limited to people who had left the USSR, often as a result of persecution. Many of her respondents were active dissenters or prominent writers and consequently much more involved in samizdat than the average reader. What is more, they naturally protected their acquaintances who had remained in the Soviet Union by not giving names. Over the space of three years, Orlova managed to conduct just over fifty interviews. At the moment, they are held in a specialist archive, not available to the general public.[44] Similar restrictions hold true for contemporary initiatives, for example the Memorial Society's annual roundtables on samizdat[45] and the interviews with samizdat activists published on the website of the Project for the Study of Samizdat and Dissidence.[46] A number of memoirs contain longer accounts of reading samizdat.[47] Yet, once again, these are individual accounts that tell us little about the workings of the networks within which samizdat flourished, and often nothing about readers other than the author themselves. So the statement made by Elena Strukova, head of the Fond netraditsionnoi pechati (Collection of Non-traditional Print) at the Russian State Historical Library (GPIB), holds true: 'Reading literature that was not even forbidden, but of which there was a deficit, was a mass phenomenon – however, there are very few testimonies.'[48] Quantitative analysis of samizdat reading on a large scale is patently impossible.

Much more than 'just' a reader

For technical reasons, I will refer to samizdat as a 'literary process' in this section, without distinguishing between literary, political, religious and other kinds of samizdat or, within literary samizdat, between new literature that existed only in samizdat and pre-existing texts that were merely copied in this way. This is solely for the purpose of illustrating the mechanism of text production, multiplication and distribution.

Any literary process requires writers, middlemen and readers. Moreover, for a text to remain accessible to new readers – in print, or in circulation – it must be endorsed by earlier readers. In this respect samizdat was no exception. However, the externalities of textual production, distribution and, ultimately, reading itself differ significantly from the ones we study when researching 'traditional' printed texts or even manuscripts. A look at these differences will afford us a shortcut in understanding why it is so crucial to study the samizdat reader if we want to understand the process as a whole.

We might want to begin by assessing the position of samizdat within Soviet textual culture and its relation to print culture in particular. Samizdat existed precisely because the state had monopolized printing. Yet it was not completely divorced from print. Rather, samizdat represents a hybrid genre[49] in technical, organizational and material terms, situated as it was within a highly developed print culture, partly overlapping with it and, for certain segments of society, increasingly replacing it. As the name 'samizdat', forming an analogy to official providers such as Gosizdat, already intimates, samizdat was an alternative variant rather than a separate phenomenon altogether.

In technical terms, samizdat was a hybrid because in its iconic form it was produced with the help of a typewriter. A typewriter is itself a hybrid, fit for private use but producing a limited number of absolutely identical copies in standardized type. In organizational terms, samizdat was a hybrid because segments of it were clearly modelled on the official literary process, leaving out censorship. This is particularly apparent when we consider the literary journals of the 1970s with their editorial procedures, subscription schemes and publication schedules; these are discussed in Chapters 5 and 6. Samizdat was a hybrid in material terms, too, because a significant proportion of the circulating literature existed in print and was merely reproduced and disseminated by hand because no new print editions were available. This concerned above all pre-revolutionary literature and contemporary texts produced in small print runs, for example the hugely popular science fiction of the Strugatsky brothers. A related issue is the fact that many samizdat writers had some publications in official print. Prominent examples include Alexander Solzhenitsyn, whose *One Day in the Life of Ivan Denisovich* caused a sensation when it was published in the official journal *Novyi mir* (New World) in November 1962, and the officially published poetry collections of Varlam Shalamov, whose famous *Kolyma Tales* circulated only in samizdat.[50] Most of the poets who defined Leningrad unofficial culture in the 1970s had published officially at some point.[51]

A further complicating factor was tamizdat, the publication abroad of texts that had no chance of publication in the Soviet Union. Tamizdat was often realized through émigré publishing houses or specialized Russian-language publishers.[52] Prominent examples of works published in this way include Leonid Pasternak's *Doctor Zhivago* and Solzhenitsyn's *Gulag Archipelago*. Copies inevitably made their way back into the USSR, where they would be typed out or reproduced by other means, thus 'returning' to samizdat. From the mid-1970s, tamizdat gradually became the most important source for obtaining longer works of literature.[53] Samizdat and print culture were thus tightly enmeshed and interdependent. A comparison between them is fruitful for the task of identifying the special characteristics of the samizdat reader.

Figure 1, the 'Communications Circuit' diagram devised by Robert Darnton will illustrate and help us to understand the magnitude of the technical differences between print culture and samizdat.[54]

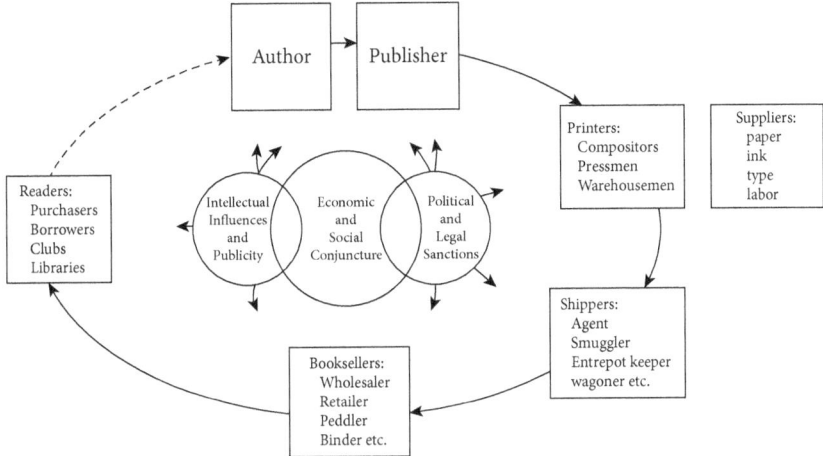

Figure 1 The Communication Circuit.
Source: Robert Darnton, 'What Is the History of Books?', *Daedalus* 111, no. 3 (1982): 68.

The diagram shows just how many intermediaries and influencing factors are habitually involved in a literary process. In this respect, neither Soviet official culture nor samizdat were exceptional. Yet in both processes the roles of intermediaries and external factors were distorted beyond recognition.[55]

Let us briefly first look at official culture, from which samizdat emerged and against which it reacted. The framework of Soviet official culture distorted, in particular, the three circles in the centre of the diagram. The need for all texts to be assessed by Glavlit, the censor's office, to ensure their conformity with the ideological and aesthetic guidelines set by the Communist Party, and the central role of the Writers' Union (which regulated who was considered a writer) both show that political sanctions played a disproportionally large role. These did not merely dwarf intellectual considerations; they were superimposed onto them. By contrast, market pressures as they were experienced in the West were largely suppressed. While Soviet publishing houses were in theory supposed to support themselves financially, the need to meet ideological and/or educational requirements usually overrode concerns for profit; readers were seen as receivers of culture rather than consumers of books.[56]

One could say that samizdat reacted to this imbalance by abolishing political (and legal) considerations altogether. The texts circulating in samizdat included anything proscribed by official culture, from erotica such as the *Kama Sutra* to poetry judged aesthetically deficient, religious texts, and material explicitly criticizing Soviet policy. Indeed, one of the definitions of samizdat literature is *nepodtsenzurnaia literatura*, literally 'literature not under censorship': that is, uncensored literature.[57] Market pressures were virtually absent. Commercial samizdat was rare, although it became more common as time went on.[58] Tamizdat books exposed unofficial publishing to political interests, some explicit, some indirect. At the same time, intellectual/aesthetic considerations were everything. In the absence of institutions such as libraries and bookshops, where a potential reader can familiarize themselves with a given text, a samizdat text had to find favour with its initial audience in order to gain even one additional reader.

The factors described above already indicate the importance of the reader and their taste above all else. However, samizdat's greatest distortion of the communications circuit concerns the outer circle of the diagram and the roles described in each individual square. All these functions, from the decision to publish in the first place to printing, shipping/distributing, selling, binding and stocking, and preserving for posterity were carried out by the reader. Incidentally, this reader might also be the author of a text, in which case they would be responsible for the entire circle; as veteran dissident Vladimir Bukovsky remarked: 'I write it myself, I edit it myself, I censor it myself, I publish it myself, I circulate it myself and I myself serve the prison sentence for it.'[59] The typewriter as a method of production and the absence of an editorial process (unless we are talking about journals) meant that the threshold for becoming a 'published' author was low. Twenty-two respondents to the samizdat reader survey report that they were samizdat authors.

Most importantly, the readers were responsible for circulating a very limited number of physical copies to the largest possible circle of readers. Many of them produced further physical copies, either solely for their own use or for others; the typewriter made it possible to do both things at once. Consequently, the reader acted as both publisher and printer. Alexander Daniel maintains that this 'secondary multiplication' at one remove from the author's own circle was instrumental to the process of samizdat.[60] Irina Tsurkova, a typist who, among many other texts, also typed a short-lived journal called *Perspektiva*, identified this ability of the samizdat text to 'live its own life' as its most important feature, actively sought by samizdat authors:

> However, samizdat had a special feature, which is why it was called samizdat, self-published – it was able to multiply by itself [*samorazumnozhatsia*]. A certain number of these twenty-four copies [the initial print run of the journal] were intercepted by the KGB; of course, some were thrown away, burnt or flushed down the toilet by people who took fright because they were being followed …

On the other hand, you would pass a copy on to somebody, and that person would reproduce it, either by typing it out again or by making photocopies. This was very important. People would photograph the text, making it possible to print from the film ... What was important was that these copies were alive – they were living a life of their own.[61]

Secondary copies were produced in great haste, as readers often kept texts for a day or a night only and during this short time typed up all or part of it. These material and temporal constraints were a major factor limiting the reach of samizdat texts, unlike in a book economy that can mass-produce copies and where circulation is determined by economic considerations such as production costs and level of reader interest. Naturally, the way in which copies were reproduced had a major impact on the state of the text as a physical object. Different copies of one and the same text often display an astonishing degree of variation, beyond obvious typos or accidental omissions. Unlike printed texts, typescripts could be, and regularly were, corrected by hand: for example, when words in Latin script had to be added.[62] This practice blurs the distinction between manuscript and typescript, placing typescript somewhere in the middle between manuscript, where each copy is unique, and print, where technology ensures that all copies are identical. Moreover, the informal way in which these texts were reproduced changed the general understanding of a text as an inviolable whole. Readers took liberties with texts, making decisions that are normally the prerogative of authors or editors.[63] Sometimes, people would copy out only part of a text or collection of poetry, to save time or for aesthetic reasons, and then circulate it, leading to a new version becoming established. One respondent to the samizdat reader survey reports cherishing handwritten copies of Akhmatova's *Requiem,* a cycle of poems which circulated in samizdat for a long time and was also passed on orally, and then discovering that it did not correspond to the version that finally made it into print.[64] In other cases, samizdat authors, translators or typists purposefully reproduced only part of a text. Natalia Trauberg, who translated, among other things, religious and philosophical texts from the English (Chesterton, C.S. Lewis), details how she would leave out large chunks of text she deemed inaccessible to her potential readers because they lacked the theological knowledge necessary to appreciate it.[65] Elena Rusakova, a samizdat typist, gives another reason why longer texts were often incomplete:

'I was typing [Andrei Platonov's novel] *Kotlovan* [*The Foundation Pit*], and I was copying from a Western edition ... In fact I wasn't typing out the whole novel, because as usual, these books had to be returned quickly and we only had parts of it. So, I was typing out some parts, while somebody else did some others.'[66]

The readers felt this effect, too. One survey respondent remembers that incomplete texts were a regular occurrence:

> Samizdat is a printed text created by an underground press rather than an official one. As a rule, texts that were banned on the territory of the Soviet Union were published in this way. The texts were printed with the help of a typewriter on poor-quality paper. Books weren't always complete – it happened that you would get part of a book and needed to wait for the next bit.[67]

Tamizdat books were read and reproduced in the same way, under extreme time pressure, with all the consequences that have been outlined above. This and the fact that many readers, including the majority of respondents to our survey, did not strictly distinguish between them justifies the treatment of samizdat and tamizdat as essentially part of the same phenomenon: as texts produced, circulated and read outside the state's monopoly on textual production. Tamizdat also throws light on a different concept of 'original' and 'copy'. Professional print was not necessarily seen as more authoritative, as Viacheslav Igrunov's observation regarding the *Chronicle of Current Events* illustrates: 'And another particularity: when it comes to samizdat, the relationship between "copy" and "original" is very difficult. The *Chronicle of Current Events* typed out on a typewriter, is considered the original, while the foreign [i.e. printed] edition is the copy.'[68]

Samizdat knew no copyright; indeed, copyright would have been counterproductive to its mission. This means that the author lost control over the text the moment he or she 'published' it; this was the price for it reaching the reader.[69] Samizdat thus challenged the 'Gutenberg model' that was established when print made it possible to infinitely reproduce identical physical copies of a text. This paradigm presupposes that the text is fixed and has been created by one or several individually known authors, and that it is the author or authors who have ultimate responsibility for the text.[70] The alterations made to samizdat texts during spontaneous reproduction – conscious or not – challenge this model; observers and scholars have used terms included 'pre-Gutenberg phenomenon',[71] 'extra-Gutenberg phenomenon'[72] and 'prä-printium'[73] to describe the relationship between samizdat and established print culture. The difficulty in establishing the authoritative version of a given text naturally shifts the focus from questions of textual authority to those of dissemination and readership.[74]

It follows that individual copies of a given journal and their digital reproductions should be treated like archival relics rather than copies of an authoritative text; digital reproductions should indicate which archive or collection holds the particular copy that is being reproduced. The handmade, improvised and almost deliberately shabby appearance of samizdat texts has become their trademark sign and is now being studied extensively.[75] At the same time there can be no doubt that the fluidity of samizdat texts was an accidental consequence of their material reality rather than the result of any deliberate action. Authors and editors actively strove for more durable formats to make the process less labour-intensive and ensure wider circulation. Tamizdat via émigré publishing houses can be seen as one such example. Copies smuggled abroad for publication and safekeeping in archives often became the authoritative version of a given text.[76] Longer texts were increasingly reproduced with the help of photography and, later, copying machines. Journal editors, too, began to use copying machines as soon as it became possible.[77] One side-effect of the emergence of authoritative versions was the loss of the individual samizdat script as a unique artefact. The modes of reproduction are discussed in detail in the subsequent chapters.

The processes described and examples given above demonstrate clearly the degree to which samizdat depended on the reader's approval for its very existence in the most direct, physical sense, blurring the line between creator and receiver, in some cases consumer, of a medium. Yet readers can fulfil the tasks usually carried out by an army of professionals only to a limited degree, and the result, including the material available to the researcher, looks very different from the picture we know from mainstream literary culture.

Networks

Samizdat and the internet

Samizdat preceded the contemporary challenge presented to the 'Gutenberg model' by the internet. It has become popular to compare samizdat to the World Wide Web, particularly to social media. The Russian term for social media – *sotsial'nye seti* – literally translates as 'social webs/networks' and is also used to describe networks of people; this coincidence invites and facilitates the comparison.[78] Articles on this topic regularly find entry into new volumes on samizdat.[79] The well-known German journal *Osteuropa* (Eastern Europe) posits samizdat and the internet as spaces that allow the free word to flourish.[80] Eugene Gorny, a leading expert on the Russian internet, has researched the significance of samizdat as one of the main metaphors used to describe the Russian section of the internet.[81] Sharon Balazs has drawn up a useful table for comparing historical samizdat and the internet.[82] Some very new research even compares the practice of file sharing to samizdat.[83] There are less enthusiastic voices, too. Henrike Schmidt, who has written widely on samizdat and the internet, warns against a facile equation between the two phenomena. Her essay 'Postprintium' – a synthesis of a rich body of research, including from Russia – posits that the comparison only holds in certain particular cases, if we consider 'samizdat' to be a metaphor for describing a space where debate is relatively spontaneous, easily accessible to those who wish to contribute, and largely free of commercial interests.[84] Comparing and contrasting samizdat networks and social media is not the purpose of this study. However, given that most of us use the internet every day, while only few have experience of samizdat, a brief consideration of certain points throws into sharp relief the particularities of samizdat and enhances our understanding of its reading, production and social environment.

The comparison usually hinges on the observation that both phenomena allow for the spontaneous generation of texts at grassroots level, without the interference of either editors or censors. Indeed, both samizdat and social media are based on network structures that are informal, fluid and capable of overlapping infinitely. On social media, users/readers can generate and circulate their own texts/content, while sharing and re-posting other people's content can be construed as an analogue to the retyping of samizdat. Moreover, texts circulated on the web are not 'fixed' in the way printed texts are; readers who share texts can and do edit, alter and abridge them. As we have seen, the same happened to samizdat texts, although for different reasons. Naturally, the limits of the comparison become clear once we begin to consider these analogies in finer detail. First and foremost there are the constraints of laborious manual reproduction, which mean that samizdat remained a scarce and therefore highly coveted commodity, while texts on the web can – and do – become 'viral' with minimal effort. In the case of samizdat, these constraints also acted as a natural mechanism of quality control, and it is safe to assume that the majority of today's social media posts would not have warranted the effort required to turn them into physical documents. Moreover, the way in which social media has changed our way of interacting with each other, introduced a habit of reducing important thoughts to sound bites, and possibly even influenced the way our brains are wired cannot easily be compared to the effect of samizdat on Soviet society.

However, the two differences between samizdat and the internet/social media that are relevant for the purpose of this study lie elsewhere. Firstly, the main issue facing the researcher who is trying to reconstruct the trajectory of samizdat texts – and thus the network of people reading them – is the lack of records. Spontaneous and illegal as it was, the samizdat process concealed the links between the origin of a text and its reader, as well as between readers sharing texts. By contrast, the internet, and social media in particular, render these links transparent. Online, the processes of reading and distribution become visible in the literal sense of the word: if not to the user themselves, then certainly to platform hosts, providers and specialists. There are also special platforms that enable users to display to each other what they are reading, recording engagement with a written text beyond mere possession.[85] Reading samizdat would have been impossible without friendship ties and personal acquaintance. While social media can be used to stay in touch across continents, facilitate new contacts and organize large-scale events, they also have an isolating effect. Social media users do not need any other social media users around them in order to indulge – a smartphone and phone signal are all that is required. By contrast, reading samizdat brought people together and created communities, not only because connections were required in order to obtain samizdat but also because people often read rare texts collectively. Leonid Zhmud' remembers: 'This literature not only formed my political worldview but also determined my social circle, connecting me with many interesting people; the exchange of books was followed by an exchange of ideas.'[86]

Research into the digital sphere yields valuable insights into the structure of networks, and some of these insights can be applied fruitfully to samizdat. Samizdat as a whole was a network phenomenon that depended on multiple overlapping networks. Researchers of internet governance, for example, point out that – unlike traditional media – the 'decentred network' that is the internet has no single point of control and is therefore hard to regulate. The result is a broader network of networks as 'communities gravitate towards other communities that share similar values'.[87] A similar kind of 'network individualism' and lack of central control is precisely what made samizdat so lively and robust; the authorities were never able to suppress it. The mechanism of communities (groups, friendship networks) to enmesh with and influence each other will become obvious in the discussion below.

An alternative to official culture?

Samizdat networks were heterogeneous groups with fluid, informal membership. Situated outside official Soviet culture, they were nevertheless part of the cultural landscape, especially once the practice of reading samizdat became widespread among intellectuals. Participation in one or several samizdat networks did not require a person to renounce participation in official life – for example, by exercising a profession, including in the field of culture – or in other informal networks, such as *blat*, the complicated system of mutual favours, at work and elsewhere. One of the best-known conceptualizations of communities whose identity depended on being 'inside-yet-outside' authoritative discourse is that by Aleksei Yurchak; his analysis is not specific to samizdat groups, although most of his protagonists would have read samizdat. Yurchak's conclusions are nevertheless helpful, as he examines the late Soviet generation's ability to '[be] simultaneously inside and outside of some context – such as being within a context while remaining oblivious of it, imagining yourself elsewhere, or being inside your own mind. It may also mean being simultaneously a part of the system and yet not following certain of its parameters'.[88] Crucially, Yurchak's study includes groups that were close to Soviet institutions – for example, the *Komsomol*, the communist youth league – as well as those that were nominally outside all these structures, such as the regulars at the cafes that proliferated in Leningrad in the 1960s, including the famous Saigon.[89] In a recent study, Ilya Kukulin criticizes as simplistic Yurchak's conception of late Soviet networks. According to Kukulin, presenting these groups without recourse to social network theory fails to account sufficiently for their heterogeneity.[90] Kukulin's observations are certainly pertinent. However, Yurchak's findings remain relevant to this study: not only does he emphasize the ambivalent relationship between official discourse and those who position themselves outside of it, but he also demonstrates how official social structures – the Palace of Pioneers, Literary Associations – could become spaces that allowed people, in particular young people, to develop a sense that they were situating themselves outside official discourse.[91] The attitude of many samizdat readers towards official culture can be summarized, in the words of Natalia Pervukhina, as 'our passive rejection':[92] underlining that, while people were willing to read forbidden literature and engage in lengthy debates in friends' kitchens, for the majority of them this represented an internal attitude rather than a call to action. This emphasizes the low threshold required to become involved in samizdat. Even mere 'passive dislike' carried the seed of outsiderdom, as the fates discussed in my study demonstrate.

Yurchak and Kukulin are not the only researchers to focus on the ambivalent social location of samizdat networks. A positive and versatile appraisal is offered by Ann Komaromi. In her article 'Samizdat and Soviet Dissident Publics', Komaromi describes unofficial groups centred on samizdat reading with the help of Nancy Fraser's concept of 'counterpublic', underscoring what she calls the 'dialectic orientation' of such groups. Her central argument is that samizdat groups operated in two spaces simultaneously, one essentially private and the other public. The private element – 'space for withdrawing and regrouping' – is easy to see. Whether or not a person was able to read (much) samizdat depended on their social environment: that is, the people they knew and the circles in which they moved. Samizdat also became currency in certain social networks. Irina Tsurkova described this phenomenon as follows: 'I was almost always typing something, for my own enjoyment and in order to give pleasure to my friends - for example, in order to be able to give a splendid birthday present. In my circles it was considered very cool to be given a collection of samizdat for your birthday.'[93] At the same time, the practice of samizdat generated new friendship networks, bringing people together on the basis of shared reading interests.[94] The public element identified by Komaromi, the groups' 'function as training grounds for agitation directed against a wider public', needs more qualification. Komaromi's argument is based on two case studies: Soviet Jews as a national minority and the Leningrad feminists of the late 1970s. These groups were much more closely delineated than the friendship networks invoked by Tsurkova; they were also explicitly socially and politically active. Many Soviet Jews were lobbying for the right to emigrate to Israel, agitating against official Soviet policy which marginalized them. The underground feminists were agitating against patriarchal norms dominating, among other spheres, the male-dominated literary underground. It might be difficult to see how Komaromi's definition could be applied to a loose friendship group exchanging poetry. However, her use of the term 'agitation' is not to be understood literally. Komaromi herself posits that cultural samizdat 'functions as a laboratory of values and identities, new and alternative ways of defining the subjectivity that public activity aims to defend'.[95] 'New subjectivity' is a category that is hard to define and even harder to quantify, and the influence of alternative civil platforms on the course of history remains contentious. However, the respondents to the reader survey confirm that samizdat reading fostered a new sense of identity, with more than a few suggesting that the ways of thinking honed by samizdat reading had some degree of impact on the demise of the Soviet Union. In this sense, samizdat groups represent counterpublics that were centred on an alternative form of media which, over the thirty-odd years of its existence, at the very least furthered a consciousness that was less influenced by Soviet official discourse.

2

Readers: An online survey for samizdat readers

Introduction

The 1960s and 1970s, when the phenomenon of samizdat was at its height, can still be considered recent history. While the founding generation – which included names such as Lev Kopelev (1912–1997), Alexander Solzhenitsyn (1918–2008), Andrei Siniavskii (1925–1997) and Larisa Bogoraz (1929–2004) – has now for the most part passed away, the historical proximity of samizdat still offers unique opportunities for research. Many middle-aged and elderly Russians alive today have had some exposure to samizdat. We can still gather empirical, first-hand data and therefore try to improve an imbalance that affects the public and researchers alike: most testimonies about samizdat feature the same dozen or so names, including those given above. These figures, many of them active dissidents, have become the default spokespeople of the subculture that was samizdat; researchers keep turning to them even today.[1] But, as a reading culture, samizdat was a mass movement. And the 'ordinary' members of this movement – those who primarily read and passed on texts and stayed away from more visible activity – have more often than not ceded the right of remembrance to those who have become the accepted historiographers of samizdat.[2]

If we want to study how samizdat functioned as a reading culture, we must research the reader. But how are we to gather data from a group that is so large, so heterogeneous and so geographically dispersed? These are not the only factors that render the traditional methods of oral history, particularly the in-depth narrative interview, unsuitable for this kind of research. More importantly, we do not know our research subject – the 'ordinary samizdat reader' – by name. Therefore, rather than actively approach a limited number of previously known respondents, our aim must be to persuade as many samizdat readers as possible to approach us and share their experience. This is only possible with the help of the internet and social media. The internet reaches all generations and compensates for the geographical dispersion of people from the former Soviet Union, including the emigration of many intellectuals to Western Europe, Israel or the United States. There are a large number of active social media accounts belonging to people who witnessed the era.

In order to target the group described above – inhabitants of the former USSR with experience of reading samizdat – Gennadii Kuzovkin, a historian and archivist and director of the History of Dissent in the USSR programme[3] at the Memorial Society in Moscow, and I designed an online survey. We were fortunate to be able to draw on the generous support of a group of Russian sociologists.[4] The survey, hosted by the Faculty of Modern and Medieval Languages at the University of Cambridge, went live on 14 March 2017 and was promoted via social media and selected Russian online media. In 2018, it found a permanent home as part of the ongoing Project for the Study of Samizdat and Dissidence at the University of Toronto.[5] The 122 replies on which this chapter is based were gathered between 14 March 2017 and 26 June 2018, the majority before December 2017. To our knowledge, this survey constitutes the first attempt to collect empirical data about (and from) the 'ordinary' reader of samizdat. By October 2019, the survey had gathered 155 replies.

The survey has two main purposes. The first is to preserve as many individual accounts of reading samizdat as possible. Secondly, we aim to create a broader knowledge base by explicitly inviting the testimony of those who were not in any way 'spokespeople' of the subculture. Of course, we do not discourage well-known figures from participating, and indeed several responses are from people who have previously assisted research into samizdat. But the threshold for participation is very low, and the survey explicitly permits anonymous submissions. Twenty-eight respondents either did not give their name or asked us not to publish any personal information. To protect their identity, we refer to all respondents by a unique number. While their narratives form the backbone of this chapter, where appropriate they have been supplemented with material from interviews and written sources.

Who are our respondents?

The point in time at which we started our research means that we surveyed the second and third generations of samizdat – the typical 'mass readers' rather than the pioneers and most important authors. Our oldest respondent was born in

1931, and the vast majority of those we surveyed were born in the 1950s and 1960s.

By the time those born in the 1970s – the youngest participant was born in 1977 – had grown into conscious readers, the political processes around Perestroika meant that samizdat and official culture were on the way to merging. This process was begun when Gorbachev announced the policy of Glasnost in 1986, which lead to a gradual relaxation of censorship and culminated in the adoption of the Law on Print in 1990, which abolished censorship altogether.[6]

Tables 1 to 4 provide a few basic statistics.

Table 1 Decade of birth

Decade of Birth	Number of Respondents
1930s	5
1940s	15
1950s	49
1960s	36
1970s	12
No DOB given	5
TOTAL	**122**

Table 2 Sex

Sex	Number of Respondents
Male	63
Female	42
Not specified/anonymous	17
TOTAL	**122**

Table 3 City of birth

City of Birth	Number of Respondents
Moscow	58
Leningrad/St Petersburg	24
Other Russian city or town	27
In the USSR but not Russia	7
Not specified/anonymous	6
TOTAL	**122**

Table 4 Education

Education	Number of Respondents
High school	5
Technical college	8
University degree	64
Postgraduate/PhD	41
Other/not specified	4
TOTAL	**122**

We should not be surprised that the largest group of respondents were born in Moscow and/or named Moscow as their residence when they were reading samizdat. That the majority have a university degree was also to be expected. Samizdat thrived in university circles as an ideal environment for socializing with like-minded peers. Soviet university students typically lived in halls of residence (*obshchezhitie*) and shared rooms. Here are a few typical stories about how the university environment fostered people's acquaintance with samizdat:

> During my studies at the Faculty of Philology I came across samizdat all the time. We would swap books, giving them to each other overnight to read and then pass on to the next person. Several of these books are still in my private library. (#9, b.1965)[7]

> I was a student at the Faculty of Philology of Moscow State University. I started there in 1966. That means that the first time somebody gave me samizdat to read overnight was no later than 1968. It was [Boris Pasternak's] *Doctor Zhivago*. (#45, b.1947)

> Somebody gave me a samizdat book at the Faculty of Philology of Moscow State University where I was a student. A book of poems by Nikolai Gumilev. Later, I was given unpublished poems by Mandelshtam. I also remember receiving some Galich, I think. (#13, b.1967)[8]

While some works circulated widely in samizdat – one thinks of 'classics' such as the works of Solzhenitsyn and Venedikt Erofeev – many towns and cities had a lively local scene of writers who wrote for themselves and their friends. Remembering his youth in Novosibirsk, the scholar Andrei Rogachevskii tells of a kind of samizdat that did not travel much beyond local circles, much of it the product of student activity; characteristically, the texts have not survived to the best of his knowledge. At the same time, these students were familiar with those same 'samizdat classics' that will be mentioned in this chapter again and again; Rogachevskii remembers that samizdat introduced him to the works of Joseph Brodsky and Daniil Kharms.[9] The journalist Vladimir Skrashchuk offers an overview of the local samizdat scene in Irkutsk, including the activity of Boris Chernykh, who published a literary journal called *Literaturnye tetradi* (Literary Notebooks).[10] But not all of these local scenes remained insular: the poet Vsevolod Rozhniatovskii describes the history of the poetry almanac *Maia* that appeared in Pskov in the late 1980s and was informed by the friendship between the authors and Leningrad-based poets, in particular Oleg Okhapkin.[11] Konstantin Kuzminskii and Grigorii Kovalev's nine-volume *Blue Lagoon Anthology of Modern Russian Poetry*, featuring samizdat from cities beyond Leningrad – in particular Kharkov and Kiev – is further evidence that scenes were interconnected beyond local limits.[12]

What people read

Since the focus of our survey is on collecting as much information as possible, there are no dedicated research questions we hope to answer with the help of the material gathered. The survey consists of sixty-three questions, the majority of which require the respondent to check a box or choose from a list of possible answers. These questions might ask in which decade the respondent first came across the word 'samizdat', whether they ever read tamizdat (ninety-eight respondents out of 122), or listened to samizdat broadcast via foreign radio stations (sixty-seven respondents). Questions like this, which elicit comparable statistical data, are always followed by open-ended questions which encourage the respondents to share what they remember about texts and people. To give an example, the question about reading tamizdat (Question 32) is followed by questions asking about dates and titles and then by an invitation to answer freely: 'How did you manage to receive tamizdat?' (Question 32.4). This setup means that the data we received is very uneven, as our respondents provided vastly different amounts of information. We deliberately refrained from making any of the questions compulsory. As a result, some people only answered the tick-the-box and multiple-choice questions, ignoring the invitation to reminisce. Others left out individual questions or blocks of questions. Yet others wrote far above average amounts of free text.

Our sample confirms a number of widely held hypotheses about samizdat reading. But the statistical data gathered from such a small sample can only ever give an indication. The limited use of a small self-selecting sample in strictly statistical terms makes it all the more clear that every statistic consists of a tapestry of personal stories that cannot be translated easily into numbers. Each of these stories is unique, and stories are precisely what we risk losing as witnesses die out – stories of how a significant minority circumvented a literature-centric society's prescriptive print culture with the help of informal networks and handmade artefacts. Here is a brief taster of the stories we gathered.

One respondent provides a rough sequence of the samizdat phenomenon, without attaching a timeline, from its origin in manual copies (*spiski*) of poetry to the time when entire volumes of prose or history were available, often through tamizdat: 'As far as I remember, first there was the poetry of [Nikolai] Gumilev and [Anna] Akhmatova (*Requiem*) and fairly neutral texts from the Writers' Union. After that came anti-Stalin texts, Solzhenitsyn's Nobel Prize lecture; and only afterwards entire books, Avtorkhanov et al.'[13] Another respondent describes how the decision about what to read was determined by the availability of texts: 'At home we only had literary texts, in homemade publications.'[14] The Russian adjective used here – *samopal'nyi* – means both homemade and counterfeit, highlighting that this was a special form of literature, produced in a manner that differed from the expected one. This reader tells us about the experience of having samizdat at home, which was evidently not a regular occurrence: 'It was a book my mum was reading. We weren't allowed to tell anybody about it. And, during the week that the book was in our flat, we weren't allowed to bring any friends home.'[15]

Particularly intriguing first encounters include:

> I think that was a typewritten copy of Erofeev's *Moskva-Petushki* [*Moscow Circles*]. In 1972, if I remember correctly. My mum and I immediately typed out another copy. And I remember that a bit later a really funny thing happened with this book. An acquaintance of the time, [name supplied], who'd borrowed the book from me, spent several hours on the phone at night dictating it to his then-girlfriend. She was a professional typist and typed it out, taking dictation. (#23, b.1955)

> Evtushenko's poem 'Pamiati Esenina' [To the Memory of Esenin] and Vysotsky's 'Navodchitsa' [The Gunlayer]. But that's something I found out only afterwards; I can't remember whether authors and titles were written on the texts. I found them in my aunt's cupboard (I don't remember whether by accident or whether I had been looking for them), on yellowing paper, and in either typescript or some other reproduction technique, with faded letters. (#98, b.1951)[16]

The sheer ubiquity of samizdat is remarked upon – 'It was in the air.'[17] – as is the fact that it was vindicated by history when censorship was abolished: 'When the formerly forbidden texts started to be published in large numbers during Perestroika (and later), it turned out that I was already familiar with the vast majority of them via samizdat and tamizdat.'[18]

Our respondents cite a range of reasons for reading samizdat. In its basic form, samizdat was a source of better literature. This is a selection of replies to Questions 20.1 ('Which textual genre was predominant in your samizdat reading? Please explain your choice or choices – why did you read those texts?') and 21.1 ('What was for you the most valuable element in the samizdat texts you knew? Please tell us why?'):

> The utter poverty of 'Soviet' theology and the limited access to literature. (#64, b.1956)

> I'm indifferent towards religion. Everything else was excellent ammunition for the battle against sensory deprivation (boredom). (#20, b.1966)

> New authors and styles were especially interesting, because I was entirely focused on literature: Brodsky, [Dmitrii] Prigov, [Lev] Rubinshtein, [Vasilii] Aksenov. (#25, b.1963)

> In those years I loved poetry ... I was enchanted by the poetry of Joseph Brodsky. (#74, b.1957)

In its entirety, samizdat satisfied a need for literature and information that arose as a result of the Soviet regime's isolationist policies and strict censorship. For many, it became an important source of information that could not be accessed in any other way:

> Any literature that contained trustworthy historical information helped us to put together the puzzle and to explain the historical process. (#63, b.1950)

> Without samizdat it was impossible to discover the history of the Soviet era. (#11, b.1952)

> [We found out] facts and pseudo-facts that were absent from official literature. (#20, b.1966)

> New and previously carefully concealed information came from outside. (#53, b.1954)

Some seem to have listed the functions of samizdat according to perceived importance:

> Samizdat provided me with information about what was going on in the country, immersed me in social and philosophical topics and acquainted me with amazing works of literature. (#72, b.1940)

Samizdat acquainted me with issues concerning the repressions under Stalin, the Thaw, the fate of the dissidents and the fate of writers in the 1920s and 1930s. (#29)

Some readers of samizdat had political motivations:

As I was busy searching for a way to transform the Soviet system, for me the most important samizdat materials were historical and sociological texts, alongside academic literature. (#21, b.1941)

The orientation towards socio-political activity with the future aim of transforming Soviet society [by] introducing a greater degree of democracy and social justice [was what motivated me]. (#57, b.1953)

Others explicitly resisted ideas these kinds of ideas:

The information and social journalism [in samizdat] seemed to be a bit biased. I wanted truth rather than howling and hysterics. The literary texts were gentler and more varied. (#48, b.1959)

I think that as a Soviet reader I disliked critical anti-Soviet texts if they belonged to the genre of journalism without outstanding artistic and philosophical merit. (#52, b.1960)

The last response shows that some saw no difference between identifying themselves as 'Soviet people' and reading samizdat.

Becoming a regular reader

By the nature of the survey, everyone who took part had some experience of reading samizdat, and they regard this experience as important enough to warrant spending upwards of one hour on filling in a survey. It is therefore even more interesting to check how many respondents considered themselves regular readers of samizdat. Question 19 asks: 'Would you say that at some point in your life you became a regular samizdat reader?' Several older respondents name the year 1968, that is, the 'era of [protest] letters and Czechoslovakia [the violent suppression by Soviet and Warsaw Pact forces of the Prague Spring]' (#81, b.1935), as the moment that made them regular samizdat readers. Respondent #21 (b.1948) specifies that he 'began to regularly receive samizdat in October 1968'. Respondent #63 (b.1950) attributes his regular reading, beginning in 1972, to his friendship with a particular individual. Respondent #105 (b.1949) identifies personal contacts as crucial to a samizdat reader. Once a text was produced, its trajectory through samizdat triggered a chain reaction the origin of which is hard to trace, as the reader who received a text from one friend would pass it on to others, in turn becoming their 'source'. By contrast, respondent #67 (b.1947) questions the validity of the question itself – the haphazard channels through which samizdat was produced and passed to the reader mean that 'the word "regularity" is inappropriate in this context'. Respondent #105 (b.1949) contributes a pertinent observation, elaborating that one of the impediments to the average samizdat reader was the inability to have a designated space for storing the texts: 'People with links to dissidence lived with the threat that their home might be searched at any moment. I believe that there were distinctive "repositories" and libraries even then. But only people in whom the KGB was not interested had them'. Incidentally, his point about libraries only being kept by people not in the sights of the KGB is incorrect (see Chapter 4, in this volume, on Samizdat libraries).

Thirty out of our 122 respondents identify themselves as only occasional readers. In fifteen of these cases, this can be attributed to age: born in the second half of the 1960s or the 1970s, in two cases as late as 1977, they simply would not have been old enough by the time the Soviet Union first relaxed and then abolished censorship, so their samizdat experience is limited to seeing samizdat, perhaps in the way one sees artworks, rather than using samizdat as a regular means of reading interesting new texts:

> August 1984. It was Bulgakov's novel *The Master and Margarita*, and next to it there were some pages with satirical poems on Gorbachev and his wife. I saw the book and the pages on the dresser in my parents' room. (#6, b.1977)

> 1988. *Skazka o troike* [*Tale of the Troika*] by the Strugatsky brothers. Somebody brought and showed the text, which was printed on the reverse side of various papers from a Scientific Research Institute. (#68, b.1977)[19]

The answer of respondent #68 stresses the material quality of samizdat as different from books. It is worth pointing out that by that time, both *The Master and Margarita* and *Tale of the Troika* were published in the USSR, albeit in unsatisfactorily small print runs.[20]

Samizdat as a literary phenomenon

Before discussing the technical and collective aspects of samizdat reading, it is worthwhile to examine what exactly it was that 'ordinary' readers read. Samizdat owes it reputation as a counterculture largely to the texts produced by the dissidents, which include certain 'sensational' literary or semi-literary works, such as the novels of Alexander Solzhenitsyn and his monumental 'experiment in literary investigation' – the subtitle of *The Gulag Archipelago*. And yet, literary texts not only preceded political, religious, philosophical and other materials but also continued to dominate samizdat. The overwhelming majority of our respondents became acquainted with samizdat via texts that can be classified as literary; literature also continued to be the most commonly read samizdat throughout their reading 'career'. Even for those born in the 1970s, this was a common way of coming into contact with samizdat: 'If we assume that samizdat is something copied out on a typewriter or by hand rather than a photocopy, then my first texts were my mum's manual copies of [Sergei] Esenin's poetry. And my uncle's computer copies of [Vladimir] Vysotsky's poems' (#22, b.1976). On the other hand, there were also those who seemed surprised that their own experience began with literature, sharing the common perception that samizdat was political by definition and/or forbidden: 'This may sound strange, but it wasn't political samizdat [but] Nabokov's novel *Dar* [*The Gift*]' (#51, b.1952).[21]

Table 5 is a breakdown of the replies to Question 4 by genre; the sum of the replies is far greater than the number of people surveyed because most respondents listed several authors.

If we bear in mind that this table divides literature into four different categories – poetry of the Silver Age, pre-revolutionary literature other than Silver Age poetry, literature written after 1917 and translations – the predominance of literature as the genre that introduced respondents to samizdat becomes overwhelmingly obvious. Only the last two items in the left-hand column denote non-literary texts. I strongly feel that separating out Silver Age poetry is warranted for two reasons. The first is the decisive role it played for the

Table 5 Samizdat texts by genre

Question 4: 'What was the first samizdat text you saw or read?'	Number of Respondents
Literature written after 1917	99
Literature – Silver Age poetry	38
Literature written before 1917 (except Silver Age poetry)	12
Translations	8
Non-literary contemporary text (e.g. protest letter)	21
Other	7

emergence of samizdat as a phenomenon. The second is more complex: Silver Age poetry exemplifies the liminal existence between the official and unofficial, legal and illegal spheres in which much samizdat literature existed, if we take 'literature' to mean literary texts as opposed to religious or political materials. This is also evident from a statement by samizdat bookbinder Lev Turchinskii, who was an avid bibliographer of twentieth-century poetry. He recalls the KGB searching his flat in 1974:

> They rummaged through my entire library but didn't find anything purely anti-Soviet [because I was only interested in poetry] ... All my samizdat copies and books published 'over there' were confiscated ... By the way, I had bought some of those confiscated books in state-owned antiquarian bookshops. There you have a Soviet paradox: you can buy it in a shop, but you can't keep it at home. Like with Gumilev before: you couldn't even mention his name in print, all mentions would be cut out and discarded, but buying his works in an antiquarian bookshop was not a problem. Later, I found my own confiscated books in a shop.[22]

The memory is almost funny in its paradox, demonstrating how semi-official networks show up the authorities' evident lack of a clear policy, as well as the limits of censorship and control. Some Silver Age poets remained firmly taboo, for example the aforementioned Acmeist Nikolai Gumilev, Anna Akhmatova's one-time husband, who was shot in 1921 as a counter-revolutionary; as a result, his work became particularly intriguing to samizdat readers.[23] In Leningrad, the literary scholar Ivan Martynov ran an annual seminar specifically on Gumilev (*Gumilevskie chteniia*, 1976–1983) which would meet on 15 April, the poet's birthday.[24] Respondent #36 (b.1968) remembers being told: 'don't tell anyone at school about Gumilev.'[25] Respondent #27 (b.1954) tells us the following anecdote:

> According to one urban legend, Raisa Gorbacheva [the wife of General Secretary Mikhail Gorbachev] absolutely loved the poetry of Nikolai Gumilev that circulated in samizdat. And – or so the myth goes – this was one of the reasons for Perestroika: yes to the KPSS [CPSU, Communist Party of the Soviet Union] and to socialism, but it must be socialism with a human face where one is allowed to read Gumilev.[26]

The Silver Age poets remained hugely popular so long as samizdat flourished, as respondent #110 (b.1962) affirms: 'Poetry, especially Gumilev, Tsvetaeva, Mandelshtam and Brodsky.'[27] Respondent #32 (b.1954) also lists them when he remembers writers that were read in a group environment: 'Poetry. Voloshin, Mandelshtam, Tsvetaeva, Gumilev etc. The Silver Age.'[28] In the case of certain modernist poets, it was primarily their post-revolutionary work that was not published and became very popular in samizdat, for example Marina Tsvetaeva's later verse, Akhmatova's *Requiem* (mentioned fifteen times), and Mandelshtam's work from the 1930s. It is common knowledge that the Soviet regime supressed the heritage of the Silver Age to varying degrees; yet it cannot but (at least mildly?) shock us to see how many authors who never wrote politically charged texts and are now on the Russian school curriculum were suppressed to such a degree that they could become samizdat 'hits'. As respondent #110 (b.1962), asked which aspect of samizdat was especially valuable, reminds us: '"New literary styles" – well, "new" in the sense that some literature that wasn't very new (e.g. the Silver Age) was available mainly in samizdat.'[29]

Alongside the question regarding genre, we asked respondents about the first authors they read in samizdat, the ones they remember reading repeatedly, and the ones that left the strongest impression. One outstandingly popular author, and clearly the most popular 'samizdat' poet of the pre-revolutionary era, was Osip Mandelshtam. His name is mentioned sixty-six times across different questions. What we can see here is a parallel between our respondents and contemporary (samizdat) poets who revered Mandelshtam and on whose work he was a key influence.[30] Also widely read were the poems and song lyrics of two contemporary bards, Alexander Galich (forty-one mentions) and Vladimir Vysotsky (thirty-seven mentions), whose music circulated in magnitizdat – samizdat on tape. In addition, fans would copy out and circulate their song lyrics, much like teenagers in the 1990s sharing CD booklets and, now, playlists.[31] Galich and Vysotsky also feature prominently as respondents' first samizdat authors. This is perhaps not surprising – they were contemporary, very popular among young people and not particularly 'dangerous', i.e. unlikely to lead to prosecution. Table 6 lists the literary authors who initiated readers into samizdat; only writers named more than three times are listed.

Those whose replies are hidden in the rubric 'others' also name predominantly literary texts. This data serves to confirm the reasons our respondents gave for their attraction to samizdat.

Table 6 Samizdat texts

Question 4: 'What was the first samizdat text you saw or read?'	Number of Respondents
Solzhenitsyn	16
Bulgakov	11
Mandelshtam	11

Question 4: 'What was the first samizdat text you saw or read?'	Number of Respondents
Vysotsky	9
Galich	8
Gumilev	8
Tsvetaeva	7
Strugatsky brothers	5
Venedikt Erofeev	4
Others	43

The prominence of Solzhenitsyn and the mention of Venedikt Erofeev are indicative of the relatively young age of our respondents. Erofeev wrote *Moskva-Petushki* (*Moscow Circles*) in 1969–1970; it became a cult text in samizdat almost immediately afterwards, but was published officially in the Soviet Union only in 1988.[32] Bulgakov's *The Master and Margarita* – and ten out of eleven respondents who mentioned the author were referring to this particular text – became prominent after the journal *Moskva* serialized an abridged, censored version in 1966–1967 and an unabridged tamizdat edition appeared in Paris almost simultaneously.[33] Copies of this foreign edition – but in particular the passages excised by the censor – circulated widely in samizdat even after a complete version was officially published in 1973; most respondents did not specify whether they saw the entire novel in samizdat or just these excised fragments. Lev Turchinskii remembers a curious incident during the KGB search of his flat in 1974: 'And the people the police made witness the search (*poniatye*) nicked a copy of *The Master and Margarita*, the first edition that was published without any cuts. The practice was rather widespread: when a book-lover's place was searched, the *poniatye* would steal books.'[34] The novel's history displays remarkable parallels to that of Alexander Griboedov's play *Gore ot uma* (*Woe from Wit*) in the nineteenth century, which widely circulated in manuscript while the censor's office was still deliberating whether to allow print publication.[35] Genuine reader demand makes it impossible to suppress reproduction of a text, even when few technical means are available. In the case of poets, our respondents rarely mentioned particular poems, with the exception of Akhmatova's *Requiem*. Usually they name the author or specify something along the lines of 'unpublished Mandelshtam'. Sometimes a specific collection is named, but most common are the authors' name or the author's name accompanied by the word 'poems'. This means that, if we want to research the history of individual texts, and poems in particular, we need additional research tools.

Respondent #52 (b.1960) provides a model answer, but unfortunately such detailed reminiscences are rare:

> Something from this list:
> - the excised parts from Bulgakov's novel *The Master and Margarita*;
> - Marina Tsvetaeva's poems from different years;
> - *Gadkie lebedi* [*The Ugly Swans*] by the Strugatsky brothers;
> - *The Gulag Archipelago* by Alexander Solzhenitsyn;
> - *Animal Farm* by George Orwell.

This list is a typical mixture of literary texts that circulated in samizdat in the 1970s: a censored text (Bulgakov); pre-revolutionary poems that were hard to find (Tsvetaeva); a suppressed text by two hugely popular contemporary fiction authors (Strugatsky); a text that was sensational and banned (Solzhenitsyn); and forbidden foreign works (Orwell). The list also faithfully reflects the growing importance of prose texts, including contemporary works, during the mature period of samizdat.

We know that the sum of self-produced texts that circulated during the later decades of the Soviet Union included many genres beyond high literature, politically significant texts and religious writings. Yoga handbooks, the *Kama Sutra*, science fiction translated for samizdat and even recipes are just some examples. However, the extent to which they were prevalent in the lives of respondents is hard to measure. The fact that our readers are hesitant to mention them indicates that their identity as samizdat texts is contentious. One respondent explicitly specified: 'Samizdat is that which you reproduce with great pleasure and for free. Of course this term does not apply to palmistry, porn, fantasies about UFOs and recipes for cat pies [*sic*].'[36] Only just over half of our respondents – sixty-six out of 122 – think that the term 'samizdat' can be applied to this kind of 'everyday' texts. Nonetheless, several of this number are uneasy with their choice. Their explanations, a few of which are given below, indicate that, while any self-produced text could be samizdat, the term nevertheless carried an association of literary quality, political relevance or even danger:

> In the general sense, yes, but not without qualification. As a rule, this term was applied in a more narrow sense to forbidden or practically forbidden literature. (#103, b.1956)
>
> It's annoying, but apparently yes. (#123)
>
> With one reservation: you didn't go to prison for it. (#119)
>
> There were different levels, just like in mainstream literature. (#53, b.1954)[37]

The last reply cited is particularly interesting: it divides the phenomenon 'samizdat' into various 'levels' in much the same way as official literature can be sorted by genre, for example high literature, light entertainment, etc. Several conclusions can be drawn here. Firstly, samizdat primarily satisfied a desire for culture, information and thought rather than easy entertainment, and this is reflected in the frequency with which our respondents mention what we might consider highbrow literature. Samizdat inverted the ordinary 'reading pyramid', a tool that visualizes the proportions of readers according to their preferred genre. In a 'regular' reading culture, readers of refined literature, philosophical texts and the like constitute a minority and are thus placed at the top of the pyramid. By contrast, the average samizdat reader expressed a strong interest in precisely this 'high' literature, philosophical and political writings and works of a similar vein.[38] The emphasis on, and preference for, serious texts is also – at least implicitly – a testimony to the Soviet background and education of the readers, who were brought up in an environment in which the written word had central importance: the Bolsheviks had attempted to use literature as a tool for forging the new Soviet man,[39] while the belief in the ability of literature to influence behaviour was enshrined in the doctrine of Socialist Realism and was arguably one of the justifications for censorship. Just like the reader according to Soviet ideology, the Soviet reader of samizdat was always a receiver of culture rather than a consumer. It just happened that they read the 'wrong' kind of texts.[40]

Literature continued to be the predominant genre throughout the entire period our respondents spent reading samizdat. Table 7 lists the replies to Question 20. Once again, respondents were free to nominate more than one genre.

Table 7 Samizdat texts by genre II

Question 20: 'Which texts did you predominantly read when reading samizdat?'	Number of Respondents
Social/political journalism	62
Literary works	106
Religious texts	20
Other, e.g. history	6
No data	4

The rubric 'other' includes historical sources and scientific and esoteric texts. Some respondents were not entirely clear about the limits of samizdat. Respondent #81 (b.1935) remembers: 'I don't know whether protest letters can be considered samizdat. I was fired from my job because of these letters.' Naturally, those who associate samizdat with political dissidence would see these letters as the quintessence of samizdat. Indeed, Igor Golomshtok remembers that his main aim in writing letters of protest was '[to] inform people by means of samizdat about what was in fact going on in this country'.[41]

The picture looks slightly different for Question 18 ('Which of the samizdat texts you read left the strongest impression with you and why?'). Non-literary texts play a much more important role, especially if we decide, as I have done, to include Alexander Solzhenitsyn's *The Gulag Archipelago* in this category. *The Gulag Archipelago* is by far the most frequently mentioned work: there are thirty-one mentions, alongside fourteen others that simply said 'Solzhenitsyn' or cited one of his other works; respondents were allowed to name more than one text.[42] Another non-literary 'text' mentioned frequently is the human rights bulletin *Khronika tekushchikh sobytii* (*Chronicle of Current Events*) (fifty-seven respondents mention it, many of them more than once). It seems that these two publications were of seminal importance to the public's understanding of samizdat as a phenomenon that could provide fuller information about current affairs in their own country. Viacheslav Igrunov, organizer of a samizdat library in Odessa that is discussed in Chapter 4, is one of many who describe how his worldview was changed when he came across the *Chronicle of Current Events*. One event that helps us to understand the intensity of feeling caused by the publication of *The Gulag Archipelago* is the 'Moscow Declaration' dated 3 February 1973. In this document, Andrei Sakharov and other dissidents put forward four demands: (1) the publication in the USSR of *The Gulag Archipelago*, (2) the publication of archival materials that would give a 'full picture of the activity of the secret services', (3) an 'international public tribunal' for the investigation of the crimes committed, and (4) a guarantee that Solzhenitsyn can work in the USSR without persecution.[43] It is worth noting that the publication of the book is the first point.

Many other 'impressive' texts are also directly or indirectly linked to the topics of Gulag, state terror and repression. These include works by the historian Abdurakhman Avtorkhanov[44] and Andrei Amalrik's *Prosushchestvuet li SSSR do 1984?* (*Will the USSR Survive until 1984?*), as well as clearly literary texts, for example Varlam Shalamov's *Kolymskie rasskazy* (*Kolyma Tales*), Andrei Platonov's *Kotlovan* (*The Foundation Pit*) and *Chevengur*, Vasilii Grossman's

Zhizn' i sud'ba (*Life and Fate*) and George Orwell's *1984*. Also mentioned are a transcript explaining the rationale behind the yearly 'rallies' on Pushkin Square on 5 December (the Day of the Soviet Constitution) (#14, b.1967),[45] the final words of those who demonstrated on Red Square on 26 August 1968 (#21, b.1948) and the Universal Declaration of Human Rights, which the USSR adopted in 1948.

Those respondents who describe their reaction broadly agree that these texts offered them new information about their own country; eighty-one respondents provided details, many, unfortunately, only very brief: 'I found out about the existence of political prisoners' (#14, b.1967); 'This was the first time I understood the system of control in the USSR' (#29); 'A part of my country's history that was completely unknown until then' (#34, b.1965); 'The sheer scope of the system, its huge size and coherence' (#48, b.1959); 'Information about resistance to the "communist" system and the scale of repression in the USSR' (#57, b.1953); 'Touching upon the truth' (#58, b.1958); 'Horror and hatred for the Soviet system' (#74, b.1957); 'Well, it's more or less clear with regard to literature about the camps and the repressions: one can't live like that.' (#105, b.1949); 'The tragic history of my Motherland (tragedy generally leaves an impression)' (#116, b.1966). Most eloquent are the explanations that refer to Orwell:

> Orwell showed me that a totalitarian regime is the greatest evil there is, and that this evil is a fundamental characteristic of the regime rather than a price to pay for its transition period. (#52, b.1960)

> In 1984, I read the novel *1984* in English and cried: just HOW could Orwell know WHAT would happen to us in 1984? (#121, b.1954)

So, while samizdat was a mostly a literary phenomenon, for many people even literary texts had an impact that exceeds strictly aesthetic criteria. It is certainly possible to conclude that for many, samizdat influenced their worldview, paving the way for a more critical stance towards Soviet ideology.

Samizdat reading as resistance

In spite of the uncontested predominance of literary texts, most respondents nevertheless attached at least a hint of political significance to samizdat reading. Question 12 ('Do you agree that samizdat emerged in opposition to certain traits of Soviet society?') was answered positively by 108 out of 122 respondents. The most commonly used term in the subsequent text field (Question 12.1, 'What is it that samizdat opposed?') is 'censorship' (thirty-eight times), accompanied by adjectives such as 'total' or 'savage'; also popular are 'control' and 'surveillance'. Here are a few examples: 'The totalitarian essence of the Soviet regime' (#2, b.1931); 'The lack of tolerance for ideas that were different, the lack of freedom, and censorship' (#5, b.1951).

In a monolithic, centrally controlled culture, samizdat represented a way of counteracting, in the words of respondent #34 (b.1965), 'the effort made by the government to control people's information sources, tastes and views'. And indeed, samizdat was an antidote to the 'greyness (in all its nuances) and the all-encompassing uniformity of thought that was imposed on us' (#7, b.1957) and to the 'impossibility of disseminating one's creative work and views outside the official institutions' (#4, b.1972). In this context, reading samizdat increased people's individual feeling of freedom and represented a personal act of resistance. Respondent #49 (b.1955) specifies: 'People wanted more information – political, art-related and religious. The authorities would oppose this and even imprison people for reading and circulating samizdat. This was opposition.'

Historians are still arguing about the degree to which civil society had an impact on the demise of the Soviet Union. This argument is neatly reflected in the replies to Question 11, 'In your opinion, what was the role of samizdat in the transformations that happened in the USSR (Russia) in the 1980s–1990s?' This question inspired a good number of longer replies, which are interesting in their own right. A basic tendency is immediately recognizable: the twenty people who reckon that the role of samizdat was negligible are invariably convinced this was the case because of samizdat's limited reach, namely, the fact that it reached only the educated strata of society in the big cities. The answers of those who are convinced that its role was significant (sixty-nine respondents) are more varied: quite a few point out that samizdat made 'truthful' information available to the 'reading public' and the 'educated elites' and therefore had an influence on the worldview of those that were involved in shaping the fate of the country:

> Samizdat widened the possibilities for education, and the reading public simply filled in the gap in both Russian literature and history of the twentieth century and in world politics and philosophy. This gave rise to questions that couldn't be answered by the usual means and led to a more profound interest in, and knowledge of, reality. (#25, b.1963)

> Samizdat formed the mentality of the elite that would become involved in the political process during Perestroika. This mentality had an impact on political developments. (#21, b.1948)

This is not the place to collect historical evidence, or argue for or against samizdat's impact on Soviet politics. What is significant here – and very hard to counter – is the argument in favour of samizdat as a unifying force that brought people together outside Soviet official culture:

> It revealed hidden knowledge and brought together people who were close to each other in spirit. (#53, b.1954)

> [It played] an important role, because it united people. (#69, b.1947)

> Even if it didn't form them, samizdat, alongside the songs of singer-songwriters and unofficial culture in general, supported an entire generation of people who were inwardly liberated from communist ideology and prepared for change. In addition, samizdat rallied, brought together and, one could almost say, created a stratum of people who understood each other by the merest hint and trusted each other, while not trusting the authorities in the slightest. (#73, b.1941)

> It prepared the soil by loosening it. (#5, b.1951)

> I think it helped bring up a generation that not only no longer believed, but also wasn't afraid. (#108, b.1960)

These statements chime with the words of several figures who were prominently involved in samizdat in Leningrad. Viacheslav Dolinin observes:

> Alongside the passive rejection of everything officious (*ofitsioznyi*), there was also a rise in unsanctioned public activity, which gradually undermined the communist regime, although it mostly lacked explicit political overtones. Aesopian language became the language of the liberal intelligentsia, unorthodox publications made it into official print, from the theatre stages came remarks that slipped the censor's attention, and at the seminars of official literary associations you could often hear daring, independent opinions.[46]

Anatolii Vershik maintains that samizdat 'changed the consciousness of people and gradually prepared [those who wanted change] for the changes that many were hoping for without believing that they would come so early'. Vershik points out that the abolition of censorship was possibly the most important real change to the internal political climate in the early 1990s.[47] Samizdat was a symptom of the growing internal emancipation of certain segments of society, as a way of self-organization that diversified a monolithic, centralized and very prescriptive cultural sphere. Read in this way, the emphasis and importance of samizdat is on the word 'sam' – self. In the midst of a centrally organized 'monoculture' that discouraged, suppressed and penalized individual initiative, samizdat depended on this initiative. Our survey garnered many statements confirming 'freedom' and 'individual freedom' as one of the most important functions of samizdat. Respondent #2 (b.1931) specifies 'The spirit of truth and freedom', while respondent #6 (b.1966) insists that the possibility of circumventing the censor was in itself more important than the content of the texts: 'Samizdat resisted the total censorship and the control the state exercised over each person. Not all the texts were of high artistic value, but the act of owning such a text or even just knowing about it made you a bit freer.'[48]

Thirty-four of our respondents experienced persecution for samizdat, either personally or in their immediate circle of family and friends. These range from invitations for a 'chat' with the KGB (fourteen mentions) to house searches (ten mentions), problems at work/losing one's job (five mentions) or at university (exclusion, not allowed to join – three mentions). Seven respondents or their next of kin served prison sentences between one and six years. The Soviet Criminal Code contained no article against samizdat per se, but many of those arrested for political activity, including the spreading of texts, in the years after Stalin would have been sentenced according to the infamous Article 70.1, 'anti-Soviet agitation and propaganda', adopted in 1960. Two respondents report that they were indicted according to this article. Respondent #23 (b.1955) tells a detailed story about how he was accused of speculation for facilitating the sale of a volume of tamizdat, although the reason for arresting him was the large amount of samizdat in his flat and the evidence that he was reproducing texts, including *The Gulag Archipelago*.[49]

These figures suggest that serious persecution for samizdat was not a very high risk for those who merely read. Moreover, most instances of persecution were haphazard and intended first and foremost to bully and scare. Yet persecution remained a real prospect, and so potentially contributed to a sense of identity that rallied samizdat readers. As an activity that could incur a prison sentence, reading was invested with heightened importance. This was in addition to the significance afforded to the written word by the long tradition of writers acting as truth tellers in Russian society.

Reading samizdat in other forms

The role of tamizdat

It is very likely that samizdat would not have enjoyed the success it did – the geographical spread, the number of readers it reached and the variety of texts it could offer – had it not been for tamizdat.⁵⁰ 'Tamizdat' – literally, 'published-over-there' – made it possible to circulate longer texts and, crucially, facilitated the reproduction of texts in large numbers. The term refers mostly to Russian-language texts that were printed abroad and then smuggled back into the Soviet Union, usually to be reproduced using 'traditional' samizdat methods and in this way merging with samizdat. However, as has been stated above, many people included texts by foreign authors that joined the samizdat process through translation in their definition of tamizdat. The unofficial literary process included many translators, only a few of whom were well known. A very touching portrait of such a translator is given by Natalia Pervukhina, who describes Elena Auslender, the woman who introduced her to samizdat, in the following terms:

> She would devote all her free time to translating English, French and German literature that was forbidden in the USSR. Elena came from a wealthy, cultured family in Odessa and graduated from grammar school before the revolution; she translated without recourse to a dictionary. During the night watches at the hospital, when everybody was asleep and you didn't have to be afraid of somebody watching what you did, she would translate Uris and Orwell, Ionesco and Malraux, sometimes just belles-lettres. But most importantly, she and [her sister] Shura would type out Russian samizdat texts.⁵¹

Here, the translation of forbidden texts for the purpose of clandestine circulation – done on a typewriter – and the reproduction of Russian samizdat texts happen simultaneously, and Pervukhina's description conveys that she regarded both activities as part of the same process.

Tamizdat became ever more important and, by the mid-1970s, it had grown into a mass phenomenon; however, it was by no means new. One of the best-known examples from the Soviet period after the Second World War is the publication, in Italy, of Boris Pasternak's novel *Doctor Zhivago*, which won the author a Nobel Prize he was forced to renounce. In the Soviet Union, *Doctor Zhivago* circulated only in samizdat and was 'very popular'.⁵² The change concerned quantity rather than quality; tamizdat became ubiquitous. Lev Kopelev remembers: 'A new quality, a new feature of the phenomenon in the 1970s was the growth of tamizdat, the increase of books that came in from abroad. They partly replaced samizdat books, but not completely. Books were less often typed out, or people almost stopped typing them out. They would reproduce only some books, or only poetry.'⁵³ Another samizdat 'hit', Anna Akhmatova's *Requiem*, was published in the United States in 1963.⁵⁴

Earlier waves of emigrants from Russia had actively promoted literature in Russian abroad.⁵⁵ But the exponential growth in tamizdat was driven by the so-called 'third wave' of emigration in the 1970s to 1980s, which saw intellectuals flee to Germany, France, Israel and the United States. To give a few examples: Andrei Siniavskii, who emigrated to Paris in 1973 after finishing his labour camp sentence for publishing abroad,[56] founded the almanac *Sintaksis* (1978–2001). Vladimir Maramzin, arrested in 1974 for compiling a five-volume samizdat edition of Brodsky's poems, also emigrated to Paris, where he co-edited the literary journal *Ekho* (1978–1986); Ekho is still a Russian-language publishing house today.[57] The human rights activist Valerii Chalidze, who was deprived of his Soviet citizenship while on a visit to the United States in 1972, set up Khronika Press – which published works originating in the USSR, including the *Chronicle of Current Events* – and a second publishing house called Chalidze Publications. Many important works, including *The Gulag Archipelago*, were published in Paris by YMCA Press, one of the publishers established after the revolution in 1925 and led for many years by Nikita Struve, the grandson of a White émigré who came to France after the 1917 revolution. Tatiana Goricheva, one of the 'hubs' of Leningrad samizdat in the 1970s, was another émigré to Paris in 1980, where she founded the publishing house Beseda. Beseda produced an eponymous journal (1983–1993) as well as monographs, publicizing the poets of the Leningrad underground.[58] However, it was not just Russian émigrés who promoted literature that could not be obtained in the Soviet Union. Ardis Publishers was founded in 1971 by Carl and Ellendea Proffer, whose principle aim was to provide scholars of Russian literature with a broad variety of modernist texts, including out-of-print or unpublished ones. They also published a journal called *Russian Literature Triquarterly*. But over the course of the 1970s, Ardis became a major producer of tamizdat that reached the USSR. Among their projects are Russian translations of Nabokov's work written in English, the work of Joseph Brodsky, Osip Mandelshtam's later collection *Voronezhskie tetradi* (*Voronezh Notebooks*), Nadezhda Mandelshtam's memoirs, and the oeuvre of contemporary prose writer Sasha Sokolov, *Shkola dlia durakov* (*A School for Fools*).[59] Some of our respondents are familiar with Ardis editions:

> Andrei Bitov's *Pushkinskii dom* [*Pushkin House*] in an Ardis edition, 1980. (#113, b.1960)

> Mandelshtam (at the time there was no Soviet edition yet) and Nabokov. (#100, b.1946) [The Mandelshtam volume might be an Ardis edition, the Nabokov almost certainly is.]

> Sasha Sokolov's *Mezhdu sobakoi i volkom* [*Between Dog and Wolf*]. (#12, b.1963)

> Many books published by the émigré publishers Posev and Ardis. (#76, b.1951)

There was (very) much literature, all the best texts [came out in tamizdat], which is why I list only the publishing houses: Ardis, YMCA Press, Posev. (#5, b.1951)⁶⁰

The overwhelming majority of our readers indeed report contact with tamizdat: ninety-eight respondents out of 122. On the other hand, not everybody clearly distinguished between samizdat and tamizdat. Question 29 asks about respondents' experience of collective reading of samizdat, i.e. people meeting to share a single physical copy of a text ('Do you remember incidents when samizdat texts were read collectively [e.g. when one person would read a page and then pass it on to the next]? Which texts were read in this way, and when was that?'). Respondent #57 (b.1953), replies: 'In 1975–1976 the first volume of [Solzhenitsyn's *Gulag*] *Archipelago* was read by groups of students in the zone E dorms of the main building of Moscow State University.' It is highly likely that the respondent is referring to a tamizdat copy or secondary reproduction thereof.⁶¹ Respondents who mentioned 'the American Mandelshtam' or 'the American Mandelshtam edition' were without doubt referring to tamizdat, although it is not clear whether they had an actual printed copy or a reproduction.⁶² Some people identified the two modes completely with one another: 'I don't know the difference' (#94, b.1960).⁶³ Some gave a more differentiated answer: 'Tamizdat literature was often retyped and turned into samizdat, which is why it is pointless to distinguish between samizdat and tamizdat' (#116, b.1966).⁶⁴ The reply of respondent #19 (b.1966) shows that by the time the younger generation came to read samizdat, tamizdat had taken over: 'See my earlier responses [with regard to specific titles] – basically everything I listed there was tamizdat.'

Perhaps these blurred or non-existent boundaries should not come as a surprise. Once a text re-entered the USSR in a foreign edition, it would inevitably be further reproduced in order to maximize its readership, often by means of either photography or photocopy (in Russian, *fotokopiia* and *kserokopiia* respectively), which had become more widely available by the 1970s. Our respondents' testimonies, as well as the reports of samizdat collectors in Chapter 4, suggest that tamizdat was increasingly the main source for longer texts and entire books, and that copies were widespread.⁶⁵

The Gulag Arkhipelago (photocopied, which means it can be counted as samizdat), as the volumes appeared one after the other. (#57, b.1953)⁶⁶

We had photo prints of *The Gulag Archipelago*, which were kept in the overhead cupboard. (#59, b.1951)⁶⁷

You would find [Vladimir] Voinovich's *Chonkin,* Platonov's *Chevengur* and *Kotlovan* [*The Foundation Pit*], works by Nabokov and Avtorkhanov, the memoirs of Nadezhda Mandelshtam and many other things. I can't say whether the literary works were photocopies or originals. But I think there were only a few originals, if we don't count periodicals like *Vestnik RKhD* [The Herald of the Russian Christian Movement], *Vremia i my* [Time and Us], *Strana i mir* [Country and World] and the newspaper *Russkai mysl'* [Russian Thought]. Those were probably originals, and I don't think they were being reproduced. (#105, b.1949)⁶⁸

They were for the most part photocopies of tamizdat editions (Pomerants, Yu. Annenkov, A. Galich, Mandelshtam, with corrections by [his widow] Nadezhda Mandelshtam) and classified editions (Djilas etc). (#50, b.1955)⁶⁹

Classified editions (in Russian, *izdanii s grifom 'Rasprostraniaetsia po spisku'*) were books that were printed in the Soviet Union, usually in very small print runs, and made available only to a narrow and select circle of people, usually government officials. They were rare compared to tamizdat, but could play a similar role if and when they were circulated. A particularly salient story involving a classified edition is related by Larisa Bel'tser. In the early 1980s, with the title year of Orwell's *1984* fast approaching, the authorities ordered the production of a classified Russian edition: 'The publishing house *Progress* published Orwell's novel as part of the so-called "White Series" in a print run of 500 copies. It wasn't produced for sale, but was intended for distribution among the top members of the nomenclature, or, in the words of Orwell, the "inner party".' Bel'tser, who worked at the Soviet Academy of Science's Institute of Comparative Political Science at the time, was part of a group tasked with monitoring Western attitudes to this book. Her colleagues managed to procure a Progress edition by clandestinely 'borrowing' it from a party official's private flat, only to lose it shortly afterwards. Desperate to cover up the loss, they managed to source a second book and set out to produce a convincing-enough copy to return to the original owner, complete with the serial number. With good contacts in the samizdat scene ('At least we had a lot of experience in how to procure forbidden stuff [*zapreshchenka*]. For us it had become our "daily bread", we were the generation brought up on samizdat'), they recruited the necessary help. This is how Beltser ends her story: 'The highly experienced samizdat veterans who bound our little book naturally didn't pass up the opportunity to make a number of copies for themselves. The demand was enormous ... This is how George Orwell "went to the people."'⁷⁰ Like tamizdat, publications intended for the party elite could also turn into samizdat.⁷¹

People sourced tamizdat (and classified editions) in exactly the same way as samizdat: via friends and acquaintances, as reported by fifty-three out of the seventy-nine respondents who specified how they obtained the tamizdat they read. But it is worth noting that only eleven respondents remember passing on texts for publication abroad, and eight respondents report receiving texts directly from abroad via their own contacts or those of acquaintances. Two others had the opportunity to bring texts into the USSR themselves, while the third respondent had a tamizdat 'smuggler' in their immediate family:

> I smuggled suitcases full of books given by [name supplied] from Paris. Friends would bring them to be sent to the Soviet Union. (#48, b.1959)
>
> I began travelling abroad in 1977 and would bring books from there. Several of my friends managed to do the same. (#81, b.1935)
>
> My father was a journalist. He regularly went abroad and sometimes would take the risk and bring back books. (#121, b.1954)[72]

Tamizdat networks inevitably required reliable foreign contacts, which were viewed with suspicion and carried a much greater risk. Moreover, tamizdat cemented the centrality of Moscow for unofficial publishing in the USSR: Moscow was the location of foreign embassies and the main destination of foreign journalists. While private connections remained pivotal for the purpose of sourcing texts, tamizdat inevitably involved a degree of politics, as Western governments, especially the United States, used their publishing prowess as a soft power tool to subtly influence public opinion in the Soviet Union.[73]

Irina Roskina, who lived in Moscow at the time, remembers: '[Georgii] Vladimov's *Vernyi Ruslan* [*Faithful Ruslan*], [Vasilii] Grossman's *Vse techet* [*Everything Flows*], tamizdat editions of the poetry of Akhmatova and Mandelshtam and others were given to us by foreign correspondents and interns. The American Embassy handed out many of these works for free.'[74] Two witnesses, both from Leningrad, explain Moscow's significance. Yurii Kolker attributes the relative scarcity of literary samizdat journals in Moscow to the fact that Moscow authors found it easier to get 'published': 'In Moscow there were more Western-published books; the manuscript of a Moscow author got to the printing shop faster.'[75] Kirill Kozyrev explains why Moscow became the capital of dissident as opposed to literary underground activity: 'This was because [Moscow] is where the embassies are, so you could pass on texts via the embassy employees ... Letters and so on – all this was passed on via Moscow.'[76] Two of our respondents explicitly name Moscow friends as their source for tamizdat. As tamizdat was often the basis for large collections of unofficially published literature, Moscow was of disproportionate importance for those collections.[77]

Tamizdat publishers also pursued political interests independent of those of Western governments. While Ardis Publishers was a primarily cultural, scholarly endeavour, and the editors produced books for friends in the USSR rather than for wide circulation, and while Tatiana Goricheva's Beseda focused on religion and poetry, some émigré publishers were openly anti-Soviet and produced and distributed literature with the aim of making a political impact. One example is the émigré organization Narodno-trudovoi soiuz (shortened to NTS, Popular Workers' Union), who had been publishing the journals *Posev* (Sowing) and *Grani* (Facets, not officially associated with the NTS) since 1945–1946 and were running the Possev [*sic*] publishing house in Munich/Frankfurt. This publisher printed pocket-sized books in Russian, for example a collected works of Solzhenitsyn (six volumes, 1971), as part of a targeted distribution campaign in the USSR.[78]

Politically sensitive literature, especially if it was 'imported' from abroad, made the owner liable to reprisals. Mikhail Meilakh, a literary scholar whose name is forever linked to the 'resurrection' of OBERIU, had longstanding links to publishing houses abroad. Meilakh had circulated the OBERIU manuscripts, which had miraculously survived the war and the Blockade of Leningrad, among his friends and in so doing introduced unofficial culture to the last avant-garde group of the 1920s. When he understood that there was no chance of publishing them in the Soviet Union he facilitated their publication abroad. Eventually, the works of Alexander Vvedenskii and Daniil Kharms were published in the United States and Germany respectively.[79] Meilakh's large collection of tamizdat literature was a key contributing factor to the prison term he received in 1984 (seven years of camp and five years of exile, freed in 1987 as part of Gorbachev's amnesty). Meilakh has told his story multiple times; his testimony provides insight into a special route for books into the USSR, using diplomatic channels, as well as into the role of the secret services on both sides:

> The collection of books in Russian, published abroad (tamizdat), for which I was imprisoned … had been collected over many years, even decades, mostly through interns who were able to receive parcels from abroad via diplomatic channels. The CIA made eager use of this opportunity. Let's say you asked for Mandelstam or Nabokov – here are the books, but they would add some Avtorkhanov to the parcel, or that strange book on Gagarin's space flight by the late Leonid Finkelshtein, *Sovetskii kosmicheskii blef* [*The Russian Space Bluff*]. And it wasn't just interns that we socialized with, but also correspondents of Western newspapers and diplomats. In Moscow there were several ladies who hosted salons where these people would congregate.[80]

Particularly interesting in this context is the observation that a person with the right contacts could 'order' tamizdat books. This is a topic that deserves further investigation. However, concentrating on the role of the secret services narrows our view of a process that was ultimately highly complex and involved a number of factors and players. Anatolii Vershik remembers that the circulation of certain books was tightly monitored: 'The movements of certain books were tracked: *V belye nochi* [*White Nights*] by M. Begin, V[ladimir] Bukovsky's *I vozvrashchaetsia veter* [*Back to its circlings the wind is returning*] or Robert Conquest's exquisite and widely known *The Great Terror* ... And for journals like *Kontinent* you could "get" several years of imprisonment.'[81] Indeed, it is these 'forbidden' editions that people remember, with Solzhenitsyn as the most frequently mentioned author (twenty individual mentions) and *Posev* (journal and publishing house) mentioned eight times and *Kontinent* nine times. Respondent #72 (b.1940) says: 'There were many titles, if I'd named any that would be accidental. There is one exception – Solzhenitsyn's *Gulag Archipelago*. For me, that was the height of tamizdat.'[82] This chimes with the memories of Lev Turchinskii, known for using his skills as a bookbinder to bind innumerable volumes of samizdat. Asked about the black book market, where book lovers traded pre-revolutionary and other rare books, but also increasingly tamizdat editions, he reminisces: 'Everything changed when *The Gulag Archipelago* came out. It passed from one person to another in the foreign edition and there was even an anecdote about a man who came and asked for *Treasure Island* and was given *The Gulag Archipelago*.' But Turchinskii also maintains that the foreign edition of *The Gulag Archipelago* marked the beginning of a new, much harsher attitude on the part of the authorities towards those who collected forbidden books, which affected people in his immediate vicinity:

> The KGB cracked down on the black market of books. Many people went to prison, including two acquaintances of mine, the poet and translator Alexander Fleshin and Volodya – nobody in the book scene knew his surname and we called him Hippo [*Begemot*] because of his large frame and height; he worked with the ambulance service. I never saw Hippo again. He was a good guy. Sasha Fleshin returned some five years later and told us he'd been tried according to two different articles – for speculation and anti-Soviet propaganda [*anti-Sovetchina*].[83]

Orwell, whose name reliably recurs among the authors who left a strong impression, was named four times as a tamizdat author, showing that, for many, tamizdat was any book that originated abroad rather than a Russian-language book published outside the Soviet Union. Our respondents confirm that the perceived 'danger' of a text determined how they treated it:

> *The Gulag Archipelago,* in a photocopy reproduction, was kept in the overhead cupboard, called 'the Tablets of Testimony' and given to close friends, while other materials were constantly in free circulation. (#59, b.1951)

> I would stash away political samizdat (microfilms, to be precise) in the basement. (#27, b.1954)

Foreign radio stations: The 'Voices' of samizdat

The physical circulation of samizdat was arduous and had its limits. One institution that greatly enhanced the reach of unofficial texts was foreign radio stations that broadcast samizdat text, read out loud, back to the Soviet Union. As these were, to various degrees, sponsored by Western governments and security services, critical analysis has often focused on the moral ambiguities created by this setup.[84] The question of which – and whose – aims these broadcasts were furthering stands out much more than in the case of books crossing the border from the West, because the process of book smuggling was nevertheless decentralized and depended on publishing houses and individual contacts.[85] There is a vast body of literature available on the subject of Western involvement in the samizdat process.[86] My aim here is limited to investigating how listening to foreign radio broadcasts of samizdat and tamizdat in Russian (as opposed to, say, Western news or news about events in the Soviet Union, such as arrests, which were also reported) influenced our respondents' experience and perception of samizdat. In this respect I will treat the 'Voices' in the spirit of the analysis of Friederike Kind-Kovacs, who has called Radio Free Europe/Radio Liberty (RFE/RL) 'the tools of intellectuals bent on spreading uncensored literature'. According to her analysis, the creators of these radio stations possessed great 'awareness of the literary underground press' great potential for the rapprochement between the intellectual communities in a divided Europe'.[87]

In the early 1970s, RFE/RL set up a section specifically for working with samizdat.[88] Texts were broadcast via shows such as *Unpublished Works of Samizdat Authors* and *Samizdat Review*. Today, these broadcasts can be accessed online via the website of the Open Society Archives.[89] Moreover, beginning in 1971, RFE/RL published an almost weekly bulletin that reproduced samizdat texts (*Materialy samizdata*, until 1992). In addition, thirty-four volumes of samizdat documents were published under the name *Sobranie dokumentov samizdata* (Collected Documents of Samizdat), catalogued as *Arkhiv samizdata* and made available to major repositories. For a long time, this was the most representative collection of samizdat documents easily accessible to researchers. However, as the station's programme was skewed towards politically significant materials, both as a result of its official mission and of the kind of texts that people would make an effort to smuggle abroad, the image of samizdat preserved by this archive lacks many facets, in particular those provided by contemporary literary texts. This factor might well have contributed to the widespread association of samizdat with dissidence at the expense of its other cultural functions.[90] Kirill Kozyrev deplores the absence of contemporary 'second culture' from foreign radio, speculating that it was motivated by a fear of causing problems for cultural figures who remained in the USSR:

> If we recall, for example, the broadcasts of Voice of America, BBC or Radio Liberty of that time – the cultural direction – perhaps they were afraid of compromising those people [in the USSR] ... What was being read there? Well, *The Gulag Archipelago,* Nabokov and some others. ... But it was impossible to hear young poets and writers writing at the time – they were simply not represented.[91]

A brief scroll through the Radio Liberty rubric *In the Land of Poetry* does indeed reveal that younger poets living in the Soviet Union were virtually absent. Instead, the broadcasts featured widely known favourites, for example Tsvetaeva and the recent émigrés Joseph Brodsky and Alexander Galich.[92]

A clear majority of the respondents to the samizdat survey, seventy-one individuals out of 122, remember listening to samizdat texts on the radio. Here are some typical answers:

> The texts of Solzhenitsyn and Siniavskii. The poetry of Akhmatova. Radio Liberty and the BBC, from the 1960s–1980s. I don't remember the details. (#56, b.1945)

> I didn't pay attention, but my parents would constantly listen to Radio Liberty, the BBC, Deutsche Welle, and Voice of Israel. (#14, b.1967)

> Everything – from Brodsky to Gorenshtein and Solzhenitsyn. The radio was on for ten hours a day, particularly at the dacha, where the jamming wasn't so noticeable. (#19, b.1966)

> 'What goes on in Russia we'll find out from the BBC.' [In Russian, the sentence rhymes: 'Chto tvoritsia na Rusi uznaem iz Bee-Bee-Cee.'] (#27, b.1954)[93]

In an interview given to researchers at Bremen University in the early 1980s, Lev Kopelev and Raisa Orlova, recently emigrated to Germany, sketched out the significance of foreign radio for the samizdat process:

Without [foreign radio] it is completely impossible to imagine the scope of what was going on. Initially, we didn't understand its significance. And once again, I'm convinced that in the beginning it was all very spontaneous. And the people who were doing it didn't understand fully what they were doing. Foreign correspondents were simply reporting on what was happening in Moscow. And this was broadcast back to us by radio, approximately from 1970 onwards. *Orlova*: It was a mass phenomenon. Here I think we can talk without exaggeration about millions of people, at the very least hundreds of thousands. Millions of listeners … [People were listening to foreign radio because] they had a need for information. The need for information was huge. And, for the first time in many years, information cascaded down to us, so to speak … For a long time, the late Anatolii Maksimovich Goldberg[94] was the best-known person. Goldberg's voice was the most famous voice in the Soviet Union. One young woman told me 'I don't live with my husband at all, I live with Goldberg, because it is only Goldberg to whom I listen all the time.'[95]

For Irina Lashchiver, whose mother Asia was an active dissident, the 'Voices' and typewriters are closely associated – two iconic sound settings in a family of samizdat activists: 'One of my first auditory impressions as a child was the noise made by the jammers and the "enemy voices" that struggled through that every night. And [there was always] the clatter of the typewriter – some books were impossible to buy even on the black market.'[96]

In some cases, it was foreign radio that helped samizdat activists living in different parts of the Soviet Union to become aware of each other. Viacheslav Igrunov remembers:

I first heard the name of Larisa Bogoraz on 25 August 1968. At that time, I began listening to foreign radio stations. Or, rather, I took it seriously for the first time, because my previous attempts at listening to the Voice of America and the BBC had always ended with me turning them off and then not listening to these stations for several years, including at least 1967 and 1968. Well, in 1966 I didn't listen to them either. Only at the very beginning I tried to. But when our troops pushed into Czechoslovakia there was no choice – I had to listen. We needed additional information and not just that which our mass media, *Izvestiia* and *Pravda*, would give us.[97]

Sometimes, it seems, even the KGB received its information from the Western radio stations. Sergei Stratanovskii, who was involved in two secret conferences on the unofficial cultural movement in Leningrad in 1979, remembers: 'the conference went on for two days, and the KGB had no idea. They found out only from the "Voices", from Radio Liberty ... A real scandal ensued: "What is going on there? A conference on unofficial culture where people are giving papers?!"'[98]

Foreign radio stations clearly constituted a source for alternative, and by implication more trustworthy, information compared to the official channels. It can be said that their function was akin to that of samizdat versus official print in the textual sphere; and indeed, the person who listened to the 'Voices' has been identified as a special kind of samizdat reader.[99] Many readers 'received' samizdat in oral form, without ever holding a text in their hands. The West, and major government agencies at that, thus had a hand in spreading samizdat and tamizdat as widely as they were spread. According to the mission statement of RFE/RL of 1982, Washington created these stations to 'project a diverse international awareness',[100] a wording that chimes with our respondents' definition of samizdat's effect on Soviet society.

How samizdat was read

Samizdat as a collective reading experience

Samizdat was an inalienable constituent of the culture of *kruzhki*, informal circles that allowed people to circumvent highly regulated and prescriptive Soviet official culture, as described by Liudmila Alekseeva: 'These groups ... often replaced non-existent or for various reasons inaccessible institutions – publishing houses, lecture halls, exhibitions, notice boards, confessionals, concert halls, libraries, museums, legal consultations, knitting circles ... as well as seminars on literature, history, philosophy and linguistics.'[101] The 'collective experience of literature'[102] created and nurtured many of these circles, the functioning of which depended on the participants being able to identify and trust each other.[103] A closely related type of group emerged later as part of the unofficial music and art scenes in the 1970s and 1980s, namely that of *tusovka*, a group with no clear distinction between authors/performers and audience.[104]

Consequently, the typical samizdat reader was a sociable networker rather than the proverbial solitary bookworm. The majority of our respondents report knowing many others who read samizdat; see Table 8.

Table 8 Readers of samizdat

Question 14: 'How many readers of samizdat did you know?'	Number of Respondents
Under 10	9
Over 10	45
Over 100	28
'Many'	27
Not specified/can't answer the question	13
TOTAL	**122**

Those who reported that the majority of their acquaintances read samizdat were counted as 'many'. Typical answers include:

> Dozens. I think that there wasn't a single one among my friends who didn't read samizdat. And many of them made and disseminated [samizdat]. (#10, b.1955)

> Very many (practically everyone I knew). (#17, b.1950)

> Quite a lot, I think that in my social circle there weren't any people who didn't [read samizdat]. (#46, b.1968)

Yet this is precisely the genre of question where practical and methodological issues specific to samizdat make it hard to obtain precise information. Depending on the kind of samizdat they read, people were secretive about it and, as respondent #119 points out, '[I knew] several dozens, but I can't give a concrete number. If you were interested in [this question] people would have considered you an informer.' A more immediate problem is that even approximate numbers are hard to compare because they necessarily relate to different years and, as respondent #50 (b.1955) underlines: 'This question must be considered in relation to time. It is impossible to put [samizdat readers] from the 1970s in with those from the 1980s.' Nevertheless, they illustrate clearly that samizdat reading was a sociable activity. Not knowing enough/the right people from whom to procure and to whom to give texts is cited repeatedly as the reason why somebody failed to become a habitual reader of samizdat, or why they did not read a particular genre of text:

> I didn't have a reliable source for obtaining samizdat. If I heard of something interesting and could get my hands on it I would read it. (#11, b.1952)

> That depended on the sources to which I had access. For example, in my immediate social circle there were hardly any serious disseminators of political literature. (#56, b.1945)

In the reverse case, being part of a specific friendship group also predisposed a person to samizdat reading: 'This is what people read and gave to others to read in my circle of friends at the time' (#19, b.1966).[105] All these factors – the limited availability of texts, the clandestine nature of the process as a whole, and the fact that texts were often lent only for a short period of time – meant that people frequently read them together. Reading samizdat brought people together in the immediate physical sense. Indeed, forty-six of our respondents remember incidents when texts were read collectively. A number of them recall poetry as especially popular in this context:

These were literary texts, mostly poetry. We read them aloud in my circle of friends. (#31, b.1963)

Poetry. Voloshin, Mandelshtam, Tsvetaeva, Gumilev etc. The Silver Age. (#32, b.1954)

Later, collective reading was common in the case of particularly topical (and definitely 'forbidden') texts:

We read one after the other. Me, my mum and my wife. An ordinary family evening. We would read Voinovich aloud, I remember that. (#24, b.1976)

We would read, for example, Solzhenitsyn's *Rakovyi korpus* [*Cancer Ward*], passing the typescript pages round in a circle. I guess that was around 1970. (#73, b.1941)

For example, a photocopy of *The Gulag Archipelago*. In the flat of my friend [name supplied], in 1977. (#75, b.1962)[106]

Those who might in theory have something rare or forbidden would offer to read it at their place. (#22, b.1976)[107]

The Gulag Archipelago was not only among the most topical, sensational and 'dangerous' texts. It also brought people together, especially just after its publication, when there were only a few tamizdat copies:

I don't remember who gave us the *Archipelago*. It happened in February or March 1974, that I remember well because I was heavily pregnant. I phoned those same faithful girlfriends; I didn't have to explain anything. When somebody phoned you just like that and invited you with the words 'Come today, my mum has made a cake', you wouldn't ask any questions, but get into a taxi and go. All three volumes were typed out on very thin onion-skin paper. They had been given to us for a very short time. And so we sat up all night, enveloped in silence, and passed each other the pages we had read.[108]

> The first chapters of the *Archipelago* I received from one of the Germans at the journal *Der Spiegel* ... And so we got together. We didn't have the text in Russian, but everyone was keen on it. And so we decided not to put it off for a minute. Our *kruzhok* got together – if you can call it that, we never called ourselves a *kruzhok* – and I translated on the spot for everybody. I simply looked at the German text and translated it into Russian and sometimes even managed to get the style more or less right ... This is how we got to know quite a number of the chapters, well, at least those that were published at that moment.[109]

The small-group culture in which samizdat flourished brings to mind another time period in which *kruzhki* were seminally important to the development of Russian literature, that is, the literary salons and circles of Pushkin's era,[110] and later, of the early Silver Age.[111] The earlier period is especially interesting for comparison because it encompassed manuscript as well as print culture and was characterized, in the words of Simon Franklin, by '[a] fluidity of the relations of the various media ... Authors and readers, reciters and listeners, producers and critics, scribes and printers were in multimedia dialogue with each other as never before.' Franklin notes that 'the elegant manuscript album was revered as an emblem of civilized pursuits' and describes the salon members' vacillation between disdain for the vulgar new-ish technology of print and aspiration for print as the more reproducible medium which could provide professional writers with earnings.[112] Samizdat – a handmade, 'backward' medium that somehow managed to become the vehicle of the most interesting, novel, daring literary pursuits and rare, trustworthy facts – was held by its practitioners in similarly high esteem. The shabbiness of the barely legible typescript on onion paper was already 'cult' in the 1960s – in the words of one eyewitness, Natalia Pervukhina, 'the era of texts typed out on onion-skin paper, which were sometimes so faint that you had to place a white sheet behind them in order to be able to make out the words'.[113] Part of society preferred samizdat to official print, seeing it as 'more truthful'. A widely known anecdote goes like this: 'A man asks a typist to type up *War and Peace*. Surprised, she asks him why, upon which the man explains: "My son's in high school, he only reads samizdat, but I want him to read this novel."'[114] Our respondents tell similar stories, without the hyperbole that makes the anecdote so funny:

> I was a school kid, and I fully understood the value and difference between the printed [party] newspaper *Pravda* and the *Chronicle* [*of Current Events*] lying on the table. Hearing the conversations of one's parents and their friends is one thing, seeing the printed text quite another. That the pages were typescript made them more convincing in my view, weightier, more truthful. (#47, b.1955)[115]

However, while Pushkin's friends despised print for its potential mass appeal, (some) samizdat practitioners held it in disdain for its dependence on official 'mass' culture, which continued to marginalize, exclude and even persecute them. A comparison of the typical barely legible onion-skin paper samizdat page and a nineteenth-century manuscript illustrates this incongruity, and the limits of this kind of comparison.

Much more than just a reader

In our sample, those who 'only' read and returned the text to the person who gave it to them are in the absolute minority. According to the data gleaned from the responses to Questions 17/17.1 ('Which samizdat activity were you involved in? You can tick several options. Please give details about your answer.') and 24/24.2 ('Did you ever reproduce samizdat texts? If so, what influenced your decision to do so?'), the most common additional function fulfilled by the reader was duplication/reproduction, including for their own use or out of 'the desire to commit [the text] to memory' (#97, b.1951). Only twelve out of our 122 respondents report that they merely read samizdat texts (for the sake of comparison: twenty-two respondents were also samizdat authors). Thirty-four respondents popularized samizdat texts by reading them and either passing on their copy or retelling the content. However, seventy-one respondents – the majority – reported that they reproduced samizdat, usually with the help of a typewriter. Table 9 clearly shows how deeply enmeshed reading and publishing functions were.

Table 9 Samizdat activities

Question 17: 'Which samizdat activity were you involved in?'	Number of Respondents
Reading only	12
Reading and … retelling/circulation	34
Reading and (any other and) … reproduction	71
Reading and (any other and) … authorship	22

The testimony of Irina Roskina, who sent a letter to the researchers instead of filling in the survey, demonstrates that samizdat was a form of cultural currency in circles that loved reading: 'Later, I also contributed by typing out poems by Brodsky and song texts by Galich and turning them into nice little books I would give to friends. But we didn't regard this activity as circulation of samizdat. We saw it as representing our love of poetry.'[116] Her words are evidence of a very casual, everyday attitude towards the reproduction of literary texts that found the reader's favour. In the mind of those who reproduced (literary) texts, 'samizdat' was not necessarily a clearly delineated category.[117]

It is tempting to regard samizdat, especially its literary branch, as a particularly 'pure' literary process, which depended solely on the reader's approval on aesthetic grounds and as a result rendered 'viable' even texts that would not stand up to commercial scrutiny. It is thus imperative to scrutinize our respondents' motivations for reproducing samizdat. Indeed, the data submitted broadly confirms the thesis that the reproduction of texts depended on personal aesthetic approval or, in the case of political samizdat, the value of the text as information. Of the seventy-one people who reported reproducing texts, thirty-two stated as their reason variations of these three answers: (1) 'Delight in the unusual language' (#51, b.1952) or even 'My conviction that it was of exceptional literary value' (#63, b.1950)[118] and (#59, b.1951) 'I was happy to reproduce true literature';[119] or, (2) 'I felt an insuperable urge to share this amazing text with my friends' (#23, b.1955); or, (3) 'I simply wanted these books for myself' (#77, b.1969) or, in greater detail: 'I was given the book for one day, but it was very long, 800 pages. I wanted to read it but there was no time, so I had to photograph the book and return it. Later we printed the photographs. They took up a huge amount of space' (#103, b.1954). This is classic reader behaviour, and indeed the latter reason is exactly why readers in an 'ordinary' literary process visit a bookshop: 'The opportunity to own a copy of Jung's lectures' (#70, b.1962). By contrast, seventeen people saw their function as closer to that of a middleman in a literary process – namely, they were acting to satisfy a demand: 'One of my dissident friends asked me to' (#10, b.1955), or because they assumed a particular function, either professionally or through friendship ties:

> I was a member of the Leningrad Rock Club. (#18, b.1967; this respondent typed the Club's journal *ROKSI*)[120]

> My close acquaintance and friendship with the editors of various journals: *Chasy, 37, Obvodnyi Kanal*, etc. (#7, b.1957; this respondent typed and circulated literary samizdat journals)[121]

or because they had access to the necessary resources, for example a typewriter:

> They brought me a book and asked me to type copies. (#55, b.1954)

> I had taken typing lessons and could type very fast. (#14, b.1967)

The account of respondent #26 (b.1969), who remembers copying a tract of traditional folk medicine in Moscow in 1983, deserves to be quoted in full:

> It was a proposal I couldn't turn down: the original typescript was divided into parts and distributed for copying during lessons by the teacher at the industrial training centre, which all older pupils had to attend in order to learn some kind of profession. The subject was typing and office administration. Well, what did we care which text we used to practice speed typing?

Only four respondents cite a straightforwardly moral and/or political reasons:

> August 1968 [i.e. the Soviet invasion of Czechoslovakia]. (#40, b.1950)

> My desire to share information and examples of moral resistance with others. (#41, b.1954)

> My friend's insistent advice to use my position as a librarian and my steadfast hatred of the Soviet authorities. (#59, b.1959)[122]

The outstanding twenty either gave no reason or one that does not neatly fit these categories.

Does this really make samizdat an exceptionally 'pure' literary process, though? When we look at Silver Age authors circulating in samizdat, we should remember that interest in them was heightened because they, belonging as they did to another era, had been suppressed; their popularity could therefore not be compared to that of present-day authors, let alone present-day authors participating in a standard literary process. 'New' samizdat authors, specifically, those writing in the 1960s to 1980s, implicitly assumed the position of people whose creativity was being thwarted by repressive official culture. Persecution, or at least the risk of it, imbued the texts with a particular aura of authenticity. Of course, this would not work if readers were not complicit; their leniency and the absence of editorial input, in the case of self-produced texts, or permissive editors, in the case of some literary journals, temper any claim that samizdat as a literary process was dependent merely on the readers' *aesthetic* judgement.

What was samizdat: Text, process, multimedia sphere

The list of definitions offered by our respondents in response to Question 7 ('Do you have a definition of samizdat, and if yes, what is it?') is as varied as that used by scholars. Perhaps predictably, samizdat is most commonly understood to be a body of texts. The majority of the fifty respondents who answered to this effect stress that these texts were 'uncensored', 'unofficial', 'banned from official publication' or 'produced without the involvement of the authorities'. It seems that content defines samizdat to a lesser degree: three respondents specify 'prose and poetry', while only one respondent is adamant that the term applies to political texts only (#72, b.1940). Others (thirteen respondents) place the emphasis on how the texts were made – most frequently 'typescript'; others accept 'photocopy', while one respondent mentions 'handwritten' or simply 'not printed'.[123] Twelve respondents focused on the 'private', 'non-public' aspects of samizdat, the fact that it was 'done in private' and that the texts were 'the work of one's close friends' (#53, b.1954; #55, b.1954). In the Soviet context, which discouraged private initiative of any kind, the emphasis on samizdat as an essentially private practice – an area shielded from the enforced 'publicity' of official culture – carries significant weight. Only one person explicitly included tamizdat in their definition as 'texts imported without state control' (#20, b.1966). Some people saw them as completely identical: 'I made no distinction between tamizdat and samizdat. It was all samizdat to me' (#45, b.1947).[124] This reader evidently regards samizdat as a mode of being of the text. If we are prepared to consider tamizdat a distinctive subsection of samizdat, we see that, within unofficial culture, hand-produced texts and print continued to overlap. In this sense, the most accepted marker for samizdat is not so much the production method of a given text but rather the question of whether or not it was a product of Soviet official culture.

While the typescript page remains the iconic material representation of samizdat, samizdat was clearly not a monomedial cultural sphere, and only a few respondents limited samizdat to the typewritten page. Indeed, our question about the methods by which respondents themselves reproduced samizdat texts shows that all media were used – handwriting, typewriting, photography, copying machine and photocopy.

Only a small minority (twelve respondents) of those who answered Question 7 and 7.1, asking for their definition of samizdat, define it as a process rather than a specific body of texts. In six cases, this definition is simply 'the circulation of typewritten and/or forbidden text', placing the emphasis on the action rather than the object. Only one person calls samizdat 'a means of resistance' (#122, b.1965). Three respondents distinguish between the product, i.e. the text, and the process, i.e. in the words of #63 (b.1950), 'In the broad sense: unofficial cultural activity during the Soviet era. In the narrow sense: the texts.' The answer of respondent #50 (b.1955) is worth quoting at length, as it encompasses all the possible definitions that we have encountered. It is worth noting that he seems to rate the process as more important than the product and by doing so emphasizes that aspect of samizdat now favoured by researchers. He also underlines that it is the reader alone who decides whether a given text is circulated and how many copies come into existence:

Samizdat is:
1. the process of producing uncensored copies of an uncensored text (it's rarer that texts are unavailable for other reasons). Unlike the 'samsebiaizdat' of Nikolai Glazkov [who gave copies of his own works to friends], the number of copies circulated is determined, not by the author, but by the readers, according to reader demand;
2. the entirety of texts produced in this way;
3. an individual copy of a text, produced using one of the samizdat techniques that can be carried out by the ordinary person (photocopy, photography, copying by hand, reading on tape etc);
4. the same thing read on tape (a variety of 'magnitizdat').

For completeness' sake, we should supplement this with the words of respondent #4 (b.1972), who calls samizdat 'an unofficial, underground network for book publishing and book dissemination'. This reply evidently has its limits, taking only books into consideration and drawing a distinction between the process of publishing and dissemination that was not as clear-cut in practice. However, he is one of the few to emphasize the network aspect, which is crucial to samizdat as a whole and an essential rather than practical difference between samizdat and official/traditional print culture.

Samizdat was both the process and the product of unofficial – i.e. non-state-sanctioned – cultural activity. It centred on written texts, but was not limited to text alone. Probably the most salient difference between samizdat and traditional print culture was the role of the reader: readers alone were responsible for every single link in the chain that is the communications diagram (p. 15.). In other words, the success of samizdat depended on the informal networks to which readers belonged and/or which they created in response to their acquaintance with samizdat. These networks were foundational to samizdat. The survey, which will remain live for the foreseeable future, constitutes a sustained attempt at researching samizdat, in particular the reading and reproduction of literary texts, as (a cluster of) social networks – the totality of acquaintanceships connecting people in a particular place and/or social environment.[125]

3

Manufacturers: Samizdat typists

Introduction

As time went on, samizdat assumed various material guises, from classical typescript to microfilm, 'photocopy' – namely, photo prints from negatives – and photocopy made on a conventional photocopier. Yet typescript on yellowing onion-skin paper, and the heavy mechanical typewriter used to produce it – a specimen of which can be seen on the cover of this volume – remains the image most people associate with samizdat. Contemporary publications often use these material artefacts to create an instant visual association.[1]

A person who wanted a physical copy of a samizdat text, either because they had written something they wanted to share or because they wanted to own and/or circulate something they had read, had the option of typing it themselves if they had access to a typewriter and the necessary skills and/or patience. Some people learned to type in order to satisfy their curiosity for reading material; this is the story of veteran dissident Liudmila Alekseeva:

> This happened in the early 1950s, in 1953–54. After the death of Stalin, yes, but straight afterwards before [the 20th Party Congress that denounced Stalinism] in 1956. I did it because certain books were simply hard to come by while others could be bought in antiquarian book shops, but were very expensive. I was not interested in bibliography. The important thing for me was poetry. And so I would type out the texts. I can even remember the first book I typed. It was a collection of Kipling's poems in Russian, a Soviet edition from 1936. It was not forbidden, but very rare and out of print. And somebody lent it to me for a few days, with all the warnings, etc. At first, I copied it out by hand because I did not have a typewriter. But it was this book that encouraged me to buy a typewriter and learn how to type. We went out and bought an Erika. They were sold openly at the time. And I started learning to type, so that I would be able to copy out the poems that I loved but could not obtain. Afterwards I typed out my manuscript

in four or five copies – on normal paper, not onion-skin paper – and had it bound. And then I kept one copy for myself and gave the others to my friends. Everybody was glad to receive a present like this.²

Indeed, as typewriters became more widespread, people would also type their own texts. Often enough, this was motivated by purely practical considerations – Leningrad poet Boris Likhtenfel'd remembers learning to type so he could show his texts to people.³ The act of sitting down and typing out one's own text marks the moment when the author takes on the role of both typesetter and printer.⁴

The other option, which will be examined in this chapter, was to engage a trusted person who more or less habitually typed samizdat. This person would usually be a member of the informal networks in which the 'client' themselves moved. Those who typed samizdat were closely involved in the entire chain of textual production. Moreover, their participation in a quasi-illegal process, which implied the risk of persecution if they handled politically sensitive material, inevitably had an impact on their everyday life. As Elena Rusakova, one of several samizdat typists I interviewed, remembers: 'after all, the most important thing was not the person's ability to use a typewriter. The most important thing was whether that person could be trusted.'⁵ Whether the typist would receive money was a separate issue and depended on the relationship between typist and 'client', the nature of the text and, crucially, the point in time: commercial samizdat became a lot more widespread as the final decade of the Soviet Union drew near.

This chapter is based on a series of interviews with samizdat typists and others who were active in Leningrad in the 1970s, as well as a limited number of secondary sources and responses to the samizdat survey. I am particularly grateful to Elena Rusakova, Tatiana Pritykina, Natalia Volokhonskaia, Natalia Dobkina and Irina Tsurkova, who sacrificed their time to initiate me into the intricacies of manufacturing samizdat. My respondents typed everyday and/or literary as well as political samizdat. When I began taking the interviews, I was particularly interested in their motivation, alongside questions on how long they had been in contact with samizdat culture before beginning their involvement. In other words, I wanted to find out whether they were recipients (to avoid the term 'consumers') before they became manufacturers of samizdat. However, it became clear even from my small sample that typists were as heterogeneous a group as samizdat readers themselves, except that the overwhelming majority were women. The same person might have typed 'everyday samizdat', such as yoga textbooks and science fiction, for payment; political texts in conditions of strict conspiracy; and new poetry for writer friends in their spare time. I have therefore opted for narrative interviews that allow typists to tell their own story rather than a questionnaire with set questions.

The women quoted here did not just occasionally type up a few texts they wished to share with friends, but produced samizdat in large quantities, on a regular basis, and usually to order. This is the definition of 'typist' I will use for the remainder of this chapter. Mature samizdat, in particular any kind of periodical edition, depended heavily on those who were willing to take on this physically taxing work, meaning that typists were absolutely integral to the fabric of samizdat networks. Typically, they would receive no or little remuneration, because samizdat remained for the most part a strictly non-commercial endeavour. Moreover, typists received only a fraction, if any, of the recognition that the underground intelligentsia afforded to samizdat writers and editors while running a not dissimilar risk of persecution.

In many cases, the names of typists are as hard to unearth as those of 'ordinary' readers; they are links in the samizdat network that have been irretrievably lost. This is certainly one of the reasons why their contribution to the phenomenon of samizdat has scarcely been researched.[6] Just as importantly, perhaps, typists played a supporting administrative, rather than creative or executive, role; they did not compose the texts and had little or no impact on the content of collections or periodicals. Since most research into samizdat to date has focused on texts and authors, this might explain our lack of knowledge about typists.

Life as a samizdat typist

Producing samizdat texts was an intensely physical process. Natalia Volokhonskaia related the following variation of the anecdote about *War and Peace* I cited in Chapter 2:

> So, a director comes to work in the morning, and his secretary is sitting there typing away, surrounded by huge piles of typewritten pages. He asks 'Maria Ivanovna, what are you doing?' – 'Typing' – 'Well I can see that you're typing, but what is it?' '*War and Peace.*' 'Why that, [Leo Tolstoy's] *War and Peace*?' 'It's for my son.' 'But why?' 'Well, the only thing he'll read is samizdat.'[7]

This version of the anecdote highlights something that might be difficult to imagine for those living in the age of the computer, internet and smartphone: the production of (serious amounts of) samizdat was slow and very labour-intensive. Typing takes time and, without the possibility easily to correct errors, insert omitted paragraphs, etc., considerable skill; moreover, operating a mechanical typewriter requires a certain amount of strength. Typists remember: 'And the carriage return makes so much noise! It's very hard to imagine the noise of a professional typist typing on a cast iron typewriter. It's very noisy! Drrrrr-bzhik, drrrrrr-bzhik'[8]; 'On a mechanical typewriter you had to type using all your strength, your shoulders would hurt like a lumberjack's.'[9]

Moreover, a typewriter only produces a small and finite number of identical copies. Popular art of the time immortalized these limitations: in 1966, Alexander Galich sang that 'Erika beret chetyre kopii' (The Erika [a famous brand of typewriter] takes four copies).[10] From the reminiscences shared with me, it seems that the average number of copies in one set was typically six or seven, depending on the typewriter itself; but more importantly, in the words of Irina Tsurkova: 'with mechanical typewriters, it depended first and foremost on the typist, on the strength in her fingers'.[11] Tsurkova and the other typists I interviewed all claimed that they were able to produce twelve copies at once; several proudly showed me their hands, well muscled even now, decades after they stopped typing samizdat. The ability to produce many copies in one sitting was the highest-prized skill of a samizdat typist: 'I could bend a five-kopeck coin with my hands. The tender hands of a typist! I was very well trained, and at the height of my activity I could type 15 copies on onion skin paper, very thin paper, and copy No. 15 would be legible.'[12]

According to Volokhonskaia, finding a typist was easy. In the Soviet Union there was no shortage of people with typing skills and access to typewriters and consumables, not just paper but also ribbon and carbon paper. Most firms and institutions – not to mention publishing houses, editorial offices and so on – would employ in-house typists. The practice of typists using their access to the means of textual production to earn money on the side, a process known as *khaltura* (hackwork), was widespread. All the typists I interviewed remember seeing this practice or engaging in it themselves. Certain types of samizdat texts were easy to produce in this context. Volokhonskaia is even convinced that 'the majority of samizdat texts were typed in the workplace', citing texts of everyday interest, from yoga to science fiction, as opposed to rare new literature or material with political content. The results of the survey confirm at least that this practice was widespread: fifty-two respondents out of 122 report knowing about samizdat being produced in the workplace, on either typewriters or photocopying machines. Here a few typical answers to Questions 26 and 26.1 ('Did you know about samizdat being reproduced in state enterprises, either using photocopy or office typewriters? If yes, please tell us more. Which texts were reproduced in this way?'):

> In the 1970s. The texts weren't political, it was all popular culture. (#10, b.1955)

> My husband told me afterwards that in the late 1970s, he used the copying machines at work. [He copied] Zinoviev's *Ziiaiushchie vysoty* [*Yawning Heights*] and [the poetry of] Tsvetaeva and Mandelshtam. (#14, b.1967)

> The forbidden texts of the Strugatsky brothers and reports about UFOs. Between 1976–1982. (#20, b.1966)

> I reproduced everything with the help of a photocopier at the institute where I worked. Later, the lady who made money on the side by allowing us to do it was fired and went to work in a different Scientific Research Institute (NII), and I would go to see her there. (#50. b.1955)

Typists who worked in this way typically stayed behind after hours to work on their private commissions: Volokhonskaia herself remembers that, initially, she was not in the habit of distinguishing between samizdat and other texts brought to her. However, many texts were typed in a private space, particularly those texts that clearly exhibited 'illegal' characteristics. Poets and writers could usually rely on somebody within their own circle who was willing to make a few copies for readings and sharing; Volokhonskaia's own activity is a case in point. A poet herself, she would also type up the work of friends.[13] Longer texts, let alone periodicals, required a more concerted approach, especially when large amounts of sensitive text needed to be copied. Those texts were typed in the home of the typist or, in some cases, in the home of the 'customer' or in specially chosen 'secret flats':

> I very often worked in 'conspiracy flats'. They weren't entirely conspiratorial. They belonged to acquaintances with whom I was not acquainted ... Somebody would take me there and tell [the occupants] that this woman was going to sit here and type. I would type for some time. Then somebody would come and collect what I had typed and take me home ... As a rule, it wasn't dangerous.[14]

None of the typists who were interviewed for this chapter used their skills exclusively for the purpose of producing samizdat. Samizdat blurred the concept of public space and time and the private equivalent, drawing simultaneously on the professional skills and private connections and convictions of the typists. As we shall see, it could also blur the boundary between typing for money and typing as a passion or civic obligation. Irina Tsurkova recalls: 'I was also working as a professional typist. You could say I worked double shifts. One shift I would work at my official job, where I would type and take care not to overexert myself, and afterwards, in the evening and at night, I would type my own things [i.e. samizdat commissions].' For her, samizdat commissions were a matter of conscience and taste: 'On principle I never took any money for samizdat. How would the people who gave me samizdat to type have had any money?' Tatiana Pritykina began typing samizdat as a quasi-hobby in the early 1970s, while working as a typist in the editorial office of the newspaper *Leningradskii rabochii* (The Leningrad Worker). Alongside samizdat, she would also type out diplomas and other texts for friends without asking for payment. In 1977, she began earning her living typing at home; among her regular commissions were articles for the official journal *Neva*. Alongside worked her friend Elena Rusakova. Rusakova was not a professional typist, but participated in the unofficial cultural scene and had been typing samizdat for her acquaintances on a 'voluntary basis', in small quantities and 'without deadlines', always for free. This is Rusakova's account of the two young women setting up their typing enterprise:

> And we bought a typewriter and told everybody in our circles: 'give us work!' We had a fairly close acquaintance, Samuil Aronovich Lur'e ... he worked for the journal *Neva* and would send us authors whose texts needed to be typed up. But that wasn't samizdat. That's how we earned our living ... And suddenly a certain Senia [Arsenii] Roginskii came to see us. We didn't know he was called Roginskii; we were told he was called Senia, and that was that. And he would bring us texts. We started typing them.[15]

It seems that those women who at some point began typing samizdat for money had amassed considerable practice beforehand, typing casually in order to satisfy their own or their friends' desire for new reading material. This is evident from the story of Olga Abramovich, co-editor and typist for the literary journal *Mitin zhurnal* (Mitia's Journal). In the 1970s, Abramovich regularly typed new poems and other texts written by her close friends, as well as texts already in circulation that she reproduced in order to increase their dissemination. She frequently kept one copy for herself and never asked for money for her services. By contrast, *Mitin zhurnal*, which emerged in 1985, was sold for a nominal sum in order to cover typing costs. During Perestroika in the later 1980s, a time when semi-official publications flourished, Abramovich turned typing journals into a profession, producing four different journals.[16]

The ability to move in different circles simultaneously, circles that exhibited different degrees of closeness to official culture and Soviet everyday practices, with different levels of personal involvement in each separate circle, characterized the lifestyle of a large proportion of the late Soviet intelligentsia.[17] The overwhelming majority of those who read and practised samizdat did not follow the exhortation to cease all participation in official Soviet culture, advocated in Alexander Solzhenitsyn's 1974 article 'Zhit' ne po lzhi' (Live not by lies), where the author posits an understanding of truth in starkly binary terms.[18] That people active in unofficial culture should increasingly combine different loyalties, switching between different versions of themselves without feeling evident conflict on a moral, aesthetic or ideological level, can be attributed to the overall disillusionment with politics in the 1970s. Viacheslav Dolinin observes: 'Among the creative intelligentsia, political indifference is becoming ever more widespread. For the vast majority, free thinking and voicing opposition in one's circle of close friends easily goes hand-in-hand with ideological conformism.'[19] However, we should not forget that samizdat became ever more common and available to a greater number of people, which naturally entailed greater diversity in the worldview of those who became involved. Samizdat typists were more immersed in the samizdat process than many 'ordinary' readers who might copy out the occasional text, but their lives were not necessarily different. Elena Rusakova remembers:

> This is how we spent our youth – during the day we worked for a Soviet newspaper feeding the Soviet propaganda mill, then in the evening and night we'd be sitting there and typing [Andrei Platonov's novel, not published in the USSR until 1987] *Kotlovan* [*The Foundation Pit*] ... First everyone would go to the cinema and watch some Soviet nonsense, then we'd go and have some vermouth and eat some cake and do things, and then we'd dance to jazz records – and afterwards we'd go home and hammer out some anti-Soviet flyers. And in the morning we'd go to work for our newspaper. We managed to combine all this somehow, you see?

Samizdat texts existed at many different degrees of remove from the official Soviet cultural sphere. This enabled typists to work at a level at which they felt comfortable; only a minority was involved in the production of politically sensitive material. Individual comfort levels did not remain static. The examples cited above already illustrate how typists would move fluidly between texts belonging to different frameworks. Let us now analyse the particularities of creating different types of samizdat texts in greater detail. Some samizdat could be created in the workplace: for example, non-forbidden literature or everyday texts that would not necessarily lead to reprisals if discovered. Whether reprisals would follow did not depend solely on the texts. Volokhonskaia tells the following story:

> Everybody can tell of some unpleasant incident. I still hadn't become a dissident and was sitting at work typing out poems by Evgenii Rein, the author from Moscow. At that moment some important superior entered, took a look, pulled the pages from my typewriter, gathered them up and left the room, cursing. But later I went to see him, took my papers and left his room. He was very surprised.

The superior's reaction shows that he was not concerned about the nature of the text Volokhonskaia was working on; it seems that he did not even take the time to study the material. Instead, his ire was likely caused by his employee typing something that was not related to her function at the office; he was policing, not samizdat, but the widespread practice of typists using office equipment to earn money on the side. Indeed, a professional typist who accepted orders on the side was not necessarily certain whether the text she was asked to reproduce was 'official'. Volokhonskaia remembers:

> I typed my first samizdat without even realising that it was samizdat. I was writing poetry and regularly attending a literary association [*literaturnoe ob"edinenie*]. [The leader] asked me to type Maksimilian Voloshin's poem 'Golod' [Hunger] for him ... Voloshin was not in print ... So I think that it was samizdat. And I had no clue – well, [it was] a poem by Voloshin, an interesting, strong, powerful poem.

Irina Tsurkova typed her first samizdat text while still a schoolgirl. Having learned to type in school, she followed the example of other girls who used the school typewriters for private purposes. According to her, the school turned a blind eye to students using equipment and consumables for their own modest projects, and indeed some of the respondents to the reader survey confirmed that they typed in school.[20] However, it is no exaggeration to say that Tsurkova's choice of text was highly unusual:

> The next day – we had to take typing lessons once a week – I brought along this copy of the first chapters from *The Gulag Archipelago* and sat down to type them. I can't remember now what fib I told the teacher, but I know that the girls in our class would often type stuff for themselves, usually something pornographic. Anyway, I told some fib and typed out those first couple of chapters – they're only a few pages long – in six copies probably, perhaps in eight.

Tsurkova was sixteen years old at this point and her carefree behaviour can be considered a result of her lack of experience. *The Gulag Archipelago* is habitually identified as a text likely to lead to persecution of those who merely read, let alone reproduced it. Possibly the most tragic case in point is that of Elizaveta Voronianskaia. Voronianskaia was one of three women (the others were Elena

Chukovskaia, daughter of the well-known writer and critic Lidiia Korneevna Chukovskaia, and Solzhenitsyn's first wife, Natalia Reshetovskaia) who typed out Solzhenitsyn's manuscript; she was also the keeper of part of this archive. She committed suicide after disclosing the whereabouts of the text to the KGB following five days of questioning in 1973.[21]

The risk a typist ran when accepting a samizdat commission varied greatly; handling politically sensitive texts normally demanded a concerted strategy of concealment, from production itself to delivery. Natalia Volokhonskaia explains:

> If a text is dangerous you need to type it more quickly so that it leaves your house more quickly. You need to hit the keys hard, from morning to night, in order to finish the job more quickly and pass on the text as quickly as possible. Then you throw out the carbon paper and hide the typewriter, because – well, what will you eat if they confiscate your typewriter?

When she became increasingly involved in dissident activities, Volokhonskaia was under constant surveillance by the KGB, which led to her adopting behaviour worthy of a spy:

> A curious thing once happened, during my dissident days. I had something that I needed to pass on. And I suspected or, rather, I was almost certain that the KGB knew that I had the item and would pass it on. And they needed to find out who I'd give it to. On that day I left the house and went round to see twenty-five different acquaintances. I was on my feet the whole day. I would drop in on people for a cup of tea or to use the toilet [so they would not be able to determine who exactly was the recipient].

Volokhonskaia is talking about dangerous individual commissions. Those who were involved in the more regular production of sensitive texts observed stricter rules of conspiracy: for example, the use of premises other than their own home, and minimal participation in the network around the publication. By thus limiting their own knowledge about the work they were doing and the individuals involved, the typists protected both themselves and their 'clients' – in the not unlikely case of arrest, they would simply not know any sensitive details to disclose. Tatiana Pritykina's testimony is illustrative while also highlighting the pivotal role of relationships of trust; the 'materials' to which she is referring relate to the almanac *Pamiat'*:

> My friends explained to me how to behave ... there was a brochure called *How to Behave during an Interrogation* which I must have typed a hundred times. We would distribute it and I learned it by heart. You must not give any information whatsoever. The less you know the better. I had no need for a close

connection with the people who were bringing me the materials ... I would never have received a person I didn't know. These people were introduced to me by Arsenii ... Arsenii was introduced to me by my husband, and I trusted my husband. So, I knew Arsenii, I knew his name and I even knew where he lived, but I had no desire to know any of the others. There was this scheme – to keep it within three degrees of separation ... My friend thought differently and befriended these people ... Later, during a different time, I became very close friends with Alexander Dobkin ... and we spent many years working together in the publishing house I headed ... But during these years, until 1983, I didn't know anything apart from their first names ... It would happen that some danger arose and we had to hide things in a different place. That means we had to put everything into bags and take it to one of our friends. Later we would take it back.

Even contact with trusted individuals required conspiratorial measures: 'I had been taught during the preceding years not to ask questions. That way it would be less dangerous for both them and myself. They would phone me first, always from a public phone booth.' The landlines in the homes of people involved in unsanctioned activities were often tapped; using public phones minimized the risk that a phone call would inform the KGB of their plans. Sergei Stratanovskii, who edited several literary journals, remembers employing similar conspiratorial tactics although literature, unlike history and politics, was a comparatively low-risk genre: 'All of this was fraught with danger. We concealed the identity of the typists who worked for us. We would never call them from work ... At the time there were no mobile phones but there were public phone booths, and we would only call from those.' Stratanovskii maintains that the typists were potentially susceptible to pressure from the authorities precisely because they did not belong to the 'inner circle' of a journal and as a result were less invested in the endeavour. On the other hand, dealing with 'outsiders' made the 'inner circle' vulnerable to infiltration by informers, which is why typists were always recruited via acquaintances:

> **JVZ:** How did you find typists for the journals?
> **Sergei Stratanovskii:** Well, I don't remember exactly now, but it was always via acquaintances ... this is also how we found the man who bound the journals. He was a person like us. It would have been dangerous to entrust those matters to just anyone ... This is because [the KGB] kept tabs on things. Once we had a problem: we gave materials to a typist and she was visited by a KGB officer who told her to stop this activity. They always tried to identify the typists as an immediate point of contact.[22]

Yurii Avrutskii, whose network for the exchange of samizdat is discussed in Chapter 4, specified that one of the typists who worked for him only ever gave her first name.²³

The question of motivation

The necessity of behaving in a conspiratorial manner affected not just the relationship between typist and 'client' but also the material circumstances of production. In the case of *Pamiat'*, the 'client' supplied all necessary materials; supplying the typist at a minimum with consumables seems to have been common practice, at least in the case of journals:

> [Arsenii] Roginskii organized everything very well. I sat at home and [Alexander] Dobkin would bring me the materials. I had a small child, so it was easy to explain why I was at home. He would come to my place in Kupchino and bring me the original text, as well as paper, carbon paper and ribbon for the typewriter – they managed to locate all that stuff somewhere. And when an urgent situation arose that made it necessary to change typewriter – that happened once when the vice-consul who was transferring our texts came under suspicion and was searched and all our materials ended up with the KGB – well, we had to get rid of that particular typewriter and get a new one, all this needed to be organized. Typewriters are heavy; women should not lift heavy things, so they collected the typewriter from my place and brought a new one.²⁴

We can see that typewriters, the main tool of production, were particularly sensitive goods; this will be discussed in the section 'Manufacture: How samizdat was made' below. The responses cited so far all stem from women who typed more or less professionally in the 1970s and were largely divorced from the creative process, that is, the collection of background material and the actual composition of the text. A very different account is given by Vera Lashkova, a human rights activist who was sentenced to a year in prison in 1968 in the case that has become known as the *Delo chetverykh* (Trial of the Four). Lashkova was tried for typing the miscellany *Feniks-66* (Phoenix-66), edited by Yurii Galanskov and Alexander Ginzburg, as well as the famous *Belaia kniga* (White Book), the collection of materials pertaining to the 1965 trial of Andrei Siniavskii and Yulii Daniel that Ginzburg had compiled.²⁵ Lashkova, who was a trained typist working at home,²⁶ became part of a circle of would-be human rights activists during the many poetry readings taking place in Moscow in the early 1960s ('back then poets would constantly read their work'). Her typing the materials for which she was later imprisoned seems to have been motivated by her own involvement and convictions. In an interview given to Gleb Morev, she remembers: '*Feniks* was already quite long, in the format of a typewritten page, on onion-skin paper, of course, but it contained a lot of material ... *Feniks* was a very thick volume. The most important thing was to find a typewriter, paper and a person who was prepared to type it out.'[27] In other words, Lashkova was already a dissident when she began reproducing politically sensitive materials, and remained true to this calling after the end of her sentence: she continued to type politically sensitive samizdat, including the *Chronicle of Current Events* and the Christian almanac *Nadezhda* (Hope), edited by Zoia Krakhmal'nikova.

It seems that Lashkova's sentence was comparatively lenient – one year as opposed to the seven years given to Ginzburg – precisely because she was presented in court as 'merely' the typist: that is, a hired hand rather than a co-conspirator who happened to type. Agreeing to play this role – which she seems to have perceived as secondary and subordinate – spared her a harsher sentence, but did not correspond to her understanding of herself:

> However, when Alik and I discussed the possibility of arrest and related issues, he said: 'You must tell them that you were working as my typist.' He wanted to protect me, of course. I replied 'No, Alik, I won't do that. What does that mean, I was working as your typist? I wasn't working as your typist, I was working as your, well, as a person who thinks like you [*edinomyshlennitsa*].' But he managed to persuade me that I should say what he told me, although I was very uncomfortable with that. Because I had received no remuneration whatsoever.[28]

Lashkova's understanding of her own role as integral to the activities that led to the group's persecution is incompatible with the self-perception of the professional typists of the 1970s and 1980s, who worked at much greater remove from the texts. Natalia Volokhonskaia emphasizes that professional typists did not necessarily limit themselves to texts they found interesting or worthwhile, and even maintained that typists producing large quantities to order rarely studied the material properly; while Leonid Zhmud', reminiscing about commissioning copies of samizdat works he wanted to keep, specifies that typists loved Andrei Platonov and Vladimir Nabokov.[29] Crucially, Lashkova interprets the fact that she did not work for payment as the main reason why her contribution should not be reduced to that of typist. Ironically, her inclusion as one of four defendants in the Trial of the Four immortalized her name and contribution in a way that has not been afforded to the professional, conspiratorial typists of later well-known samizdat.

For some, it was their encounter with particular texts that cemented their decision to make a contribution to the process. As we have seen above, Irina Tsurkova was a sixteen-year-old schoolgirl when her boyfriend gave her excerpts from *The Gulag Archipelago* to read. This event changed her life:

> It was nothing less than *The Gulag Archipelago*, a few chapters from the first volume. I read it and remember going to school in the morning not having slept one minute because I'd been up all night reading those faint pages, which naturally had the effect of a bomb going off. It really felt like something had exploded inside my head ... 'I don't know anything and nobody around me knows anything. And then there are some courageous people who dedicate themselves to reproducing books like that.' My decision came immediately. I was a typist, after all.

After copying out these pages, Tsurkova began to type other texts supplied by Arkadii Tsurkov, the boyfriend who would become her husband. By the time she finished school, she was an experienced samizdat typist and joined Tsurkov and other friends who had decided to produce a samizdat journal in a kind of commune in a clandestine location. By contrast, Tatiana Pritykina did not express any outspoken ideological motivation. Her involvement in samizdat production was initially driven by reading and the desire to read more:

> Both my husband and I read a lot of samizdat; it constituted most of our reading matter. So we always had something in the house. Moreover, people would give me samizdat because I would promise to copy it. This was valuable, because I could obtain everything I wanted, immediately. I would promise people that if they gave me a text, in a week's time they would receive five copies.

While Pritykina experienced no desire to be involved in human rights/dissident activities in an active capacity, with time she came to see her role as a typist as a contribution to the opposition and resistance others were organizing: 'for the first ten years I did it for free, because I considered that, for me, this was the only possible way of resistance ... I liked the texts I typed'. Pritykina's testimony is significant because it demonstrates how reading – which in her circles was a low-threshold, essentially passive way of appreciating alternative media – and the decision to become involved in production could lie very close to each other. Of course, certain texts – we have already read about *The Gulag Archipelago* – had more potential to inspire a critical stance. Elena Rusakova offers an illustration of how the effect of a text depended not exclusively on its content but also on the material form in which it reached the typist:

It was one thing to type out Vysotsky's collection *Nerv* [The Nerve] for money and a different thing to reproduce Brodsky's poems. But you wouldn't get into serious trouble for Brodsky. Well, there might be some, but not much. The *Chronicle [of Current Events]*, now that was something else altogether. And apart from that, when you take the original material in your hand ... Have you seen it? No, you can't have seen it. I don't think that those things survived. Imagine cigarette paper of the kind used for *Belomor* papirosy [a kind of cigarette consisting of a disposable mouthpiece and section of rolled tobacco]. The mouthpiece is made from thick paper that you can take in your mouth, but the tobacco is wrapped in cigarette paper. So, people would remove the tobacco and write in minute handwriting on that paper, things such as who's been put into the punishment cell, or who's been beaten to near death ... And then they would fold that piece of paper one hundred and eighty two times and the result was a little ball, the size of a pearl. And that was your source text. It's impossible to not be affected, you would need to be some kind of ... the content, that's what affects you, you can't just let that go ... And you are also affected when you receive poetry from a camp, and sometimes even good poetry. That does affect you.

Rusakova's testimony highlights a clear hierarchy of preference: some samizdat was produced for money and without emotional involvement, and other texts were aesthetically significant, while topical material was capable of changing one's worldview. In the case of the *Chronicle of Current Events*, the extreme ends to which the prisoners went in order to pass on their testimony clearly played a role.

Manufacture: How samizdat was made

My interviewees provided detailed information about the physical production of samizdat at the 'coalface'. Some of this detail, especially the comparative aspects, is worth sharing.

The most important piece of equipment that a samizdat typist required was a typewriter. Irina Tsurkova remembers that, by the late 1970s, it was possible to freely buy typewriters, but that they were expensive. However, the shortage (and/or forbidding price tag) of good typewriters remained an issue. A 'good' typewriter was one that allowed for as many legible copies as possible to be typed simultaneously. Natalia Volokhonskaia points out that portable typewriters were particularly unsatisfactory in that respect but highly prized by those working in a way that was effectively 'freelance', which might entail transporting their typewriters from one place to another. Konstantin Kuzminskii, editor of

The Blue Lagoon Anthology of Modern Russian Poetry, also reminisced about samizdat production and remembers a rare stroke of luck: 'It was Boria Taigin who bought a typewriter for Ester [Joseph Brodsky's typist] in Moscow, made by the Czech company "Konsul". And although it was portable, it would make eight, and sometimes even nine copies!'[30] There was a second issue connected with typewriters: the type of each typewriter is unique.[31] People who typed sensitive materials needed to ensure that the device could not be traced back to them, and if they also typed other materials – 'harmless' samizdat or commissions, etc. – they needed to use separate typewriters for each task. Tatiana Pritykina recalls:

> I always used two typewriters. At home I had a 'clean' typewriter and a 'dirty' one. On the 'clean' one I would type all kinds of other casual texts. A dissertation for a friend, books and other things. On the 'dirty' typewriter I would produce flyers, [issues of the journal] *Pamiat'*, etc., because the KGB investigated typeface. When my friend Valerii Repin[32] was arrested and I was called for interrogation, they [the KGB] came to my flat afterwards to take a sample of my typewriter's type. That means I had to type a page in their presence. Every typewriter had some kind of fault. One letter would not come out properly, or askew or something, and that's how they would identify different typewriters. For some reason they didn't carry out a search. I typed the page on the 'clean' typewriter, while the 'dirty' one stood under the bed, where it wouldn't have been at all difficult to find! I never had any trouble with typewriters, because my friends got them for me.

Elena Rusakova did not keep the typewriter on which she produced the *Chronicle of Current Events* at home – it stayed with the man who brought her the material: 'As far as the *Chronicle* is concerned, certain rules were observed. Firstly, the *Chronicle* was never typed on the same typewriter as other samizdat, which is why our acquaintance who was, well, curating us and had got us involved, would always bring a typewriter under his arm, wrapped up in some kind of blanket.' As mentioned above, by no means all typists produced samizdat in their own homes. Irina Tsurkova reports typing only inconspicuous texts in her own flat. She would type samizdat in different locations and on different typewriters. Paper and other consumables needed to be procured and were in short supply depending on place and time. Paper was pivotal; and not every type of paper was equally suitable. The number of copies that could be produced in one sitting depended not only on the typewriter and the skill of the typist but also on the kind of paper used. Thinner paper meant each set would yield more copies, although the quality, i.e. readability, would inevitably suffer; this is why barely legible typescript on 'onion-skin paper' has become a symbol of samizdat.

Alexander Galich's song about the Erika typewriter, quoted above, immortalized the idea that a set contained four copies. My interviewees were a bit more generous:

> **Natalia Volokhonskaia:** On thick paper the normal volume is around five or six copies. That costs around 10 kopecks per page, prose rather than poetry. Our paper was 210 mm by 297 mm, standard A4 format, 210 by 297; I remember that to this day. The best paper cost 46 kopecks, but there were two kinds of paper. One kind was a bit rough, the other smooth. Text came out better on the rough paper.[33]
>
> **JVZ:** Did your clients bring the paper?
>
> **NV:** No, no. The cost of the paper was included in the price, or I charged for it separately.
>
> **JVZ:** Was it difficult to obtain paper?
>
> **NV:** Sometimes there wasn't any. You would go to a shop and there wouldn't be any. Well, [they say] I was born with a receiver in my hand. So while other typists ran around the city in search of paper and carbon paper, I'd pick up the phone and make calls, 'Hello, do you have any paper at 46 kopecks?' I had a list with the phone numbers of all shops selling stationery and I just rang round. Sometimes I would have to go to the other end of the city to pick up the paper.

Rusakova remembers that in the case of fairly spontaneous samizdat, the typists sometimes had to source consumables themselves: 'All this we did absolutely for free, and what's more, we often had to source paper and carbon paper ourselves, and that was hard to find.' Pritykina recalls additional details: 'It was hard to buy paper myself; sometimes Sasha and Feliks would bring it. Good paper was easier to come by, but it wasn't suitable for samizdat, because you couldn't make many copies on that. So there was paper for doing beautiful work. But the paper necessary for samizdat was hard to find.' The translucent paper commonly used for samizdat is referred to in Russian as *papirosnaia bumaga*, literally 'paper for papirosy', i.e. cigarette paper, but was sold in shops selling stationery and in fact continues to be sold under this name.[34] In English, the most frequently used term in the literature on samizdat is 'onion-skin paper,' referring to the brittle, translucent appearance, and this is this term I use throughout this study.

The most memorable stories told to me concerned the carbon paper that is needed to make a set of copies. Carbon paper retains the imprint of the typewriter's letters, making it possible to reconstruct what was being typed, and is therefore potentially incriminating. Typists sometimes went to considerable lengths to rid themselves of it.

Natalia Volokhonskaia: Yes. Carbon paper was harder to find, but as a rule, we all brought carbon paper from work. We would simply steal it.

JVZ: And what did you do with it afterwards? Did you throw it away?

NV: The carbon paper? Of course.

JVZ: But it retains the imprint of the text ...

NV: Ah! That was during the dissident times – yes, then people didn't simply throw it away. Burning carbon paper is an awful idea, because those black flakes fly and will go everywhere. Because of that, we had to tear it into tiny pieces and throw them into the toilet. There was even a designated word for it: 'unitazirovat" [a verb derived from the noun 'unitaz', toilet].[35]

JVZ: A good solution ...

NV: Yes. Ordinary paper you can burn, but carbon paper is a different matter. And there was good carbon paper and bad carbon paper. I don't know how the factories did that – sometimes, you would use the carbon paper once and everything would come off. The best carbon paper came from Czechoslovakia. It was longer than an ordinary page, so you could wrap it around and grip the top of the page and pull the whole set out in one go.

Irina Tsurkova: There were usually big reams of paper in the typing cabinet [in school], and carbon paper, too.

JVZ: And what did you do with it afterwards?

ITs: I burned it because I understood that certain conspiracy measures had to be observed. That someone could hold the carbon paper up against the light and spot anti-Soviet texts. That's why I always burned the carbon paper – I remember well.

JVZ: What did you do with the carbon paper?

Tatiana Pritykina: Carbon paper was easier to buy. We were supposed to destroy it.

JVZ: Because it could be used to restore the text?

TP: As a rule that was impossible, because we were poor, and so we used the carbon paper until it gave out. If you use it ten times it becomes practically illegible. But still, we made the effort to destroy it.

The accounts of the typists show that those who physically produced samizdat often had access to the means of (re)production in a professional capacity. The story below is by Irina Tsurkova and describes the manufacture of translations from Polish journals, which she undertook together with two friends in 1979–1980; the friends were native speakers of Polish and the three of them would translate the texts together:

> Lilya was a typist and there were two typewriters in the house. I mean, at some point she had two, at other times she had only one. And Valera was a

photographer and preferred photographic samizdat. The result was that we turned their flat into a printing workshop. A publishing house. Lilya and I would type, sometimes taking turns, sometimes simultaneously on two typewriters, Valera would photograph the pages, [develop the prints] and take them to a friend of his who would bind them. That is, we would make and bind entire photo books.

This is a rare instance where those who typed were also closely involved in, or witness to, the remainder of the production process. Similar accounts will be discussed in Chapter 5; however, they give the point of view of journal editors and do not involve the typists. Moreover, Tsurkova's account introduces two further technical aspects of samizdat production, i.e. multiplication by photograph – enabling a theoretically infinite number of prints – and the binding of texts into books. The practicalities of multiplication using photography (in Russian, this is often called *fotokopiia*, 'photocopy', as opposed to *kserokopiia* or 'kseroks', a copy made using a photocopier; the Russian term is derived from the brand name *Xerox*) will be discussed in detail in Chapter 4. The other aspect is the binding of typescript or photocopy into some kind of cover. People would bind samizdat texts (or have them bound) for different reasons: for example, in order to protect the pages and increase their lifespan; to make reading them more comfortable; to make them resemble professional editions; or to turn them into attractive presents. Binding required more technical equipment and skill than typing. As a result, it was mostly the remit of people who had access to the necessary tools through their workplace, highlighting once again the degree to which the workplace was tied into the phenomenon of samizdat. But covers were not essential for a text to circulate; binding a samizdat text remained an optional extra.

Lev Turchinskii, a bibliographer of twentieth-century poetry and prolific binder of samizdat, worked as a book restorer and therefore had both the professional knowledge and access to materials and equipment.[36] Turchinskii's trajectory towards becoming a well-known figure in the Moscow samizdat scene began with his bibliophilia and love for poetry. His story is published on the website of the online academy Arzamas.[37] In the late 1950s and 1960s, his keen interest in pre-revolutionary poetry drove him to the second-hand bookshops of Leningrad and Moscow where people bought and exchanged these books; the shops heavily overlapped with the 'black market' in books where people would 'exchange books in the street'. After he moved to Moscow in 1961, friends helped him find a job as a book restorer and binder at the Pushkin Museum, and over the years he used his workshop there to bind books and other samizdat texts brought to him. While Turchinskii was an avid reader whose prized skill guaranteed him a steady supply of topical samizdat texts, it seems that samizdat binding was, at least at some point, merely an additional source of income that helped him finance his passion for rare antiquarian poetry books:

> I myself was no dissident, but I knew many of them ... I simply loved reading, and forbidden fruit is always sweeter. Moreover, I had many friends who would ask me to bind manuscripts, including illegal ones ... on one of these days an acquaintance asked me to bind the samizdat journal *Evrei v SSSR* [Jews in the USSR]. I didn't even read it, it was just some work on the side that I did to earn money to buy books.

The company of intellectuals with similar interests introduced Turchinskii to samizdat and dissident ideas: 'After all I moved not only among scholars of philology, but also in dissident circles. I was friends with Vladimir Kormer, Vadim Borisov, Vladimir Gershuni, Father Alexander Men; I socialized with Alexander Galich and Yulii Kim. These people were not just book lovers but, from the KGB's point of view, dissident groups.' For others, the accumulation of rare and forbidden texts in Turchinskii's workshop made this room something akin to a library. The art historian Igor Golomshtok, who worked at the Pushkin Museum between 1955 and 1963, remembers:

> From everywhere in Moscow people would bring books and manuscripts to Leva for binding, and his room was full of illegal literature. Stacks of books published abroad, sets of émigré journals, rare pre-revolutionary editions and, most importantly, samizdat towered from floor to ceiling. Leva would readily give his friends samizdat to read for a short period. It was here that I first read typewritten copies of Solzhenitsyn's *Avgust chetyrnadtsatogo* [*August 1914*], Iuz Aleshkovskii's *Nikolai Nikolaevich,* and Venichka Erofeev's *Moskva-Petushki* [*Moscow Circles*].[38]

Naturally, this activity did not remain undetected by either the authorities or his superiors. The KGB took a lively interest in Turchinskii:

> Many times I was dragged to the KGB for interrogation – they wanted to find out what kind of books I was binding. I had bound hundreds of books; it is impossible to remember them all. Those considered seditious by the Soviet authorities included Gorky's *Nesvoevremennye mysli* [*Untimely Thoughts*], Arthur Koestler's *T'ma v polden'* [*Darkness at Noon*], the poetry of Osip Mandelstam and Joseph Brodsky, Varlam Shalamov's short stories, Iuz Aleshkovskii's *Nikolai Nikolaevich*, Solzhenitsyn's *Avgust chetyrnadtsatogo,* and Venichka Erofeev's *Moskva-Petushki*.

Antonova, the director of the Pushkin Museum, an otherwise liberally minded woman, warned him repeatedly, '[demanding] I not bring anti-Soviet literature into the museum. How can poetry be considered anti-Soviet literature?' Nevertheless, Turchinskii continued to work, and bind samizdat, at the Museum until 1974. In that year, his workshop was searched twice by the KGB. After the second search, he was dismissed from the Museum. The ostensible reason was a single issue of the journal *Evrei v SSSR*, which the officers found in his binding press, the glue not yet dry.

Turchinskii's account is rare for the amount of detail it provides, but samizdat being bound – and even reproduced commercially, on the premises of a Soviet institution – was certainly not a singular occurrence. One respondent to the samizdat survey remembers: 'In the building of the TsNIIPROM there was a section for "multiplication". The rules in this institute were relatively lax even during the strictest years. People would regularly use the commercial photocopier there to reproduce any text that was in demand (for commercial aims). The texts were also bound there and then.'[39] Binding samizdat was no less physical than typing, especially when no professional workshop was available. Natalia Lazareva, active in the Leningrad samizdat scene and involved in the production of the feminist journal *Mariia*, left a detailed account of the technicalities involved in binding a samizdat journal. When she was interrogated by the KGB on 28 April 1982, she was asked to explain the function of certain contraptions. The following is an excerpt from the interrogation protocol, which also contains a drawing of the instruments:

> I used all these items to stitch x copies of the collection *Mariia* while I was living in the flat of K(.........) A(......) on the Moika Embankment. In particular, I took two ... wood-fibre boards and put pages on top and underneath ... At the edge of the table I would fasten them with clamps. Then I sewed them together ... punching openings in the pages with a square awl. ... I did not use these awls. I did not use a scalpel for this. ... I would use it only when I carved the logo of the collection ... I glued the pages into the finished cover using 'PVA' glue. [With a brush] and a pen I would draw the logo of the collection and write the title ... In the section 'Attention, children' I drew a street sign and ... the heading of the section. I did not use the awl with the wooden handle. The awl with the white plastic handle was too thin and would bend when you used it to make holes, which is why I stopped using it.[40]

The majority of samizdat texts were not bound in any way. A loose-leaf binder or file remained the most widespread device for holding together loose pages. There were also other creative ways of keeping a large number of pages in one place, as this example shows: 'One item that stood out amidst this archival splendour was a little volume of the *Gulag Archipelago*. It was printed on photo paper and placed into a small cardboard box covered with grey canvas. A black-and-white photograph of the writer had been glued onto the canvas.'[41]

Commercial samizdat

The testimonies above demonstrate that, at some point in time, samizdat became a potential source of income for those producing it in large quantities. Typists working to commission and people hiring typists were symptoms of a process that was becoming increasingly well organized and professionalized.[42] All the testimonies I collected in person describe the 1970s and 1980s – that is, the decades when samizdat had become an everyday occurrence and tamizdat facilitated the reproduction of longer texts. Natalia Volokhonskaia, who treated samizdat for the most part like other commissions, points out an interesting detail: 'People made money with all this – everybody, including the typists there. This was a way of making money. Unlike poetry. With poetry, people might pay the typist or not. I was sometimes paid and sometimes not. But since, at some point, typing became for me the only way to earn a living, people would usually pay me.'

There remained a difference between 'everyday samizdat' – handbooks, song texts, etc. – which became increasingly commercialized, and 'high' literature, especially new texts by contemporary authors that needed to find a readership. Human-rights-related materials were a different matter altogether and were very rarely sold.

Twenty-five respondents to the survey discussed in the previous chapter remember buying or selling samizdat, while forty-eight respondents report knowing about samizdat being sold or produced for sale. Several refer explicitly to the practice of typists charging for their work:

> The typing and dissemination were done by a male friend. He lived on the money he got for disseminating texts and would type everything that readers might find interesting ... He would type and sell uncensored literary and political texts; I sometimes helped with dissemination, selling texts to people I knew ... That was in the early 1980s. (#25, b.1963)

> I set the price myself, corresponding to a typist's fee based on the going rate per page depending on the difficulty of the text (many footnotes and words in foreign languages that needed to be inserted cost more, etc.). (#26, b.1969)[43]

The commercial element involved in many of the literary journals of the 1970s and 1980s was usually intended to cover the costs of typing. Some recovered these costs via a subscription fee; in other cases, the editors found some means of absorbing the costs themselves and paying their typists. In any case, the fee remained very small. Poet and journal editor Sergei Stratanovskii remembers the women who typed *Obvodnyi kanal*, one of the journals he co-edited:

> **Sergei Stratanovskii:** I must say that [the typists] were enthusiasts.
> **JVZ:** Did they work for free?
> **SS:** No, well, we paid them a small fee because the volume [of the journal] was large, after all, but it was a minimal fee. That was all.[44]

Natalia Volokhonskaia confirms this: 'I did not type Viktor [Krivulin]'s journal [*37*]. I typed one issue of *Chasy* [The Clock]; every issue was typed by several typists. And Boris Ivanov always paid. However, the money was a pittance.' It is thus clear that, even when money exchanged hands, samizdat was not a lucrative source of income and remained a labour of love, undertaken for motivations that included ideology, aesthetics and friendship. The making of journals is discussed in detail in Chapter 5.

A different matter is samizdat for sale, i.e. when the finished product is sold for a profit. This remained rare, although it became more common as time went on, and often involved reproduction via copying technology. Survey respondents remember:

> In the second half of the 1970s, I regularly came across books that had been photocopied; these were literary and religious samizdat. At the time, it was fashionable to use photocopiers to multiply texts on yoga, Hinduism, meditation techniques and nutrition. A phenomenon arose that you could call commercial samizdat – those copies were for sale. (#105, b.1944)

> Silver Age poetry, late 1970s, 5–10 roubles per book. Siniavskii's *Strolls with Pushkin* [*Progulki s Pushkinym*], mid-1980s, 10 roubles. (#27)

> Albert Camus's *Myth of Sisyphus,* around 10 roubles in 1978 and Nikolai Berdiaev's *Proizkhozhdenie i smysl russkogo kommunizma* [*The Origin of Russian Communism*] in 1984, I don't remember the price. (#59)

> This happened as late as the mid-1980s. We clubbed together and bought a photocopied volume of Nabokov (this means it was either samizdat or tamizdat) as a birthday present for a friend, for a sum that was huge in those days: 40 roubles. (#77)[45]

Commercial samizdat is mentioned in passing in Larisa Bel'tser's colourful description of how she and a group of friends reproduced George Orwell's *1984* from an official Russian edition intended for high government officials in the early 1980s:

> According to our plan we now had to pass on the typed-out pages to our friends who made 'samizdat' – they had agreed to bind them and make a cover ... The highly experienced samizdat activists who bound our little book naturally didn't pass up the chance to make many copies for themselves. The demand was huge, and these samizdat professionals knew exactly how to make money with forbidden literature [*zapreshchenka*].[46]

Elena Rusakova states: 'at the stage [in the mid-1970s] at which I joined the process, [samizdat] was no longer spontaneous at all'. The commercial element represents a degree of organization that marked a departure from the earlier, more basic phase. It also constitutes evidence of a gradual rapprochement between samizdat and more 'regular' forms of textual production. It is worth noting, though, that commercial samizdat reflects a basic market mechanism and is therefore not modelled on the planned economy of Soviet book production and circulation.

The question of gender

Investigating the role of samizdat typists from the angle of gender provides important additional insight into the social structure of samizdat networks. Typists, as a distinct subgroup within samizdat networks, raise the gender question with particular urgency. They played a pivotal role in the samizdat process, yet their testimonies are rarely recorded and their achievements rarely researched, if at all. Most samizdat typists were women; at the same time, women were in the minority in other active roles. The combination of these two factors means that the contribution of women to the samizdat process remains catastrophically underappreciated.

The encyclopaedia *Samizdat Leningrada* (The Samizdat of Leningrad), the main reference work on Leningrad samizdat, which lists individuals, publications and groups, does not feature separate entries for people who 'merely' typed, even if they were well known to the editors. Viktoria Apter is a case in point. The main typist of the longest-existing literary journal, *Chasy*, for many years, she later married Boris Ivanov, who was not just *Chasy*'s founder and editor-in-chief but also one of the editors of *Samizdat Leningrada*. And yet Apter's name is absent from the crucial reference volume. Neither Elena Rusakova, Tatiana Pritykina or Natalia Dobkina are mentioned in *Samizdat Leningrad*, although the men who curated them – Arsenii Roginskii and Alexander Dobkin – feature prominently.[47] In view of this it can be concluded that typists who do have a personal entry, such as Olga Abramovich and Natalia Volokhonskaia, are included, not for their activity as typists, but for other reasons: Abramovich was editor or co-editor of *Mitin zhurnal* and the three other Perestroika-time periodicals which she also typed, while Volokhonskaia was a poet who published her own verse in samizdat.[48] A 2017 volume on the almanac *Pamiat'* provides another illustrative recent example of how typists are overlooked even when researchers are studying the particular network these typists served.[49] Researchers Barbara Martin and Anton Sveshnikov painstakingly collected interviews with many members of the editorial board but did not consider the typists at all, although at the time of writing they were alive and easy to trace via the *Pamiat'* editors or the Memorial Society in St Petersburg; three of my respondents for this chapter are *Pamiat'* typists. In another article, Martin and Sveshnikov casually mention the typists in passing and without giving names or an approximate number: 'they [the editorial board] benefited from the help of a few hired samizdat typists'.[50] Konstantin Kuzminskii left an enraptured appraisal of typists' contribution to samizdat, but only gives three names while admitting that

> The ones who distributed and typed the poems were women … countless numbers, I met dozens of them at the house of Grisha [Grigorii Kovalev, co-editor of the *Blue Lagoon Anthology of Modern Russian Poetry*] … so these women played a role in Russian poetry, too … How many of them there were, those selfless female typists slaving over the texts of Brodsky, [Mikhail] Eremin, [Dmitrii] Bobyshev and [Viktor] Sosnora.[51]

Of course, men also used typewriters in order to produce samizdat, and we can draw on several high-profile testimonies. This is Konstantin Kuzminskii's affectionate memory of his friend Boris Taigin:

> [He] published his friends. On a Kolibri typewriter (which is still in working order now), which barely makes three copies, and typing with one finger, he typed up more than 40 copies of Gleb Gorbovskii's collection … several collections of my poetry, the collections of Stanek Kiselev, Bob Bezmenov, Bob Biriulin – impossible to name them all – and [he typed all of them] with one finger and on that Kolibri typewriter.[52]

But Taigin was not 'just' a typist but a samizdat publisher and, crucially, a poet, and Kuzminskii's reminiscences form part of an introduction to Taigin's poetry.

Viacheslav Igrunov's memory of how he learned to type in order to reproduce longer texts precedes a description of how this experience inspired his search for better copying methods: 'Of course, we couldn't type out *Doctor Zhivago* in four copies ... We wanted to have the whole book, but we weren't up to it – it is very thick and I couldn't type. This, and later [Bulgakov's] *Sobach'e serdtse* [*Heart of a Dog*], helped me learn to type.'[53] Igrunov is best known for his 1970s samizdat library and his present-day efforts to keep the memory of samizdat alive as editor of the collection *Antologiia Samizdata* and the corresponding website. Mikhail Meilakh, whose efforts introduced the 1920s avant-garde group OBERIU to the Soviet public, remembers the process of preparing the manuscripts of Alexander Vvedenskii and Daniel Kharms for publication as extremely labour-intensive: 'It took a very long time. Volodya Erl and I copied the entire archive by hand. Back then there were no photocopies and all work was done by hand. Later the texts were typed out on a typewriter and proofread many times.'[54] In this case, typing was a technical process that underpinned the two men's painstaking work as editors of extremely valuable material pertaining to a genre in which they were experts: Meilakh was a philologist, and Erl was a poet writing in the tradition of the avant-garde of which OBERIU formed part.

As we see from these examples, when men typed, it was often only one part of their samizdat activity, and not the central one at that. Of course these examples are only snapshots. What is known is that those who typed in bulk and to order, including for money, were mostly women. Perhaps this should not surprise us. *Mashinistka* – the Russian term for typist – was a typical ancilliary profession and therefore a female domain, in the Soviet Union as well as in the West during those years.[55] Moreover, as a flexible activity that could be done from home, typing was particularly suitable as a source of income for mothers of young children. Elena Rusakova and Tatiana Pritykina, cited above at great length, set up their typing enterprise after they both had babies, and they took turns providing childcare and working at the typewriter. Kirill Kozyrev provides anecdotal evidence that various journals would recruit typists from among 'single mothers who stayed home with their small children'.[56]

A number of prominent women are habitually associated with both literary and human rights samizdat. There is Liudmila Alekseeva, identified in the pre-publication of her 1983 interview as 'the most famous samizdat typist';[57] however, it is not her service as a typist that made her famous. She was a very active dissident, forcibly exiled to the USA in 1977, chair of the Moscow Helsinki Group, and the author of the first systematic study of the phenomenon of dissidence.[58] There are also: Larisa Bogoraz, veteran dissident and member of many editorial boards; Natalia Gorbanevskaia, the fearless editor of the *Chronicle of Current Events*; Tatiana Goricheva, the journal editor and patron whose work is discussed in Chapters 5 and 6; the prodigious poet Elena Shvarts; and several dozen more. However, the vast majority of well-known samizdat figures – poets, writers, editors, human rights activists who communicated via samizdat, and political prisoners who suffered for it – were men. A visual impression of male predominance can be gleaned from the group photos at the back of *Samizdat Leningrada*; in *The Blue Lagoon Anthology of Modern Russian Poetry* editor Konstantin Kuzminskii assigned separate sections to only a handful of female authors and artists. The achievements of prominent female figures notwithstanding, the majority of women who participated in samizdat networks clustered around men, taking on the role of muse, facilitator, typist, archivist, hostess, emotional support and general aide, often in the time-honoured fashion of writer's wives or widows who edit and preserve their husband's work. As prominent examples, we might name Natalia Solzhenitsyna, the writer's second wife and editor of his manuscripts, who tirelessly promotes her late husband's work to this day; or indeed Nadezhda Mandelshtam, who ensured the survival of her husband's poetic legacy. Researchers, as well as the women themselves, have sketched these relationships many times; here are a few examples. In their introduction to the *Collected Works* of Leonid Aronzon, editors Petr Kazarnovskii and Ilya Kukui describe, at great length, the poet's relationship with his wife Rita Purishinskaia, who is, correctly, cast as his poetic inspiration and 'support in the struggles of everyday life'.[59] Alena Basilova, the wife of poet Leonid Gubanov, was a poet in her own right but is remembered as one who made her contribution to unofficial culture as a generous hostess, welcoming Moscow's underground poets into her home.[60] Human rights activist and typist Vera Lashkova, who spent time in prison on political charges herself, made an interesting point when she said that 'all of us wives of political prisoners became friends',[61] identifying women's loyalty towards their politically active men as the social glue that brought them together.

Relationships with men, be they friendships or romantic relationships, are also what inspired women to start typing samizdat in the first place. Above, we saw how typists Irina Tsurkova and Tatiana Pritykina were basically curated by their partners/husbands at the beginning of their 'career' as producers of samizdat. Natalia Dobkina was another *Pamiat'* typist and affectionately known as 'Klava', a nickname that triggers associations with the Russian words for 'key' (*klavishche*) and a well-known songtext by Nikolai Vil'iams in which it belongs to an underground typist. She would type up manuscripts and various materials to support her husband, Alexander Dobkin, who was one of the editors of *Pamiat*.⁶² Galina Drozdetskaia, who associated with the poets around the journal *37*, sometimes helped type new issues. She later married poet Alexander Mironov and identified her reason for involvement as admiration for the young men and the texts that they wrote, specifying she wanted to make sure that people read them.⁶³

In 1979, a group of women who had been involved in samizdat in various roles produced the almanac *Zhenshchina i Rossiia* (Woman and Russia) the first feminist publication in the USSR, if we define feminism as the discourse that gained traction in the West in the 1960s and 1970s. The almanac – alongside the journal *Mariia*, which was in some sense a continuation of *Zhenshchina i Rossiia* – has recently drawn much interest from researchers.⁶⁴ It is beyond the scope of this chapter to analyse the journal or late Soviet feminism in general. Rather, I will concentrate on the fact that the women behind *Zhenshchina i Rossiia* – Tatiana Mamonova, Tatiana Goricheva, Yuliia Voznesenskaia and Natalia Malakhovskaia – had been involved in unofficial culture and samizdat in various capacities for several years. Goricheva and Malakhovskaia in particular were closely acquainted, as editor and copy editor of the journal *37* respectively. It seems that their own observations of the attitude towards women in their social circles played a not insignificant role in their decision to set up a feminist publication. Malakhovskaia remembers:

> In the Leningrad samizdat milieu, people were happy to leave the technical side of the job (typing out and binding samizdat journals) to women.⁶⁵ When it came to publishing their own texts, only those women who had 'a man's mind' or wrote 'manly poetry' stood a chance (at the time, this assessment sounded like the highest kind of praise). Consequently, a woman's only chance to reach the reader in some way or other was to renounce and deny herself. The same dynamics were at work in the nonconformist art scene.⁶⁶

Malakhovskaia's diagnosis is astute in many ways: while the Soviet Union had comprehensive equal rights legislation,⁶⁷ much more progressive than that of Western countries at the time, patriarchal attitudes continued to dominate people's mentalities and therefore also everyday life.⁶⁸ And samizdat culture reflected the order of the society in which it was embedded. The feminists agree that sexism was rife in their surroundings; in the words of Tatiana Mamonova: 'The dissident artists present themselves as nonconformists only in their art; in their attitude towards women, they are absolutely conformist.'⁶⁹ Malakhovskaia tries to find an explanation, noting that 'these patriarchal attitudes towards women, which in the USSR exist in hidden mode and never vanished, came to light at the very moment people began to consider, in the most tentative manner imaginable, how these ideals of freedom might be realised'.⁷⁰

Malakhovskaia's comments illustrate that it is a fallacy to assume that a liberation movement will necessarily be liberal within its own structures. It should perhaps not come as a surprise that the networks of samizdat reflected the structures of the society of which they remained part – a society that was considerably less egalitarian in practice than its progressive legislation might tempt us to think. In conclusion, from a gender point of view, the structures of samizdat networks – which reserved supporting roles for women and in which women were underrepresented in active roles – corresponded to those in wider society. Samizdat networks offer much opportunity for further research, including research from a feminist perspective. This kind of analysis should begin with typists as a subgroup that particularly clearly exemplifies the gender-specific issues.

4

Collectors: Samizdat libraries

Introduction

Samizdat texts, and the networks within which these texts were produced, circulated, read and discussed, satisfied a demand for reading materials and discussion space that state-sanctioned official culture could not fulfil. This chapter discusses networks that aimed specifically to increase the circulation of samizdat texts and attract new readers.

Firstly, I will analyse responses to the reader survey on the topic of collecting samizdat. The data shows that most samizdat readers were avid bibliophiles who lived in spaces filled with (not necessarily samizdat) books. Some also collected samizdat texts, often specific genres. The replies also demonstrate that samizdat bibliophilia was beset by a specific set of issues that included the availability of material, the danger of keeping certain kinds of texts in the house, and the moral duty to share rare and/or topical material. Secondly, I will offer case studies of two special collections of samizdat; these are usually referred to as 'samizdat libraries'. While most people would share their samizdat with trusted friends, these 'libraries' were collected with the explicit aim of increasing the number of people who read alternative texts. They fulfilled the traditional functions of a library in extremely adverse conditions, which included the absence of fixed premises and the need to carefully vet new readers. In effect, the libraries were highly mobile, adaptable networks of committed samizdat readers. Thirdly, I will examine a unique samizdat publication: the review journal *Summa* that appeared in Leningrad between 1979 and 1982, offering its readers overviews, summaries and critical reviews of new samizdat publications. The aim of its makers was to increase the number of people with access to alternative reading, in this instance by providing information about texts many people would not have been able to access physically.

The analysis of library networks adds depth to our understanding of samizdat because these networks employed practices that are characteristic of the process as a whole, but exceedingly difficult to study in the absence of documentation.

Collecting samizdat

The analysis of reading habits in the preceding chapters has shown that samizdat reading fits into the pattern of Soviet literature-centrism and bibliophilia. During the early decades of the Soviet Union, which involved a large-scale literacy campaign, mass reading was mainly confined to libraries, many of them newly founded. From the 1950s onwards, private collections grew in importance as leisure activities migrated to the private sphere. The demand for books rose sharply, as did the demand for more varied reading materials, which was one of the factors fuelling samizdat.[1] And, of course, intellectuals have always been proud of their home libraries. 120 out of our 122 respondents boast of collecting books or growing up in homes filled with books.

Samizdat was a written rather than an oral culture. Yet the texts were highly mobile, constantly passing from hand to hand, read in short bursts, often overnight. If we add in the fact that the possession of samizdat, especially politically relevant texts, put the keeper at risk, it is evident that samizdat could never form part of readers' private libraries in the same way as printed books. Yet almost all of our respondents (102 people) kept samizdat at home. Those who named texts (ninety-three people) usually list works of literature, alongside two political texts, the *Chronicle of Current Events* and *The Gulag Archipelago*, as in this example: 'I think I would have kept more samizdat if I had been able to obtain these texts – they were normally given to be "read by tomorrow", more rarely for a couple of days, and in those cases I felt the need to share them with my friends' (#75, b.1962). Others queried the very concept of 'preserving samizdat':

> Samizdat and tamizdat were not supposed to be kept at home. They needed to be disseminated. (#7, b.1957)

> I actually tried hard to not keep the books at home for too long. It was a pity, as there were no copies. I acted according to the principle of reading as fast as I could and then passing the book on. (#105, b.1949)[2]

> Finally, it was rare that a beautiful edition from YMCA Press remained somebody's private property. It would be passed on to others and lost – this was

the general fate of books. What was important was not the book but the text itself. Not 'I possess this or that book' but 'I read this or that book.' This sums up the character of the period. (#116, b.1966)³

Yet others made a distinction according to the topicality of the text – information ought to be passed around in real time, while belles-lettres could be kept: 'Why should one not keep literature at home? But to keep, for example, a regularly appearing dissident chronicle about what was going on in the camps in Mordovia would have been silly. The *Chronicle* was immediately circulated so that people could read it, not keep it in their bookcase' (#116, b.1966).⁴ The perceived danger of a text also played a role:

> *The Gulag Archipelago,* in a photocopy reproduction, was kept in the overhead cupboard, was called 'the Tablets of Testimony' and given to close friends, while other materials were constantly in free circulation. (#59, b.1951)

> We burned the most dangerous part [of the samizdat archive], including copies of *The Chronicle of Current Events,* in the Ismailov Forest. (#63, b.1950)

> I would stash away political samizdat (microfilms, to be precise) in the basement. (#27, b.1954)

> A photocopy of the tamizdat Mandelshtam was openly displayed on our bookshelf. And a few typescripts were kept in the cupboard, hidden from view. (#75, b.1962)⁵

The nature of samizdat left its imprint on the primary private and public habits of reading. By this I mean book collecting and solitary slow reading in the peace of one's own home, and reading in a public library, established to preserve and disseminate knowledge. Nevertheless, there were people who amassed large collections of samizdat.

> I had very many books – almost everything by Solzhenitsyn, including *Bodalsia telenok s dubom* [*The Oak and the Calf*], the American Mandelshtam edition, Pasternak ... Well, once again, I was a keeper and disseminator of illegal literature. (#89, b.1950)⁶

> Books kept flooding in, but sooner or later I had to give them back, which I considered very annoying. I tried to photocopy or type out the most valuable ones. As a rule I sent the novels of Nabokov and Platonov to be typed out, because typists loved them, while Solzhenitsyn and Zinoviev were photocopied. After a few years, I had amassed a veritable 'dissident library' that I could use as I saw fit.⁷

Often, collections of samizdat were not only significant to the collector. In many cases, they supplied the owner's friends with reading matter and enabled the secondary copying of texts that was pivotal to keeping the phenomenon alive. Our respondents confirm this; below are typical replies to Question 8./8.1 ('Did you know about any museums, libraries, private collections etc. that were used as sources for copying and circulating literature or documents that were not in print in the USSR? Your personal experience is especially valuable.'; 'If yes, can you name these institutions or private collections? If you visited them, we would be grateful for details.'):

> Many people had personal collections and I gradually found out more about them. (#63, b.1950)

> The libraries of Sergei Smirnov (Moscow) and Tatiana Kotliar (Obninsk). (#86, b.1959)

> As early as 1996 I visited the house of A. Evdokimov, who was an old friend of Vysotsky and who has since died, whose entire library consisted of samizdat and tamizdat. From the veteran samizdat activist L. Turchinskii I found out about the collection of L.E. Pinskii, which disappeared more than once in the bowels of the KGB. (#50, b.1955)

> The personal collections of my friends, and books from the special collections [*spetskhran*] of state libraries. (#76, b.1951)

> Some things were available in the collections of the Lenin Library [Leninka, now the Russian State Library] and the Library of Foreign Literature [Inostranka]. [Then there were] the personal collections of friends and acquaintances. (#46, b.1968)

> University, different Scientific Research Institutes, especially those with older archival collections. (#53, b.1954)

> For example, the library of my uncle, Professor Geptner. He had collections of Silver Age poetry and a Remington typewriter that was not always in use. My uncle would not lend his books to anyone. I would type out selected poems. (#73, b.1941)

Question 30 of the survey asked for the names of passionate samizdat collectors. This question caused a lot of controversy among the respondents, which can partially be attributed to historic fear of persecution. I have decided against listing any names here, not only to honour the wishes of those who specifically asked not to publish their replies but also because the names alone – most of them supplied with minimal contextual information – contribute little to the understanding of how individual networks functioned.

The replies above illustrate the importance of historic, pre-revolutionary collections as a source for samizdat; they would supply, for example, Silver Age poetry and religious philosophy. These texts could also be accessed in public libraries, in particular by people with access to special holdings (*spetskhran*),[8] and/or knowledge of foreign languages in the case of books not written in Russian. Tatiana Goricheva, editor of the samizdat journal *37* and a keen translator, remembers how she and her friend Boris Groys sourced texts for translation in the State Public Library (*Publichka*) in Leningrad. Goricheva, who at that point was working in the *Publichka* as a bibliographer, used her privileged access to read and translate theological literature from German for subsequent circulation in samizdat:

> Everything, absolutely everything was available in the *Publichka*, but few people were reading there [in foreign languages ...] I had learned German at school and was able to read freely almost from Year 5 onwards ... I would sit in the *Publichka* from 9am to 9pm.[9]

Some enthusiasts amassed collections of a specific author or genre. A well-documented example is Lev Mnukhin's collection of materials relating to Marina Tsvetaeva. Although rather haphazard selections of Tsvetaeva's writing continued to appear in the official press, following a first republication in the miscellany *Tarusskie stranitsy* in 1961, she remained a marginal figure – not forbidden, but also certainly not showcased – and her immense popularity in the last decades of the Soviet Union is the result of samizdat. Mnukhin, who became passionate about Tsvetaeva's work in the early 1960s, systematically collected her writings and associated paraphernalia. Beginning in 1978, he also organized regular, semi-official seminars dedicated to the study of Tsvetaeva. These seminars were virtually the only platform for serious study of the poet in the Soviet Union, and possibly contributed to the rehabilitation of Tsvetaeva in the 1980s. Mnukhin's actions are one example of how grassroots activism promoted and advanced literary study.[10]

Samizdat collections today

Archives in Russia and abroad that nowadays hold sizeable amounts of samizdat texts – examples include the branches of the Memorial Society in Moscow and St Petersburg and the Research Centre for East European Studies at Bremen University – most frequently received these as gifts from private individuals. One of these repositories, the International Memorial Society in Moscow, has made public the process that is triggered when an individual entrusts their private archive to Memorial. From the point of view of archival practice and cataloguing, a number of interesting bibliographical challenges arise when handling private samizdat collections. In particular, the archivist needs to determine how to catalogue the material – like a museum collection, like an archive, or according to library conventions? Over many years of practice, the archivists of Memorial devised categories to record how each text came to be in the possession of the person who handed it over to the archive. Were they the author of the text? A reader who managed to preserve some of the samizdat they read, perhaps by typing their own copy and giving others to friends? This person would not have collected samizdat in any organized fashion. Or were they a disseminator (*rasprostranitel'*) – somebody who was actively circulating texts and exchanging them with others? Disseminators did not necessarily keep large amounts of texts at home but, according to Memorial's classification, they might have been involved in large-scale reproduction; unlike the final category, the 'librarian' of samizdat who collected texts and passed them on to readers without receiving a text in return and with the text scheduled to return to them. Depending on the category of the owner, the submitted material is then classified as either an accidental collection (*sobranie samizdata* – this refers to material that ended up in the personal archive of a reader), a systematic collection (*kollektsiia samizdata* – these are texts that were collected purposefully for private use) or a samizdat library (*biblioteka samizdata* – texts collected purposefully in order to be shared).[11]

Equipped with this knowledge, we tried a similar approach in the survey and asked our respondents about different roles within the samizdat process. Question 16 listed a number of roles – much larger than the archival list given above – and invited respondents to tick the list if they fulfilled these roles or knew anybody fulfilling them; see Table 10.

Table 10 Roles in the samizdat process

Roles in the Samizdat Process	Number of Mentions
Reader	120 (with two missing answers)
Author	57
Keeper/custodian	79
Disseminator	93
Involved in reproduction	92
Editor/compiler	42

Roles in the Samizdat Process	Number of Mentions
Correspondent for samizdat periodicals	27
Translator	30
Collector	13
Organizer of a samizdat library	16
Organizer of commercial reproduction	11

It should be noted that we did not offer an explanation of the terms. The order in which they are arranged, and the way we used them in preceding questions, would have directed respondents in a particular way. So people who identified themselves as a keeper/custodian (*khranitel'*) most probably 'merely' kept samizdat at home. Within the context of our survey, the term 'disseminator' (*rasprostranitel'*) clearly includes those who haphazardly passed on texts to close friends only, as opposed to doing so on a large scale. This is reflected in the fact that more people identified as disseminators than as keepers. 'Involved in reproduction' (*tirazhirovanie*) applies to those who retyped individual texts as well as those who might have done so in a systematic way (as opposed to reproduction for sale, which is a separate category). From the information provided by some of our respondents, for example Boris Khersonskii, already quoted above – 'I had very many books – almost everything by Solzhenitsyn ... Well, once again, I was a keeper [*khranitel'*] and disseminator [*rasprostranitel'*] of illegal literature' (#89, b.1950)[12] – it is clear that those heavily involved in the circulation of samizdat were important social 'hubs' that deserve much closer investigation. Documentation of their activity, however, is very scarce.

We did not use the term 'librarian', as we foresaw it causing confusion. We did, however, ask: 'Did you know of any samizdat libraries (associations which regularly exchanged texts)?' (Question 34). As it was, twenty respondents gave a positive answer. The cities mentioned are Odessa, Moscow, Leningrad, Obninsk, Kazan, Vilnius and Chelyabinsk. Pavel Naumov, the owner of the Chelyabinsk library, responded: 'There were thousands of texts, and my samizdat library was used by several dozen readers in Chelyabinsk; people would also come from the surrounding area.' He also claims that his library was the largest of at least four libraries in Chelyabinsk, used by 'informal politicians [*sic*], punks, hippies and counter-cultural activists'.[13] It is worth noting that Naumov was born in 1969, so his library was active in the 1980s, when censorship had softened and more material was available.

Aleksei Makarov, research associate at Memorial, lists the names of several samizdat librarians in Moscow (Vladimir Shaklein; Valerii Balakirev and Alexander Bolonkin with their *Prosvetitel'skoe obshchestvo* [Society for Education]) and mentions Dmitrii Markov's library in Obninsk.[14] Moreover, Makarov lists collections that fulfil his definition of a samizdat library in Akademgorodok in Novosibirsk and (unconfirmed) in Rostov on Don.[15]

According to Memorial's categorization, what distinguishes a samizdat library from a collection is that collections were not circulated in an organized way. This means the owner did not use their texts in order to create a purpose-bound network and was not motivated by any desire to recruit or educate new readers. This definition has informed my choice of case studies.

What is a samizdat library?

When we hear the word 'library', the first association is usually with a particular locality – national libraries in the capital cities around the world, the Bodleian Library in Oxford, the *Publichka* in St Petersburg, or our local library. A library is a building that houses stacks of books and reading rooms. Some libraries allow registered readers to borrow books to read at home and record this fact in a borrowing register. This definition needs to be adapted significantly in the case of samizdat libraries.

By the time samizdat libraries emerged, in the late 1960s or 1970s, samizdat was dynamically evolving from an informal subculture into a parallel culture that provided those things official culture would not provide: varied reading matter that was in high demand from a significant substratum. Some respondents to the survey questioned the identification of this kind of structure as a 'library': 'How could libraries of samizdat exchange texts? Your question is a dead end. The way in which they were disseminated means that samizdat and tamizdat were not a library but a network.'[16] This respondent puts his finger on the issue. As a rule, samizdat libraries were sophisticated networks around one or several people who organized the procurement, exchange and circulation of forbidden or otherwise unavailable texts. The organizers pursued the aim of making unofficial texts available to as many people as possible while maintaining measures to safeguard both texts and distributors.

As part of a clandestine subculture, these libraries had to exist without an actual building that would offer a repository for archives and holdings, or reading rooms that readers could visit. In the case of the libraries studied for this chapter, several people ('librarians') would keep the physical texts in decentralized locations: samizdat libraries were lending libraries. The task of a samizdat librarian consisted in passing texts on to readers from a pre-approved circle; in some cases, members of this circle would curate their own sub-circle in order to maximize circulation.[17] An important element that distinguished library networks from other ways of exchanging samizdat texts was that the text in question would normally be returned to the librarian who supplied it. It follows that samizdat libraries were semi-closed associations and as a result existed in an irresolvable field of tension. The aim of widening the circle of samizdat readers, and therefore being open to new people, had to be carefully counterbalanced against the need to protect the librarians and existing readers against persecution and the texts against confiscation. Trust between individuals replaced commercial or educational considerations in the process of procuring or lending library stock. Viacheslav Igrunov remembers how these relationships worked in practice:

> [Bella Ezerskaia] in turn introduced us to the Averbukh brothers, Igor and Isai, and most importantly to Isidor Moiseevich Gol'denberg, a teacher of Russian language and literature, with whom Sasha met and to whom he offered *Doctor Zhivago*. In return, Sasha received from him [Mikhail Bulgakov's] *Sobach'e serdtse* [*The Heart of a Dog*] and some other books. Ultimately, he offered us a very large number of texts.[18]

This overview demonstrates that, while individual library networks might have been elusive, the existence of such institutions – and I am choosing this term deliberately – was certainly not a closely guarded secret. The claim made by Gleb Morev in the comments to his interview with Viacheslav Igrunov – namely, that Igrunov founded the first and only samizdat library in the USSR – is patently incorrect, at least without further qualification.[19]

Viacheslav Igrunov's widely known library, which began operating in Odessa in 1967 and also supplied literature to order for other libraries in other cities, will be one of the two case studies considered below. The second is the less formal association organized by Yurii Avrutskii in Moscow in 1974. These samples have been chosen consciously: firstly, both libraries held sizeable collections comprising several hundred texts and had clearly defined frameworks for safeguarding, circulating and enlarging these collections. Secondly, the networks making up these libraries were large and complex enough to require some of the organizational traits of 'ordinary' libraries, like a subscription and a cataloguing system, as well as (encrypted) borrowing records. This documentation has at least partly survived and is accessible to researchers. Thirdly, the organizers of both libraries were motivated to pursue social or political goals, however loosely defined, by way of educating the public with the help of their libraries.

The library of Viacheslav Igrunov, Odessa (1967–1982)

Igrunov gives the birth date of his library as January 1967.[20] This library was the 'result' of an underground circle he had set up in 1965 with a political aim: to 'change the existing political order, because it makes the achievement of communism impossible'.[21] The members of this circle began to collect reading matter for their educational seminars, primarily on history and sociology, but also the works of Marx and Lenin in commented editions.[22] Books were needed in order 'to understand what is going on';[23] Igrunov himself stresses repeatedly that, in spite of his close links with many prominent dissidents, he saw himself as a politician rather than a human rights activist.[24] What began as a collection amassed by a group who wanted to educate themselves and others grew into a formidable network linking a heterogeneous group of individuals and groups across various towns and cities throughout the Soviet Union:

> Viktor Matizen ran a small branch of the library in Novosibirsk; Vladimir Kirichenko another small branch in Zaparozhe. Besides, we delivered many texts to order, to Riga, Petersburg [sic] and Moscow; sometimes we would send something to Ukraine – Kiev, Lvov, Simferopol, rarely to Tiraspol. Some individual copies travelled further, for example to Chita or Erevan; they would also end up in Nikolaev, and sometimes in Kherson. But the main spots were: Crimea, Odessa, Zaparozhe, Kiev, Novosibirsk, Leningrad.[25]

This network involved many outstanding individuals, including Igrunov himself, the poet Boris Khersonskii, the political scientist Gleb Pavlovskii, the dissident and historian Alexander Daniel and others, as well as different and partially overlapping groups: Moscow dissidents, Jews aiming to emigrate to Israel, and Ukrainian nationalists. The library's many sources of texts included not just well-connected individuals but also public and university libraries:

> Our group would reproduce barely accessible texts from the Gorky Regional Library in Odessa, from the Public Library in the city and from the Academic Library at the university. Moreover, we regularly received samizdat from many individuals in Moscow. Those who provided the largest number of texts were Vladimir Tel'nikov, Alexander Ginzburg, Kronid Liubarskii – who passed them on through Shikhanovich – Irina Maksimova and Leonard Ternovskii.[26]

Educating the public was the goal that determined the kind of texts that were collected in the first instance. Igrunov recalls the following works as forming the basis of the library: Milovan Dzhilas's *New Class,* Boris Pasternak's *Doctor Zhivago,* Nikolai Berdiaev's *Istoki i smysl russkogo kommunizma* (*The Origins of Russian Communism*), Mikhail Bulgakov's *Sobach'e serdtse.*[27] The *Chronicle of Current*

Events had a particular impact on the development of Igrunov's worldview after 1968 and became a central 'exhibit' of the library, which Igrunov and his fellow activists 'reproduced in huge quantities' once they had managed to establish reliable channels for sourcing the bulletin, which included the *Chronicle*'s founding editor, Natalia Gorbanevskaia. Later, Igrunov himself became a trusted channel for passing on information about human rights violations for inclusion in the *Chronicle*.[28] Providing education to bring about social change remained the dominant long-term goal of the library's chief organizer. In 1972, Igrunov identified difficulty in obtaining information as the greatest obstacle faced by the democratic movement or any other social movement lobbying for change in the USSR. He put down on paper his ideas on how to remedy the situation, in a treatise in which he outlined the tasks of repositories that offered access to alternative sources of information (i.e. samizdat libraries). It was entitled 'Neofitsial'naia literatura i nekotorye voprosy praktiki' (Unofficial Literature and some Practical Questions) and was appended to a longer essay on the civic movement in the USSR, 'K problematike obshchestvennogo dvizheniia' (On the Issue of the Civic Movement), which circulated in samizdat signed with the pseudonym EGO. Here, Igrunov stipulates that unofficial institutions have a crucial role to play and must aim for the 'greatest possible distribution of samizdat' while ensuring the 'safeguarding [of] the sources of information'.[29] Indeed, although his political underground circle had become defunct, he and his associates continuously undertook practical attempts to provide systematic education rather than just offer reading matter: 'Moreover, our library provided the basis for several long-lived *kruzhki*. People didn't just read out of interest; our library had founded a little school.'[30]

Igrunov's library lends itself to study not only on the basis of its size and durability – it existed for fifteen years after all – or the fact that the organizers maintained links to several prominent circles of dissidents. It is also exceptionally well documented. Igrunov himself maintains a website that is one of the leading primary sources of samizdat on the internet. Much of this website is based on the three-volume *Antologiia samizdata* published in 2005,[31] and it can be assumed that most of the texts featured on the web formed part of the physical library at some point.[32] A different section of the large and complex website constitutes a repository of memoirs, interviews and other materials relating to the history of the library, compiled by Igrunov and others who were involved, for example Petr Butov, the man responsible for the library between 1975 and 1982, Boris Khersonskii, who was himself an avid collector and distributor, and Bella Ezerskaia, who was an important source for procuring texts.[33]

In the last fifteen years, the library has attracted the attention of researchers, and there is plenty of scope for more specialized study. Scholarly interest has created the extensive interviews with Igrunov on which this discussion is based, and which detail the motivation behind the library, its history and structures, as well as its demise. Surviving materials from the library – physical texts as well as film – have been passed on to research centres specializing in the history of samizdat: the Russian State Historical Library, the International Memorial Society (both in Moscow) and the Research Centre for East European Studies at Bremen University all hold sections of this remarkable institution.[34] Much valuable work has been undertaken by Elena Strukova, head of the Collection of Non-traditional Print (*Fond netraditsionnoi pechati*) at the Russian State Historical Library (GPIB), who accepted the library materials into the archive in 1998. Strukova is the author of a useful historical overview that includes an index of all library materials now in the State Historical Library and draws, among other sources, on the case files relating to the criminal cases brought against Igrunov and Petr Butov, who were arrested in connection with the library in 1975 and 1982 respectively.[35] Her readiness to accept this collection, to the apparent bewilderment of certain colleagues – who pointed out that the texts had for the most part been published and asked her 'what [she] need[s] this junk for'[36] – has made it accessible to others in the first place. She describes its condition upon arrival as follows: 'In 1998, a collection of samizdat was given to the archive of the Russian State Public Historical Library. It contained more than 50 crumbling rolls of film, several texts produced on a typewriter, books and journals published abroad (tamizdat of the 1960s–1970s).'[37]

Seen in this light, its size and organizational structure, as well as the unwavering political commitment of its organizer, make Igrunov's library an exception. However, it allows us to study many processes that were typical of samizdat libraries and illustrate the problems faced by anybody who tried to make samizdat available in large quantities and to large numbers of people. It also exemplifies how the desire to read and obtain samizdat furthered the development of new networks that overcame significant geographical challenges, connecting like-minded people in different cities who would otherwise not have had much reason to seek direct contact.

The library of Yurii Avrutskii, Moscow (1974–late 1980s)

The Moscow-based network of Yurii Avrutskii is little known by comparison and is an example of a library that was much more modest in size, mission and geographical reach. Avrutskii did not pursue political aims and did not supply samizdat to other towns and cities. Nevertheless, there are distinct parallels in form between the two libraries.

In the early 1960s, Avrutskii and his co-librarians were part of the circle around the dissident Alexander Ginzburg, but they did not become outspoken dissidents. Avrutskii quickly abandoned the idea of collecting and distributing samizdat texts for educational purposes that had motivated him in the beginning: 'At first I thought that these books were needed by some special people who were ready to fight Bolshevism.' However, realizing that there were no such people in his immediate surroundings, he changed his attitude: 'Gradually I came to the understanding that these books were needed by the people around me, simply for their life.'[38] These words acknowledge the often-described hunger for information experienced by Soviet intellectuals. For Avrutskii and his friends, their hunger did not translate into any form of open protest, but rather an 'internally free' civic position that found the parameters prescribed by official culture too narrow and, rather than actively seeking to remove the proscriptions, simply disregarded them. Alexander Rabinovich, one of Avrutskii's fellow librarians, remembers that the circle was motivated by intellectual curiosity in a pure form, namely: 'how can it be that there are books that one isn't allowed to read?'[39] Avrutskii states that, since most of the library's readers had degrees in technical subjects (they represented the 'technical intelligentsia'), reading samizdat for them was effectively a supplementary higher education in humanities subjects, for example politics, literature and religion.[40]

Avrutskii submitted part of the library's holdings to the archive of the International Memorial Society in Moscow, alongside important supplementary documents. His unpublished memoir (eleven pages of manuscript) details his motivation as well as the library's organizational structure, and lists the names of those who, over the years, helped procure texts and carried out technical tasks, for example supplying paper and other materials, copying, and binding. Two exercise books contain the encoded borrowing records. The several dozen samizdat 'books' surrendered to Memorial reveal a detail that physical samizdat copies normally carefully conceal: in most of these cases, the name of the person who reproduced and/or bound the text is known. Avrutskii's archive thus allows the reconstruction of two distinct but overlapping networks that are normally notoriously hard to pin down: the network of those involved in the physical production (Avrutskii names them in his memoir), and the network that maps the journey of texts among readers (their names can be reconstructed via the encoded borrowing records). This makes the collection exceptionally valuable to researchers.

Much of the information I rely on here is gleaned from the essay by Alexei Makarov that I cite earlier in this chapter. Makarov bases his discussion not only on Avrutskii's memoir, which can be accessed in Memorial's archive and which I have seen, but also on an unpublished interview with Alexander Rabinovich which I have not accessed; Rabinovich is the man who devised the library's system for copying and producing books. Makarov has worked hard to publicize the existence of Avrutskii's little-known collection, not just to the highly specialist audience who would read the essay cited but also to the broader public. A publication he created for the website of the Russian online academy Arzamas uses Avrutskii's library to help readers understand what samizdat was and how the process was organized: 'Normally it is very difficult to reconstruct the circulation of samizdat texts, but there are instances where people systematically collected samizdat and amassed entire libraries.'[41] The article is accompanied by high-quality photographs of actual items from the library, including the exercise books containing the borrowing records. Incidentally, this use of a samizdat library – Avrutskii himself called his organization a 'club'[42] – as a shortcut towards explaining the functioning of samizdat networks chimes with my argument advanced at the beginning of this chapter: samizdat libraries represent samizdat in its more advanced, professionalized manifestation.

The everyday life of samizdat libraries

The following discussion uses material pertaining to both libraries under study interchangeably. Igrunov, who replied to the samizdat reader survey, describes his library in these terms: 'In a special repository we had collected several hundred books (I think around 500), a certain number of periodicals, both samizdat and foreign, and several thousands of articles, letters, poems, stories, essays etc.'[43] On his website, he expounds in greater detail. Significantly, the collection featured rare and pre-revolutionary editions:

> In the context of that period the library was very large and very serious. Of course, we also held books that were not completely illegal. We had books published in the Soviet Union in a limited print run of 120 copies for members of the Central Committee apparatus. We had books intended for academic libraries, some of which were openly available for sale while others were not. We also had, of course, books that had been freely available previously but then disappeared, for example Jung, Freud, Nietzsche and Lev Shestov. We had acquaintances who would allow us to borrow them from academic libraries for copying. So, alongside those several hundred illegal books we also had a fairly decent library of rare editions, for example lots of minor memoirs.[44]

The extent to which this collection is different from a library in the usual sense becomes apparent when we examine the functions and activities of the people involved:

> In technical terms, the library was organized as follows: there was one person, the courier, who delivered the literature. Before 1972 this role was fulfilled by Alexander Rykov, who had introduced me to Rezak. Alongside him there was a technical operator, Rezak, who would photograph all the texts. There was one archivist who stored the films, the originals. In a word, it was an entire system.[45]

Igrunov mentions three separate roles here: courier, technician and archivist. Let us begin our analysis with the role of the courier, a task Igrunov himself carried out in the early 1970s. The courier was much more than just a person who procured and delivered books. In order to be entrusted with the material, they had to enjoy the trust of their sources. In other words, the courier needed to be a person with excellent connections in circles that could supply samizdat. In the earlier years of the library in particular, the ability to procure new texts heavily depended on Igrunov's own links to particular dissidents. When an individual relationship soured or was interrupted due to a source's arrest or emigration, the library was left without texts. Only in 1974, following a stay in Moscow, did he manage to establish multiple stable connections that ensured a reliable supply of literature to Odessa and other cities in which the library was operative.[46] Both libraries maintained extensive connections in dissident circles and also abroad; the latter helped them procure tamizdat editions. Yurii Avrutskii sourced some of his literature via Igrunov's courier, Alexander Rykov, but seems to have been oblivious to the fact that he had tapped into a much larger network.[47] He merely remarks that Rykov had a very good system of reproduction that included access to a copying machine and marvels that the other man never asked for money, as he evidently had his own library.[48] Rykov is not the only point of contact between the two libraries: Igrunov and Avrutskii both name dissident Yurii Shikhanovich as a contact.[49] The supply of the library was therefore dependent on personal connections and reputation, rather than on the expert knowledge of subject librarians and bibliographers. The librarians' collection efforts were dictated by the availability of rare texts rather than thematic principles.

The second person mentioned by Igrunov, the technician, was tasked with an activity modern libraries do not carry out, leaving it to publishing houses instead: 'For some time, the one to keep literature at his home was Valerii Rezak; he was the main activist, the main re-printer, the main photographer. He would photograph all books. He developed a brilliant system of printing photographs.'[50]

In their effort to copy a large number of texts, the libraries gradually left behind the typewriter as the iconic tool of samizdat textual (re)production. Typing out full-length novels took far too much time, while the number of copies that could be produced in one sitting remained limited. Instead, librarians relied heavily on different technologies to 'photocopy': large texts. The original might well be typescript, but longer books (e.g. Solzhenitsyn's novels) were increasingly multiplied from printed tamizdat editions instead. There were two ways in which a text could be 'photocopied': using a photocopier or a camera. In the latter case, the individual shots were developed like photos, on photo paper. Avrutskii's library, which at first had relied on typists typing for free or for very little money,[51] soon began using the former option. The librarians produced photocopies (*kserokopii*) with the help of an ERA copying machine, using technical paper that was intended for measuring variations in the earth's magnetic field and which one of the librarians was able to procure (that is, take or steal) through his work at IZMIRAN (Institute of Earth Magnetism, Ionosphere and Distribution of Radio Waves). While these copies looked fairly professional, they were essentially an improvisation that illustrates the contingency of samizdat's material form upon whatever materials were available. The copies were held together by string and often also bound into hard covers to increase their durability.[52] In contrast, the reading matter of Igrunov's library consisted mostly of photo prints (*fotokopii*), illustrating that people made do with the means at their disposal:

> After the negative was created, we would develop prints. The person who did this was Valerii Rezak, and he did so in horrible material circumstances. He is a truly heroic man, who produced many hundreds of books and many, many thousands of articles and journals. Most importantly, we would read the *Chronicle of Current Events* in photo print, while the original was kept in the archive in case 'it was needed'.[53]

The archive (as opposed to the reading copies) did indeed consist largely of negatives from which books could be reproduced if necessary:

> Our storage system was rather convoluted. For example, the archive containing the source materials was not kept in one place. There was the film archive – we would photograph most of our holdings and keep the film separate. And then there was the library, which consisted mostly of prints. Of course, there were many books that were impossible to reproduce in this way because you would end up with a thick stack. Something like [Avtorkhanov's] *Proizkhozhdenie partokratii* [*The Origins of the Partocracy*] made up an entire bag or briefcase. And yet we distributed *The Gulag Archipelago*, as well as Avtorkhanov and many other books, in precisely this format.[54]

The system of double-copying that Igrunov describes – the practice of keeping a copy on film for the archive while circulating photo prints – created a system of 'indestructible' (*neunichtozhimyi*) samizdat that was protected against confiscation of the reading copy and thus achieved Igrunov's goal: the source of information (i.e. the source text) was protected while the information it contained was made available to a large number of people.

Certain features we have identified as typical of samizdat, which in their entirety give samizdat its 'pre-Gutenberg' character, do not completely apply to the texts produced and circulated by the libraries precisely because libraries increasingly relied on semi-professional means of reproduction. Photocopiers and negatives have many advantages: using them, it is possible to produce a theoretically infinite number of identical copies, just like print. They eliminate the potential for mistakes inherent in the practice of typing and promote the circulation of one single version of a given text. Cameras were accessible to private individuals, but the development of film and the subsequent printing required significantly more equipment and skill than operating a typewriter. By contrast, photocopiers, while certainly less formal than a printing press, were not normally available to private individuals, and those who used them for samizdat had access to them in some professional capacity. Their contingency and mobility notwithstanding, libraries constituted comparatively formal systems within a culture that drew its energy from spontaneity, informality and secrecy. Moreover, libraries exhibited an attitude towards texts that was at least partly driven by practical considerations and strove towards more durable formats. This supports a reading of samizdat libraries as a symptom of samizdat's inexorable professionalization.

The third function Igrunov mentions is that of the archivist. The most prized skill of samizdat archivists was not their knowledge regarding the sourcing, handling or cataloguing of rare texts, but rather their ability to safeguard a collection against discovery and their willingness to participate in conspiratorial behaviour. The keepers had to be inconspicuous, and the archive was divided up between several locations:

> The conspiratorial measures were very simple. Firstly, some things were kept in the homes of people whom I had a reason to visit if I went there. It would appear that I had gone there for a reason other than to fetch literature. For example, for a long time the film archive was kept in the flat of my form teacher, Dina Samsonovna Tochilovskaia. I went to see her very rarely, once every few months, and the archive was simply lying there. If I needed to add something I would go and bring the item, add it and leave again. There were also interim archives.

... At the very beginning, when we were devising the safety measures, I had an entire page with instructions on how it should work. For me, the main point was that there should be an alternative reason for every meeting; there should always be some professional relationship or other easy-to-explain reason for why I was meeting with this person in that place and what he was doing ... I very much wanted to avoid a system that was orientated exclusively towards passing on or reading samizdat.[55]

The practices employed by the network that made up Avrutskii's library were to a much lesser degree dictated by the need for secrecy, and the functions individuals fulfilled were not distinguished so clearly. However, the principle of decentralized stock keeping was observed. Each librarian was responsible for safeguarding a comparatively modest number of texts, around twenty to twenty-eight books per person. Moreover, each librarian would collect texts on a specific topic: books on political themes (Avtorkhanov, Zinoviev and others), historical books (this rubric included memoirs and Solzhenitsyn's *The Gulag Archipelago*), religious and philosophical texts (the Gospels, the 1905 essay collection *Vekhi* [*Signposts*], Nikolai Berdiaev, Grigorii Pomerants) and literary texts (Vladimir Nabokov, Sasha Sokolov, Andrei Bitov's *Pushkin House*). Some librarians preferred to hold thematically mixed stock; journals were also part of the library's provision.[56] This way of spreading library holdings across a number of people prevented the risk of losing the entire library should one of the librarians be arrested.

But the network of librarians also fulfilled a practical function. Avrutskii recalls that it became increasingly difficult to schedule meetings with the growing number of people who wanted to borrow one of the around 100 titles he possessed. Moreover, remembering who had taken which texts was very difficult without a register. The network of librarians was founded to facilitate this task '[we had to try] to organize ourselves somehow, at least into a club. One of the attempts involved issuing 10–20 books, dividing them between people and according to topic, and then numbering both the participants and the books. That means you only had to call up a few numbers and you would be able to arrange a meeting and find out who had the book.'[57] The encoded borrowing register was a practical necessity, and it seems that practical necessity also informed the decision to divide the texts between librarians.

Samizdat libraries were compelled to compromise in many ways in order to carry out their mission, and the absence of premises or a central archive was only part of the issue. The organizers had to prioritize safety over accessibility. The shortcomings of the conspiratorial approach were evident, and this approach hampered the ambition to 'make [the library] accessible to as many people as possible'.⁵⁸

Commercial samizdat in libraries

In Chapter 3 we touched briefly on the question of commercial samizdat, mainly from the perspective of typists charging for their work. We have also seen that numerous respondents to the samizdat survey report buying samizdat or tamizdat editions. And, indeed, there was a lively black and grey market.⁵⁹ Irina Roskina remembers: 'Sometimes something you couldn't live without was impossible to find in circulation and had to be bought for horrendous amounts of money from one of the "bookmen" [*knizhniki*] (they didn't like to call themselves "speculators"). For example, we bought Nadezhda Mandelshtam's *Vtoraia kniga* [*Hope Abandoned*] for 60 roubles, which was half of my monthly salary at the time.'⁶⁰

Tamizdat editions offered the most in-demand long texts in an authoritative format. Avrutskii remembers that in the mid-1970s, when more and more texts started to appear, one book would cost around 30–40 roubles, which was expensive even when he and his friends clubbed together. And so, the forbidding cost of tamizdat became a major motivating factor for developing a reliable and efficient system for multiplying texts.⁶¹ On the other hand, libraries could not exist without tamizdat, if only because they were better suited for photocopying than any homemade typescript. Igrunov remembers a particular adventure in the very early days of his library's existence, which illustrates the extraordinary impression the availability of illegal texts for sale made on him:

> And after that there was a fairly long period of silence, until August 1968. A student from the MGU biology faculty, Alexander Zhivlov, was selling all kinds of books next to an antiquarian bookshop in Odessa. My friend Anatolii Glants was amazed by these books. They included Antokol'skii's memoirs, a book of Brodsky's poems published in New York and some other things. Zhivlov was simply standing in the street and selling them. My friend had no money on him and so he asked Zhivlov for his contact details, so that he would be able to go see him and buy these books. Zhivlov replied: 'I have many other things too, *Doktor Zhivago* for example.' This seemed fantastical – how easily a person could sell on something that could put you in prison.⁶²

In this particular case, Igrunov's plan to buy Solzhenitsyn's works were foiled because, by the time he had made it to Moscow, the authorities had arrested the small group of activists who had protested on Red Square against the Soviet invasion of Czechoslovakia to crush the Prague Spring. The repression of the demonstrators instilled fear in unofficial circles, and people who had engaged in forbidden activity, like selling tamizdat, became much more cautious. Igrunov expresses a sceptical attitude towards the widespread practice of crucial information being offered for sale: 'By the way, the tamizdat market already existed at that time. And the traders, for example, the smugglers who sold the treasures of our national art – icons and other rare things – also traded in tamizdat.'[63] Irina Roskina, cited above, explains that the book traders tried to avoid calling themselves 'speculator[s]' (*spekulant*), a term with a distinctly negative connotation, indicating that not just the authorities, but the customers, too, were critical of their activity. This did not stop them from buying the books on offer, however, and so the trade continued to flourish. Igrunov's network sourced tamizdat texts to a large degree via trusted sources (e.g. Yurii Shikhanovich, who sourced them from Kronid Liubarskii in Moscow) who would lend the originals to be copied and subsequently returned: 'afterwards [the texts] returned to Moscow, with the exception of those that were given to us as gifts and those that we had bought'.[64] This statement makes it clear that the library could not fulfil its mission entirely without commercially sourced texts.

The issue of size

As could be expected, the users of Igrunov's library were mostly intellectuals:

> Who were the readers? I already named a few people. They were mostly students, those who taught at higher education institutes and schoolteachers, that is, ordinary members of the intelligentsia. Staff from the faculty of A. Uemov (the philosophy faculty at the university) were steady readers. I would take books to Yurii Iosifovich Zuev, and he would distribute them.[65]

The way Igrunov's library organized its borrowing process makes it possible at least to count the readers, if not name them. Igrunov maintains that in Odessa – the city with the largest readership due to the library having its origins there – the circle of library users comprised only around 200 people in the period 1973–1974.[66] Between 1977 and 1979, the year in which the library enjoyed its highest popularity, this number at least doubled and possibly even rose to 600.[67] Thanks to its connections and branches in other cities, the library's overall network boasted a truly impressive number of readers: 'According to my calculation, there were around 1,500 readers, but not in Odessa alone. The steady readership of the library comprised around 1,500 people [in an area ranging] from Novosibirsk to Lvov.'[68]

But in reality nobody, not even Igrunov himself, had direct contact with, or an overview of, all the readers. To reach such a large number of readers, the core organizers used a snowball system: 'The reading process was organized as follows: I would give books to several people, each of which had their own audience. And often those *kruzhki,* like little stars, were surrounded by their own scene. So I can say that I handed books directly to about two dozen people [a list of names follows].'[69]

This snowball system was very popular within organized samizdat networks as a natural way to ensure wider circulation; some of the literary journals discussed in Chapter 5 employed a similar system. However, it has consequences for record keeping. Even a meticulous chronicler such as Viacheslav Igrunov could not know his network in its entirety:

> Around two thousand. Of course I didn't know all [the readers] in person, we had a many-tiered system: the librarian would pass books to a dozen people who would actively circulate them in turn. This number is based on the information given by the distributors. It can be compared to those figures which, in libraries, are called 'reader records'. One reader might take one or two books, while others were continuous readers.[70]

We recall that, in the earlier quotation above, Igrunov estimates the overall number of readers to be 1,500: a difference of 500 people, or 25 per cent. While even his crude estimate is valuable – it tells us that the library's readers numbered in the low thousands, not the hundreds and not the tens of thousands – the parallel he draws between this roughly calculated number and the records kept by a regular library is not convincing. The issue is not just that an ordinary library can give exact numbers and knows the names and addresses of its readers. Rather, practices common to samizdat – which was an economy of scarcity, after all – such as secondary copying and borrowers passing on the books to friends before returning them, mean that the actual number of people who read a text supplied by the library was simply impossible to calculate. Conversely, it is very likely that some end readers never knew that Igrunov's library was the source of their texts, especially when there were several additional links in the chain between them and the relevant librarian.

The end of the libraries

In 1974, Igrunov was implicated as the supplier of the copy of *The Gulag Archipelago* that had been confiscated from V.A. Alekseev-Popov, a lecturer at Odessa University, and warned to stop his activity linked to the 'acquisition, storage and distribution of ideologically harmful and anti-Soviet literature'.[71] In 1975 he was arrested and sentenced to forced treatment in a psychiatric hospital. In his absence, the library was run by Petr Butov, a young physicist. Butov took a much more cautious approach towards distributing literature, in particular because the library was now squarely in the KGB's line of sight.[72] He managed to preserve the collection; however, Igrunov considers that the mission of the library as a social institution suffered because it no longer brought people together: 'reading literature was [no longer] conducive to the formation of a certain social circle. Rather, it satisfied the need for individual education.'[73] It seems that Butov's caution increased the library's vulnerability, as the decentralized system of preservation was abandoned and texts would amass in the flats of individuals. Igrunov was released in 1977, but did not resume his position as main organizer of the library. In 1981, Butov's flat was searched and much literature confiscated;[74] his arrest in 1982 spelled the effective end of the library. Searches at the houses of other librarians further decimated the holdings.[75]

For a concise testimony to the inherent risk of making available a collection of unsanctioned literature – both to the owner and to the collection itself – we can turn to Mikhail Meilakh. By 1984, the year of his arrest, Meilakh was already a philologist and poetry specialist whose contacts abroad had allowed him to accumulate a sizeable collection of tamizdat books. While he was not an active dissident, he had been under KGB surveillance for a while; the discovery of his collection gave the security services an additional reason to arrest him:

> And so, I had amassed around two hundred books that were kept by a woman of the intelligentsia, Sof'ia Kazimirovna Ostrovskaia; we had known each other a long time. When I asked her whether she could hide the books she said 'yes, of course'. The books were in her flat, in two suitcases inside her wardrobe. I would come from time to time, take some and put others back. Right up until her death. She suffered from cancer and was about to die, and I had to collect the books. I gave them to a man who turned out to be untrustworthy. He started something like a library with reading room [*izba-chital'nia*], complete with a catalogue and reader register, and of course he was caught quickly. We had agreed that in case of a blunder he would say that he'd received the books from somebody who had emigrated. But this didn't work; they beat my name out of him and he received a lighter sentence.[76]

Meilakh was sentenced to seven years in a camp and five years of exile; the collection was lost. Confiscation of texts during house searches spelled the end of many a splendid collection. Igrunov maintains that failure to observe the correct conspiratorial measures was what foiled the efforts of other samizdat collectors, citing in particular the example of Kronid Liubarskii in Moscow, who at some point supplied Igrunov's library.[77]

Yurii Avrutskii's library escaped this fate, surviving until the late 1980s when the necessity of circulating reading materials in secret vanished as these texts began to appear in the official press. However, the increase in house searches among unofficial intellectuals, and the fear of these searches, took a toll on this collection, too, because the librarians began hiding their stock in the flats of distant acquaintances. These secondary keepers were not always committed to preserving the collection. Avrutskii deplored the unavoidable loss of stock that occurred because books were circulated in a haphazard manner and not returned. However, he also conceded that this might have been one of the best ways to increase the texts' chance of a wide readership.[78]

Samizdat libraries are living proof that a library can operate without repositories and reading rooms; however, before the internet age it could not possibly operate without physical copies of texts. These physical copies made the librarians – and through them the library itself – vulnerable. While decentralized archiving, which was laborious and inefficient in practice, minimized the risk that the discovery of a single hiding place being discovered jeopardized the entire library, it was simply impossible to neutralize this risk entirely.

Summa for free thought: A review of samizdat

Samizdat libraries, their individual differences notwithstanding, carried out their mission in two distinct but overlapping ways: by reproducing texts, they increased the number of copies in circulation, and by devising lending schemes they gave a larger number of people the opportunity to read these texts. The makers of the samizdat review journal *Summa: Referativnyi zhurnal samizdata* (The Sum: A Review Journal of Samizdat), eight issues of which were published between 1979 and 1982, took a fundamentally different approach. When *Summa* emerged in 1979, samizdat had become a mass phenomenon, with new texts and periodicals appearing frequently. In the absence of informational resources such as bibliographies and library catalogues, it was hard even for committed and well-connected readers to keep track of the developments. The haphazard circulation of samizdat texts compounded the problem. *Summa* constituted an attempt to remedy the problem.

Summa was produced by a group around the Leningrad mathematician Sergei Maslov and his wife Nina. The journal was discontinued after Sergei Maslov died in a car accident in 1982, the causes of which have never been satisfactorily established.[79] It is discussed in this chapter, rather than alongside the other Leningrad journals in Chapters 5 and 6, because it represented a network-based alternative institution founded to increase the number of people reading existing samizdat texts, rather than a platform for new writing. In the mid-1970s, Maslov and his friend Anatolii Vershik, who would serve as one of several co-editors for *Summa*, came up with the idea of a review journal to help orientate the reader in an increasingly diverse field and ensure that, in the absence of physical texts, potential readers had a maximum amount of information at their disposal. Both men were mathematicians, and their concept for the journal was clearly based on scientific publications designed to help scientists stay on top of new information. Their journal would pursue two aims. The preface proclaims: 'The modest aim of this publication is to provide a means of orientation for the stormy and contradictory spiritual life of our country.'[80] It is worth noting that this is a rather vague statement that does not sound at all scientific. The eight issues of *Summa* were republished in book form in 2002, supplemented with analytical materials prepared by Vershik and other participants.[81] This edition is an invaluable source; moreover, I am fortunate to have been granted a long interview by Anatolii Vershik. In his foreword to the book edition, Vershik formulates the need for a review journal in more specific terms: 'in the 1960–1970s, this entire torrent crashed down on those who had previously heard only Soviet propaganda, mendacious and dreary, but who knew things the knowledge of which was forbidden'.[82] The second aim behind *Summa* was to popularize samizdat, and tamizdat as its inalienable constituent. Vershik remembers: 'in the 1970s, many of us experienced a natural desire to *share* all this new knowledge, tell everything to those who did not have direct access to uncensored literature'.[83] After all, 'people can't possibly read everything; they won't be able to obtain it'.[84] Vershik's words echo those of our survey respondents who insisted that being able to obtain samizdat entailed a duty to share it further, as well as Yurii Avrutskii's insight, cited above, that samizdat books were vitally important to those around him. *Summa* was a unique undertaking. It featured neither literary texts or analytical essays, nor factual information in the style of the *Chronicle of Current Events*. Instead, the authors reviewed unofficial journals, longer texts, and books, regardless of genre or geographical location. As an overview of unofficial publications as they emerged, *Summa* is a vital source of insight into mature samizdat culture.

Each issue of *Summa* consisted of three separate sections, and each section published a different genre of review. The first was called 'Referaty i vypiski' (Summaries and Extracts). Here, the authors presented concise information about individual texts and collections that were circulating in samizdat, as well as about periodicals and individual texts within them.[85] Many of the summaries presented tamizdat and journals of the émigré press: further evidence of the ever-growing importance of texts produced beyond the Iron Curtain as sources of information. That these texts were discussed alongside samizdat shows that the makers of *Summa* perceived them as part of the same phenomenon. The 'Summaries and Extracts' section resembled the format of scientific review journals published by the Russian Academy of Sciences' All-Russian Institute of Scientific and Technical Information (VINITI RAN). Unlike a scientific review journal, which informs specialists about texts they have no time to read, *Summa* provided information about texts that were hard to come by.

The second section featured reviews/points of view and encouraged the exchange of opinion, while the third section was dedicated to new editions of existing samizdat periodicals, literary as well as political, supplemented by émigré journals: *37* and *Chasy* (The Clock) as Leningrad-based forums for new writing alongside the *Chronicle of Current Events*, *Poiski* (Search), *Evrei v SSSR* (Jews in the USSR), the almanac *Pamiat'* (Memory) and émigré journals like *Kontinent* and *Russkoe vozrozhdenie* (The Russian Revival).

As a review journal, *Summa* depended on the availability, firstly, of a representative number of publications for review, and secondly, of authors to write the reviews. With no predictable way either to source texts or recruit authors, the makers of *Summa* called on their readers – people who, presumably, had an active interest in samizdat. The first edition of the journal featured the following call: 'If you've been reading [a samizdat text] and want to respond, argue, or publish an excerpt – you can do that through us.'[86] On the one hand, this sounds very much like a call for reader contributions in an ordinary journal – Soviet journals, like journals in other countries, invited readers to send in letters and similar materials. However, it also represents a pattern familiar from other samizdat publications. Soliciting material from the reader was an approach also employed by *Pamiat*[87] and the *Chronicle of Current Events*. For all its professional outlook, *Summa* exemplifies a paradox or contradiction inherent in many later samizdat, which is the sharp contrast between a highly sophisticated idea that is gleaned from official practice and its necessarily amateurish execution. This feature was common to many mature samizdat journals and will be discussed in detail in Chapter 6.

According to Anatolii Vershik, there was no standard procedure for procuring texts for review. Periodicals were reportedly easy to obtain, including the *Chronicle*, for which they had 'a distinct channel'. Ultimately, the process by which *Summa* sourced material – review copies as well as finished reviews – strongly resembled the one employed by the samizdat libraries discussed above: the members of the small core group of editors each used their own contact network; these networks might overlap, but were not normally disclosed among the editors; the information flow was conspiratorial, and sources were disguised. This means that those involved in the journal did not know other participants by name, and the editors did not discuss their sources among themselves. In the case of *Summa*, these precautions were all the more necessary, since the texts under review included politically sensitive publications, possession of which could entail persecution. This level of secrecy led to curious incidents. Anatolii Vershik recounts how friends would not necessarily know that they were both contributing to the same publication.[88] In some cases, many years passed before this information emerged. Sergei Levin, another co-editor, discovered that Vershik was also involved in *Summa* only after Vershik published an article on *Summa* in 1991 – nine years after *Summa* was discontinued.[89] Sergei Maslov did not know about Vershik's Moscow sources,[90] while Vershik himself was not informed about the technicalities of the finished journal's distribution in Moscow.[91] While Vershik had his contacts for procuring material, he remembers that many texts were submitted spontaneously rather than commissioned.[92]

Nevertheless, a few names keep recurring. A very important contact was Maslov's friend Lev Kopelev. Himself an active dissident, he was a key link to Moscow dissident circles and the literature they circulated, which included the journal *Poiski*. Via his professional contacts in the Federal Republic of Germany (FRG), Kopelev – who was a leading Germanist – was able to obtain tamizdat, which he shared with his friends.[93] Generally, obtaining tamizdat was a haphazard undertaking that depended on many factors, not least whether the respective émigré publisher had the necessary contact network to smuggle books into the USSR.[94] Another well-known dissident who made a significant contribution to *Summa* was Revolt Pimenov. Living in exile in the city of Syktyfkar (Komi, North West of Russia), he managed to circulate the journal there, as well as index the first four issues.[95] Nikolai Kaverin, who used to keep and circulate Solzhenitsyn's texts, was also heavily involved.[96]

Since the review authors used pseudonyms, even Sergei and Nina Maslov did not know all of them by name. When Maslov and Sergei Levin collected the materials, they were already signed with a pseudonym.[97] Moreover, the number of authors was much smaller than the variety of pseudonyms used throughout the journal suggests: the author index in the print edition lists only eighteen names. All authors used several pseudonyms, a practice also employed by the literary critics of unofficial culture. By far the most reviews were written by Maslov himself, who used thirteen different pseudonyms, including ones he shared with co-authors.[98] Pseudonyms have three functions: they disguise the author's identity when discretion is paramount; they allow an author to keep separate identities for different genres, for example poetry and literary criticism; and they suggest that the number of active contributors to a given publication is larger than it actually is. In the case of *Summa,* the reason for the use of pseudonyms is likely a mixture of functions one and three.

Summa depended on the Maslovs, who would collect, collate, type and bind the first sets of copies. Sergei Maslov was primarily known in Leningrad's unofficial culture for the seminar that regular met in his flat;[99] several members of this seminar were also involved in the production of *Summa* at various stages. The editors tried to distribute the issues in a manner that guaranteed that they would be read by the greatest possible number of people in Moscow, Leningrad and other cities they physically visited. At the same time, they explicitly relied on secondary reproduction: in Moscow, the journal was retyped by D.G. El'gort, a woman with much experience in reproducing and circulating samizdat.[100] Tamizdat books were read for review in the same way as most sam- and tamizdat generally, that is, under immense time pressure and often over a single night. Vershik remembers how he failed to copy out more than the table of contents and a few remarks from John Barron's book *KGB*.[101] Time pressure, added to the constraints imposed by the need for secrecy, invariably had an effect on the quality and depth of the reviews and commentaries, which is indeed very varied. Vershik remembers that not all reviewed books had actually been read by the editorial collective when they were reviewed by outside authors, so there was an implicit relationship of trust.[102] The journal kept no library, and no one person would have had access to all necessary texts, although some individuals had collections – Vershik remembers keeping a lot of things at home, including 'dangerous' texts.[103] *Summa* is proof that a scholarly treatment of samizdat was possible without the existence of large repositories. At the same time, the varying quality of the published material, as well as the eclecticism of the subject matter – no professional review journal would cover a similarly diverse breadth of material – locate the journal firmly in an alternative cultural sphere.

Libraries as models of samizdat networks

Networks that collected samizdat with the concerted aim of increasing people's awareness of this source of alternative information are a rewarding topic of research. The case studies presented here, but also the phenomenon as a whole, invite more detailed investigation, from a variety of angles that include sociology, social anthropology and book history. Studies of this kind will necessarily be fieldwork-intensive and require a good personal network; they become increasingly difficult as time goes on and people with personal experience of the phenomenon die. For the purpose of the current study, several conclusions are key.

Firstly, samizdat libraries help us gain a better understanding of the mechanics by which texts were circulated and multiplied. As organized networks they existed over some time and often kept records, which makes them significantly more accessible than the fluid friendship groups that constitute the typical samizdat environment. Libraries demonstrate in exemplary fashion the workings of samizdat networks, in particular the snowball-like pattern by which texts were passed on among people who were personally acquainted and had been judged reliable. In the case studies discussed, the existing records allow us to trace part of a text's trajectory, and personal memory shines light on connections between individuals. However, the samizdat-specific circulation pattern means that ultimately, even a library's reader network cannot be reconstructed in its entirety.

Secondly, libraries and initiatives like the review journal *Summa* are evidence of the growing professionalization of samizdat as time wore on – by the mid-1970s samizdat had evolved into an alternative culture with its own institutions that were effectively modelled on the equivalent in official culture. In the conditions of de facto illegality, the organizers of samizdat initiatives managed to compensate for the lack of resources such as buildings and stable information streams by harnessing the energy and commitment of like-minded individuals. This means there was necessarily a large gap between theory and practice, between a professional idea and its necessarily improvised physical execution and material circumstances. Perhaps this gap can be regarded as characteristic of all the institutions of samizdat that developed as the 1970s wore on. The gap, as well as the tendency of samizdat groups to replicate official structures, will be discussed in greater detail on the example of Leningrad literary journals in Chapter 6.

5

Patrons: Samizdat journal editors

Introduction

In the 1970s, networks of poets in Leningrad began producing typewritten periodicals for the circulation of their own texts and other writings that were of interest to them. Some of these journals were short-lived, while others existed until the collapse of the Soviet Union in 1991. Literary journals are a symptom of mature samizdat, signalling that what had started as a spontaneous phenomenon was becoming a more and more professionalized literary process. As periodical publications they depended on a more or less stable group of individuals who conceived, compiled, produced and distributed them; they appeared more or less regularly, at the very least more than once, in a similar format. This makes them an excellent primary source for the researcher seeking to reconstruct the mechanisms by which certain kinds of texts were made and circulated, from the concepts informing them to the technical details of their production and, importantly, the issue of how their editors conceptualized their readership.

If we take into account the adverse circumstances in which they were created, the periodicals under study in this chapter appear to be highly professional ventures. Each journal was divided into various sections featuring, for example, different literary genres, criticism, essays on contemporary culture, and translations of foreign literary, theological and philosophical works. Moreover, they chronicled unofficial cultural events such as readings, informal seminars, art exhibitions in private flats et al. Along with the outward appearance of (some) journals, this suggests an ambition on the part of their editors to produce something more than simple pamphlets for sharing texts with friends. In the absence of professional equipment, some editors carefully bound their creations by hand, producing veritable works of art.[1] The journals themselves, as material artefacts, allow us to speculate, and often draw informed conclusions, with regard to the conceptual framework and technical processes that brought them into being. However, the most substantial information is contained in the memory of their founders and readers.

The editors of the literary journals I explore in this chapter are known by name. Indeed, most journals publicized their makers' real names in the front matter. In addition, most journal editors have subsequently published memoirs, given interviews and/or produced scholarly writings on their experience in the underground.[2] These figures tended to be social 'hubs' with a talent for connecting people; some of them regularly organized informal seminars and similar events, and retain memories of those who attended. Consequently, personal acquaintance can help us today to retrace at least some features of the samizdat journal networks.

Much of the data on which this chapter is based was collected during a series of interviews conducted in St Petersburg in 2015. I was fortunate enough to be able to speak to the editors of several journals, in addition to the typists whose recollections are featured in Chapter 3, and others who were more loosely involved in journal making. I am deeply grateful to Tatiana Goricheva (*37*), Boris Ostanin (*Chasy*), Sergei Stratanovskii (*Dialog, Obvodnyi Kanal*), Dmitrii Volchek and Olga Abramovich (*Mitin zhurnal*) and Anatolii Vershik (*Summa*), who freely shared their knowledge with me. Additional information was provided by published sources (memoirs and interviews), as well as the growing body of critical literature on Leningrad samizdat. My respondents replied to questions about the concepts behind the journals and the technical details involved in production, as well as editorial policy. What motivated the choice of texts to be included? How was the material identified, procured and, in some cases, translated? What was the editing process like? Who physically produced the journal and in what conditions? How was the finished journal distributed? A second line of enquiry concerned the target audience – for whom were the journals made? As it turned out, this question needed to be modified to be relevant to the situation in the 1970s. I shall return to the reasons for this at the end of this chapter.

Why 1970s Leningrad?

Samizdat periodicals, including literary ones, existed in many cities of the Soviet Union, although the largest scenes were in the two capitals, Moscow and Leningrad. The Project for the Study of Dissidence and Samizdat at the University of Toronto has created an online map visualizing samizdat periodical activity across various cities in the Soviet Union. For Moscow, the map records 108 periodicals, with Leningrad featuring 58 entries; other cities had significantly fewer journals (e.g. Kaunas with 22 entries, Novosibirsk with 15). However, the numbers given represent the total number of periodicals that existed at any given point during the period under study, as the map cannot at this point reflect different time frames.[3]

What, then, were the features that make it possible to speak of Leningrad samizdat as a recognizable 'scene' with distinct characteristics?[4] In particular, what distinguished the 1970s literary underground in Leningrad from its Moscow counterpart, with its strong tradition of dissidence? Eyewitnesses such as Yurii Kolker, point to 'connectedness and coherence' (*sviaznost'*) between different Leningrad circles as the main reason while, in Moscow, samizdat groups maintained separate identities originating in specific interests:

> The common feature of the 'second literature' [one of several terms used for literature not published officially] of Leningrad, which distinguishes it from its Moscow analogue, is connectedness and coherence [*sviaznost'*]: [in Leningrad], writers who have distinguished themselves to the necessary degree form one single circle and live in the same informational field, which has only a few poles. By contrast, in Moscow the members of one circle often do not know about the existence of other circles.[5]

Anecdotal evidence confirms this: respondents to the samizdat reader survey in Chapter 2 who were familiar with Leningrad journals tend to refer to them as a group, while other journals mentioned in the survey, for example the *Chronicle of Current Events* or *Evrei v SSSR* (Jews in the USSR), were specified by name.[6] This phenomenon is partly explicable by circumstance, most importantly greater publication opportunities for Moscow-based literary writers, including the opportunity to send manuscripts abroad for tamizdat publication. By contrast, Leningrad official culture was much more hermetic, which heightened the importance of samizdat as an outlet:

> The difference between Russia's two cultural centres can be explained by the fact that in Moscow you can breathe more freely, regardless of the proximity of the Kremlin. Moscow has more books that are published in the West; the manuscript of a Moscow author reaches the printing press more quickly. This is why the significance of samizdat is so much greater in Leningrad.[7]

> Leningrad was a terribly stale place that boasted neither the cosiness of the province nor the freedoms of the capital. It was impossible to set out as a writer in Leningrad.[8]

Perhaps the most salient feature of Leningrad's underground was the predominance of cultural, rather than political, interests among its intellectuals. Stanislav Savitskii, in his study *Andegraund* – an attempt to write the cultural history of Leningrad unofficial culture – correctly emphasizes the essentially apolitical character of almost all literary groupings in the 1960s and 1970s. The majority of samizdat published in Leningrad journals or almanacs was literary, which is reflected in the existing publications on Leningrad samizdat as an integral phenomenon.[9] Even non-literary periodicals, like the historical almanac *Pamiat'*, which set out to provide an alternative to official historiography, fit into the pattern of cultural rather than political opposition that was so characteristic of Leningrad by maintaining a neutral, factual tone.[10] The time frame plays a role, too: in the 1970s, Leningrad was the undisputed capital of poetry; the most interesting new texts were being written there. Moscow conceptualism, the innovative current created by writers such as Dmitrii Alexanderovich Prigov and Lev Rubinshtein, only gained prominence in the early 1980s.

And, lastly, the cultural underground in Leningrad engendered a unique mixture of seminars and salons.[11] Despite being unofficial – and this means for the most part confined to individual's cramped private flats – many of these ventures maintained high literary or otherwise professional standards. Moreover, several venues in Leningrad's compact centre helped creatively minded young people meet each other: there was the often-invoked smoking room (*kurilka*) of the State Public Library (*Publichka*),[12] as well as the cafe on Novaia Sadovaia Street and, later, the famous (and infamous) cafe Saigon on the corner of Nevskii and Vladimirskii Prospekt.[13] These groups created an informal, mostly oral infrastructure, and it was this environment that later sparked and sustained the journals.

I start my survey in the mid-1970s, when the phenomenon of samizdat periodicals first became widespread. It is true that the first literary samizdat periodical, Alexander Ginzburg's short-lived *Sintaksis* (Syntax), had appeared in Moscow in 1959, and similar efforts were underway in Leningrad. However, until the mid-1970s, most publications of new underground literature were individual brochures containing poetry and uncollected articles, or more substantial, multi-author almanacs.[14]

The poetry anthology *Lepta* (Contribution) was a typical example of the trend described above, as well as a unique experiment. *Lepta* is mentioned here because it is commonly held that the anthology's fate precipitated the emergence of Leningrad's literary samizdat periodicals. In 1974, a group of five Leningrad poets – Yuliia Voznesenskaia, Boris Ivanov, Viktor Krivulin, Konstantin Kuzminskii and Evgenii Pazukhin – submitted the volume, featuring preselected work by thirty-two unofficial poets, to Sovetskii pisatel' publishing house. This means that *Lepta* was an attempt to legalize the unofficial poets' contribution to the literary process, or, in the words of Sergei Stratanovskii: 'We did not come together to create *Lepta* as a samizdat edition. Our idea was to have an official publication in order to confront the Writers' Union with the fact that there were poets who were trying to break through this wall.'[15] The anthology underwent the editorial review process but was ultimately turned down, an event that marked the end of the era of unofficial anthologies in Leningrad.[16] *Lepta* was the final attempt of unofficial writers to collaborate with the cultural authorities for a long time: the next such attempt would come almost a decade later.

The literary journals of Leningrad samizdat

The mid-1970s: Breadth and eclecticism

The following overview is by no means comprehensive; rather, I have chosen representative samples from each 'generation' of samizdat journals in Leningrad.[17] The first two, entitled *37* and *Chasy* (The Clock), were effectively sister journals and characterized by an unprecedented breadth with regard to the materials they published. Their connection to the revival of religious ideas, which took a particular form in the Leningrad underground, will be discussed in a dedicated section towards the end of this chapter.

Tatiana Goricheva and Boris Ostanin, editors of *37* and *Chasy* respectively, both maintain that the initial plan was to set up a single journal. Ostanin explained to me that there was a consensus that the members of the unofficial cultural scene should unite their efforts after the failure of the *Lepta* project; Goricheva remembers that this journal was to be called *Chasy*.[18] However, divergent ideas about the journal's ultimate purpose, and especially about the mechanisms for procuring texts for publication, meant that Goricheva and her then-husband, the poet Viktor Krivulin, together with their friend Lev Rudkevich left the planning group and published their own journal, *37*, the first issue of which appeared a few months before the first issue of *Chasy*. The early issues of both *37* and *Chasy* featured material scheduled to appear in *Lepta*.[19]

37 was named after the number of the flat its three editors shared at 20 Kurliandskaia ulitsa.[20] They thus advertised the journal's origins in an informal, even domestic environment, typical of unofficial cultural life in the 1970s, when the audience for new writing consisted of friends and acquaintances. Twenty-one issues of *37* appeared between January 1976 and March 1981: nine in 1976, four in 1977, three each in 1978 and 1979, and one each in 1980 and 1981.[21] Initially the journal appeared monthly, but this ambitious goal was soon abandoned. *37* embraced an eclectic mixture of texts. Daring and playful speculations about avant-garde tendencies in art, experimental poetry, philosophical and theological tracts – many of them in translation – and the religious-philosophical ruminations of the journal's makers and their close friends featured side by side.

This eclecticism can at least partially be explained by individual editors pursuing their own distinctive interests. While the journal's sections varied slightly from issue to issue, there were usually several literary ones featuring poetry, prose and essays, as well as literary scholarship and criticism and translations. Literary editor Viktor Krivulin was one of the Leningrad underground's most prolific and original poets, as well as a man with a legendary gift for drawing people together. Under his editorship, *37* became a springboard for many poets from Leningrad and beyond. The journal regularly included selected poetry by a single author in the form of a separate booklet.[22] For most of *37*'s existence, Krivulin also edited the "chronicle" section, an overview of unofficial cultural events in Leningrad. On the other hand, Tatiana Goricheva, an ardent neophyte who was baptized into the Orthodox faith in 1973,[23] maintained that 'All the members of the editorial board of "*37*" want the journal to serve the cause of Orthodox education.'[24] A closer look at the journal's history disproves this claim: the 'religious' part, which featured variously under the headings 'Philosophy, Theology' (nos. 3, 4, 10), 'Christianity and Art' (nos. 14, 15) and 'Philosophy and Religion' (nos. 11, 18), was only one of several distinctive sections, each of which had its designated editor. Lev Rudkevich, who edited the science section until his emigration in 1977, was an atheist.

Perhaps the most convincing explanation for the eclecticism of both material and opinion is the objective proclaimed in the first issue: 'To lead the culture of conversation beyond its pre-written stage'. 'Culture of conversation' refers not only to the cherished practices of the cultural underground, but more specifically to the sessions of the Religiozno-filosofskii seminar (Religious-Philosophical Seminar), initiated by Goricheva and Sergei Stratanovskii in 1974 and meeting regularly until 1980.[25] This seminar, which was by no means limited to a narrowly religious agenda, was only one of many informal, semi-private seminars in Leningrad; but it is exceptionally well documented, not least because its hosts produced a samizdat journal. During the first year of its existence, *37* served as a mouthpiece for this particular seminar, publishing papers and summary reports.[26] However, the intimate origin of these discussions and their limited thematic reach meant that they were not always comprehensible to outsiders. With the exceptions of rare Orthodox texts and translations of Western twentieth-century theology, most of the 'Christian' texts were generated by the editors and their friends and very personal in nature. Some took the form of 'conversations' – that is, stylized epistolary exchanges – the 'Evangelical Dialogues' between Goricheva and Krivulin in nos. 1 and 2 and 'Issues of Contemporary Christianity' between 'A and B' in no. 2, continued by 'A, B, V, G, and D' in no. 3.[27] These texts were not really geared towards giving even determined neophytes a grounding in Orthodox theology or practice – Goricheva's stated goal – and some readers deplored the inaccessibility of parts of *37*. This respondent to a 'reader survey' published in no. 17 stated: 'I think that … materials that are written for oneself or a very narrow circle of readers ought to be curtailed.'[28]

The resulting impression of 'elitism' on the part of the editors was a seminal feature distinguishing *37* from *Chasy* and, if we believe Goricheva, it was intentional and indeed necessary in order to maintain standards of quality: 'Our aims were elitist, because there were many graphomaniacs, there are always those … So we made an elitist journal and that is why considerably fewer issues appeared, we selected very carefully.'[29] It is worth noting that Goricheva explicitly denies any desire to reach out to a bigger audience, or even an audience beyond their immediate circle: 'Our journal was created elitist. We did this consciously, because you can't do everything at once, as they say. Moreover, in one sense we also did it just for ourselves, that is, for a narrow circle.'[30]

Goricheva emigrated in 1980, another victim of the persecution campaign the authorities unleashed against unofficial intellectuals in the period 1979–1980.[31] Her departure led to an almost complete overhaul of the editorial board for the last three issues (nos. 19–21): Viktor Krivulin took over as editor-in-chief, while Boris Groys and Suren Takhtadzhian assumed prominent roles. New sections for cultural studies (no. 20) and fine art (nos. 20, 21) appeared; the Moscow conceptualists started to dominate the poetry section. Evgenii Pazukhin and Viktor Antonov, who had co-edited the theology section, resigned from the editorial board; this meant that with Goricheva's departure the theology section disappeared completely. The reborn *37* lasted only three issues. In 1981, the journal was discontinued. KGB pressure, especially against Krivulin, played a decisive role.[32] Yet Krivulin also concedes that, by 1981, both the journal's key authors and its main readers had left the country.[33] It is worth noting that the more robust *Chasy*, with its broader conceptual and personal base, would continue to thrive for nine more years.

The stumbling block that prevented the unification of the journals was neither *37*'s eclecticism nor its close association with the Religious-Philosophical Seminar. After all, *Chasy* also published Western philosophy and theology in translation,[34] and sometimes even brief annotations about sessions of the Religious-Philosophical Seminar.[35] Indeed, the close relationship between *37* and *Chasy* was not limited to the initial idea. The two journals continued to overlap significantly with regard to the material and authors they promoted; prolific poets in particular regularly appeared in both journals, as did *Chasy*'s founder, Boris Ivanov, an influential critic. *Chasy* sometimes reprinted materials from *37* in the form of a digest.[36] This willingness to reproduce material from other sources is a reflection of *Chasy*'s editorial policy, which aimed closely to mirror the existing literary process underground. And it was this objective that separated it from its sister journal.[37]

Just like *37*, *Chasy* was produced by an editorial committee. Alongside Ivanov, this consisted of Boris Ostanin and, over the years, several others, including Arkadii Dragomoshchenko, Sergei Korovin, Igor Adamatskii, Yurii Novikov and Viacheslav Dolinin. From the very beginning, *Chasy*'s editorial policy acknowledged the special situation of culture in Leningrad/the Soviet Union. Rejecting the 'elitist' stance adopted by *37* – the endeavour to finding the 'best' new texts as defined by the editors, in the words of Ostanin, 'as the journal emerged from a small circle [*kruzhkovyi zhurnal*], there was a closely defined community' – the makers of *Chasy* deliberately aimed for breadth. Their position was driven not merely by aesthetics, but by social considerations, too:

> We had a certain principle … that if somebody from our circles brought us poetry, well, we were selective, but we would publish them once. If we didn't like their work we would turn them down in the future. But it was a good thing that they were published, that they felt good about themselves, that they didn't … drown themselves because they had no readers.[38]

This approach was contentious and the risks were apparent: Boris Ostanin remembers that the editors faced constant criticism from within their own circles for being too accessible and 'democratic' and therefore putting literary quality in jeopardy. One of those who were critical of *Chasy*'s 'democracy' for precisely this reason was Yurii Kolker, even though he published his own work in the journal: 'the quality of the publications has been consciously sacrificed for the sake of regular appearance: according to their idea, the journal must …

reflect the *literary process* as it is'.³⁹ The risk of pandering to the 'graphomania' – prolific textual production by writers of little talent – of the underground⁴⁰ was certainly high in a city where 'every second person considers themselves a poet'.⁴¹ But 'graphomania' was only one of the issues the journals faced. Part of *Chasy*'s objective was to widen the textual base their readers could access, and so they actively looked for new writers and translators.⁴² Ostanin reports travelling regularly to Moscow to source texts from poets there, and remembers that at certain points 'I … would lose heart a bit, because I had thought that the range would be greater, that dozens of similar journals would spring up, that there would be a Union of Independent Writers'.⁴³ The body of suitable new texts was, in fact, smaller than the enthusiastic unofficial intellectuals from Leningrad had hoped. It is worth noting that Ostanin chooses to compare his own hopes for the underground with the Writers' Union, the organization that strictly regulated who was considered a writer in the Soviet Union.

And yet *Chasy* succeeded in its mission to be the written organ of unofficial culture as a whole.⁴⁴ True to its name, the journal appeared with reliable regularity between 1976 and 1990, publishing eighty issues overall. As a result it managed to chart the entire development of the mature underground. This was not a coincidence. Founder Boris Ivanov consciously created his journal to be an institution, maintaining that the only way to resist unsatisfactory institutions – by which he meant the official agencies of Soviet culture – was by setting up one's own, more appropriate ones.⁴⁵ The journal's clockwork-like publishing schedule provided an element of predictability in an otherwise insecure environment. In the words of Ostanin: 'we were creating a certain long-term institution, a certain venture, and the name *Chasy* – The Clock – was no coincidence. We were regular like clockwork. And "bong", we've struck again.'⁴⁶

This approach was extremely effective: the editors of *Chasy* were instrumental in creating other institutions of unofficial culture, some of which survive today. In 1978, they inaugurated a literary prize, the Premiia Andreia Belogo (Andrei Belyi Prize), in the categories of poetry, prose and essay. The prize is still awarded today and has become very prestigious as the longest-serving independent literary prize in Russia.⁴⁷ In 1979, *Chasy* hosted two conferences on the significance of the unofficial cultural movement; the specifics of these conferences illustrate the movement's curious situation between officialdom and underground. On one hand, the conferences were professionally organized, with formal papers that were later reproduced in *37* and *Chasy*.⁴⁸ On the other, they took place in private flats and, in the case of the second conference – which involved participants from Moscow, Lvov and other cities – were shrouded in conspiratorial silence; even the participants did not know the exact location.[49] Sergei Stratanovskii remembers: 'It was kept well secret, the participants didn't know where to go. They had been told to come to Petrogradskaia metro station, where they would be picked up and taken to the venue.'[50] Moreover, Boris Ivanov was the driving force behind the foundation of the Klub-81 in 1981, an association that existed under the auspices of the Writers' Union and the KGB with the explicit aim of giving a legal space to independent writers. Klub-81 is discussed briefly in Chapter 6. As late as 1993, Viktor Krivulin kept insisting on the fundamental differences between *37* and *Chasy*:

> *37* and *Chasy* were different types of publication. *37* pursued the aim of creating a certain language that would be able to describe the present state of culture and the historical moment in Russia from the point of view of the individual, while *Chasy* set itself the task of 'gathering mushrooms', i.e. [ensuring] survival in the cultural environment that existed at that moment.[51]

In this statement, Krivulin addresses what is perhaps the most important function of literary samizdat journals: they actively created a new cultural field, complete with its own language. I will address this trait at the end of this chapter. For now, let us note that, despite the stated differences, the material records left behind by *37* and *Chasy* are remarkably similar. Far from being merely a platform for new writing, they documented what preoccupied young intellectuals in a stifling environment. By announcing and publicizing unofficial events before they took place and publishing transcripts and reports afterwards, they helped create a cultural milieu that amounted to something greater than the sum of separate events and made this milieu accessible to those who were not directly involved in organizing the events in question. In addition, they recorded what had started out as an informal subculture for posterity, marking the transition from a largely spontaneous process to a much more deliberate system of interactions. The difference between these two journals is far less obvious than the editors would like us to think. Perhaps this is only natural given the closeness of their editors and their initial joint purpose.[52]

The late 1970s: Literary criticism and the rise of institutions

The late 1970s and early 1980s saw the emergence of a new wave of literary samizdat journals at the same time as the KGB intensified its struggle against unofficial culture. Boris Ostanin interprets the emergence of the second- and third-generation journals as a result of the 'institutional' approach of *Chasy*.

While a correlation is likely, it is simplistic to assume that other editors simply 'copied' the *Chasy* model, as he claims. Rather, the new journals are evidence that the literary process that *37* and *Chasy* had begun to document was entering a new phase.

Firstly, their differences notwithstanding, the new journals moved away from the all-encompassing concepts that had inspired both *37* and *Chasy*. The reason was most likely a change in the needs of both authors and readers: the publication of rare texts and provision of alternative reading material was no longer a priority. Rather than cater for a maximally broad mixture of interests ranging from patristic theology to avant-garde poetry under a single cover, the new journals focused more strictly on original literary work by unofficial writers.

Secondly, the new journals operated under much more strictly defined editorial policies, shaped by a narrower focus and the editors' personal tastes. To give an example, Sergei Stratanovskii remembers his decisions as editor of *Obvodnyi kanal* (the name, literally 'Bypass Canal', referes to a main waterway in the centre of Leningrad-Petersburg) as primarily motivated by taste: 'Kirill Butyrin and I had a right to our own taste ... of course journals, especially your own, are always a subjective affair.'[53]

Thirdly, unofficial journals began to devote more space to literary criticism, a trend that is evident from the very titles of the second-generation samizdat journals. *Obvodnyi kanal* (nineteen issues, 1981–1993), for example, bore the subheading 'Literaturno-kriticheskii zhurnal' (Literary and Critical Journal); its short-lived predecessor, *Dialog* (three issues, 1979–1981) was called 'Zhurnal kritiki i polemiki' (Journal for Criticism and Polemic) and *Severnaia pochta* (The Northern Post, eight issues, 1979–1981) was founded as 'Zhurnal stikhov i kritiki' (Journal for Poetry and Criticism). Unofficial culture produced a handful of first-rate literary critics. Viktor Krivulin and Sergei Stratanovskii in particular were prolific scholars and critics who discussed historic works as well as contemporary writing. Other figures who played an important role include the now well-known art historian and critic Boris Groys[54] and of course Boris Ivanov, the founder of *Chasy*.

The choice of *Obvodnyi kanal* and *Severnaia pochta* for discussion is not accidental. With Krivulin and Stratanovskii as their respective editors, both journals were run by people who were heavily involved in the first generation of journals. In this way the two journals highlight the continuities and changes undergone by the very current of unofficial culture that had found its first home in *37* and *Chasy*. At the same time, the prominence of the same few individuals as key figures in the journal scene can be read as a symptom of the extreme self-referentiality of the Leningrad underground.

Obvodnyi kanal emerged as the successor to *Dialog*, an essentially private (*domashnii*) journal in source if not in readership, which was based on written exchanges between editors Kyrill Butyrin and Sergei Stratanovskii. Butyrin specified that *Dialog* was in part a reaction to the 'elite' of the underground bohème with Viktor Krivulin at the centre and an attempt to introduce a degree of pluralism into the scene.[55] This is a curious statement to say the least, in particular if we consider that Stratanovskii, Butyrin's interlocutor, was a key representative of that very 'elite' as one of the instigators of the Religious-Philosophical Seminar and regularly sat on the editorial board of *Chasy*. At the same time, Butyrin's indignation indicates that the underground had formed a literary hierarchy that invited a degree of resistance from those who found themselves outside it.

The purpose behind *Obvodnyi kanal*, the second-longest surviving journal after *Chasy*, remains contentious, depending on which eyewitness we consult. Butyrin reports that *Obvodnyi kanal* was founded when 'Sergei Stratanovskii and I understood that our journal was outgrowing the domestic framework and had developed an objective cultural dimension.'[56] Yet the creative exchange between editor-in-chief Butyrin and Stratanovskii that had inspired *Dialog* effectively continued in *Obvodnyi kanal*, where it evolved into the two sections dedicated to philosophical publications and literary criticism. Yurii Kolker, who published his poetry in both *Chasy* and *Obvodnyi kanal*, maintains that the latter journal emerged in the wake of the discontinued *37* and was 'created and supported by representatives of the same literary-philosophical *kruzhok*'.[57] Evgenii Gollerbakh, who has compiled a most useful annotated table of contents for *Obvodnyi kanal*, stipulates that the journal's objective was 'to publish the work of the authors of the "second culture" who had united to form the literary group Klub-81 and had no opportunity to publish in official print.'[58] Neither of these affirmations constitutes a wholly balanced reflection. We have already noted that Sergei Stratanovskii had close personal ties to *37*, although not in an editorial function. He was head of the poetry section of Klub-81; however, Gollerbakh's statement is the only one known to me that sees a direct link between *Obvodnyi kanal* and Klub-81. Stratanovskii himself maintains that the journal grew out of the idea to 'expand our activity', while providing an alternative to the lax editorial policy of *Chasy*: '[we wanted] to provide a contrast to another, already existing samizdat journal, namely *Chasy*. The issue was that we didn't like the principle of *Chasy* – there was hardly any critical selection of texts … Our principle was a bit different, and we would select poetry and prose.'⁵⁹ The process of procuring texts for *Obvodnyi kanal* was more deliberate; many hopeful writers would submit work, but the editors were not afraid to turn down poetry that was not to their taste – 'I didn't like his poems, I turned him down and I think he took offence' – while actively encouraging certain writers to submit: 'I remember paying a visit to Lapenkov, who featured in the second issue, and specifically offering to publish him.'⁶⁰ By the time *Obvodnyi kanal* appeared, samizdat editors could allow themselves to be guided by their taste; Moscow conceptualism was one current that was actively promoted in *Obvodnyi kanal*. Rather than committing to regular publication, the editors would wait until they had amassed enough material that satisfied their aesthetic criteria before producing a new issue.⁶¹

A commitment to an objectivity that avoids 'the market place of both officious [*sic*] and unofficial culture'⁶² seems to have remained central to the mission of *Obvodnyi kanal*. For Kyrill Butyrin, this was at the heart of the journal's name: the region around the *Obvodnyi kanal* is a major industrial area. At the same time the journal was 'a timeline of Leningrad underground literature; [a tool for] organising the literary process.'⁶³ This statement exemplifies a tension at the heart of the journal's mission, between the goal of reflecting accurately what is happening in literature and the goal of actively shaping the literary process. Ironically, the makers of *Obvodnyi kanal* would soon themselves be accused of 'officiousness' by a different current within samizdat culture. In 1987, Stratanovskii left the journal, citing growing ideological differences between him and Butyrin, who continued to publish until 1993.⁶⁴

While *Obvodnyi kanal* continued, to some degree, the established tradition of a mixed-genre 'thick journal', *Severnaia pochta* specialized in poetry only. As a 'Journal for Poetry and Criticism' it was designed to compensate for the lack of a journal exclusively dedicated to poetry and related theoretical and critical issues.⁶⁵ First published in 1979, its founder Sergei Dediulin recruited Viktor Krivulin as co-editor and 'public face' of the journal, as he himself was under heightened KGB surveillance for his involvement in the historical almanac *Pamiat'*; he had been subject to several house searches. Krivulin's name graced the physical copies of *Severnaia pochta*, but the journal was Dediulin's brainchild, and he was responsible for its conception, realization and physical production.⁶⁶

The editorial policy of *Severnaia pochta* throws light on a fascinating process that was evident in other journals, too, if to a lesser degree. Poems and archival materials relating to classics of the Russian and Western tradition were published alongside new poetry and criticism, suggesting implicitly that the unofficial poets were part of this lineage. A particularly fine and subtle example of this technique can be found in *Severnaia pochta* no. 6, which was a themed issue dedicated entirely to Joseph Brodsky on the occasion of his fortieth birthday. Brodsky had been a trailblazer for younger poets before he was forced to leave the Soviet Union in 1972, embracing an intellectual, metaphysically orientated poetry that looked back to the Silver Age. He settled in the USA, where he became a prominent man of letters; he would go on to win the Nobel Prize for literature in 1987. Dediulin placed Brodsky's texts on his native city next to the 'Leningrad poems' of Brodsky's mentor Anna Akhmatova, alongside thematically related verse by thirteen underground poets. Among them were Dmitrii Bobyshev and Leonid Aronzon. Bobyshev, who had emigrated only in 1979, had been mentored by Akhmatova at the same time as Brodsky. Aronzon had died through suicide in 1970, but his poetry continued to inspire many of his fellow unofficial poets. In this way the editor created a thematic block that linked the unofficial poets to one another, to their native city, to literary greatness and to the pre-revolutionary poetic tradition. Another example of the same strategy is critical rather than poetic: in his long article 'Dvadtsat' let noveishei russkoi poezii' (Modern Russian Poetry of the Last Twenty Years), Viktor Krivulin confidently maps out the place of Leningrad unofficial poetry within twentieth-century literary history, arguing for the continuities between modernism and 1970 poetry and elaborating on the renewal of poetic language after 1960.[67] In this way the editors made both implicit and explicit statements about the value of unofficial poetry – a position that was subsequently accepted by researchers.[68]

The fate of *Severnaia pochta* resembles that of *37*, and both journals were discontinued in 1981. Sergei Dediulin was one of those forced to emigrate when the government increased its pressure on unofficial circles in the early 1980s, mainly for his involvement with *Pamiat'*, which had attracted the ire of the KGB because it was being reprinted abroad.[69] At the same time, Krivulin was also being persecuted and told to close down *Severnaia pochta* if he did not want to put the Klub-81 project in jeopardy.[70] *Severnaia pochta* was discontinued after the eighth issue; Krivulin provides a touching report of how Dediulin spent the last two weeks before his emigration typing up the final two issues.[71] Dediulin's role in the physical production of the journal will be discussed in the section 'How samizdat journals were made' below. The fate of *Severnaia pochta* and *37* illustrates the vulnerability of a journal scene that ultimately depended on the commitment of a few highly visible individuals and the networks around them.

The newest generation: The proliferation of niche interests

Another phenomenon that developed around the turn of the decade was the proliferation of ever more specific interests that found expression in specialist journals. In 1979 the avant-garde journal *Transponans* (thirty-six issues, 1979–1987, edited by Ry Nikonova [Anna Tarshis] and Sergei Sigei [Sergei Sigov]) was born,[72] which appeared in Eisk but is commonly regarded as a Leningrad journal due to Sigei's close ties to the city.[73] The same year saw the birth of *Summa*, the review journal discussed in Chapter 4. Also in 1979, Natalia Malakhovskaia, Tatiana Goricheva and Tatiana Mamonova published the feminist almanac *Zhenshchina i Rossiia* (Woman and Russia), evidence of a growing preoccupation with questions of human rights in Leningrad, too. Feminism was here to stay: subsequently, the newly founded feminist club Mariia published six issues of an eponymous journal (1980–1982, edited by Galina Grigoreva and Natalia Lazareva). In the case of Malakhovskaia, Goricheva, Mamonova, and their friend Yuliia Voznesenskaia, their activism gave the authorities a reason to persecute them and ultimately push them into emigration in 1980.[74]

The stratification, or fragmentation, within unofficial culture was set to intensify. Between the onset of Perestroika in 1985 and the collapse of the Soviet Union in 1991, the number of grassroots periodicals exploded. Most of them were even more highly specialized and short-lived, exemplifying the variety of writing and reading tastes that had been fostered by unofficial culture and could now be expressed in the climate of relaxing censorship. These journals fulfilled the criteria of samizdat in the sense that they were self-produced but, by this time, the line separating official and unofficial culture had become very porous. Examples of niche journals of the Perestroika years include Boris Ivanov's satirical journal *Krasnyi Shchedrinets* (The Red Shchedrinets, ten issues, 1986–1990), poking fun predominantly at traditional rubrics in Soviet newspapers and journals, such as 'Workers' Letters';[75] and *Topka* (Furnace, four issues, 1988–1992), which published works by authors who worked in boiler rooms, a menial job popular among the unofficial intellectuals.[76]

In this place I will discuss one journal of the Perestroika years: *Mitin zhurnal* (fifty-nine issues, 1985–2001, in its old format). On one hand, it was a straightforward literary journal that shared some characteristics of the earlier periodicals. On the other, it was a prime example of the increasing individualization of unofficial culture at the cusp of Perestroika. This is already evident in the journal's title, which translates as 'Mitya's journal', Mitya being the diminutive of 'Dmitrii'. The 'Dmitrii' in question is Dmitrii Volchek, founder and main editor. *Mitin zhurnal* was a small venture, run by Volchek himself and Olga Abramovich, a woman with much samizdat experience and the journal's sole typist. Volchek states that his main motivation in founding the journal was aesthetic: the literary taste of the older samizdat generation was very unlike his own, which he describes as 'avant-garde'; he was also sceptical of the focus on the Orthodox revival and Christianity that he observed in the established journals.[77] Volchek himself commissioned most articles and reviews and resolved to publish exclusively literary texts that conformed to his own taste; he reports turning down very many submissions on aesthetic grounds.[78] *Samizdat Leningrada* cites him as saying 'the journal was initially conceived of as a publication for a narrow circle of admirers of non-traditional literature'.[79]

The term 'non-traditional' (*netraditsionnyi*), here supposedly meaning 'following the example of the avant-garde', is rare as a descriptor for samizdat literature, which tends to be referred to as 'uncensored' (*nepodtsenzurnyi*) or 'unofficial' (*neofitsial'nyi*). Hence it marks a decisive shift of perception, identifying texts by their formal properties rather than their social position or origin. *Mitin zhurnal* had thus moved away as far as possible from the imperative of a 'social institution' that guided the editorial policy of *Chasy*. And indeed, during the early years of its existence, the journal's readership consisted of a small circle of people personally known to the editor. Volchek admits that the reality did not correspond to his ambition, which had been to attract young people living an oppositional lifestyle: '[My ideal readers were] punks, but they don't read.'[80] Nevertheless, *Mitin zhurnal*'s audience subsequently expanded, not least because of a subscription scheme similar to the one operated by *Chasy*. By the second half of the 1980s it was possible to post self-made publications via ordinary mail, and so the editors were able to send their journal directly to subscribers in various cities: '*Mitin zhurnal* had subscribers in various towns, to whom we would send the journal by mail, for money. Even to Tashkent in Uzbekistan. They were ordinary people.' The journal became the hub of a network of people with similar interests: 'Thanks to the journal we discovered that there were people out there who shared our interests.'[81]

The time of its foundation meant that *Mitin zhurnal* felt the changing mood particularly acutely. The relaxation of censorship and the decriminalization of independent publishing triggered a crisis for the journal. In an increasingly pluralistic media landscape where official and 'second' culture were progressively converging, *Mitin zhurnal* had to reinvent itself. Abramovich became very active during this time. Asked about the boom in cultural activity, she remembers that the social stratum attending this kind of event had changed: 'Professionals – not members of the bohème! – would meet, organize conferences, give papers ... I would go there, record, transcribe and type out what was said – all for the journal. After all, living thought is the most interesting thing. Dmitrii Volchek left me free rein in this.'[82] Technological advances allowed *Mitin zhurnal* to adapt to the changes: while the first issues were typewritten, with Abramovich typing out up to three sets of the 400-page journal, the increasing availability of photocopiers allowed the makers to increase the 'print run'. By the time it became possible to have the copies professionally printed through a privately owned printing press, this print run had increased to 500 copies. At this time, the journal was also delivered to libraries – an impressive example of how a publication with its origins in a small informal network managed to bridge the divide between official and unofficial.[83]

Of the samizdat periodicals that survived into the 1990s (*Chasy* ceased publication in 1990, *Obvodnyi Kanal* in 1993), only *Mitin zhurnal* successfully reinvented itself. Volchek remembers a period of doubt in the 1990s when he was unsure what to publish,[84] and Abramovich stopped working for the journal in 2001. However, when Volchek set up his own publishing house, Kolonna Publications, *Mitin zhurnal* became part of his 'empire'. It continues to appear and can be read online or bought.[85] Perhaps this reinvention was possible because the editor's purpose never did depend on the underground literary process.

Mitin zhurnal represented a true change of generation. Volchek's oppositional stance, directed against the samizdat 'establishment' whose representatives continued to dominate the scene ('The main authors remained the same: Sergei Stratanovskii, Oleg Okhapkin, Alexander Mironov, that is, the acknowledged masters of the unofficial culture of the 1970s.'[86]), was symptomatic of a younger generation's rebellion against their overbearing fathers: Volchek was born in 1964, while the founders of the other journals discussed here were born in the 1940s, with the exception of Boris Ivanov, who was born in 1928.

However, older intellectuals also rebelled against the predominance of the circle around Krivulin and Stratanovskii. One instructive case is that of *Transponans*, a journal preoccupied with the influence of the early twentieth-century avant-garde on contemporary literature.[87] Editor Ry Nikonova accused those she called 'our Leningrad elite' not only of dominating the space but also of aping official culture, a point that will become very significant for our subsequent analysis. The occasion for this condemnation – and a condemnation it was, with her calling the editors of *Obvodnyi kanal* 'more orthodox than officious [*sic*] culture'[88] – was a questionnaire that invited unofficial writers to express their views on Velimir Khlebnikov. The questionnaire, distributed on the occasion of the centenary of Khlebnikov's birth in 1985, was intended to counterbalance the barrage of tendentious material in the official press, which had only just readmitted the Futurist poet to the canon.[89] Factional strife of this kind is to be expected in a developed literary scene; curiously, both Nikonova and her co-editor, Sergei Sigei, filled in the questionnaire, and their responses were published in *Obvodnyi kanal* no. 9 (1986) alongside those of many others. To examine the reasons for and validity of Nikonova's criticism is not the goal of this chapter. However, Nikonova's spite highlights a specific feature of the late Soviet underground, which is the constant presence of official culture as a realm situated outside samizdat that nevertheless had the power to define the value of most things said or written by samizdat authors. Indeed, canvassing the opinion of readers and/or important cultural figures on a variety of topics was common practice in the official press. The questionnaire is yet another structural and practical parallel between samizdat periodicals and Soviet 'thick journals' – the main topic of the final chapter of this study.

The relationship between culture and religion

The abundance of texts published in the journal *37* that were either religious, specifically Christian Orthodox or more broadly spiritual can be explained by the journal's close ties to the Religious-Philosophical Seminar. However, *Chasy* (and other journals, too) published similar materials, indicating that this issue had wider relevance.

In the pronouncedly atheist Soviet Union, which marginalized the Orthodox Church and repressed other denominations, 'being religious' was a form of dissent.[90] In European Russia, interest in religion implied, for the most part, interest in Orthodox Christianity as one of the cornerstones of Russian cultural heritage. For many, including Communist Party members, this heritage became an alternative source of values and identity after Khrushchev's Secret Speech at the 20th Party Congress in 1956 effectively dismantled the quasi-religious cult of the Communist Party. But as a result of the limitations on religious life, the most ardent debates involving Orthodoxy took place in the underground. The existence of the Religious-Philosophical Seminar, which was originally founded for the purpose of exploring the roots of the Christian tradition but which quickly turned to the concerns of Soviet neophytes, must be seen in this light.[91]

For historical reasons, Russian Orthodoxy is inherently susceptible to close association with national, and politically nationalist, sentiment and ideology, and these form the backbone of the close alliance between the Orthodox Church and the present-day Russian regime.[92] However, Leningrad neophytes of the 1970s, for the most part, lacked the national and nationalist concerns that were so central to the revival of Orthodoxy elsewhere; at least, nationalist sentiment found little reflection in underground publications. All the main nationally minded underground periodicals of the 1970s were based in Moscow. *Veche* (Popular Assembly), founded in 1971 and closed down under KGB pressure in 1974, was the major unofficial organ for Russian national sentiment in the early 1970s. Its successor, *Moskovskii sbornik* (Moscow Collection),[93] was focused more specifically on problems of nation and religion, and was also discontinued owing to the persecution of its editor. The Orthodox circle that most resembled the Religious-Philosophical Seminar, which was called Khristianskii seminar po problemam religioznogo vozrozhdeniia (literally, the Christian Seminar for Issues to do with the Religious Renaissance, or Christian Seminar), was also Moscow-based, although its members came from all over the Soviet Union and it had a dedicated Leningrad representative. While the Religious-Philosophical Seminar at one point even staged a joint conference with the Christian Seminar, ultimately the Christian Seminar was much more strictly focused on Orthodoxy proper, and its manifesto resounded with Slavophile overtones.[94]

We can conclude that Leningrad was home to the 'cultural faction' of the 1970s neophytes, whose interest in Russian Orthodoxy was entwined with developments in literature, art and thought rather than national or nationalist sentiment. In their eyes, both religion and culture were part of a mindset that acknowledged the existence of a reality transcending the two-dimensional, materialist setup of Soviet ideology. This approach risked an identification of culture with religion (or rather, culture-as-religion), and many intellectuals implied a connection between the two: Tatiana Goricheva called *37* 'a cultural-religious journal',[95] Kyrill Butyrin talks about 'the matter of the cultural-spiritual, and therefore ultimately political, opposition to the communist Leviathan'.[96] The interest in religion in general, and Orthodox Christianity in particular, was part of a lifestyle which was simultaneously steeped in high culture, and marginal. Its importance as one of the most distinctive features of the Leningrad underground has been acknowledged by researchers. The scholar Stanislav Savitskii identifies religious syncretism as a function of unofficial literature and calls *37* the journal 'on whose pages the religious-artistic mythology was formed'.[97]

How samizdat journals were made

We are fortunate to have detailed accounts of the production of several samizdat journals, including *37*, *Chasy* and *Severnaia pochta*. They are worth quoting at some length, as they highlight issues that anyone preparing samizdat in large quantities would have encountered. Moreover, it is by looking at the production process that we understand a key feature: individual differences notwithstanding – number of primary copies, copy-editing process and the question of salaried typists – ultimately, all samizdat journals remained the product of the individual or very small group who founded them.

Back in 1985, Tatiana Goricheva described the production of *37* as a social event, a spectacle: 'It was, of course, an event that went beyond us simply sitting there, typing something out and editing (there were always some girls there helping us). It was a community event.'[98] Thirty years later, her account remains similarly enthusiastic:

> We also had copy editors; there was an entire army of intellectuals … everything was scattered around, the whole floor would be covered in journal pages. For example, the first print run would be 100 copies. So we would collate those 100 copies and tie them together with some string. 100 copies. And then they would do a second print run and a third. It was that serious.'[99]

Lev Rudkevich, the third member of *37*'s original editorial team, seems to have been in charge of procuring paper and other consumables: '[At first, the journal came out] in a fairly large print run, because Rudkevich, our third editor, had become something like a publisher … He had lots of money (he had received an inheritance), and he basically published the journal at his expense.'[100]

It is difficult to establish the factual exactitude of eyewitness accounts decades later and in the absence of material evidence. What seems beyond doubt is that the 'print run' of *37* varied widely from one issue to the next. Goricheva herself stated in 1985 that 'In the first few months we would publish 200 copies. That is, of course, a lot, but we didn't know that.'[101] Thirty years later this number had halved to 100 (see above). Written sources, compiled using information provided by the editors, also vary: *Samizdat Leningrada* reports a print run of between five and 100 copies,[102] while *Antologiia Samizdata*, which has a more detailed entry on *37*, mentions between fifteen and 200 copies each, evidently reiterating a variable figure that was given by Krivulin.[103] Goricheva claims that the editors made sure to send the journals 'to different corners of the country, from Tallin to Novosibirsk and Moscow'.[104] Other sources confirm that the editors of *37* reported sending out their journal to faraway places.¹⁰⁵ However, it is extraordinarily hard to find copies of *37* in either specialist archives or private collections, casting at least a shadow of doubt over this claim. Some materials evidently reached the émigré press abroad and were reproduced in a haphazard manner, but there is no evidence that complete journals were sent abroad.¹⁰⁶ Luckily, advances in digital technologies over the last couple of years have helped overcome the issue of inaccessibility.

An interesting detail is the journal editors' attitude towards their typists, the one human resource needed for the production of any samizdat journal. The journals were thick and, in order to produce them fast, with a minimum of errors that would require correction by hand, the person typing them needed professional or near-professional skills. Krivulin specifies that 'the typists who received money from the editors of *Chasy*, worked for us for free. Their remuneration was the awareness that they were participating in a creative process. And the typists (there were three of them) made an honest effort, producing five or even ten sets each.'¹⁰⁷ Conversely, Goricheva attributes lacunae in the texts and other errors to the work of unpaid volunteers. A practical example: the first issue of *37* features Goricheva's own article on Max Scheler and naturalism. In the copy held in the archive of the Research Centre for East European Studies at Bremen University, this article carries multiple references.¹⁰⁸ However, the text of the footnotes is missing. It is not usually possible to type footnotes on a typewriter; these would need to be inserted by hand. Asked whether she could explain the absence of the notes, Goricheva replies: 'Some women did the typing for us. They did not really work, because they were doing it for free.' She concedes that this must have been a copy that slipped her editorial scrutiny: 'If I [had seen that], I would have added the notes in pencil, naturally. They simply didn't know.'¹⁰⁹ One person who remembers typing some materials for the journal is Galina Drozdetskaia. She volunteered out of sheer enthusiasm: 'I was prepared to type whatever they gave me, I considered it an honour … no, I was never explicitly asked whether I would type for the journal … The typists were simply people who had typewriters, those were hard to come by.'¹¹⁰

In accordance with the editors' institutional ambitions and more professional stance, the *Chasy* team organized the typing process differently. Boris Ivanov managed the supply of consumables mostly through informal contacts, but the editors also invested their own money in their venture:

> Boris Ivanov would obtain the materials, he knew people who worked in a printing shop. Liderin, PVA glue – amazing stuff that glued paper really well, cutters, a metal ruler, those vice clamps – all of this was simply taken from there.

> ... We would buy special thin paper. I think a large ream cost 96 kopecks, if I remember correctly. And we would buy carbon paper ... Sometimes Boris Ivanov and I would add photographs and other things; we did that at our personal expense.[111]

Most importantly, the main typist was a salaried professional, Viktoria Apter. The salary enabled her to concentrate on this work and deliver on time. 'We made it clear that [the typist] was our employee. This was her job ... and she made her living doing it. She received 120 roubles for two months ... She would do this year in, year out, she had a decent typewriter.'[112]

Kirill Kozyrev, who was closely involved with several journals, remembers that Ivanov and Ostanin would take turns binding alternating issues; according to him, differences in binding style can be attributed to the personal technique of the respective editor.[113] Surviving copies of *Chasy*, of which there are plenty, are creatively and solidly bound in hardcover. This is Ostanin's account of how the journal acquired its cover:

> So, there would be eight or ten copies ... the typist typed it all, then she would take out the carbon paper and spread it all on the floor ... Binding is sheer physical work. Binding alone took two or three days. All of it needed to be cut with a knife ... it would take a long time to explain, but it's a real feat ... We did real covers; this is one I made [holds up a bound copy of *Chasy*]. I used these threads, red ones, they were a bit woolly, but strong ... here you see a little hole, I used ... not quite an awl, but a very fine drill to push through, and then I joined up the pages.[114]

Viktoria Apter was not the only typist working for *Chasy*, although she was the longest-serving one. Natalia Volokhonskaia remembers that at one point she also typed *Chasy*. Crucially, since she earned her living by typing, she declined to work for *37* precisely because the editors did not offer payment.[115] The editors of *Chasy* organized the distribution of their journal very deliberately, through a subscription scheme: 'we had a good system. We had so-called subscribers. Every subscriber would pay twelve roubles for a copy. That's not a huge sum, but expensive for a book ... These 12 roubles we gave to the typist, the whole sum.'[116] Kirill Kozyrev remembers a slightly different scenario according to which only some copies were reserved for the subscribers: 'four copies were given to people who had subscribed to the journal; they provided the salary for the typists. And the other copies, let's say six copies, were given away for free, to everybody. Well, I mean, they were passed around.'[117] In any case, this scheme ensured effective circulation of the journal in Leningrad and beyond:

We chose our subscribers so that each would serve a large group of people. This is how Revolt Pimenov could read it there [in Syktyfkar, Komi Republic, where he had been exiled] – people would pass the journal to others to read and then give it back. There was a constant exchange going on. We tried to estimate – Boris Ivanov thinks that *Chasy* had around 200 regular readers. Perhaps a bit more, because sometimes it travelled to Moscow or even Saratov, but 200 readers, that's the minimum. Perhaps individual issues were read by more people.[118]

Curiously enough, Ostanin is very cautious about the possibility that readers might have produced secondary copies ('There were cases where somebody copied it, but not many') although this is almost certainly the case. While I have not come across a report of *Chasy* being retyped, we have indirect proof of secondary reproduction. Not only is the journal present in many archives,[119] but individual copies of the same issue show marked digressions: the copy of *Chasy* no. 12 that is held in the archive of the Research and Information Centre Memorial in St Petersburg features a report about a session of the Religious-Philosophical Seminar. In the copy from the archive of the Research Centre for East European Studies at Bremen University this report is not only absent, but not even mentioned in the table of contents; it follows that the two copies cannot have been part of the same set and were most probably typed by different people. In any case the practice of secondary reproduction of journals, or parts of journals, was common. Irina Tsurkova, who typed the two existing issues of the leftist journal *Perspektiva*, remembers:

> So, you gave somebody a copy, and that person would make another copy, either on a typewriter or with a camera. That happened a lot. Somebody would photograph a journal and then you could print from the film ... I saw photocopies of *Perspektiva* only much later, but I had already heard from different people that they had come across the journal in faraway places, for example in the Urals, in Sverdlovsk, and in Chelyabinsk.[120]

Even though several people were involved in the production of both *37* and *Chasy*, ultimately the editors were responsible for every aspect of the journal's physical production apart from the typing itself; to quote Kirill Kozyrev: 'The only thing [the editors] didn't do was type ... Binding and everything else was done by them. They procured paper and carbon paper and supplied it to the typists.'[121]

In the case of *Severnaia pochta,* editor Sergei Dediulin acted as editor, proofreader and typist at once. This means that the journal was literally 'home-made'; but, at the same time, *Severnaia pochta* was a highly professional venture.

Dediulin, a detail-loving bibliography specialist who had much experience in producing samizdat, and poetry samizdat in particular,[122] held himself to exacting standards. Krivulin exulted that '*Severnaia pochta* was the only samizdat journal without typos, those birthmarks of samizdat.'[123] *Severnaia pochta* reached its readers unbound because Dediulin would not bind the pages. However, Yurii Kolker remembers that '[the pages] were made so carefully and contained such interesting material that the readers automatically felt a desire to preserve them, and many would have them bound. I remember how I was given a bound full set of the journal to read – all eight issues – and the solemnity with which it was handed to me.'[124] Kolker speculates that there was only one set produced (i.e. five to seven copies), while Dediulin himself remembers that he produced two sets.[125] *Samizdat Leningrada* cites a 'print run' of over twenty-three to twenty-seven copies, which would correspond to three sets.[126]

Even though some journals circulated widely, they remained small ventures, usually run by one or two individuals. In the words of Kirill Kozyrev, 'if a certain issue [of *Chasy*] was done by Boris Ivanov, then he would do all of it. If it was done by Boris Ostanin, he would do all of it. And that's it, there was no one else. One person on his own.'[127] Samizdat networks achieved impressive feats in the absence of any of the middlemen normally involved in a literary process, but they depended on the selfless commitment of individuals so few in number that we know them by name. In this sense, the production story of the literary samizdat journals highlights the contingency of the process of text circulation 'by hand'.

Translation, world culture and the reality

The presence of translated texts alongside new writing in the samizdat journals can be read as an attempt by the editors to inscribe their friends (and frequently themselves) into a context that transcended their locality, native language and cultural context. But ultimately it is the field of translation that evinces most clearly the limitations the Soviet Union's isolationist policy imposed on the evolution of culture. Awareness of these limitations may have been what prompted Viktor Krivulin to define the translation policy of *37* as an attempt to counteract this tendency and to strive for 'Russian culture's inclusion in the context of contemporary world culture'.[128] As evidence he cites the translations of 'key artefacts of the present' in the journal, maintaining that the choice of texts to be translated was not accidental, and claiming that 'it was important to us to recreate the integral context of contemporary culture and not just individual elements'.[129] It is reasonable to assume that his aim for *Severnaia pochta* was broadly the same, with the focus more exclusively on poetry.[130] The quantity of translated literature on the pages of *Severnaia pochta* was minuscule – one very small selection of poems by Czesław Miłosz and another by Emily Dickinson, both in no. 8 – but this does not invalidate Krivulin's point outright. The publication of works by writers of the Russian emigration, for example Vladimir Nabokov in no. 4, and reviews of foreign poetry books strengthen it. After all, by featuring Miłosz – the current Nobel Prize winner (1980) – *Severnaia pochta* proved that it could react to events on the world literary stage in a timely manner, and the translations were accompanied by the original – a very professional detail. Krivulin, who had translated Miłosz, was a reluctant translator of poetry, claiming that translation negatively affected the poet-translator's own creative work.[131] Krivulin's statements should be taken with a pinch of salt: despite having published a translation of William Butler Yeats in 1977,[132] he later maintained that rendering poetry in another language was impossible in the first place.[133]

The scarcity of skilled translators certainly contributed to the overall dearth of translations in samizdat journals. Starting with issue no. 5 (1983), *Obvodnyi kanal* included a regular section for translations, although not all of them were new; for example, three of the five poems by Emily Dickinson and translated by M. Soboleva that featured in no. 5 were reprints from *Severnaia pochta* no. 8. But the reasons run deeper. Let us look at the two 'generalist' journals, *37* and *Chasy*. *37* no. 11 featured the first-ever Russian translation of three stories from the famous collection *Ficciones* by Jorge Luis Borges; these were republished in *Chasy* no. 9.[134] The story of how Borges ended up on the pages of *37*, rendered into Russian from a French translation rather than the original Argentinian Spanish, is worth quoting:

JVZ: You were the first to publish Borges. So you didn't just reproduce him?
Tatiana Goricheva: No, Boris Groys translated him, I think from the French.
JVZ: Was Borges permitted?
TG: I think he was starting to appear, after all this was the time when there were already Kafka and Sartre and Camus. Evidently Borges was available, too, somewhere, at least some stories ... I no longer remember what exactly Boris [Groys] translated, but we really liked Borges. I would read him in German translation while Boria would read him in French.

Goricheva was a prolific translator, mostly of philosophical and theological literature, and her efforts were supported by Groys and others who also translated foreign works. But what they could cover was necessarily limited by both their own number and the availability of texts.[135] Even though the *Publichka* increasingly collected key contemporary or near-contemporary foreign texts, the supply remained random.[136] The editors of *Chasy* pursued a translation policy that resembled that of *37*, even if they refrained from formulating a similarly lofty conceptual aim. Like its sister journal, it published key texts of the twentieth century from the fields of theology, philosophy and cultural theory, alongside some highlights of Western literature.[137] Just as problematic as the difficulty to obtain texts was the young intellectuals' lack of contextual knowledge necessary to assess and interpret the texts they chanced upon. The 'lack of erudition' diagnosed by Boris Ostanin, who curated the translation section of *Chasy*, as well as insufficient language skills, seriously hampered any effort to publish a representative number of good translations:

> It was mostly I who did that section, and I did a lot of editing, a lot ... And back then I got very upset, as I had expected that the journal would attract more material, especially translations ... We often received rather weak translations ... and sometimes it was all accidental ... For example, Volodia Kucheriavkin and I translated the *Tibetan Book of the Dead* ourselves ... Yes, of course, [you could borrow the English edition in the library], you could even buy it in English at the antiquarian bookshop, *Staraia kniga*, for four roubles. Valera Molot translated both Beckett and Robbe-Grillet ... [You would often find] an elementary lack of knowledge, a lack of erudition ... Boris Ivanov loved Protestant thinkers, Bonhoeffer, Barth, and Tillich; I think he spent a long time translating one of Tillich's books together with Tatiana Goricheva and published some fragments, *The Courage to Be*. All this was put together very gradually.[138]

There is no doubt that samizdat editors had high hopes for the genre of translation and worked hard to turn these ideas into reality. And yet, all they could ultimately achieve was to provide samples of individual key texts.

Translation only became a real strength of samizdat journals as the 1980s progressed. *Mitin zhurnal*, which emerged in 1985, included translated texts in the regular poetry and/or prose section of every issue rather than in an individual section. A dedicated section for translation appeared only in 1984. The translation journal *Predlog* (eighteen issues, 1984–1989) was the 'imprint' of the translators' section of Klub-81, which means it was a semi-official publication from the very start; significantly, Viacheslav Dolinin likens it to *Inostrannaia literatura*, the Soviet Union's official journal for translation.[139] Sergei Stratanovskii – who headed Klub-81's poetry section – points out that the focus on texts that can be called 'philosophical', in the broad sense of the word, was particularly welcome: '[*Predlog*] published only translations. Most were of philosophical texts because, during the Soviet era, hardly any philosophy or theology was translated.'[140] Stratanovskii's memory is too narrow. The journal featured translated poetry and prose as well as a section for foreign works broadly relating to the humanities – these are the texts 'missing' in the Soviet Union to which Stratanovskii is referring. The semi-official initiative that created *Predlog* seems to have radiated 'back' into samizdat, as the makers of *Obvodnyi kanal*, including Stratanovskii, established a translation supplement to the journal, pointedly entitled *Most* (Bridge, six issues, 1987–1991).[141] The focus was broadly similar to that of *Predlog*, including philosophy, psychology, cultural theory and philology. The proliferation of translation at this particular point in time – towards the end of the Soviet era – marks foreign texts as part of the wave of 'lost literature', twentieth-century classics never published in the USSR, that inundated the pages of journals both official and unofficial during Perestroika.

A unique atmosphere

What this discussion shows is that, ultimately, the reach of each journal remained limited. The conditions of unofficial culture placed limitations on the readership that could be reached, as well as on the range of texts that could be sourced or commissioned. The difficulties besetting the genre of translation expose the lofty dream of linking contemporary Russian culture to world culture with the help of handmade journals as a utopian one, undercut only by the underground's trademark irony.

However, it is a mistake to focus on the failure of the utopian idea. This kind of focus misses two crucial features of the journals. The most important function of the journals was sociocultural. Unlike library networks, which sought to increase the readership of already existing texts and had an implicit educational function, journal networks were primarily a platform for authors. In the context of these networks – group discussions and readings, friendship and publication – those who were excluded from and/or eschewed the official process could create freely. It seems that those who made the journals were aware of this. Let us look at a statement Viktor Krivulin made in 1993:

> The important task of the journal [37] was not to show everybody that it was possible for independent culture to exist, but to become aware of the limits of permissible speech and to chart the limits of a person's intellectual freedom under the reigning circumstances ... what was more important was the creation of an atmosphere in which the person of culture could live.[142]

In other words, quantifiable results – for example, the number of texts published or translated, or the number of readers reached – were of secondary importance. The journal editors I was able to interview in 2015 repeatedly stressed that the main function of the journals was to foster a certain atmosphere. The journals were successful primarily through the position their very existence afforded to intellectuals. 'Creative freedom' is only a very approximate definition. As discussed above, Boris Ostanin maintained that *Chasy* was created to give marginalized writers the opportunity to experience themselves as writers. Boris Likhtenfel'd's assessment is similar, stressing the importance of readership rather than publication: 'the emergence of samizdat journals enabled fully-fledged communication between us and readers from the same milieu'.[143] Sergei Stratanovskii effectively invalidated my research question that sought to define a target audience for each journal when he said: 'You know, these journals created an environment, and that was very important. We didn't really think about the addressee. We made an effort so that the greatest possible number of people would read our texts'.[144] It seems that Krivulin's idea about using the journals to bring world culture to Russia should be read in this vein, too: the opportunity to read international texts that were otherwise unavailable helped foster an atmosphere that was radically different from the one offered by the official cultural environment, and this was the main point. What was important was not that the cultural underground managed to create journals, but that these journals, started by a handful of people, managed to create the milieu in which, in the words of Kyrill Butyrin: 'something forced dozens of people who had no professional training to take up the pen, the paintbrush, or the guitar, or to lead a half-bohemian, half-dissident existence in those 1970s in Leningrad, approximately in the time between the emigration of Brodsky (in 1972) and the forced exile of Tatiana Goricheva in 1980s'.[145]

However, these sober assessments were made retrospectively. Perhaps we should see the evident gap between aspiration and reality as a special feature of Soviet samizdat, caused by a vast cultural hunger experienced by young people during the sixth decade in the Soviet Union. And yet the evident self-confidence shown by samizdat editors – Krivulin's high-flying aims for his journals, Ivanov's preoccupation with creating alternative institutions – has implications for the theoretical analysis in Chapter 6. As it turns out, they tackle the same issue in Soviet culture from different angles.

6

Institutions: Literary samizdat and official culture

Literary samizdat journals as communities of practice

In this chapter, I will provide a theoretical framework for the literary samizdat journals which appeared in Leningrad in the second half of the 1970s and first half of the 1980s and which were discussed in the previous chapter. The central element of this framework is the highly complex, fraught and ambivalent relationship between unofficial journals and official culture. The literary journals of mature samizdat demonstrate with particular clarity how a system of informal networks came to fulfil, for a certain segment of society, tasks that are normally fulfilled by official institutions. Moreover, as the Soviet Union began to unravel, these networks became increasingly entwined with some of their official counterparts.

A viable framework for describing distinct groups engaged in producing literary samizdat on a regular basis is that of 'communities of practice'. This concept was originally developed in the field of education science, as a social theory of learning, but has been adapted and gained currency, for example, in the study of management and virtual networks.[1] It carries echoes of Pierre Bourdieu's idea of 'habitus', which is a way of identifying the shared outlook, values and behaviours defining particular social groups.[2] In their most basic form, communities of practice are characterized by interaction ('mutual engagement'), common endeavours ('joint enterprise'), and a shared repertoire of common resources of language, styles and routines by means of which participants express their identities as members of the group.[3] The journals fulfilled all these criteria: their members interacted in the pursuit of a common endeavour, which can be defined either as the publication and promotion of unofficial literature or, more broadly, as non-sanctioned cultural activity. In addition, their 'shared repertoire' involved not only aesthetic preferences regarding reading and writing but also certain lifestyle choices. When using criteria relating to 'communities of practice' as a sociological concept, my aim is not to carry out a detailed analysis of the degree to which journal networks comply with these criteria. Rather, I am employing the terminology in a strictly descriptive sense. The semantic field that has evolved around the concept of 'communities of practice' provides accessible vocabulary for describing certain specific aspects of samizdat journal networks – most fruitfully so when we examine the relationship between these networks and Soviet official literary culture. David Barton and Karin Tusting posit that a community of practice is a group of people coming together in a particular context to carry out activities while remaining distinct from the formal structures of the workplace, place of education or other institution which generated these activities in the first place.[4] As the subsequent analysis will demonstrate, the communities that practised literary samizdat around the journals were orientated towards the institutions of official literature, such as publishing houses and official journals, even when deliberately opposing some of their processes.

Journal networks in the 1970s

As we have seen in the previous chapter, literary journals are particularly suitable for research into samizdat networks. The more or less regular production of an entire periodical required a higher degree of organization than the spontaneous reproduction of individual texts. Journals depended on the reliable collaboration of authors, editors, typists and those who circulated the finished product to the readers. While the editors of journals with a political or religious agenda, for example the *Chronicle of Current Events*,[5] or *Veche* (Moscow)[6] and *Obshchina* (Moscow/Leningrad),[7] were subject to systematic persecution at the hands of the authorities, literary journals were often able to exist relatively undisturbed for prolonged periods of time. Yet, as the previous chapter has shown, the authorities periodically increased the pressure on literary journals, too, to such a point that editors were forced into emigration and journals discontinued.

In Leningrad, the typewritten periodicals that became the most popular form for circulating literary samizdat from the mid-1970s onwards created communities of 'makers' and 'readers' that were more or less stable over several years. These communities offered a platform to intellectuals, many of them young, who eschewed the official Soviet cultural process, allowing them to showcase their work, but also to meet for discussion and exchange. At the same time, the overlap between journal authors/editors and readers was considerable.

The literary journals were a key element of a cultural environment that set itself up to be distinct from official Soviet culture. At the same time, the attitude towards officialdom of those who made and read these journals was fundamentally different from that of the older generation that had popularized the culture of informal associations and samizdat in the 1960s. Many of these 'people of the 1960s' (*shestidesiatniki*) had believed and/or hoped that the Soviet regime was open to reform; theirs was a generation of civic activists who sought dialogue (or confrontation) with the authorities, and this means they implicitly assumed that such a dialogue was possible. Those who wrote letters of protest or debated the Soviet government's shortcomings were essentially engaging with the regime on its own terms. Sergei Oushakine has dubbed the discourse of dissident activists 'mimetic resistance', a discourse that 'uses the same vocabulary of symbolic means and rhetorical devices' as that of the regime.[8] In practice this means that dissidents, just like Soviet official culture, advanced a 'grand narrative', just one with the roles of the protagonists inverted.

By contrast, the unofficial cultural scene of the 1970s was dominated by a new generation that had come of age under Brezhnev. Its members did not harbour the hopes of the 'people of the sixties'. Not politically minded, they tended to refrain from oppositional activities, seeking instead to escape Soviet reality for an alternative sphere where they would not have to engage with official ideology by either conforming to it or confronting it.[9] Poet, editor and critic Sergei Stratanovskii observes: 'We were what you could call people of the seventies. In the 1970s, we no longer had any of the illusions that the people of the sixties had.'[10] Meanwhile, his colleague Boris Ostanin remarks upon the difference between the 'current political apathy [in the early 1980s]' and the 'politicized 1960s'[11] in an article that labels the 1960s the era of 'lightning' and the tamer 1980s, characterized by a will towards compromise, as the era of 'the rainbow'.[12] The typical representative of a journal network from the 1970s has been exceptionally well characterized by Yurii Kolker:

> Of course, a randomly chosen representative of the circles close to the journal *Chasy* would never even contemplate collaboration with the regime. As a rule, they are a very well educated person working as a guard or boiler room attendant; they have friends among the émigré community as well as in exile and in the camps; they themselves could have their flat searched or be arrested at any moment in connection with any of the political trials that are going on in Leningrad all the time and they know it, just as they know that they didn't break

any laws; they might be indicted, and therefore sentenced, for *possessing and distributing literature that discredits the Soviet social or political order.*[13]

This description suggests that the Leningrad journal communities offered their members an opportunity for inner emigration: that is, detachment from Soviet lifestyle and values. In confirmation, Sergei Dediulin, editor of *Severnaia pochta,* formulates his aspirations as follows: 'I wanted to live and dedicate myself to my work, that is, converse, read and write as if the so-called Soviet regime didn't exist at all. I had to get so many things done, after all!'[14] Yet this dream was patently unachievable, and not just because the Soviet authorities continued to persecute those who were involved in samizdat (as we recall, Dediulin himself was forced to emigrate). Significantly, Kolker considers the existence of personal networks that include other marginal communities (émigrés, those exiled to remote parts of the Soviet Union, those in prison or camps and those in danger of persecution) as characteristic of the *Chasy* reader. At some point these networks might have been local but, as time went on, political and social developments – in particularly imprisonment and (forced) emigration – extended them to other localities within and outside the Soviet Union to form a 'transnational literary community'.[15]

The unofficial writers devised and idealized their own system of values. Outwardly, their distance from Soviet values was manifest in a bohemian lifestyle, not unlike that of Western hippies, but with a few Soviet peculiarities. In a society that prioritized collective labour, punished dissenters by excluding them from their professions and persecuted those who were unemployed as 'social parasites' (*tuneiadtsy*), an outsider existence was fraught with particular difficulty. Many intellectuals worked in menial roles, including night watchman, lift attendant or boiler room stoker. While for some this was a deliberate choice, allowing them to leave behind an ideologically charged professional environment and devote more time to their literary pursuits, for others it was the only option left. Most importantly, the unofficial intellectuals afforded a heightened significance to the written word, which came to dominate everyday existence and was central to the narrative they constructed about themselves:

> Their non-recognition [of Soviet values] was expressed in a lifestyle that differed sharply from that of the ordinary Soviet one. Going to work every three days, and books — that is how one could casually describe the non-Soviet lifestyle. Books were the greatest joy and keenly sought after. Refined and profound knowledge of Russian – but especially of foreign – literature and history was considered the trademark of the aristocrat, a highly artistic person who had nothing in common with the working masses … This is how the myth of the

marginal poet emerged, of the poet-outcast, the heir of the travelling minstrel [*skomorokh*], the wandering aristocrat. Conflict with society was unavoidable.[16]

The features outlined here, especially if read in conjunction with Kolker's characterization of the underground writer above, indicate that the lives of those involved in journals were shaped to a significant degree by samizdat activity. I would like to suggest that the 'underground' nature of the journals was, in fact, secondary. These individuals were united by their fascination with literature and culture and by a certain aesthetic. That the literature they favoured could only exist outside official culture was a contingency, albeit a contingency that had the power to shape the lives of an entire generation.

The concept of literature embraced by official culture invested the written word with an enormous degree of power. This was evident in the exhortation to writers to be 'engineers of the human souls',[17] the rigid censorship, and the rote learning of literary classics in schools. In the 1950s and 1960s, official literature and literary groups that did not seek contact with literary institutions had developed side by side. Groups outside official institutions were not systematically persecuted at that point, and it was not too difficult to cross from one sphere to the other. What is more, official organizations, including the Writers' Union, provided targeted programmes to promote young writers, especially in the field of poetry. This means that the poets who made unofficial Leningrad culture so vibrant in the 1970s grew up in an environment that afforded great importance to literature, expected everybody to read, and encouraged young people to write. More specifically, the protagonists of the Leningrad underground, including the influential editors, Viktor Krivulin and Sergei Stratanovskii, all began writing as adolescents under the influence of senior literary figures who headed LITOs (literary associations attached to Palaces of Culture and similar institutions) and related circles for budding writers; the LITO led by Gleb Semenov in the 1960s was particularly important to the community that created the journals under study in this volume.[18] Another 'hotbed' was the literary club Derzanie (Daring) located at the Palace of Pioneers. Samizdat typist Elena Rusakova remembers it as a place where teachers introduced their young charges to Silver Age poetry, including forbidden names, for example Nikolai Gumilev. For her, Derzanie was the place that acquainted her with the practice of passing around typed copies of poems that were hard to find in print; some of the girls would regularly copy out parts from pre-revolutionary and rare editions, and she remembers copying out texts she wanted to read on her mother's typewriter.[19] Without the stranglehold of ideological considerations on art, some of these young people would surely have risen to literary fame. As it was, an entire generation whose aesthetics did not conform to official norms was deprived of publication opportunities and a wider audience. However, the years spent in clubs and literary associations established complex personal networks, which later became the foundation for the flourishing unofficial seminars and circles that created and nourished the journals and other informal institutions.

It follows that the 'literature-centricity' that is the trademark of the underground was a perfectly ordinary product of a Soviet education, arguably mirroring the stance of official culture. Both official culture and the underground accepted literature as having a value beyond itself; it just so happened that the unofficial writers read and wrote the 'wrong' kind of texts. And, in Russia, tradition was on the side of those who read and wrote the 'wrong' texts. The cult of the poet as a visionary who pays for their initiation with exclusion from society, which had its origin in Romanticism and grew exponentially during the Silver Age, survived in Soviet Russia virtually unbroken. As Svetlana Boym has observed, this cult thrived on political oppression, fuelled by the fact that many of the greatest poets of the twentieth century fell victim to persecution by the state. A writer suffering for their literary activity was a tragic figure, and their texts bore witness to their truth.[20] In this sense, the underground poet is the quintessential Russian poet, a Romantic outsider who is hounded for the sake of the 'truth' he or she has to tell. In the 1970s, a further notion was added to this myth, which is that of the underground writer as the preserver of authentic literary culture in an age that was doing everything to stifle this culture with a barrage of tendentious and formulaic prescriptions.[21] Understanding their role in this way helped unofficial poets – the main contributors to the journals under study – to justify and even idealize their social marginality, imbuing it with metaphysical significance.

What is more, the writers around the 'Leningrad school'[22] who dominated the journal scene before Perestroika were engaged in a project to restore to its fullness a literary language they judged seriously deficient. Official propaganda surrounded citizens with statements the content of which contradicted observable reality, for example claims about the Soviet Union's prosperity that clashed with the experience of the majority of the population, who remained confined to cramped communal flats. Those claims were presented in elevated language and with a pathos unrelated to the nature of the claim. In the eyes, or rather ears, of the unofficial poets, this practice had compromised the high register of contemporary Russian and led to a kind of *dvuiazychie* (double-speak) that deprived words of genuine meaning and creative vitality. And since many aspects of reality were excluded from official discourse – for example, spirituality or sexuality – the words referring to these experiences were excised from language, too; at least from written language. The language that was available to writers who worked in the official sphere was therefore both tainted and incomplete. Viktor Krivulin described the double nature of language as tantamount to a crack in the wall of one's home, and he deplored that 'a fissure within the Russian language became audible'.[23] The literary experiments of the underground did much to restore the creative vitality of literary language, rediscovering suppressed registers of language and reclaiming forbidden subject matter.[24]

Literary language and dependence

Literary language, the central preoccupation of the alternative cultural sphere, perfectly illustrates this sphere's freedom from, and simultaneous dependence on, official discourse. All the names used to describe the literary samizdat of Leningrad – unofficial culture, second culture, underground, alternative culture and even counterculture – point to the close and possibly hierarchical relationship between literary samizdat and Soviet official culture.[25] Artistically, this disengagement from official culture was arguably fruitful because it enabled aesthetic developments that could not have existed in the official domain, and therefore added to the diversity in Russian literature in the late Soviet years. However, even the unofficial intellectuals were divided in their assessment of their own creation's value. A vigorously positive evaluation that echoes the idea that unofficial poets are the guardians of genuine literary culture is given by Anna Katsman, who was once married to Viktor Krivulin: 'The cultural chasm that came after the poetic pleiad of early twentieth-century Petersburg had to be filled – by us. And this impression was correct, as time has shown.'[26] Others were much more sceptical. Arkadii Dragomoshchenko, who sat on the editorial board of *Chasy* and whose poetry, found to be in dialogue with American Language Poetry, achieved considerable fame after the collapse of the Soviet Union, provides a pessimistic assessment: 'I would call this a shattered generation, because it did not create anything. It was an alternative generation. Alternative generation means that it was a negative. There was no change in configuration. It was the same stuff, only black instead of white.'[27] In Dragomoshchenko's eyes, cultural production emerging from the underground is irredeemably derivative, condemned to be the shadow image of the culture it seeks to avoid. Centrally managed cultural policy meant that, in the Soviet Union, any cultural activity was either officially sanctioned or de facto illegal and as a result necessarily defined by its relation to official culture. However, the discussion below will show that reducing the cultural underground to an inferior obverse side of official culture, be it in positive or negative terms, is ultimately simplistic.

Alongside language, there were conceptual and structural aspects of dependence on official culture that became apparent in what I would call the underground's institutional drive. Over the three decades of its existence, Leningrad samizdat managed to mature into a fully fledged literary process, with institutions such as journals effectively promoting their house authors, a school of literary criticism, conferences, the review journal *Summa* and, ultimately, the semi-official Klub-81, discussed below. Kirill Kozyrev explains the drive to self-reflection in relation to the sheer richness of unofficial culture:

> More and more exhibitions took place in quick succession, including those infamous ones in people's flats [*kvartirnye vystavki*]. And then there were the exhibitions in Nevskii [Palace of Culture] and Gaza [I.I. Gaza Palace of Culture] and some others. The result was a growing demand for critical articles on these artists and exhibitions, which indicated that they were also part of cultural life.[28]

It is rare for a countercultural movement to survive long enough to reach such a stage of sophisticated self-reflection, and the existence of a large body of analytical materials compiled by the unofficial writers themselves complicates any assessment of literary samizdat as a purely countercultural movement. Sergei Stratanovskii clearly identifies the point of intersection between the two cultures, maintaining that the emergence of an alternative cultural scene, complete with its own institutions, was mainly the result of the inflexible attitude of the existing literary institutions, because writers need mechanisms that facilitate interactions with the readership: 'We – that is, our scene – we did not specifically write for the desk drawer. We naturally wanted [our texts] to be known at least to a certain circle.'[29] The ambitions of individual writers,[30] and ultimately the eagerness of so many unofficial poets to join Klub-81, are evidence that many members of this scene never completely renounced their aspiration to become officially published writers: that is, to gain access to a readership not limited to their own circle.

Between seriousness and dilettantism

However, it seems naïve to assume that it was spontaneous desire for reflection alone that generated the large amount of well-preserved and already categorized material on which researchers can draw today. In its mature stages, the unofficial cultural scene in Leningrad exhibited a high level of organization and practical functionality, and many practices it employed were evidently gleaned from official culture. It is fair to conclude that it was not the wish to create a self-contained cultural space that inspired the communities of practice around the journals. In other words, the unofficial intellectuals did not seek a complete break with the 'primary' culture; in particular, their desire to reach out to a broad readership remained unchanged. The elements that articulate the highly ambivalent relationship between the two cultures can be divided into two broad categories. Official culture functioned as a natural point of reference. Yet, more often than not, the unofficial intellectuals disregarded or inverted the priorities set by official culture.

While late Soviet official culture was imbued with solemn pathos, unofficial culture revelled in a dilettantism that can be read as a form of resistance to this very pathos. At the same time, dilettantism was a natural consequence of the underground's marginal status and precarious material situation. When we look at the literary journals, dilettantism is evident everywhere: the journals were self-bound, printed on onion-skin paper and often barely legible, with handwritten corrections. The readings and seminars that were part of the journal culture happened in private flats, were frequently accompanied by plenty of drink and were attended by an ever-changing, unpredictable crowd.[31] Some praised this casual informality and playfulness as a key constituent of unofficial culture.[32] With playfulness so much at the heart of this culture, one might be tempted to describe the unofficial writers' attitude towards officialdom simply as *steb* (pronounced 'styob'). *Steb* undermines or ridicules established discourse – cultural, literary, political or other – by copying and then transplanting that discourse's symbolism into an alien context. In their choice of texts and authors, as well as their aesthetic and pronounced informality, the journals evince 'absolute non-belonging, radical alienation' from the official literary process. At the same time, the very institution of thick literary journals is a reference to official culture and, as such, demonstrates 'an unconscious and obtrusive dependence on the object from which one is distancing oneself'; this aspect will become ever more apparent over the course of this chapter. Moreover, this entire study, and the present chapter in particular, show that unofficial culture's alienation from the official literary process can hardly be called 'total'; this incomplete alienation constitutes the third characteristic of *steb* according to Boris Dubin.[33] Alexei Yurchak added an important element to this definition, pointing out that it can be difficult to distinguish *steb* practitioners' ironic attitude towards the established discourse from genuine identification with this discourse.[34] In the case of the journal communities, this conundrum is particularly difficult to resolve. The journals existed in a field of tension between playfulness and utter seriousness: they parodied established models of behaviour and forms of cultural production while emulating selected elements without any ironic distance whatsoever.

Many examples illustrate this tension. The Andrei Belyi Prize, instituted by the editors of *Chasy* in 1978, was a genuine literary prize awarded to underground writers whose work had won acclaim among their peers. A list of the first laureates shows them to be the heavyweights of underground literature, not limited to the immediate circle around *Chasy*.[35] Unlike official prizes, this one did not – and, for obvious reasons, could not – offer any material benefits or privileges. However, rather than receive nothing at all apart from a certificate, winners were given one rouble, a bottle of vodka and an apple, a fact that playfully highlighted the different attitude towards material goods of those active in the cultural underground. At the very least, it underscored that these people could not possibly be writing for material gain – unlike official writers, who would gain significant material benefits if awarded a prize.

The informal seminars and readings organized by some journal editors constitute an important performative aspect of samizdat culture.[36] Their distinction from university seminars, for example, was evident in the setting, which was usually a private flat or even a room in a *kommunalka*, a flat shared by multiple families. They also abandoned the clear hierarchy that governed events in official institutions. Seminar groups – at least the core participants – were extremely close-knit, and the roles of author, performer and audience were fluid. Those who were present would perform for each other, which meant they would take turns in reading their work and give speeches and papers.[37] However, in sharp contrast to the informal, everyday setting, the material presented at those seminars tended to be of high quality: evidence of careful and even scholarly preparation on the part of the presenter. A good example is the Shimpozium. This group convened in the flat of the poet Elena Shvarts between 1975 and 1982 to discuss history and literature. Attendants would prepare scholarly papers. As a counterpoint to the serious subject matter, every participant was known by a monkey-related nickname, gesturing to both the modernist tradition of 'literaturnoe-parodiinoe obshchestva' (literary parodic associations) that included Aleksei Remizov's Obezian'e tsarstvo (Kingdom of Monkeys) and the playfulness of the contemporary underground.[38] Kirill Kozyrev, who was very close to Shvarts, attributes this to the fact that many of the young intellectuals had experience of university study and would replicate the format of lectures and seminar or conference presentations.[39]

Perhaps the most compelling example of the underground's oscillation between irony and seriousness are the journals themselves. While their physical appearance was incomparable to that of an official publication, the conception of most journals was highly professional. One glance reveals the structural similarities between samizdat journals and their official counterparts: 'thick' literary journals such as *Novyi mir* (New World), *Zvezda* (Star) or *Moskva* (Moscow). Just like them, samizdat journals featured sections for poetry, prose, essays, translations and other genres. Just like them, they had overarching editorial principles. Just like them, they left space for criticism and analysis. Some, for example *37*, had dedicated section editors. Individual issues featured rubrics for direct interactions with readers, such as 'letter to the editor'[40] and 'polemics'. *37* and *Chasy* regularly published booklets, showcasing a particular writer in the manner of the 'literary supplements' operated by some large official journals.[41] While the emergence of a school of literary criticism towards the late 1970s doubtlessly signified that the Leningrad underground had grown into a distinct branch on the tree that is Russian literature, as opposed to an accidental association of writers united only by the fact that they were unpublished in the official press, it can nevertheless be read as a – belated and perhaps subconscious – reflection of developments in official culture. In the 1970s, criticism had moved into the spotlight. In January 1972, the Central Committee of the Communist Party passed the resolution 'On Literary Criticism', resulting in literary criticism becoming a priority for the official institutions in their quest to shape the mass readership's literary preferences. The critical journal *Literaturnoe obozrenie* (The Literary Review), which was addressed to a non-specialist audience, was founded in 1973 in order to promote the agenda set by the Party resolution.[42] The subscription scheme operated first by *Chasy* and later by *Mitin zhurnal* was an ingenious way to raise funds and ensure wider circulation. However, it constituted another parallel to official culture, as subscribing to one or several journals was a very common practice in the Soviet Union.

Editorial policy is another example of the underground's oscillation between serious emulation and ironic subversion of official customs. Certain underground-specific practices notwithstanding – in particular, the policy of *Chasy* aimed at giving the largest possible number of writers a chance of publication – samizdat journal editors performed the usual functions of curators or gatekeepers who can grant or deny publication and in this way ensure a minimum of quality control. The literary journals of late Soviet samizdat offered writers the opportunity to publish informally, which means without the interference of the prescriptive Soviet cultural institutions, but each journal had its own editorial policy, and even the broad-minded *Chasy* did not publish indiscriminately.[43] Editors, as individuals wielding considerable control, promoted or limited authors' access to publishing opportunities and so to a readership, even the small readership the journals could reach. In this respect, as in others, samizdat journals were much more similar to traditional print journals than to modern-day social media.

Russia has a long tradition of writers editing literary journals, and the underground was no exception.[44] However, due to the small size and the interpenetration of different circles within the Leningrad underground, the journal scene was effectively dominated by just a few individuals who sat on the editorial board of more than one periodical. Viktor Krivulin, Sergei Stratanovskii and Boris Ivanov in particular, accumulated considerable power: Krivulin as co-founder and literary editor of *37* and editor-in-chief of *Severnaia pochta*; Stratanovskii as co-founder and/or co-editor of *Chasy*, *Dialog* and *Obvodnyi kanal* and board member of Klub-81; Ivanov as founding editor of *Chasy* and driving force behind initiatives like the Andrei Belyi Prize and Klub-81. Alongside their editorial work, each of them published copiously in their own and each others' journals, and their centrality to Leningrad literary samizdat becomes all the more evident when we consider both their creative output and their critical pieces, a large number of which were published under pseudonyms. The widespread use of pseudonyms by samizdat literary critics is a curious phenomenon. It seems that this practice was less motivated by a need to avoid detection and persecution; after all, the journals featured the editors' real names on the first page, and poets also tended to publish under their real names, which means that the identity of samizdat writers was readily available to the law enforcement agencies. Rather, pseudonyms had the function of veiling the fact that a given journal actually published only a handful of authors, as well as the degree to which certain voices dominated the scene. Krivulin published most of his criticism under the name A. Kalomirov, while Stratanovskii used N. Golubev.[45] Boris Ostanin had several pseudonyms, among others I. Bonch and O. Vladimirov. Boris Groys, another prominent critic, who became a professor of art history after emigrating, published his critical writings as Igor Suitsidov and Boris Inozemtsev. If we cross-reference the output of Krivulin and Stratanovskii alone, and consider only journals in which they held editorial posts, the picture looks like this: Krivulin published poetry in two out of twenty-one issues of *37* and one out of eight issues of *Severnaia pochta*; also in seven out of eighty issues of *Chasy* and four out of nineteen issues of *Obvodnyi kanal*; he also published literary criticism under the pseudonym of A. Kalomirov or A. Berezhnov in four issues of *37*, one issue of *Severnaia pochta*, four issues of

Chasy and four issues of *Obvodnyi kanal*. Stratanovskii published poetry in one issue of *37*, one issue of *Severnaia pochta*, five issues of *Chasy*, and four issues of *Obvodnyi kanal*, and literary criticism under the pseudonym of N. Golubev in one issue of *37*, and ten issues of *Obvodnyi kanal*. As a result, to the unsuspecting reader the circle of authors might seem larger than it is. It appears that a certain 'size complex' continued to be keenly felt.

There is certainly an element of playfulness involved when writers publish and review themselves and their friends in handmade publications. However, it is patently impossible to reduce the relationship between unofficial journals and their official counterparts to one of *steb*. The wider context of unofficial culture suggests an alternative interpretation. The temptation to make a journal look more weighty and multifaceted than it actually was shows the degree to which the unofficial intellectuals longed to emulate 'ordinary' work practices: publishing their work in a variety of outlets and being reviewed by different critics. In this sense, the emergence of literary criticism merely underscored the self-referentiality of the literary underground.

Institutions

Klub-81

The Leningradskoe professional'noe ob"edinenie literatorov (Leningrad Professional Association of Writers) – better known under its short name, Klub-81 – existed from 1981 to 1988, and illustrates the ambivalent yet ultimately symbiotic relationship between official and unofficial culture like no other organization. By studying Klub-81 we can study in detail the interaction of certain unofficial networks with official institutions.[46] The Klub's very existence testifies to the rapidly increasing professionalization of the underground in the 1980s. At the same time, it highlights the members' burning desire for recognition and the opportunity to engage a broader readership.

There are several accounts of the emergence of Klub-81, each placing the emphasis on a different facet. What is known is that, in 1981, Boris Ivanov – the man behind *Chasy*, the most 'institutional' of the samizdat journals – co-founded an association for unofficial writers that pursued the explicit aim of providing them with a legitimate (that is, officially sanctioned) space. 'Legitimate' in this sense implies protection from the persecutions that had marred journal activity in recent months and years, along with access to a broader public. To this end, the unofficial writers reached an agreement with the very agencies that continued to persecute and exclude their kind: Klub-81 was founded under the auspices of both the KGB and the Writers' Union, with Union member Yurii Andreev taking on the role of the Klub's official curator.

Klub-81 was allowed to use the lecture hall at the Dostoevsky Museum, among other venues, to host literary evenings. These regularly attracted very large crowds and significantly heightened the visibility of unofficial writers. In his memoirs, Ivanov describes Klub-81 as a logical progression from the principle behind *Chasy* – that is, the opportunity for writers to freely interact with their readers:

> What were we, the people around *Chasy* [*chasovshchiki*, literally 'watchmakers'], doing by organising samizdat periodicals and conferences, inaugurating the Andrei Belyi Prize and seeking out the possibility of creating an independent literary club, if it wasn't giving structure to the cultural movement, if it wasn't establishing an open relationship with the reading public?[47]

In Ivanov's eyes, the time was ripe to tackle unofficial culture's greatest issue, the lack of a legitimate organization: 'We *chasovshchiki* had broached the most pressing issue of unofficial culture: the acquisition of a legitimate institution.'[48] It is therefore highly significant that the Klub's official name includes the word 'professional'.

While some, including Yurii Kolker, refused to join an organization that collaborated with the authorities they despised, many of the underground's now best-known writers and key figures became active members, including Viktor Krivulin, Sergei Stratanovskii and Arkadii Dragomoshchenko.[49] Writers jostled for space in the publications of Klub-81, which produced its own newspaper called *Reguliarnye vedomosti* (Regular Bulletin); however, the publication opportunities on offer were ultimately limited. Out of four proposed collections, only one eventually came out with Sovetskii pisatel' publishing house, a rather slim miscellany called *Krug* (Circle, 1985).[50] It is worth noting that eight of the fourteen authors featured in *Krug* had contributed to the unsuccessful *Lepta* venture eleven years previously. This indicates that the desire to leave behind the confines of semi-clandestine seminars and conferences and access the institutions of official literary culture remained strong among unofficial writers, overridden only by the even stronger desire to remain true to their own aesthetic standards. Klub-81 seemed to offer an opportunity to realize some of these ambitions, even though it ultimately remained a niche association.

The very existence of a literary association for unofficial writers under the auspices of the KGB seems an oddity. It is easy to read it in a negative light, interpreting the willingness of writers to compromise in this way as a sell-out: an indication that, in their desperation for public recognition, the unofficial poets were willing to cooperate with their most odious enemy. However, this assessment is overly simplistic. It is true that the KGB remained a powerful enemy of those operating outside official structures. Examples of KGB persecution of unofficial intellectuals in the early 1980s are rife; in Leningrad these include the emigration under pressure of Dediulin, Goricheva, Pazukhin, Voznesenskaia, et al. and the camp sentences meted out to those active in the Public Foundation for Political Prisoners and their Families (Solzhenitsyn Foundation) and the Christian Seminar.[51] In some sense, the foundation of Klub-81 itself was also linked to KGB pressure. According to Boris Ivanov, the precondition for Klub-81 was the discontinuation of *Severnaia pochta*; the KGB demanded that Krivulin sign a document to the effect that he would not continue producing the journal, otherwise he would be made to emigrate.[52] A potential discontinuation of *Chasy* was discussed, too; however, Ivanov managed to preserve his journal, which ultimately outlived Klub-81 by two years.[53] This leads us to the question of how it was possible that the KGB and the Writers' Union tolerated and even encouraged an association of unofficial writers instead of simply suppressing the entire movement. According to the recollections of several writers – I have not had access to relevant documents from the KGB archive – the reason for effectively legalizing and protecting the cultural underground was the authorities' desire to limit the number of texts these writers circulated in samizdat or, worse, sent abroad for publication.[54] It seems that the KGB were convinced, very possibly by Ivanov himself, that law enforcement would never be able to curtail the spread of unofficial culture and that it was therefore advisable to provide a local 'outlet' to exert a degree of control. For the KGB, then, the collaboration with unofficial writers was only a limited success, since the same authors that gave readings during the officially sanctioned Klub-81 events continued to circulate their work in samizdat and texts originating in Leningrad's second culture continued to appear in émigré publications. Ivanov justified his friends' behaviour by citing the continued lack of opportunities for publication, a lack that Klub-81 failed to address with the necessary urgency. Seen in this light, Klub-81 can be read as an act of self-assertion on the part of the underground writers rather than as an admission of defeat.

The timing of the club's emergence is significant. By 1981, unofficial literary networks, with the journals at their centre, had proliferated very far despite the pressure exerted on individuals and certain journals. Many of those who were forced to emigrate continued to participate in and strengthen these networks from abroad: once he was settled in Paris, Sergei Dediulin collaborated with several émigré publications, among them *Russkaia mysl'*[55] while Tatiana Goricheva founded Beseda, a publishing house with a focus on Leningrad poetry, which is discussed below.

Seen in this light, the official side's readiness to tolerate the underground under certain circumstances appears to confirm the latter's vitality. This is corroborated by the emergence of two more semi-official associations at the same time, for artists (Tovarishchestvo eksperimental'nogo izobrazitel'nogo iskusstva – Association of Experimental Visual Art) and rock musicians (Leningradskii Rok-Klub – Leningrad Rock Club). If this proliferation of institutions in which official and unofficial structures overlapped was indeed the official side's attempt to co-opt unofficial culture, it was unsuccessful: the Rock Club was a stepping stone for bands that would make Soviet/Russian rock famous, for example Alisa, Akvarium and Kino. Moreover, the key writers of Klub-81, which included Krivulin and Dragomoshchenko, did not lose their credentials as unofficial writers, as Kolker had feared;[56] the club did not censor its members' writing. With hindsight, we can see that the emergence of Klub-81 marked the point at which unofficial culture began its journey towards an official readership that would culminate in the abolition of censorship in 1990, two years after the club had ceased existing.

The anthology *Ostrova* (1982)

Some witnesses concluded that the emergence of Klub-81 marked the end of the 'obscure underground times for the second culture',[57] and this perception seems to have been the impulse behind the poetry anthology *Ostrova* (Islands), published in 1982 after over a year of editorial work. Yurii Kolker and Eduard Shneiderman, who were part of the editorial team, told of an acute need for a conclusive picture of thirty years of samizdat poetry. According to them, this period was definitively in the past,[58] especially as a new generation of poets, with their own set of aesthetic criteria, emerged on the scene.[59] In this sense, *Ostrova* was the reverse side of the development that produced Klub-81: while the Klub represented a new stage in the engagement with both the authorities and a wider audience, the anthology indicates that the self-reflection of the unofficial culture scene had now reached the retrospective stage.

According to Kolker, *Ostrova* was conceived as an answer to the monumental nine-volume *Blue Lagoon Anthology of Modern Russian Poetry*, published in the USA between 1980 and 1986.[60] Following his emigration to the USA in 1975, Konstantin Kuzminskii – a colourful figure in Leningrad unofficial culture who had run his own literary salon in the late 1960s[61] – devoted himself to reproducing Soviet samizdat, from memory as well as microfiche and recordings; he was helped in this endeavour by Grigorii Kovalev. Kolker saw what he decried as lack of editorial scrutiny in *The Blue Lagoon* as a major shortcoming, one the *Ostrova* project was supposed to rectify: 'Many people thought it important to have something to set off against K. Kuzminskii's anthology, which had been published in the USA, and which was unsatisfactory from a textological point of view and compiled without the necessary critical selection.'[62] However, ultimately the two anthologies served different purposes. While the majority of texts hail from Leningrad, *The Blue Lagoon* reflected other facets of the contemporary samizdat scene, too, for example by dedicating volumes 3a and 3b to Kharkov and Kiev respectively. As it was published in the West, in print, the anthology circulated widely and made a significant body of underground poetry available to the Western reader. It remains an important primary source: while literary texts have been reissued in professional editions that eliminated the infelicities naturally resulting from Kuzminskii's method of 'exporting' the texts, the letters, photos, collages and supplementary material he published alongside the texts convey a complex picture of the atmosphere at the time. Just like the 'broad' samizdat journals, *Chasy* and *37*, and to a lesser degree *Obvodnyi Kanal*, *The Blue Lagoon* preserved not just texts, but an entire segment of culture. By contrast, *Ostrova* was wholly focused on Leningrad and poetry. The materials span three decades, from the 1950s to the 1970s, but the emphasis on selection and quality control show that the editors did not primarily aim to publish as many authors as possible. Neither did they favour a particular aesthetic. 6,200 poems by 172 authors were initially considered, but only 413 poems by 80 authors were ultimately included. *Ostrova* drew on a wide number of sources that included the journals (mostly *Chasy*, *37*, *Obvodnyi kanal*), the various samizdat almanacs that had appeared over the years, tamizdat and also private archives. The original 'print run' was twenty-seven copies, but further copies were typed and circulated in Moscow, Riga and Sverdlovsk. A second, extended edition was begun in the 1980s and finished in 1997, but never published.[63] The appearance of a retrospective 'definitive' almanac marks a further caesura in the consciousness of the unofficial cultural scene in the early 1980s.

Scholarship and journal networks

Scholarly interest in the underground runs high in a number of different disciplines. Literary scholars regard the Leningrad underground as an important stage in the development of Russian poetry.[64] The social and artistic relationships within this culture are now being investigated from a variety of angles. Leningrad samizdat regularly inspires conference panels at international conventions, for example ASEEES, and more specialist events;[65] Facebook groups facilitate exchange between researchers,[66] and the prestigious Oxford Handbooks series will bring out a volume on Soviet underground culture with a dedicated section for the Leningrad groups.[67] This belated and relative fame was of course precipitated by the course of history: the gradual abolition of censorship in the second half of the 1980s and the collapse of the Soviet Union in 1991. However, the unofficial intellectuals made a significant contribution by manoeuvring themselves into the best possible position to be studied.

The journals themselves are a repository for unofficial culture that has facilitated as well as directed the scholarly attention this culture has been receiving since the mid-1990s. Here, the researcher finds representative collections of texts in their original surroundings. As Sergei Stratanovskii correctly observes: 'And later [the journals] became important for researchers: if they didn't exist, your task would be much harder. In that case you would have to collect all these crumbs, but as it is, [the journals] present an image of literary life.'[68] The 'image of literary life' offered by the journals did not only consist of literary texts. The journals also collated contextual information that would otherwise be lost to anybody without an excellent contact network and was, in any case, highly vulnerable to the erosion of time. Much of this information – in the form of reports on the sessions of informal seminars and other materials that provide insight into the heady atmosphere of the period – would not have been recorded without the journals as a platform. In the words of Kirill Kozyrev, 'there was so little of it that it had to be reflected in those journals, otherwise all of it would have disappeared somewhere'.[69] The long-serving journals, in particular *Chasy* and *Obvodnyi Kanal*, are especially valuable as a chronology of the unofficial literary process, while *Chasy*'s policy of publishing as wide a number of writers as possible presents indeed a broad, multifaceted image of unofficial culture. Stratanovskii suggests that the creation of a record was part of the original principle behind *Chasy*: 'This principle vindicated itself in part, because as a result of the eighty issues of the journal *Chasy* the researcher is presented with a complete, or nearly complete, image.'[70]

However, we must not forget that the image of unofficial literature offered by *Chasy* and related institutions has been shaped by the very people that are the object of research. It is self-evident that the researcher who relies on them runs the risk of neglecting alternative versions. *Chasy* portrayed the 'underground mainstream', whose aesthetics and lifestyles followed certain patterns that became somewhat routine as time went on.[71] Far from offering mere platforms for publication, the overlapping communities of the 'mainstream' samizdat journals set themselves up to be studied, partly because they emulate official structures so clearly. It is my contention that the symbiotic push-and-pull relationship between samizdat journals and official institutions make Leningrad samizdat journals such a rewarding topic of research, with so much primary material preserved and local knowledge and memories recorded. Ironically, perhaps, my study confirms the success of the Leningrad journal editors' project.

In a print culture, the institutions of publishing houses and literary criticism shape the literary canon, and Soviet unofficial culture was no exception. The literary institutions of the underground created a distinctive canon that was separate from the Soviet canon of the time, but which is now part of the canon of late twentieth-century Russian literature.[72] The activity of those who had created the journals did not stop with the collapse of the Soviet Union and the demise of the journal scene. By continuing their critical activity, they made a significant contribution to the reception of Leningrad unofficial culture in the years after 1991. Unofficial poets put their expertise on each other's work to good use, and their efforts effectively decided which names would come to the attention of a broader audience, including both Russian and Western researchers.[73] What is more, their conceptualizations of the recent past were eagerly taken up by scholars. All of the first academic or semi-academic volumes on the literary underground were compiled and edited by the stalwarts of samizdat criticism of the 1970s and 1980s, from the slim volume of papers on samizdat journals given at a conference at the Memorial Society in 1993 (co-edited by Boris Ivanov)[74] to the substantial encyclopaedia *Samizdat Leningrada* (Leningrad Samizdat), featuring entries on individuals and groups, as well as a chronology and detailed thematic essays (2003, edited by Dmitrii Severiukhin, Boris Ostanin, Viacheslav Dolinin and Boris Ivanov). *Samizdat Leningrada* has become the standard reference work on Leningrad unofficial culture, and it is perhaps not surprising that two of its editors, Ivanov and Ostanin, used to edit *Chasy*. In the same year, Severiukhin and Dolinin also published a slim but informative volume of chronological narrative under the title *Preodolenie nemoty: Leningradskii samizdat v kontekste nezavisimogo kul'turnogo dvizheniia 1953–1991* (Overcoming Silence: Leningrad

Samizdat within the Independent Cultural Movement), with short chapters on key events, places, groups, institutions and publications.[75] Boris Ivanov, on the other hand, remained true to his calling as a patron of unofficial literature and promoted literary scholarship: *Istoriia leningradskoi nepodtsenzurnoi literatury* (The History of Uncensored Literature in Leningrad), a collection of essays he compiled in collaboration with Boris Roginskii and published in 2000, is an excellent source on individual writers. Ten years later, Ivanov edited and contributed to a volume of more sophisticated literary biography, *Peterburgskaia poeziia v litsakh* (Petersburg Poetry: Faces). Ivanov's many individual essays were instrumental for the conceptualization of unofficial culture as an integrated phenomenon; his work post-1991 clearly continues an effort he began in the 1970s.[76] His case also shows how certain well-defined perspectives that originate in the 1970s persist into post-Soviet times – perhaps an unavoidable consequence of the bias of critics writing about their own circle of acquaintances and about events that form part of their own biographies.[77] In order for new perspectives to emerge, a new generation of researchers had to appear, yet without the pioneering work of the original protagonists it is highly likely that much of this culture would have been lost to posterity.

As we have seen in the preceding chapters, tamizdat played a significant role in promoting the voices of unofficial writers and was often driven by so-called Third Wave émigrés. Those who belonged to the Leningrad journal communities had a personal advocate in Tatiana Goricheva, a tirelessly committed editor and prolific critic. Pushed into emigration in summer 1980, after her move to Paris she seized upon the chance to introduce her contemporaries to a wider international audience by setting up the publishing house Beseda (Conversation). Beseda produced thirty issues of an eponymous literary journal that promoted writing by and about those active in Leningrad samizdat; this goes to show that Goricheva continued her activity as a curator of her own community of practice. In addition, Beseda published single-author collections of many Leningrad samizdat poets, including the first collections by Elena Shvarts and Oleg Okhapkin and the fullest collection of Viktor Krivulin's early work that exists to date. Significantly, the place of publication is given as 'Paris-Leningrad'. Beseda provided a bridge between fully official and unofficial publication before the two spheres began to merge in Soviet Russia, while Goricheva became an early catalyst for the canonization of the Leningrad underground. By compiling these trailblazing works, the individuals discussed here almost certainly directed the attention of younger Russian and foreign researchers, who have been studying samizdat literature and culture since roughly 2000, towards the formers' own circles.

The journals and their target audience

The discussion in this and the previous chapter has shown that the question of a neatly defined target audience for the journals was of limited relevance in the circumstances of 1970s and 1980s Leningrad. This is not only because people's hunger for reading material beyond what official culture could offer means that samizdat journals did not have to compete for readers. More important is that the journals were set up to serve first and foremost those who published in them. In this sense, they were orientated towards the writers rather than the readers. The increasing variety of journals, as well as emerging additional institutions, was driven by journal makers and writers rather than readers. The growing need of writers for more sophisticated outlets reflected the increasing complexity of their own literary practice. In his article 'Dvadtsat' let noveishei russkoi poezii' (Twenty Years of Modern Russian Poetry), Viktor Krivulin reflects on the situation of the unofficial Russian poet in the early 1970s, before the emergence of the journals studied here. For him, the defining characteristic of that time was the historically unprecedented isolation of the poet from his or her readers:

> The poet's rejection (conscious or unconscious) of the ability to influence the listener or reader directly is a fundamentally new phenomenon in the history of Russian poetry. A generation has entered literature which did not just emerge, but took shape and reached creative maturity in the conditions of the 'underground', and some already died there: that is, conditions that excluded any professional contacts between the poet and the outside world by means of their books.[78]

The emergence of samizdat journals rectified this problem to a certain degree, providing writers with the opportunity to engage more or less regularly with a circle of readers, albeit one that was limited to people who read/could access samizdat. As Sergei Stratanovskii observes: '[We] made an effort so that the greatest possible number of people would read [our texts] – and this created a certain environment. People appeared who were interested, and younger poets who were looking for a tradition followed suit.'[79] Once again, Stratanovskii emphasizes the importance of the journals for creating a suitable environment (*sreda*) for creative pursuits; the communities of practice that produced journals established a tradition – patterns of behaviour and a recognizable aesthetic that served as a point of reference for younger writers.[80] This environment fostered the self-confidence that resulted in two conferences debating 'the significance of unofficial culture' and the ability to negotiate with the KGB when it came to establishing Klub-81.

Yet, despite the ambition the editors harboured for their journals, their reach remained limited. And, for writers, being read exclusively by members of one's immediate circle is fraught with a specific set of difficulties. The reader of literary samizdat was unusually benevolent, for reasons that might have included the lack of alternative reading materials as well as a feeling of solidarity towards the authors.[81] In addition, Leningrad was a city where many unofficial poets had placed literary pursuits at the centre of their lives. Finally, when readers and writers share the same background, there is less demand on the writers to make their material accessible or appealing to a varied audience that does not necessarily understand references to topics and discourses relevant only to the writer's own community (of practice).

Yurii Kolker's negative view of the underground literary process focuses on this issue. According to him, unofficial culture produced uncritical admirers instead of readers, hampering poets' creative evolution: 'For a poet, admirers [*pochitateli*] cannot replace readers [*chitateli*].' Kolker regards the self-referentiality of the underground as an insurmountable obstacle to a professional literary process, because underground writers rely exclusively on each other for affirmation. By contrast, the literary process in a print culture requires the writer to surrender their text. Editorial scrutiny and other processes that take place before the text appears in print create a distance between author and text that prevent the author from overestimating their own significance.[82] Kolker's critique adds complexity to a discussion that is too often focused on the literary quality of underground writing as if it were a fixed category independent of context. By pointing out that freedom from censorship and creative freedom are separate phenomena with no obvious causal connection, Kolker identified one of the main risks run by those who create culture within the context of a small, enthusiastic group that cannot grow significantly beyond its initial circle, and that is the risk of creative entropy.

One community of practice

If we designate the networks that generated and were in turn nourished by Leningrad samizdat journals as a community of practice, then the journals themselves – that is, the objects produced by the community – are evidence of 'reification': 'the process of giving form to our experience by producing objects that congeal this experience into "thingness".[83] Reification, defined in those terms, is both a process and a product and, as we have seen, the social significance of the journals consisted as much in the act of making them – the exchange of texts and ideas, debate, friendship ties and organization – as in the finished product, that is, the alternative platform for publication.[84]

Each of the journals, with their individual editorial policies and processes related to production and distribution, constitutes a separate community of practice. However, the groups making individual journals overlapped significantly, and it is certainly productive to regard the groups pertaining to the 'mainstream' journals and institutions, starting with *Chasy* and ending with Klub-81, as a single community of practice. The practice of underground-specific behaviours – centring on, but not limited to, the reading, production and circulation of samizdat literature – created a feeling of belonging to a collective. In the everyday, this collective was limited to a circle of acquaintances, but it had the power to transcend this limit both geographically and temporally/conceptually. In geographical terms this collective included, for example, the Moscow-based poets, because their work regularly featured in the journals and they participated in certain other events. The list of laureates of the Andrei Belyi Prize also includes Moscow-based poets. And temporally and conceptually, the collective extended back into the past to include the literary idols and role models from the Russian (and Western) tradition whose works found their way into the pages of some of the journals.[85]

The 'secondary' nature of the literary underground held many pitfalls, primarily for writers but also for readers. However, the discussion above has shown that the relationship between official and unofficial culture in Leningrad was complex and ambivalent on many fronts, including structures, institutions, habits and language. Persecution notwithstanding, points of contact remained, in stronger or weaker form, depending on the point in time and the historical circumstances, and any 'secondariness' cannot be reduced to a simple binary. In its entirety, the community of practice represented by the 'journal scene' entertained a symbiotic relationship with official culture throughout its entire period of existence.

The ultimate convergence between the two cultures was characterized by a degree of mutuality: with the onset of Perestroika and the relaxation of censorship, a large number of often short-lived journals emerged that were neither officially sanctioned in the sense of being the publication of an official Soviet body, nor samizdat and so at risk of persecution.[86] By this time, official culture had submitted to the plurality that was inherent in the culture of samizdat. The ultimate goal of the unofficial writers was originally access to a broader readership, albeit without having to conform to the aesthetic and political standards required by official bodies in the 1970s. Once these standards fell, they transitioned easily to being writers published in their own country, perhaps because being part of a scene which, while an underground one, had nonetheless fostered all aspects of writerly practice and instilled in them the confidence that they had a legitimate place in Russian literature.

Conclusion

This study has thrown light on an underestimated and under-investigated aspect of samizdat: its social significance. Samizdat depended on networks, and it created and sustained networks in turn. All the specific groups I investigated for this study underlined the absolute centrality of personal relationships to their samizdat activity: those who filled in the reader survey confirmed that their reading was defined by whom they knew – the anecdotal lonely bibliophile would have found it difficult to source significant amounts of samizdat. None of the typists I interviewed would have accepted a commission from a stranger. Samizdat libraries, which needed to vet potential readers carefully to avoid persecution, worked on the principle that 'librarians' would distribute texts to their own acquaintances. Literary journals, deprived of the promotion channels available to official publications, depended on personal networks for sourcing texts and distributing the finished product.

It follows that, far from being concerned merely with the production and circulation of textual material, samizdat networks were important social spaces, straddling the private and public spheres in a unique way. Originating in domestic environments, they allowed people to interact around topics deemed inappropriate or unimportant by an environment that advocated collectivism and a single, tightly regulated cultural space, thus forming alternative publics. Moreover, samizdat networks were open to outsiders vetted through personal acquaintance, and they distributed information beyond their immediate circle through a 'snowball' system according to which each participant involved their respective acquaintances outside the immediate network. Thus, the contribution of samizdat to the ever-increasing stratification of Soviet society in the last decades of the Soviet Union's existence should be assessed in social as well as informational or political terms.

Studying samizdat with an emphasis on social aspects yields arguments in favour of the influential thesis put forward by Harvard sociologist Harrison

White to the effect that human beings are defined relationally: that is, by who they associate with, for example colleagues and friends, rather than by their attributes, for example a particular political stance. According to this thesis, society should be understood not as an aggregate of individuals but as defined by networks.[1] The data analysed for this volume convincingly demonstrate that it was not necessarily a person's political opinion, or their taste in reading material, that determined whether they read samizdat or how much and what kind of samizdat they read. Rather, their exposure and access to samizdat depended on whom they knew and interacted with: that is, the social circles in which they moved. Samizdat emerged from personal relationships and fostered new contacts at the same time. In other words, an individual's belonging to the intellectual underground was defined by the company they kept, rather than any one attribute such as political or aesthetic opposition to the Soviet system. This finding runs against prevailing assumptions, especially with regard to dissidents, and might be one of the reasons why samizdat and dissidence are so often conflated.

As we have seen, only a minority of reading networks grew into and/or overlapped with groups that openly expressed some form of protest against the practices of the Soviet government. The fact that some samizdat was deemed explicitly 'anti-Soviet' does not stop us from concluding that the phenomenon itself was perfectly 'Soviet'. Much of late Soviet society used informal channels to satisfy various needs rather than rely on official institutions that were widely deemed inefficient. The best-known system of this kind is probably *blat*, the elaborate system of mutual favours; the black-market economy is another example of a widely used unofficial channel. And samizdat constitutes yet another such system, or cluster of systems. The networks that produced samizdat provided reading material, satisfying some of the hunger for information in an effectively closed society. They also created publishing platforms that provided a marginalized generation of creative individuals with some opportunities for writerly fulfilment. With an often extraordinary degree of commitment and creativity, the participants in samizdat managed to overcome adverse conditions and compensate for a chronic lack of resources by mobilizing others who desired the same objects, activities or spaces. In this respect, samizdat is a very Soviet phenomenon. Moreover, as a reading culture, late Soviet samizdat was fuelled to no small degree by a specifically Soviet bibliocentrism – worship of the written word – combined with a social sphere in which informal networks played an ever-increasing role. In the field of samizdat, the evolution of informal networks was driving a process of professionalization that resulted in the emergence of alternative institutions such as libraries of samizdat and samizdat periodicals.

I would argue that samizdat's gradual disappearance – or absorption into 'ordinary' culture – during Perestroika is a further indicator of its 'Soviet' nature. When official culture began to admit plurality of opinion and privately owned printing outlets, the binary opposition between 'official' and 'unofficial' culture that had characterized the late Soviet period was undermined, and ultimately obliterated altogether. With Perestroika, the heterogeneous community around samizdat lost the framework that had defined it. Without the quasi-illegal situation, and the concomitant scarcity of material resources and the need for discretion, there was no longer any need for self-referential groups that tended to admit only those who were already to some degree insiders. This process can be seen particularly clearly in the example of the literary journals discussed in this volume. At first they furnished an alternative to official literary culture, as its obverse or shadow side, providing writers not published in the official press with an outlet. In the 1980s, official and unofficial culture began a process of ever-accelerating rapprochement, when Gorbachev's government relaxed censorship as part of its reform policies. As a result, previously forbidden texts began to appear in official editions and the ban on publishing without state control was lifted. The proliferation during these years of small presses and journals that were very similar to still-existing samizdat periodicals suggests two conclusions: samizdat practice had prepared a significant group of people for action as independent writers, journalists and publishers. The second conclusion is more narrowly based on my observations regarding the literary journals in Leningrad: once this became possible, samizdat-type journals and the collectives around them found their way into official culture so easily precisely because they had been modelled on the familiar forms of official culture all along. Perhaps paradoxically, then, the moment the journals had achieved their purported goal – to bring new literature to a larger readership – their existence became superfluous.

This study has also shown that existing sociological models are of limited use for describing all of samizdat (reading). Differentiated theoretical conclusions can only ever apply to one particular network, or to groups that share closely defined characteristics. An example of a network cluster that can be studied effectively with the help of a theoretical model is, once again, the literary periodicals. The groups that produced and read these journals share enough characteristics to enable us to conceptualize them as communities of practice. But this model, and all others, loses plausibility when applied to samizdat as a whole. This is because the phenomenon was heterogeneous, not only with regard to the material being read but also the origin and motivation of those involved and the level of involvement itself, which ranged from occasional reading to authorship, dissemination and conspiracy to running an illegal library. Even simply 'reading' is not a satisfactory common denominator. It is true that, on the most basic level, different kinds of people felt an attraction to samizdat because it satisfied a desire for information that was not otherwise available due to censorship and cultural isolation. In this sense, samizdat meets the definition of a reading community, or a cluster of related reading communities. Broadly defined, a reading community is formed by a social process based on shared reading. Moreover, as DeNel Rehberg Sedo points out, 'reading communities of the past often exposed their members to learning opportunities that were not available within the institutionalized education system'.[2] The social aspect, combined with the emphasis on education in the broadest sense, applies to samizdat as a whole, and the attentive researcher will certainly find individual groups/networks that can be classified exclusively as reading communities. However, samizdat explodes the theoretical framework of the reading community; at least, as long as we do not find a way to expand this framework to encompass production and distribution of texts.

Let us now return to the social aspect of samizdat. As we have seen, reading and other activities centred on samizdat texts brought people together and created community. However, samizdat readers shared these activities not just with a local circle of friends that were known by name. Often, samizdat provided readers with a sense of belonging to a bigger, imagined community. Samizdat was essentially what sociologist Boris Dubin has called 'literature as information and initiation', the latter term emphasizing the way in which reading samizdat functioned as a token of belonging to a particular cultural sphere.[3] Anatolii Vershik, co-editor of the samizdat review journal *Summa*, describes this community when he says that 'any person of our mindset would have chosen the same books'.[4] The books Vershik is referring to are the iconic titles of samizdat. It is no accident that reading preferences were the bottom line of community belonging. One Russian idiom that can be used to describe a like-minded person is: 'We have read the same books' (*my chitali te zhe knigi*). Effectively, samizdat created an 'imagined community': a 'mass-mediated collectivity where members may not all know each other but where each shares the idea of a common belonging'.[5] This quotation has been lifted from its context, but it fits the phenomenon of samizdat; the capacity of samizdat to create a feeling of belonging is a persuasive argument in favour of its power as a medium.

Notes

Introduction

1   Lev Kopelev and Raisa Orlova, *My zhili v Moskve. 1956–1980* (Moscow: KNIGA, 1990), 31–7, 36.

Chapter 1

1   An early example is the first (re-)publication of forty-two poems by Marina Tsvetaeva in the literary miscellany *Pages from Tarussa* (*Tarusskie stranitsy*) in 1961.
2   For the survey, see Gennadii Kuzovkin and Josephine von Zitzewitz, '*Neskol'ko voprosov o samizdate*' ('A Few Questions About Samizdat'), Project for the Study of Dissidence and Samizdat. Available online: https://samizdatcollections.library.utoronto.ca/content/survey (Accessed 13 May 2020). In reply to Question 4: 'What was the first samizdat text you saw or read?'
3   Respondent #64 (b.1956), in reply to Question 54.1: 'If you came across samizdat in school or university (for example, if your peers were interested in or reproducing samizdat texts) please give details.'
4   Described by Alexander Daniel in 'Istoki i smysl sovetskogo samizdata', in V. Igrunov, M. Barbakadze and E. Shvarts (eds), *Antologiia samizdata: nepodtsenzurnaia literatura v SSSR 1950-e – 1980-e* (Moscow: Mezhdunarodnyi institut gumanitarno-politicheskikh issledovanii, 2005), vol. 1, 18. Five respondents to the samizdat survey explicitly identify this episode as the origin of samizdat (#4, #11, #50, #56, #57; questions 3.1 and 7.1).
5   The first eleven issues were published in one volume as *Uncensored Russia*, edited and translated by Peter Reddaway (London: Jonathan Cape, 1972). In 1971, Amnesty International began publishing individual issues in English translation.
6   Founded in 1951 and 1953 respectively; RFE broadcast to Czechoslovakia, Bulgaria, Hungary, Romania and Poland, RL to the Soviet Union. The two stations were merged in 1976.
7   V. Igrunov, M. Barbakadze and E. Shvarts, *Antologiia samizdata*. Available online: http://antology.igrunov.ru/ (accessed 15 May 2020).
8   M. Ishkov, I. Akhmet'ev, V. Kulakov and T. Gromova (eds), *Samizdat veka: Neofitsial'naia poeziia; Antologiia* (The Samizdat of the Century: Unofficial

Poetry; An Anthology) (Minsk: Polifakt, 1998). Available online: http://rvb.ru/np/ (accessed 15 May 2020).

9 OSA Catalog, 'Russian'. Available online: http://catalog.osaarchivum.org/?f%5Blanguage_facet%5D%5B%5D=Russian&f%5Brecord_origin_facet%5D%5B%5D=Digital+Repository (accessed 13 May 2020).

10 Memorial Moscow/International Memorial, 'Overview of the Archives of the History of Dissent'. Available online: https://www.memo.ru/ru-ru/collections/archives/dissidents/guide/ (accessed 15 May 2020). Research and Information Centre Memorial St Petersburg, 'Public Archive on the History of Soviet Terror: Electronic Archive'. Available online: http://iofe.center/elarch (accessed 15 May 2020). In both cases, the majority of documents is not online.

11 Research Centre for East European Studies at the University of Bremen (Forschungsstelle Osteuropa, FSO), 'Archives and Research News'. Available online: https://www.forschungsstelle.uni-bremen.de/en/9/20110606113229/Archive_Library.html (accessed 15 May 2020). The archive itself is not online.

12 For the main website of the project, see Project for the Study of Dissidence and Samizdat. Available online: https://samizdatcollections.library.utoronto.ca/ (accessed 15 May 2020). For the database of samizdat periodicals, see Soviet Samizdat Periodicals. Available online: https://samizdat.library.utoronto.ca/ (accessed 15 May 2020).

13 For information, see Keston Center for Religion, Politics and Society. Available online: https://www.baylor.edu/kestoncenter/ (accessed 15 May 2020).

14 The Centre is now using a wiki platform for its growing archive, see Andrei Belyi Centre, 'Index of Authors', last updated 13 December 2013. Available online: http://samizdat.wiki/%D0%97%D0%B0%D0%B3%D0%BB%D0%B0%D0%B2%D0%BD%D0%B0%D1%8F_%D1%81%D1%82%D1%80%D0%B0%D0%BD%D0%B8%D1%86%D0%B0 (accessed 15 May 2020).

15 'Second Literature': Andrei Siniavskii Electronic Archive of Foreign Countries. Available online: https://vtoraya-literatura.com/ (accessed 15 May 2020).

16 The stenogram is published in *Acta Samizdatica: Zapiski o samizdate*, 2nd edition (Moscow: GPIB Rossii – Mezhdunarodnyi 'Memorial', 2015), 10–39.

17 Friederike Kind-Kovacs and Jessie Labov, 'Introduction', in Friederike Kind-Kovacs and Jessie Labov (eds), *Samizdat, Tamizdat and Beyond: Transnational Media during and after Socialism* (New York: Berghahn, 2013), 2.

18 Alexander Daniel, 'Istoki i smysl sovetskogo samizdata'.

19 Elena Strukova, 'Samizdat kak pamiatnik knizhnoi kul'tury vtoroi poloviny XX veka', in *Acta Samizdatica*, pilot edition (Moscow: GPIB Rossii – Mezhdunarodnyi 'Memorial' – 'Zvenia', 2012), 7–13.

20 Ann Komaromi, 'Samizdat and Soviet Dissident Publics', *Slavic Review* 71, no. 1 (2012): 70–90, 72.

21 Ann Komaromi, *Uncensored: Samizdat Novels and the Quest for Autonomy in Soviet Dissidence* (Evanston, IL: Northwestern University Press, 2015).
22 Valentina Parisi, *Il lettore eccedente: edizioni periodiche del samizdat sovietico, 1956–1990* (Bologna: Società editrice Il mulino, 2013).
23 See International Samizdat [Research] Association. Facebook community, created 22 October 2012. Available online: https://www.facebook.com/samizdat.community/; and Samizdat. Facebook group. Available online: https://www.facebook.com/groups/353375628083079/ (both accessed 16 May 2020).
24 Information about the case, the transcript of the trial and many of the letters of protest, were collated by Alexander Ginzburg and circulated in samizdat. Ginzburg, who had signed this *White Book* (*Belaia kniga*) with his own name, sent one copy to the KGB and another abroad. It was ultimately published by Posev Publishing House in Frankfurt in 1967. For this he and three friends received labour camp sentences. In English collected in Leopold Labedz and Max Hayward (eds), *On Trial: The Case of Sinyavsky (Tertz) and Daniel (Arzhak)* (London: Collins and Harvill Press, 1967). For information about the demonstration inspired by the case, which became an annual event, and this arrest, including many interviews, see D. Zubarev, N. Kostenko, G. Kuzovkin, S. Lukashevskii and A. Papovian (eds), *5 dekabria 1965 goda* (Moscow: Obshchestvo 'Memorial', Izdatel'stvo 'Zvenia', 2005).
25 For information, see Natalia Gorbanevskaia, *Polden': Delo o demonstratsii 25 avgusta 1968 goda na Krasnoi ploshchadi* (Moscow: Novoe izdatel'stvo, 2007).
26 The history of the group, including historical documents, can be found on their website, see Moscow Helsinki Group. Available online: https://mhg.ru/ (accessed 17 May 2020).
27 The Foundation was set up by Alexander Solzhenitsyn, who pledged all present and future royalties he would receive for *The Gulag Archipelago*. It became operative in 1974 and ceased open activity in 1983, following intense persecution. Khodorovich tells his story in an interview with Gleb Morev: Sergei Khodorovich, 'My nakhodili v sebe sily protivostoiat' idiotskomu bezumiu', interview with Gleb Morev, in Gleb Morev (ed.), *Dissidenty: Dvadtsat' razgovorov* (Moscow: Izdatel'stvo AST, 2017), 247–75.
28 Leonid Zhmud', 'Studenty-istoriki mezhdu ofitsiozom i 'liberal'noi' naukoi', *Zvezda*, no. 8 (1998): 204–09, 205.
29 Igor' Golomshtok, *Zaniatie dlia starogo gorodovogo. Memuary pessimista* (Moscow: AST, 2015), 150–51; all ellipsis in brackets are mine.
30 Olga Sedakova and Slava I. Yastremski, 'A Dialogue on Poetry', in Olga Sedakova, *Poems and Elegies*, edited by Slava I. Yastremski (Lewisburg, PA: Bucknell University Press, 2003), 15.
31 The *Chronicle of Current Events* – founded in 1968 to document human rights abuses and with an information and distribution chain that was highly

conspiratorial – was heavily persecuted. The editors changed regularly, usually due to arrest. For information, see Liudmila Alekseeva, *Soviet Dissent: Contemporary Movements for National, Religious, and Human Rights*, translated by Carol Pearce and John Glad (Middletown, CT: Wesleyan University Press, 1985), 285–87.

32 Golomshtok, *Zaniatie dlia starogo gorodovogo*, 149.

33 The *Miting glasnosti* (Rally for Transparency), the first human rights demonstration, took place on 5 December 1965, the day of the Soviet constitution. Organized by Alexander Esenin-Volpin, the participants held banners bearing the slogan 'Respect the Soviet Constitution!' (*Uvazhaite sovetskuiu konstitutsiiu*) and demanded an open trial for Andrei Siniavskii and Yulii Daniel. See D. Zubarev et al., *5 dekabria 1965 goda*; also cf. n. 24, above. On dissidents acting on a moral imperative and a certain passivity among the dissidents of the 1960s, see Vera Lashkova, 'U nas ne bylo zhelaniia uvidet' zariu svobody', interview with Gleb Morev, in Gleb Morev (ed.), *Dissidenty: Dvadtsat' razgovorov* (Moscow: Izdatel'stvo AST, 2017), 111. Solzhenitsyn's famous exhortation to 'Zhit' ne po lzhi' (Live not by lies), a three-page essay published in samizdat in 1974, was a call to boycott the Soviet way of life and placed the emphasis on individual moral responsibility.

34 Liudmila Alekseeva, *Istoriia inakomysliia v SSSR* (New York: Khronika Press, 1984; New edition, Moscow: RITs Zatsepa, 2001), 112.

35 Liudmila Alekseeva, *Soviet Dissent: Contemporary Movements for National, Religious, and Human Rights*, translated by Carol Pearce and John Glad (Middletown, CT: Wesleyan University Press, 1985), 283 ff.

36 Gleb Morev (ed.), *Dissidenty: Dvadtsat' razgovorov* (Moscow: Izdatel'stvo AST, 2017).

37 Lev Losev, 'Samizdat i samogon', in *Zakrytyi raspredelitel'* (Ann Arbor, MI: Hermitage, 1984), 170–74. Attentive readers will notice that the first three categories named by Losev roughly correspond to the three categories of dissent identified by Liudmila Alekseeva, which are national, religious and civic dissent (see Alekseeva, *Istoriia inakomysliia v SSSR*, 1).

38 Elizaveta Starshinina, 'Iz istorii irkutskogo samizdata', report on a lecture by Vladimir Skrashchuk, 21 March 2014. Available online: http://baikal-info.ru/iz-istorii-irkutskogo-samizdata (accessed 17 May 2020).

39 On *Kolokol*, see S. Peskov [pseudonym of V. Iofe], 'Delo "Kolokola"', *Pamiat', istoricheskii sbornik*, no. 1 (1976); published New York, 1978: 269–84.

40 Natalia Volokhonskaia, interview with the author, 12 July 2015.

41 Alekseeva, *Istoriia inakomysliia*, 112.

42 For example, Kopelev and Orlova, *My zhili v Moskve*; Liudmila Alekseeva, *Pokolenie ottepeli* (Moscow: Zakharov, 2006); Natalia Trauberg, *Sama zhizn'* (St Petersburg: Izdatel'stvo Ivan Limbakha, 2008); Liudmila Miklashevskaia, *Povtorenie proidennogo* (St Petersburg: Zvezda, 2012); Golomshtok, *Zaniatie dlia starogo gorodovogo*.

43 Archive of the International Memorial Society in Moscow. Fond 175, opis 4. Avrutskii's organization is the subject of Chapter 4, in this volume.
44 Archive of the Research Centre for East European Studies, University of Bremen, Fond I-86. The interviews are presently being prepared for publication as a commented edition with *Novoe Literaturnoe obozrenie*, under the direction of Gennadii Kuzovkin. Updates are published regularly on 'Memorial: Soviet History Project', Facebook group. Available online: https://www.facebook.com/groups/235003858273/ (accessed 13 May 2020).
45 In collaboration with the Russian State Historical Library (GPIB), proceedings published in *Acta Samizdatica*. The roundtable on 'Cultural Life of Unofficial Moscow in the 1960s–1980s' contains detailed accounts of samizdat experience by a number of invited guests. See *Acta Samizdatica*, no. 3 (2016): 195–220.
46 Seven interviews are available, see Project for the Study of Dissidence and Samizdat, 'Interviews'. Available online: https://samizdatcollections.library.utoronto.ca/interviews (accessed 17 May 2020).
47 For example: Andrei Rogachevskii, 'Novosibirskii samizdat glazami podrostka: (Konets 1970-kh – seredina 1980-kh)', *Solnechnoe spletenie* (Jerusalem), no. 16/17: 208–12; also, Aleksei Smirnov, 'Biography'. Available online: http://gendirector1.blogspot.com/p/blog-page.html (accessed 15 May 2020). On his website, Viacheslav Igrunov not only details his own extensive experience of samizdat but also provides a platform for accounts by others: 'Dissidentism: The Origins and Meaning'. Available online: http://igrunov.ru/vin/vchk-vin-dissid/smysl/1058065392/ (accessed 15 May 2020).
48 Elena Strukova, 'Delo ob odesskoi biblioteke samizdata', *Bibliografiia*, no. 2 (2012): 50–9, 51.
49 Simon Franklin uses the term 'hybrid' in order to describe a writing culture situated between manuscript and print in 'Mapping the Graphosphere: Cultures of Writing in Early 19th-Century Russia (and Before)', *Kritika* 12, no. 3 (2011): 531–60.
50 Five collections of poetry were published during his lifetime, in 1961, 1964, 1967, 1972 and 1977.
51 For a study of how the authorities curated young writers in the 1960s, see Emily Lygo, *Leningrad Poetry 1953–1975: The Thaw Generation* (Berne: Peter Lang, 2010). For bibliographical information on the Leningrad poets see the personal entries in D. Severiukhin, V. Dolinin, B. Ivanov and B. Ostanin (eds), *Samizdat Leningrada: 1950e—1980e gody; Literaturnaia entsiklopediia* (Moscow: Novoe Literaturnoe Obozrenie, 2003).
52 These publishing houses included Ann Arbor, Grani, Posev, YMCA Press, Beseda. Their role is discussed in detail in Chapter 2, in this volume.
53 The process of tamizdat gradually replacing samizdat during the 1970s is described by Alexander Daniel in 'Istoki i smysl sovetskogo samizdata'. An eloquent

confirmation is the interview Lev Kopelev gave to a group of researchers from Bremen University in the 1980s (unpublished). Archive of the Research Centre for East European Studies, University of Bremen, Fond I-86.

54 Robert Darnton, 'What Is the History of Books?', *Daedalus* 111, no. 3 (1982): 65–83. For an alternative, simplified model that emphasizes the role of external influences (intellectual, political, social and commercial, see Thomas R. Adams and Nicholas Barker, 'A New Model for the Study of the Book', in *A Potencie of Life: Books in Society* [London: British Library, 1993], 5–44.)

55 The insights offered by this diagram have been used by Valentina Parisi in 'Scribes, Self-Publishers, Artists: Performing the Book in the Samizdat Writing Scene', in Annette Gilbert (ed.), *Publishing as Artistic Practice* (Berlin: Sternberg Press, 2016), 156; and Olga Zaslavskaya in 'Samizdat as Social Practice and Alternative "Communication Circuit"', in Valentina Parisi (ed.), *Samizdat: Between Practices and Representation; Lecture Series at Open Society Archives, Budapest, February–June 2013* (Budapest: Central European University/IAS, 2015), 92. Darnton specifically pointed out that reading remains the most difficult phase in the circuit to understand and describe.

56 The mechanisms of Soviet book publishing after Stalin are discussed by Stephen Lovell in *The Russian Reading Revolution: Print Culture in the Soviet and Post-Soviet Eras* (Basingstoke: Macmillan, 2000), ch. 3, in particular p. 55 ff.

57 This term is also used in reference works, for example, B. Ivanov and B. Roginskii (eds), *Istoriia leningradskoi nepodtsenzurnoi literatury* (SPb: DEAN, 2000). Fifteen respondents to the samizdat survey used this term in order to define samizdat.

58 Described by Alekseeva, *Soviet Dissent*, 285.

59 Cited in Aleksei Makarov, 'Putevoditel' po vystavke 'Ot tsenzury i samizdata k svobode pechati: 1917–1990', *Acta samizdatica*, no. 3 (2016): 224.

60 Daniel, 'Istoki i smysl sovetskogo samizdata', 17.

61 Irina Tsurkova, interview with the author, 13 August 2015. As early as 1975, F.J. Feldbrugge described this phenomenon, where control over circulation rests with the reader rather than the publisher or author, as 'snowballing'. See F.J. Feldbrugge, *Samizdat and Political Dissent in the Soviet Union* (Leyden: A.W. Sijthoff, 1975), 7. Ann Komaromi likens the circulation to 'mushroom spores' (in 'Samizdat and Soviet Dissident Publics', 74). Olga Zaslavskaya discusses both in 'Samizdat as Social Practice and Alternative "Communication Circuit"', 89.

62 To give one single, easily verifiable example, the Leningrad poet Alexander Mironov wrote a prose piece entitled 'Pietà', published in the journal *37*, no. 3 (1976). The title, in Latin script, complete with the accent grave on the letter 'a', was inserted by hand in the journal's table of contents as well as above the actual piece. See Project for the Study of Dissidence and Samizdat, 'Tridtsat' Sem' [Thirty-Seven] No 03'. Available online: https://samizdatcollections.library.utoronto.ca/islandora/object/samizdat%3A3675 (accessed 17 May 2020).

63 This phenomenon is discussed by Dar'ia Sukhovei, 'Krugi komp'iuternogo raia', *Novoe Literaturnoe Obozrenie* 62 (2003).
64 Respondent #120 (b.1949): 'Akhmatova's *Requiem* – I typed it myself and I still remember manuscript versions that didn't always correspond to the final published text.' In reply to Question 23/23.1: 'Did you keep any samizdat at home?; If yes, can you remember the name of any texts you kept at home and/or the approximate number of texts?'
65 See Natalia Trauberg, 'Vsegda li pobezhdaet pobezhdennyi?', in *Sama zhizn'* (St Petersburg: Izdatel'stvo Ivan Limbakha, 2008), 411–12.
66 Elena Rusakova, interview with the author, 9 August 2015.
67 Respondent #6 (b.1977), in reply to Question 7.1: 'Do you have a definition what samizdat is? Please explain your definition?'
68 Viacheslav Igrunov, 'Odesskaia biblioteka samizdata: 1967–1982', interview with Elena Strukova, July–August 2005. Available online: http://igrunov.ru/cv/odessa/dissident_od/samizdat/1123138219.html (accessed 4 September 2019).
69 On the topic of authorial control, see Valentina Parisi, 'The Dispersed Author: The Problem of Literary Authority in Samizdat Textual Production', in Valentina Parisi (ed.), *Samizdat: Between Practices and Representation; Lecture Series at Open Society Archives, Budapest, February–June 2013* (Budapest: Central European University/IAS: 2015), 63–72.
70 Printing as a means of standardization is discussed by Elizabeth Eisenstein, *The Printing Press as an Agent of Change: Communication and Cultural Transformations in Early Modern Europe* (Cambridge: Cambridge University Press, 1979).
71 Konstantin Kuzminskii, 'O Grigorii Kovaleve', in Konstantin Kuzminskii and Grigorii Kovalev (eds), *The Blue Lagoon Anthology of Modern Russian Poetry* (Newtonville, MA: Oriental Research Partners, 1980–1986), vol. 1, 23. Also, Boris Belenkin, '"Rukopisnoe" ili "pechatnoe"? "Pechatnoe" kak "rukopisnoe"? Malotirazhnye izdaniia v kontekste sovremennogo kul'turnogo protsessa', in Acta Samizdatica, pilot edition (Moscow: GPIB Rossii – Mezhdunarodnyi 'Memorial' – 'Zvenia', 2012), 14–23.
72 Komaromi, 'Samizdat as Extra-Gutenberg Phenomenon'; see also Ann Komaromi, 'Ardis Facsimile and Reprint Editions: Giving Back Russian Literature', in Friederike Kind-Kovacs and Jessie Labov (eds), *Samizdat, Tamizdat and Beyond: Transnational Media During and After Socialism* (New York: Berghahn, 2013), 45.
73 Sabine Hänsgen, 'The Media Dimension of Samizdat: The Präprintium Exhibition Project', in Valentina Parisi (ed.), *Samizdat: Between Practices and Representation; Lecture Series at Open Society Archives, Budapest, February–June 2013* (Budapest: Central European University/IAS: 2015), 47–62.
74 On such dynamics see D.F. McKenzie, *Bibliography and the Sociology of Texts* (Cambridge: Cambridge University Press, 1999), 9.

75 For example by Ann Komaromi, 'The Material Existence of Samizdat', *Slavic Review* 63, no. 3 (2004): 597–618.
76 On readers as publishers who ensured that copies ended up in Western archives, see Komaromi, 'Samizdat and Soviet Dissident Publics', 74–5.
77 The editors of the Leningrad journals *Chasy* and *Mitin zhurnal* remember this practice and described it: Boris Ostanin and Dmitrii Volchek, interviews with the author, 2015.
78 Ilya Kukulin comments on this in Ilya Kukulin, 'Prodistsiplinarnye i antidistsiplinarnye seti v pozdnesovetskom obshchestve', *Sotsiologicheskoe obozrenie* 16, no. 3 (2017): 136–74, 137.
79 In her volume *Russische Literatur im Internet: Zwischen digitaler Folklore und politischer Propaganda* (Bielefeld: transcript Verlag, 2011), Henrike Schmidt includes a three-essay section on 'Internetliteratur und die Tradition des Samizdat: Historischer Kontext'.
80 The journal *Osteuropa* devoted issue number 11 (November 2010) to the topic of 'Blick zurück nach vorn: Samizdat, Internet und die Freiheit des Wortes'.
81 Eugene Gorny, *A Creative History of the Russian Internet* (Saarbrücken: VDM Verlag, 2009), 189. Gorny hosts the Russian Virtual Library (https://rvb.ru).
82 Quoted in Henrike Schmidt, 'Postprintium? Digital Literary Samizdat on the Russian Internet', in Friederike Kind-Kovacs and Jessie Labov, *Samizdat, Tamizdat and Beyond : Transnational Media During and After Socialism* (New York: Berghahn, 2013), 221–44, 222.
83 Maria Haigh, 'Downloading Communism: File Sharing as Samizdat in Ukraine', *Libri* 57 (2007): 165–78.
84 Schmidt's, 'Postprintium? Digital Literary Samizdat on the Russian Internet' is a significantly expanded version of a chapter from her German study *Russische Literatur im Internet*.
85 One such platform is LibraryThing, discussed in detail by Julian Pinder, 'Online Literary Communities: A Case Study of LibraryThing', in Anouk Lang (ed.), *From Codex to Hypertext: Reading at the Turn of the Twenty-First Century* (Amherst: University of Massachusetts Press, 2012), 68–87.
86 Zhmud', 'Studenty-istoriki mezhdu ofitsiozom i "liberal'noi" naukoi', 205.
87 Andrew D. Murray, *The Regulation of Cyberspace: Control in the Online Environment* (Oxford: Routledge, 2006), discussed in Melissa de Zwart and David Lindsay, 'Governance and the Global Metaverse', in Daniel Riha and Anna Maj (eds), *Emerging Practices in Cyberculture and Social Networking* (Amsterdam: Rodopi 2010), 74.
88 Alexei Yurchak, *Everything Was Forever, until It Was No More: The Last Soviet Generation*, (Princeton, NJ: Princeton University Press, 2005), 127–28.
89 Ibid., chs. 3 and 4.

90   Kukulin, 'Prodistsiplinarnye i antidistsiplinarnye seti v pozdnesovetskom obshchestve', 151.
91   On this topic also see Emily Lygo's *Leningrad Poetry*. Appendix 1 lists (official) LITOs as well as (unofficial) literary groups.
92   In an extended Facebook post dedicated to the woman who introduced Natalia Pervukhina to samizdat, see Facebook post, 2 August 2017. Available online: https://www.facebook.com/natalia.pervukhin/posts/1658603657483763 (accessed 17 July 2019).
93   Irina Tsurkova, interview with the author, 13 August 2015.
94   Ann Komaromi writes about this in 'Samizdat as Extra-Gutenberg Phenomenon', 656.
95   Komaromi, 'Samizdat and Soviet Dissident Publics', 85 ff. She is referring to Nancy Fraser's critique of Habermas in 'Rethinking the Public Sphere: A Contribution to the Critique of Actually Existing Democracy', in Craig Calhoun, *Habermas and the Public Sphere* (Cambridge, MA: MIT Press, 1992).

Chapter 2

1   For example journalist Gleb Morev in his recent volume of interviews with dissidents, which includes prominent names such as Sergei Grigoriants, Vera Lashkova, Pavel Litvinov, Sergei Khodorovich, Viacheslav Igrunov and Alexander Daniel: Morev, *Dissidenty*.
2   One such historiographer is Alexander Daniel. A founding member of the Memorial Society, where he set up the History of Dissent in the USSR programme, he is the son of Yulii Daniel, whose arrest and camp sentence in 1964 for publishing literature abroad was one of the decisive moments in the history of the dissident movement, and the prominent dissident Larisa Bogoraz. Born in 1951, he is old enough to have participated in samizdat himself. His many published articles are a popular source for scholars, including myself. He is regularly interviewed on human rights in the USSR (a list of interviews given to Ekho Moskvy radio station is available online: https://echo.msk.ru/guests/8880/ [accessed 13 May 2020]) and has recently given a lecture series on 'The Human Being against the USSR' for the online academy Arzamas, including a lecture on the dangers of literary samizdat and another on the *Chronicle of Current Events*, available online: https://arzamas.academy/courses/40 (accessed 15 June 2018).
3   International Memorial, 'Research Program "History of Dissent in the USSR: 1954–1987"'. Available online: https://www.memo.ru/ru-ru/history-of-repressions-and-protest/protest/dissidents/programma-istoriya-inakomysliya-v-sssr-1954-1987-gg/ (accessed 15 June 2018).

4 We are most grateful for the expert advice of Andrei Alekseev, Leonid Blekher, Liubov' Borusiak, Natalia Vasil'eva, Dmitrii Ermoltsev, Natalia Kigai and Margarita Samokhina.
5 Kuzovkin and von Zitzewitz, 'Neskol'ko voprosov o samizdate'.
6 For a timeline, see Aleksei Makarov, 'Putevoditel' po vystavke "Ot tsenzury i samizdata k svobode pechati: 1917–1990"', *Acta samizdatica*, no. 3 (2016): 221–39.
7 In reply to question 6.1.: "What did you do after reading your first samizdat text? Please provide details".
8 The two last quotations are in reply to question 2.: "When did you first hear the term 'samizdat'? When did this happen, and how?"
9 Rogachevskii, 'Novosibirskii samizdat glazami podrostka', 211–12.
10 Starshinina, 'Iz istorii irkutskogo samizdata'.
11 Vsevolod Rozhniatovskii, 'Vlianie Olega Okhapkina na krug pskovskikh poetov: Miroslav Andreev, Evgenii Shesholin, drugie avtory', in Tat'iana Koval'kova (ed.), *Okhapkinskie chtenie: Almanakh No 1* (St Petersburg: Oriental Research Partners, 2015), 17–27.
12 Konstantin Kuzminskii and Grigorii Kovalev (eds), *The Blue Lagoon Anthology of Modern Russian Poetry* (Newtonville, MA: Oriental Research Partners, 1980–1986). Available online: http://kkk-bluelagoon.ru/(accessed 15 June 2018).
13 Respondent #120 (b.1949), in reply to Questions 20.1: 'Which textual genre was predominant in your samizdat reading? Please explain your choice or choices – why did you read those texts?' and 21.1: 'What was for you the most valuable element in the samizdat texts you knew? Please tell us why?'
14 Respondent #83 (b.1968), in reply to Question 20.1.
15 Respondent #6 (b.1977), in reply to Question 4: 'What was the first samizdat text that you saw or read?'
16 Both replies to Question 4.
17 Respondent #113 (b.1960), in reply to Question 20.1.
18 Respondent #98 (b.1961), in reply to Question 19: 'Would you say that at some point in your life you became a regular samizdat reader?'
19 Both replies to Question 2: 'When did you first hear the term "samizdat"? When did this happen, and how?' and/or Question 4.
20 *The Master and Margarita* (written 1929–1940) was serialized in the journal *Moskva*, in a heavily censored version, in 1966–1967. The first unabridged book edition appeared in tamizdat (Paris: YMCA Press, 1967). In 1973, the novel, which had become a cult book, was published in the USSR in a print run of 30,000 copies. *Tale of the Troika* was published in 1968 in the almanac *Angara*, which was removed from public libraries a year later. A longer version was published in book form in 1989.
21 Both replies to Question 4.

22 Lev Turchinskii, 'Kollektsioniruite tekh, kto neizvesten i nedootsenen', *Arzamas*, 13 June 2018. Available online: https://arzamas.academy/mag/551-turchinsky (accessed 5 March 2019).
23 The cult of Gumilev in the Soviet Union is charted by Roman Timenchik in *Istoriia kul'ta Gumileva* (Moscow: Mosty kul'tury, 2018).
24 Severiukhin et al., *Samizdat Leningrada*, 401–02.
25 In reply to Question 6.1: 'What did you do after reading your first samizdat text? Please provide details.'
26 In reply to Question 11: 'In your opinion, what was the role of samizdat in the transformations that happened in the USSR (Russia) in the 1980s–1990s?'
27 In reply to Question 28: 'Which samizdat texts were particularly popular and circulated widely in your opinion? In other words, which texts would you call "samizdat hits"?'
28 In reply to Question 29.1: 'Do you remember incidents when samizdat texts were read collectively (e.g. when one person would read a page and then pass it on to the next)? Which texts were read in this way, and when was that?'
29 In reply to Question 21/21.1.
30 Emily Lygo describes his popularity in *Leningrad Poetry 1953–1975*, 7 ff. I discuss his influence on the poetics of poets prominent in the 1970s in Josephine von Zitzewitz, *Poetry and the Leningrad Religious-Philosophical Seminar 1976–1980: Music for a Deaf Age* (Oxford: Legenda/MHRA and Routledge, 2016), esp. ch. 2.
31 The sheer popularity of Vysotsky can be gleaned from Wikipedia, 'List of works by Vladimir Vysotsky', last edited May 12, 2020. Available online: https://ru.wikipedia.org/wiki/%D0%A1%D0%BF%D0%B8%D1%81%D0%BE%D0%BA_%D0%BF%D1%80%D0%BE%D0%B8%D0%B7%D0%B2%D0%B5%D0%B4%D0%B5%D0%BD%D0%B8%D0%B9_%D0%92%D0%BB%D0%B0%D0%B4%D0%B8%D0%BC%D0%B8%D1%80%D0%B0_%D0%92%D1%8B%D1%81%D0%BE%D1%86%D0%BA%D0%BE%D0%B3%D0%BE (accessed 13 May 2020).
32 The poem-in-prose was first published in print in Israel in 1973 (in Russian).
33 Cf. Note 20 of this chapter.
34 Turchinskii, 'Kollektsioniruite tekh, kto neizvesten i nedootsenen'.
35 As told by Simon Franklin in 'Mapping the Graphosphere', 554.
36 Respondent #59 (b.1951), in reply to Question 7/7.1: 'Do you have a definition for samizdat? If yes, please explain briefly.'
37 In reply to Question 9: 'Do you thing that the term samizdat can be applied without qualification to the following: books on palmistry, erotica, crime fiction, reports on UFOs and similar texts?'
38 Discussed by Olga Zaslavskaya in 'Samizdat as Social Practice and Alternative "Communication Circuit"', 92.
39 Compare the statement that 'writers are engineers of the human soul', popularized by and attributed to Stalin, who used it in 1932 at a meeting with Soviet writers. In

fact he was quoting the novelist Yurii Olesha. See 'Inzhenery chelovecheskikh dush', in *Entsiklopedicheskii slovar' krylatykh slov i vyrazhenii* (Moscow: Lokid-Press, 2003). Available online: http://dic.academic.ru/dic.nsf/dic_wingwords/1087/Инженеры (accessed 13 May 2020).

40 For a chronological analysis of the 'Soviet reader', see Lovell, *The Russian Reading Revolution*.

41 Golomshtok, *Zaniatie dlia starogo gorodovogo*, 130.

42 *The Gulag Archipelago* is also mentioned as a seminal text by individuals whose memoirs I have used for this monograph and/or who have given me interviews, cf. Rogachevskii, 'Novosibirskii samizdat glazami podrostka', 209; Irina Tsurkova, interview with the author, 13 August 2015.

43 V. Glotser and E. Chukovskaia (eds), *Slovo probivaet sebe dorogu: Sbornik state ii dokumentov ob A.I. Solzhenitsyne: 1962–1974* (Moscow: Izdatel'stvo Russkii put', 1998), 459–60.

44 *The Gulag Archipelago* and Avtorkhanov's *Technology of Power* are among the texts frequently mentioned on the pages of the *Chronicle of Current Events*. The list, as well as a description of the process of indexing, can be found in Gennadii Kuzovkin, 'Nauchnoe izdanie "Khroniki tekushchikh sobytii" i novye vozmozhnosti dlia izucheniia samizdata', in *Acta Samizdatica*, pilot edition (Moscow: GPIB Rossii – Mezhdunarodnyi 'Memorial' – 'Zvenia', 2012), 36–45.

45 For information on the rallies, see A. Podrabinek, '10 dekabria: Moskva; Pushkinskaia ploshchad'; 18 chasov', 6 December 2015. Available online: http://www.cogita.ru/a.n.-alekseev/kontekst/10-dekabrya-moskva-pushkinskaya-ploschad-18-chasov (accessed 15 June 2018).

46 Viacheslav Dolinin and Dmitrii Severiukhin (eds), *Preodolenie nemoty: Leningradskii samizdat v kontekste nezavisimogo kul'turnogo dvizheniia (1953–1991)* (St Petersburg: Izdatel'stvo N.I. Novikova, 2003), 61–2.

47 Anatolii Vershik, '"Summa" za svobodnuiu mysl', in *'Summa' za zvobodnuiu mysl'* (St Petersburg: Zvezda, 2002), 6.

48 Both replies to Question 21.1.

49 In reply to Question 44: 'It is well-known that during the Soviet era people were persecuted for samizdat. Were you affected by persecution?'

50 A major new research project, led by Yasha Klots from Hunter College of the City University of New York, is underway. See the Tamizdat Project's website, http://tamizdatproject.org/en (accessed 13 May 2020), which lists and links institutions, imprints and individuals who produced and promoted tamizdat. The papers given at the project's inaugural conference can be listened to at Russian and East European Cultures at Hunter College, https://www.reechunter.com/tamizdat-conference.html#Program (accessed 6 March 2019).

51 See Natalia Pervukhina, Facebook post, 2 August 2017. Available online: https://www.facebook.com/natalia.pervukhin/posts/1658603657483763 (accessed 17 July 2019).
52 The novel was published in Italy in Italian translation in 1957. The first Russian-language editions appeared in the Netherlands in 1958 and Italy in 1959. The edition in Holland was produced with the support of the CIA and distributed for free to Russian tourists at the World Exhibition in Brussels and the VII World Youth Festival in Vienna. The novel was published in the USSR only in 1988. Twenty-five respondents remember reading it, seven of which specify a tamizdat edition. Anatolii Vershik talks about the novel's popularity in '"Summa" za svobodnuiu mysl', 9.
53 Lev Kopelev and Raisa Orlova, unpublished interview, Archive of the Research Centre for East European Studies, University of Bremen, Fond I-86.
54 For details, see Gleb Struve, 'Kak byl vpervye izdan "Rekviem"', in Anna Akhmatova, *Rekviem: 1935–1940*, 2nd edition (New York: Tovarishchestvo zarubezhnykh pisatelei, 1969). A collection of reminiscences about the fate of the cycle, including how Akhmatova typed out the first copy in 1962, uniting the poems into a cycle, and planned to offer them to *Novyi mir* journal, whose editor turned them down, see Iakov Klots, '"Rekviem" Akhmatovoy v tamizdate: 56 pisem' COLTA, 24 June 2019. Available online: https://www.colta.ru/articles/literature/21637-rekviem-ahmatovoy-v-tamizdate-56-pisem?fbclid=IwAR0CTmzFHK_QlQGB_slVbQkabMytb_KS3QA12aHqgIUz1_PfOjaBw5deimw (accessed 4 August 2019).
55 For example the YMCA Press, transferred from Russia to Berlin in 1925. Initially focused on Christian works, in the 1970s it published a range of contemporary texts, including Solzhenitsyn's *First Circle* (1969) and *The Gulag Archipelago* (1973). For an account of the early years, see Matthew Lee Miller, *The American YMCA and Russian Culture: The Preservation and Expansion of Orthodox Christianity, 1900–1940* (Lanham, MD: Lexington Books, 2012). For a list of titles plus images, see Tamizdat Project, 'Publishers: YMCA-Press; Paris'. Available online: http://tamizdatproject.org/en/publisher/ymca-press (accessed 6 July 2019).
56 For details on the case see Labedz and Hayward, *On Trial*.
57 The case against the compilers of the Brodsky samizdat edition is described by Efim Etkind, one of the participants, in his memoir *Zapiski nezagovorshchika* (London: Overseas Publications Interchange, 1977). For some of the books published by *Ekho* after 2000, see 'Izdatel'stvo "Ekho"'. Available online: http://russianemigrant.ru/tag/izdatelstvo-eho (accessed 7 October 2019).
58 For example, Viktor Krivulin, *Stikhi*, 2 vols. (Paris and Leningrad: Beseda, 1988); Elena Shvarts, *Stikhi* (Leningrad: Beseda, 1987); Oleg Okhapkin, *Stikhi* (Leningrad: Beseda, 1989). Also discussed in Chapter 6, in this volume.

59 The history of the publishing house has been studied by Ann Komaromi in 'Ardis Facsimile and Reprint Editions', 27–50. For a list of titles see pp. 333–38. For title images, see Tamizdat Project, 'Publishers: Ardis; Ann Arbor, MI'. Available online: http://tamizdatproject.org/en/publisher/ardis (accessed 13 May 2020). For a statement by publisher Ellendea Proffer herself, see Ellendea Proffer Teasley, 'How Censorship Leads to Samizdat: Ardis Publishers', keynote lecture, 'Tamizdat: Publishing Russian Literature in the Cold War' conference, Russian and East European Cultures at Hunter College, New York, 10 December 2018. Available online: https://www.reechunter.com/tamizdat-conference.html#Keanote1 (accessed 6 March 2019).

60 In reply to Question 32/32.2: 'Did you have contact with tamizdat? If you can, give a precise date.'

61 *The Gulag Archipelago* was published in Paris in 1973 by YMCA Press; this publication was instrumental in the decision of the authorities to force Solzhenitsyn into exile in February 1974.

62 Four respondents mention this edition, which is most likely the three-volume collected works that came out in 1967, six years before the much more modest Soviet edition: Osip Mandelshtam, *Sobranie sochnineniia v trekh tomakh*, introduction by Clarence Brown, G.P. Struve and B.A. Filippov (Washington, DC: Inter-Language Literary Associates/Mezhdunarodnoe Literaturnoe Sodruzhestvo, 1967).

63 In reply to Question 32.3: 'Did you ever come across tamizdat, and when?'

64 In reply to Question 32.3.

65 For a timeline and general description of the process, see Alekseeva, *Soviet Dissent*, 284–85. Andrei Rogachevskii describes specifically how his first source of samizdat texts in 1970s Novosibirsk would have longer texts in tamizdat editions, sometimes photographed or photocopied, for example Georgii Vladimov's *Vernyi Ruslan* (*Faithful Ruslan*), or the works of Zinoviev, in Rogachevskii, 'Novosibirskii samizdat glazami podrostka', 209.

66 In reply to Question 18: 'Which of the samizdat texts you read left the strongest impression with you, and why?'

67 In reply to Question 23/23.1: 'Did you keep any samizdat at home?'; 'If yes, can you remember the name of any texts you kept at home and/or the approximate number of texts?'

68 In reply to Question 32.3.

69 In reply to Question 4.

70 Larisa Bel'tser, 'Operatsiia "Gutenberg-1984"', Cogita, 9 March 2017. Available online: http://www.cogita.ru/a.n.-alekseev/publikacii-a.n.alekseeva/operaciya-gutenberg20131984 (accessed 20 June 2018).

71 For a detailed account of how books that were reserved for various members of the social hierarchy ended up on the black market, see Losev, 'Samizdat i samogon', 152–55.

72 All replies to Question 32.4: 'How did you manage to obtain tamizdat?'
73 For information on CIA involvement in Russian-language book publishing, see, for example, John Matthews, 'The West's Secret Marshall Plan for the Mind', *International Journal of Intelligence and Counter Intelligence* 16 (2003): 409–27.
74 Irina Roskina, letter to Gennadii Kuzovkin, July 2017.
75 Yurii Kolker, 'Ostrova blazhennykh: Vtoraia literatura i samizdat v Leningrade', *Strana i mir*, nos. 1–2 (1985). Available online: http://yuri-kolker.com/articles/Ostrova_blazhennykh.htm (accessed 21 September 2018).
76 Kirill Kozyrev, interview with the author, 7 July 2015.
77 Viacheslav Igrunov's samizdat 'library' operated mainly from Odessa, but the material was mostly procured via Moscow. See Viacheslav Igrunov, 'O biblioteke Samizdata, o Gruppe sodeistiia kul'turnomy obmenu i o Larise Bogoraz-Brukhman', interview with E.S. Shvarts, 2001. Available online: http://www.igrunov.ru/cv/vchk-cv-memotalks/talks/vchk-cv-memotalks-talks-bogoraz.html (accessed 20 August 2019).
78 *NTS: Mysl' i delo; 1930–2000* (Moscow, 2000). I owe this reference to Ann Komaromi. One of our respondents seems to have known these editions: 'In the 1970s, when I caught a glimpse of a volume of Solzhenitsyn in pocketbook format, which my father had borrowed in order to make a copy' (#93, b.1966, in response to Question 32.2).
79 The two-volume selection of Alexander Vvedenskii was published with Ardis between 1980 and 1984. The first collected poems of Daniil Kharms Meilakh published together with Vladimir Erl with K-Presse (Bremen) between 1978 and 1988.
80 Mikhail Meilakh, 'Pervym moim sledovatelem byl Viktor Cherkesov', interview with Gleb Morev in Gleb Morev (ed.), *Dissidenty: Dvadtsat' razgovorov* (Moscow: Izdatel'stvo AST, 2017), 332; also Mikhail Meilakh, 'Kak zhizn' pobedila smert'', interview with Vitalii Leibin, *Russian Reporter*, no. 16 (455), 11 August 2018. Available online: https://expert.ru/russian_reporter/2018/16/kak-zhizn-pobedila-smert/ (accessed 26 June 2019).
81 Anatolii Vershik, '"Summa" za svobodnuiu mysl', 9.
82 In reply to Question 32.3.
83 Turchinskii, 'Kollektsioniruite tekh, kto neizvesten i nedootsenen'.
84 The BBC is funded by the British taxpayer and out of the TV licensing fee, and is nominally independent of the government; the Russian Service is part of the BBC World Service's foreign-language output, which is provided in about forty languages. Voice of America, in Russian *Golos Ameriki*, is the US government's official international broadcasting arm. One major sponsor of Radio Free Europe and Radio Liberty was the CIA. Friederike Kind-Kovacs, 'Radio Free Europe and Radio Liberty as the "Echo Chamber" of Samizdat', in Friederike Kind-Kovacs and Jessie Labov (eds), *Samizdat, Tamizdat and Beyond: Transnational Media during and after Socialism* (New York: Berghahn, 2013), 90 n.54.

85 On the Free Europe Press and its efforts to increase the exchange of written texts across borders, see Kind-Kovacs, 'Radio Free Europe and Radio Liberty as the "Echo Chamber" of Samizdat', 73–9; she uses mostly the example of Poland.
86 For an overview of studies that consider this angle, see ibid., p. 89, n. 15, n. 16.
87 Ibid., 73, 72. See ch.1, n. 6.
88 By 1971, as detailed during the conference *The Future of Samizdat: Significance and Prospects,* transcript of conference held in London, by Radio Liberty Committee. 23 April 1971, HIA, RFE/RL Corporate Records, see Albrecht Boiter, 'Radio Liberty's Present Use of Samizdat', sheet 3. I owe this reference to Friederike Kind-Kovacs.
89 OSA Catalog, 'RFE/RL Russian Broadcast Recordings'. Available online: http://catalog.osaarchivum.org/?f%5Bdigital_collection%5D%5B%5D=RFE%2FRL+Russian+Broadcast+Recordings (accessed 13 May 2020).
90 According to research carried out in the year 2004, 62 per cent of *Arkhiv Samizdata* (3,284 items) consist of material that can be classified as political. Hyung-Min Yoo from the University of Chicago used the published Arkhiv Samizdata as a basis for a quantitative analysis of samizdat documents by genre, applying Liudmila Alekseeva's classification of different kinds of *dissent* (national, religious and political/human rights) to samizdat *texts*. This approach itself is not without problems. More importantly, Yoo was aware that '*Arkhiv Samizdata* as a rule did not include literary writings' and that only about 50 per cent of samizdat texts mentioned in the *Chronicle of Current Events*, which was itself orientated towards human rights, found their way into RFE/RL's archive. But although he concluded that '*Arkhiv Samizdata* covered less than 50% of the entire samizdat phenomenon', he claimed that 'The best source of samizdat is without doubt *Arkhiv Samizdata* … it is the best collection of samizdat available.' Hyung-Min Yoo, 'Voices of Freedom: Samizdat', *Europe-Asia Studies* 56, no. 4 (2004): 573–74.
91 Kozyrev, interview.
92 OSA Catalog, 'Literary Readings'. Available online: http://catalog.osaarchivum.org/?utf8=%E2%9C%93&f%5bgenre_facet%5d%5b%5d=Literary+Readings&f%5bprimary_type_facet%5d%5b%5d=Audio&q=poetry (accessed 13 May 2020).
93 All replies to Question 37/37.1: 'Did you listen to samizdat texts on the radio? Could you tell us about the texts you heard? Which radio stations broadcast them?'
94 Goldberg was the main voice of the BBC Russian service in the 1970s, succeeded by Seva Novgorodtsev.
95 Lev Kopelev and Raisa Orlova, unpublished interview, Archive of the Research Centre for East European Studies, University of Bremen, Fond I-86.
96 Irina Lashchiver, 'Posleslovie' to Asia Lashchiver, "Dissidentskie vospominaniia"', in *Acta Samizdatica*, pilot edition (Moscow: GPIB Rossii – Mezhdunarodnyi 'Memorial' – 'Zvenia', 2012), 120.
97 Igrunov, 'O biblioteke Samizdata, o Gruppe sodeiztviia kul'turnomu obmenu i o Larise Bogoraz-Brukhman'.

98 Sergei Stratanovskii, interview with the author, 14 August 2015.
99 R. Eugene Parta, *Discovering the Hidden Listener: An Assessment of Radio Liberty and Western Broadcasting to the USSR during the Cold War; A Study Based on Audience Research Findings, 1970–1991* (Stanford, CA: Hoover Institution Press, 2007).
100 *The Mission of Radio Free Europe and Radio Liberty Broadcast*, reprint in A. Buell, 'Radio Free Europe/Radio Liberty in the Mid 1980s', in K.R.M. Short (ed.), *Western Broadcasting Over the Iron Curtain* (London: Croom Helm, 1986), 85.
101 Liudmila Alekseeva, *Pokolenie ottepeli* (Moscow: Zakharov, 2006), 91.
102 Schmidt, 'Postprintium?', 225.
103 The process people used to establish to whom they could give texts is described in great detail by Lev Kopelev, unpublished interview, Archive of the Research Centre for East European Studies, University of Bremen, Fond I-86.
104 The origin of the term is discussed by Polly McMichael, '"A Room-Sized Ocean": Apartments in Practice and Mythology of Leningrad's Rock Music', in William Jay Risch (ed.), *Youth and Rock in the Soviet Bloc* (Lanham, MD: Lexington Books, 2015), 183–209, 187 ff. Also see Artemy Troitsky, *Tusovka: Who's Who in the New Soviet Rock Culture* (London: Omnibus Press, 1990).
105 All three replies to Question 20.1.
106 In reply to Question 29.1.
107 In reply to Question 23/23.1.
108 Pervukhina, Facebook post, 2 August 2017.
109 Raisa Orlova, unpublished interview with Elena Vargaftik, 30 April 1983. Archive of the Research Centre for East European Studies, University of Bremen, Fond I-86. Excerpts from *The Gulag Archipelago* were published in the German weekly *Der Spiegel*, nos. 1–5 (1974).
110 Franklin, 'Mapping the Graphosphere', 552. Studied in detail in M. Aronson and S. Reiser, *Literaturnye kruzhki i salony* (1929; St Petersburg: Akademicheskii proekt, 2001); Irina Murav'eva, *Salony pushkinskoi pory: Ocherki literaturnoi i svetskoi zhizni Sankt-Peterburga* (St Petersburg: Kriga, 2008).
111 One of the best-known salons of the Silver Age, Viacheslav Ivanov's 'Tower', is researched in great detail in V. Bagno et al., *Bashnia Viacheslava Ivanova i kul'tura serebrianogo veka* (St Petersburg: Filologicheskii Fakultet Gosudarstvennogo universiteta, 2006).
112 Franklin, 'Mapping the Graphosphere', 552.
113 Pervukhina, Facebook post, 2 August 2017.
114 Sergei Semanov, *Russkii klub: Pochemu ne pobediat evrei* (Moscow: Litres, 2017, ebook).
115 In reply to Question 5: 'What was the impression left by your first encounter with a samizdat text? Give details if possible.'
116 Irina Roskina, Letter to Gennadii Kuzovkin, July 2017.

117 For a very similar statement, see Viacheslav Igrunov, 'Ia byl dissident v dissidenstve', interview with Gleb Morev, in Gleb Morev (ed.), *Dissidenty: Dvadtsat' razgovorov* (Moscow: Izdatel'stvo AST, 2017), 195–218, 205.
118 Both replies to Question 24/24.2: 'Did you ever reproduce samizdat texts? If so, what influenced your decision to do so?'
119 In reply to Question 20.1.
120 This and the previous replies in this section are to Question 24/24.2.
121 In reply to Question 17/17.1: 'Which samizdat activity were you involved in? You can tick several options. Please give details about your answer.'
122 This and the previous replies in this section are to Question 24/24.2.
123 When respondents combined two definitions, i.e. 'forbidden literature in typescript' (e.g. #16, b.1959), their answer was counted in both categories.
124 In reply to Question 32.3.
125 For a criticism of the way in which sociology describes late Soviet social networks, which includes the absence of systematic research into samizdat as a system of social networks, with the help of social network theory, see Kukulin, 'Prodistsiplinarnye i antidistsiplinarnye seti v pozdnesovetskom obshchestve', 136–74.

Chapter 3

1 Examples include the title pages of the encyclopaedia *Samizdat Leningrada* and the specialist series *Acta Samizdatica*, published by the Memorial Society in collaboration with various partners.
2 Interview with Liudmila Alekseeva, taken by Raisa Orlova in August 1983. Archive of the Research Centre for East European Studies (Forschungsstelle Osteuropa, FSO), University of Bremen. Publication forthcoming in the volume *Neskol'ko interv'iu o samizdate*, edited by Gennadii Kuzovkin. Partial pre-publication available online: https://urokiistorii.ru/article/55967?fbclid=IwAR1JJqennOLl27L5OONaHeaENVYs0N_bNcR3j3cRP0X_D_Z_rAeDba_eLxs (accessed 15 May 2019).
3 Boris Likhtenfel'd, interview with the author, 25 July 2015.
4 For the role of the author as typesetter, see Hänsgen, 'The Media Dimension of Samizdat'.
5 Elena Rusakova, interview with the author, 9 August 2015. All further quotations by Elena Rusakova are from this interview and will not be referenced in this chapter unless necessary.
6 One researcher who draws attention to this is Ilya Kukulin, see 'Prodistsiplinarnye i antidistsiplinarnye seti v pozdnesovetskom obshchestve', 159. I consider this issue from a gender angle in the final section of this chapter.

7   Natalia Volokhonskaia, interview with the author, 12 July 2015. All further quotations by Natalia Volokhonskaia are from this interview and will not be referenced in this chapter unless necessary.
8   Tatiana Pritykina, interview with the author, 13 July 2015. All further quotations by Tatiana Pritykina are from this interview and will not be referenced in this chapter unless necessary.
9   Rusakova, interview.
10 'My ne khuzhe Goratsiia' (1966), music and text available online: http://www.bards.ru/archives/part.php?id=4132 (accessed 4 June 2019).
11 Irina Tsurkova, interview with the author, 13 August 2015. All further quotations by Irina Tsurkova are from this interview and will not be referenced in this chapter unless necessary.
12 Tsurkova, interview.
13 Her personal entry in Severiukhin et al., *Samizdat Leningrada*, 249, features a list of works she typed – most of it Silver Age, but also new editions. Among the poetry she typed was the samizdat journal *Golos* in 1978 (ten issues, see Severiukhin et al., *Samizdat Leningrada*, 398).
14 Pritykina, interview.
15 Arsenii Roginskii (1946–2017), human rights activist and historian, one of the founders of the Memorial Society, from 1998 to 2017 chairman of the executive board of the International Memorial Society. Between 1975 and 1981 he edited the samizdat historical almanac *Pamiat'* (Memory), which was published abroad from 1978. In 1981, Roginskii received a four-year camp sentence. The texts mentioned by Rusakova were intended for *Pamiat'*.
16 Olga Abramovich, telephone interview with the author, 27 August 2015.
17 Ilya Kukulin analyses this phenomenon using French sociologist Laurent Thevenot's theory of 'engagement'. For details on how people regulate different types of engagement, see Laurent Thevenot, 'The Plurality of Cognitive Formats and Engagements: Moving between the Familiar and the Public', *European Journal of Social Theory* 10, no. 3 (2007): 409–23.
18 Published in samizdat on 13 February 1974, the day after Solzhenitsyn's arrest. For the text, see Alexander Solzhenitsyn, 'Zhit' ne po lzhi!'. Available online: http://www.solzhenitsyn.ru/proizvedeniya/publizistika/stati_i_rechi/v_sovetskom_soyuze/jzit_ne_po_ljzi.pdf (accessed 8 October 2019). The story of the essay's publication is described in Alexander Solzhenitsyn, *Bodalsia telenok s dubom: Ocherki literaturnoi zhizni* (Moscow: Soglasie, 1996), 388–89.
19 Dolinin and Severiukhin, *Preodolenie nemoty*, 61.
20 The practice is confirmed by respondent #26 (b.1969) to the samizdat survey, who remembers copying a tract of traditional folk medicine in Moscow in 1983.

21 See A.V. Korotkov, S.A. Mel'chin and A.S. Stepanov (eds), *Kremlevskii samosud. Sekretnye dokumenty Politbiuro o pisatele A. Solzhenitsyne* (Moscow: Rodina Edition 'Q', 1994), 250–51.
22 Sergei Stratanovskii, interview with the author, 14 August 2015.
23 Yurii Avrutskii, unpublished memoir – manuscript. Archive of the Memorial Society in Moscow, Fond 175, opis 4.
24 Rusakova, interview.
25 Cf. Chapter 1, n. 24.
26 Vera Lashkova, 'Vera Lashkova – zhivoi golos russkoi istorii', interview with Iaroslav Gorbanevskii, 2011. Available online: http://ru.rfi.fr/rossiya/20111113-vera-lashkova-zhivoi-golos-russkoi-istorii (accessed 14 April 2019).
27 Lashkova, 'U nas ne bylo zhelaniia uvidet' zariu svobody', 103–04.
28 Ibid., 104–05.
29 Zhmud', 'Studenty-istoriki mezhdu ofitsiozom i "liberal'noi" naukoi', 205–06.
30 Kuzminskii, 'O Grigorii Kovaleve', 22.
31 An iconic example is the one used by Viktoria Apter, typist of the literary journal *Chasy*, which punched through the letter 'o'. I myself own a table of contents for the journal, where this fault is clearly visible. Boris Ostanin maintains that only the first copy of any set was marked in this way. (Boris Ostanin, interview with the author, 20 August 2015).
32 Repin was the Leningrad coordinator for Alexander Solzhenitsyn's Foundation for Political Prisoners and their Families. See Chapter 1, n. 27.
33 Volokhonskaia is possibly referring to two types of paper commonly used for tracing, rough 'pergament' and smooth 'kal'ka'. I am grateful to Irina Flige for the clarification.
34 Both Tsurkova and Rusakova use it frequently. For written sources see Lashkova, 'U nas ne bylo zhelaniia uvidet' zariu svobody', 108; for Natalia Pervukhina's story see Facebook post, 2 August 2017.
35 The term as well as the general practice of disposing of carbon paper down the toilet are also remembered by Natalia Dobkina, interview with the author, 11 August 2015.
36 The activity of another prominent samizdat binder from Moscow, Sergei Lar'kov, is described by Ann Komaromi in 'The Material Existence of Samizdat', 600–03.
37 Turchinskii, 'Kollektsioniruite tekh, kto neizvesten i nedootsenen'. All quotations by Lev Turchinskii are from this publication and will not be referenced in this chapter unless necessary.
38 Golomshtok, *Zaniatie dlia strarogo gorodovogo*, 68.
39 Respondent #82 (b.1948), in reply to Question 26/26.1: 'Did you know about samizdat being reproduced in state enterprises, either using photocopy or office typewriters? If yes, please tell us more. Which texts were reproduced in this way?'

40 'Leningradski feminism 1979', Facebook post, 26 April 2019. Available online: https://www.facebook.com/kulturwerkstatt.zhaba/posts/1698022777162868?__tn__=KH-R (accessed 14 May 2020). The case documents are held in the archive of the Memorial Society in St Petersburg.
41 Strukova, 'Delo ob odesskoi biblioteke samizdata', 50. The copy of the *Archipelago* she describes used to form part of Viacheslav Igrunov's samizdat library in Odessa, studied in Chapter 4.
42 For a description of this process, see Alekseeva, *Soviet Dissent*, 285.
43 Replies to Question 21.1: 'What was for you the most valuable element in the samizdat texts you knew? Please tell us why?'; and Question 15: 'If you feel that your interest in samizdat arose as the consequence of certain events in your life, could you name these events?'.
44 Sergei Stratanovskii, interview with the author, 14 August 2015. Names of typists supplied.
45 All replies to Question 43/43.1: 'Did you ever have to buy samizdat? If yes, can you remember the works and their price?'
46 Bel'tser, 'Operatsiia "Gutenberg-1984"'.
47 It is worth noting that Irina and Arkadii Tsurkov are not mentioned.
48 For Abramovich, see Severiukhin et al., *Samizdat Leningrada,* 69–70; Volokhonskaia features under her maiden name, Lesnichenko, p. 249.
49 Barbara Martin and Anton Sveshnikov, *Istoricheskii sbornik 'Pamiat'*, *Issledovaniia i materialy* (Moscow: Novoe literaturnoe obozrenie, 2017).
50 Barbara Martin and Anton Sveshnikov, 'Between Scholarship and Dissidence: The Dissident Historical Collection *Pamiat'*, *Slavic Review* 76, no. 4 (2017): 1003–026, 1022.
51 Kuzminskii, 'O Grigorii Kovaleve', 22.
52 Konstantin Kuzminskii, 'Boris Taigin', in Konstantin Kuzminskii and Grigorii Kovalev (eds), *The Blue Lagoon Anthology of Modern Russian Poetry* (Newtonville, MA: Oriental Research Partners, 1980–1986), vol. 1, reprint edition, 2006 (pagination different from original), 25.
53 Igrunov, 'Ia byl dissident v dissidenstve', 205.
54 Meilakh, 'Kak zhizn' pobedila smert''.
55 The only mention of male typists – *mashinisty* – alongside women that I have come across is Zhmud', 'Studenty-istoriki mezhdu ofitsiozom i "liberal'noi" naukoi', 205.
56 Kirill Kozyrev, interview with the author, 7 July 2015.
57 Alekseeva, interview with Raisa Orlova, see Gennadii Kuzovkin, 'Samaia znamenitaia mashinistka samizdata', Uroki istorii: XX vek, 22 July 2019. Available online: https://urokiistorii.ru/article/55967?fbclid=IwAR1JJqennOLl27L5OONaHeaENVYs0N_bNcR3j3cRP0X_D_Z_rAeDba_eLxs (accessed 14 May 2020).

58 Alekseeva, *Istoriia inakomysliia v SSSR*.
59 Petr Kazarnovskii and Ilya Kukui, 'Vmesto predisloviia', in Leonid Aronzon (ed.), *Sobranie Proizvedenii*, vol. 1 (St Petersburg: Izdatel'stvo Ivana Limbakha, 2006), 11.
60 For details, see Genrikh Sapgir, 'Sapgir ob avtorakh i gruppakh', RVB, 21 August 2019. Available online: http://rvb.ru/np/publication/sapgir5.htm#67 (accessed 21 October 2019).
61 Lashkova, 'U nas ne bylo zhelaniia uvidet' zariu svobody', 108.
62 Dobkina confirmed this in the interview she gave me; this detail is also remembered by Volokhonskaia.
63 Galina Drozdetskaia, interview with the author 10 July 2015.
64 For a general overview, see Natalia Pushkareva, 'Feminism in Russia', in *Encyclopaedia Round the World*. Available online: https://www.krugosvet.ru/enc/istoriya/FEMINIZM_V_ROSSII.html (accessed 14 May 2020); Natalia L. Pushkareva, 'U istokov russkogo feminizma: skhodstva i otlichiia Rossii i zapada', in G.A. Tishkin (ed.), *Rossiiskie zhenshchiny i evropeiskaia kul'tura* (St Petersburg: Sankt-Peterburgskoe filosofskoe obshchestvo, 2001), 79–84; Alexandra Talaver, 'Samizdat of the Soviet Dissident Women's Groups, 1979–1982', submitted MA thesis (Central European University Department of Gender Studies, Budapest). The German-Russian culture workhop *Zhaba* is preparing a travelling exhibition on the occasion of the fortieth anniversary of the appearance of *Woman and Russia* that will open in December 2019 in St Petersburg. See https://www.leibniz-gwzo.de/de/transfer/ausstellungen/leningradski-feminism-eine-wanderausstellung?fbclid=IwAR2YAgLb_YF7Tcndpbj28BhKk4En8zNXflIxokUyh8E_lbmS_glI345pteM (accessed 21 October 2019). The project's Facebook page ('Leningradski feminism 1979'. Available online: https://www.facebook.com/kulturwerkstatt.zhaba/ [accessed 14 May 2020]) collects and displays related materials.
65 As we have seen in this chapter, binding was often done by men, more examples will follow as part of the discussion on the journals *Chasy* and *Severnaia pochta* in Chapter 5.
66 Natalia Malakhovskaia, 'Feministskii samizdat: zhurnal "Mariia"', *Live Journal*, 24 January 2013. Available online: https://feministki.livejournal.com/2499778.html (accessed 5 May 2018). Malakhovskaia observes that women themselves have imbibed the hostile atmosphere and turned against women.

   A rare example of a woman poet who was a full participant, an active agent rather than a facilitator for others, was Elena Shvarts. Very feminine in her appearance, she claimed several male domains of behaviour as her own: she drank and smoked heavily, failed to turn up for readings and publicized her notorious love life. For detail, see Josephine von Zitzewitz, 'From Underground to Mainstream: The Case of Elena Shvarts', in Katharine Hodgson and Alexandra Smith (eds), *Reconfiguring the Canon of Twentieth-Century Russian Poetry, 1991–2008* (Cambridge: Open Book Publishers, 2017), 225–64.

67 In 1917–1918, the Bolsheviks decreed equal political and property rights; women were obliged to work; in the 1977 Constitution, Article 53 declares men and women equal; Article 36 specifies the need to protect women.
68 Malakhovskaia, 'Feministskii samizdat'.
69 Tatiana Mamonova, 'Introduction', in Tatiana Mamonova (ed.), *Women and Russia: Feminist Writings from the Soviet Union* (Oxford: Blackwell, 1984), xiv.
70 Malakhovskaia, 'Feministskii samizdat'. She is referring to, for example, the fact that while women did have workers' rights and obligations, they were expected to do the housework and look after the children.

Chapter 4

1 Discussed in Lovell, *The Russian Reading Revolution*, 60–9.
2 All replies to Question 23/23.1: 'Did you keep any samizdat at home?'; 'If yes, can you remember the name of any texts you kept at home and/or the approximate number of texts?'
3 In reply to Question 32.3: 'Did you ever come across tamizdat, and when?'
4 In reply to Question 23/23.1
5 In reply to Question 23/23.1.
6 In reply to Question 23/23.1.
7 Zhmud', 'Studenty-istoriki mezhdu ofitsiozom i "liberal'noi" naukoi', 205–06.
8 For a exposition of how books and periodicals, including foreign ones, might end up in a *spetskhran* special collection, see Losev, 'Samizdat i samogon', 158–62.
9 Tatiana Goricheva, interview with the author, 4 July 2015.
10 On Mnukhin's activity, see Anastasia Kostriukova, 'Chitat' i slyshat' nastoiashchuiu literaturu', in *Acta Samizdatica: Zapiski o samizdate*, pilot edition (Moscow: GPIB Rossii – Mezhdunarodnyi 'Memorial' – 'Zvenia', 2012), 84–94. This publication contains excerpts from an interview with Lev Mnukhin in Paris on 3 November 2007, see 'Lev Mnukhin', interview with Ann Komaromi, Project for the Study of Dissidence and Samizdat, August 2014. Available online: https://samizdatcollections.library.utoronto.ca/interviews/ru/lev-mnukhin (accessed 2 October 2019).
11 This categorization is described in Aleksei Makarov, 'Ot lichnoi kollektsii samizdata k obshchestvennoi biblioteke. Trudnosti granits i definitsii', in *Acta Samizdatica: Zapiski o samizdate*, pilot edition (Moscow: GPIB Rossii – Mezhdunarodnyi 'Memorial' – 'Zvenia', 2012), 24–35, esp. 28–9.
12 In response to Question 23/23.1. The importance of such figures is confirmed, for example, in Rogachevskii, 'Novosibirskii samizdat glazami podrostka'; see also Turchinskii, 'Kollektsioniruite tekh, kto neizvesten i nedootsenen'.

13 In response to Questions 23/23.1 and 34: 'Did you know of any samizdat libraries (associations which regularly exchanged texts)?'.
14 One respondent remembers a further library in Obninsk that functioned as late as the early 1990s. Respondent #86 (b.1959), in reply to Question 34.
15 Makarov, 'Ot lichnoi kollektsii samizdata k obshchestvennoi biblioteke', 30–1.
16 Respondent #116 (b.1966), in reply to Question 34.
17 The process is described in Viacheslav Igrunov, 'Beseda o "Khronike tekushchikh sobytii" i biblioteke samizdata', interview with Gennadii Kuzovkin and Nikolai Kostenko, 31 January 2004. Available online: http://www.igrunov.ru/cv/vchk-cv-memotalks/talks/about-chronika-et-samisd.html (accessed 4 September 2019) and in 'Odesskaia biblioteka samizdata'. Yurii Avrutskii also describes it in his unpublished memoir. Manuscript, archive of the Memorial Society in Moscow, Fond 175, opis 4. Cited after Makarov, 'Ot lichnoi kollektsii samizdata k obshchestvennoi biblioteke', 34.
18 Igrunov, 'Odesskaia biblioteka samizdata'.
19 Igrunov, 'Ia byl dissident v dissidenstve', 196.
20 Igrunov, 'Odesskaia biblioteka samizdata'.
21 Ibid.
22 Here we can see an intriguing parallel between Igrunov's group and the nationalist and monarchist underground VSKhSON (Vserossiiskii sotsial-Khristianskii soiuz osvobozhdeniia naroda; All-Russian Social-Christian Union for the Liberation of the People). This group, whose members professed the intention of overturning the Soviet system, started as a reading group and collected large amount of contemporary and pre-revolutionary literature for the purpose of self-education. It never developed beyond this stage: founded in 1964, it was uncovered by the KGB in 1967 and its members were sentenced to lengthy labour camp terms. For information, see Alekseeva, *Istorial inakomysliia v SSSR*, chs. 'Stanovlenie' and 'Russkoe Natsional'noe dvizhenie', esp. 200–02. Materials relating to the group, including their manifesto, are compiled in John Dunlop (ed.), *VSKhSON: Materialy suda i programma; Vol'noe slovo; Samizdat. Izbrannoe*, vol. 22 (Frankfurt: Posev, 1976).
23 Igrunov, 'Beseda o "Khronike tekushchikh sobytii"'.
24 For example, in Igrunov, 'Beseda o "Khronike tekushchikh sobytii"'.
25 Igrunov, 'Beseda o "Khronike tekushchikh sobytii"'.
26 Igrunov (#21, b.1948), in reply to survey Question 8/8.1: 'Did you know about any museums, libraries, private collections etc that were used as sources for copying and circulating literature or documents that were not in print in the USSR? Your personal experience is especially valuable.'; 'If yes, can you name these institutions or private collections? If you visited them, we would be grateful for details.'
27 Igrunov, 'Odesskaia biblioteka samizdata'.
28 Igrunov remembers: 'Through the *Chronicle of Current Events* I not only found out about people I needed to become acquainted with because their views and

behaviour were close to my own, but also about books and articles. It represented a truly free view of the world. All other samizdat was something like an appendix to the *Chronicle of Current Events*. The *Chronicle of Current Events* represented the pivotal aspect of my life back then, and everything else revolved around it' (Igrunov, 'Beseda o "Khronike tekushchikh sobytii"'). The editors of the *Chronicle* observed strict conspiratorial principles. In soliciting information from their readers, they exhorted contributors to pass material on to the person from whom they had received their copy rather than try to find the editors, to avoid being taken for an informer. See *Khronika tekushchikh sobytii*, no. 5 (1968), cited after Maria Fokin (ed.), 'Chronicle of Current Events', translated by Julie Draskoczy. Available online: http://www.memo.ru/history/diss/chr/ (accessed 4 September 2019).

29 Viacheslav Igrunov, 'Neofitsial'naia literatura i nekotorye voprosy praktiki' and 'K problematike obshchestvennogo dvizhenia', Available online: http://igrunov.ru/cv/vchk-cv-chosenpubl/vchk-cv-chosenpubl-ego.html (accessed 1 October 2019).

30 Igrunov, 'Odesskaia biblioteka samizdata'.

31 *Antologiia samizdata*. Available online: http://antology.igrunov.ru/ (accessed 15 May 2020).

32 As asserted by Elena Strukova, a leading expert on the library, in 'Delo ob odesskoi biblioteke samizdata', 51.

33 On the structure of the library, including the names of the main keepers and distributors, see Viacheslav Igrunov, 'Primernaia struktura biblioteki samizdata v Odesse'. Available online: http://igrunov.ru/cv/odessa/dissident_od/samizdat/library-structure.html; Petr Butov's three-part memoir about the dissidents in Odessa, 'Vospominaniia ob Odesskikh dissidentakh', parts 1 and 2. Available online: http://igrunov.ru/cv/odessa/dissident_od/samizdat/1109017845.html; Boris Khersonskii, 'Beseda s Borisom Khersonskim 1. iuniia 2002 g. Odessa', interview with E.S. Shvarts. Available online: http://www.igrunov.ru/cv/vchk-cv-side/vchk-cv-side-stories-herson.html; Khersonskii's memoir 'Pamiati semidesiatykh', *Vestnik*, 2 November 2008. Available online: https://magazines.gorky.media/interpoezia/2008/2/pamyati-semidesyatyh.html; Bella Ezerskaia's memoir 'Kak eto bylo v Odesse', *Vestnik*, no. 11 (348) (2004). Available online: http://www.vestnik.com/issues/2004/0526/win/ezersky.htm. I am grateful to Elena Strukova for pointing me to Ezerskaia's text. (All sources accessed 14 September 2019.)

34 As specified by Makarov, 'Ot lichnoi kollektsii samizdata k obshchestvennoi biblioteke', 30.

35 The overview in question is Strukova's 'Delo ob odesskoi biblioteke samizdata'. The criminal case files she accessed are held in the archive of the Sluzhby Bezpeky Ukrayiny (SBU; Security Service of Ukraine) for the Odessa region ('Delo ob odesskoi biblioteke samizdata', 51 n. 6). Also see her paper 'Odesskaia biblioteka samizdata Igrunova-Butova i "Masterskaia khudozhestvennykh promyslov" Avraama Shifrina', given at the *Chteniia pamiati A.B. Roginskogo*,

Moscow, 30 March 2019. See International Memorial, 'Chteniia pamiati Arseniia Roginskogo: Den' vtoroy', YouTube, 30 March 2019. Available online: https://www.youtube.com/watch?v=JwnRcfDkWbk (accessed 17 September 2019).
36 Strukova, 'Delo ob odesskoi biblioteke samizdata', 57–8.
37 Ibid., 50.
38 Avrutskii, unpublished memoir, quoted in Makarov, 'Ot lichnoi kollektsii samizdata k obshchestvennoi biblioteke', 33–4.
39 Quoted in Makarov, 'Ot lichnoi kollektsii samizdata k obshchestvennoi biblioteke', 33.
40 Avrutskii, unpublished memoir.
41 Aleksei Makarov, 'Zhurnal domashnei biblioteki: Kak bylo ustroeno virtual'noe sobranie zapreshchennykh knig', Arzamas. Available online: https://arzamas.academy/materials/1155 (accessed 13 June 2018). This article forms part of a thematic section entitled 'The Anti-Soviet Museum'.
42 Makarov, 'Ot lichnoi kollektsii samizdata k obshchestvennoi biblioteke', 34.
43 Igrunov (#21, b.1948), in reply to survey Question 23/23.1.
44 Igrunov, 'O biblioteke Samizdata'.
45 Igrunov, 'Beseda o "Khronike tekushchikh sobytii"'.
46 Igrunov, 'Odesskaia biblioteka samizdata'. The difficulties of obtaining literature after multiple arrests among his sources in the 1970s are also described in Igrunov, 'O biblioteke Samizdata'.
47 Makarov 'Ot lichnoi kollektsii samizdata k obshchestvennoi biblioteke', 33.
48 Avrutskii, unpublished memoir.
49 Makarov 'Ot lichnoi kollektsii samizdata k obshchestvennoi biblioteke', 33; Igrunov, 'Beseda o "Khronike tekushchikh sobytii"'.
50 Igrunov, 'Odesskaia biblioteka samizdata'.
51 Avrutskii, unpublished memoir.
52 As seen on Makarov, 'Zhurnal domashnei biblioteki'; also described in Makarov, 'Ot lichnoi kollektsii samizdata k obshchestvennoi biblioteke', 32, 34.
53 Igrunov, 'Beseda o "Khronike tekushchikh sobytii"'.
54 Ibid.
55 Ibid.
56 Makarov, 'Ot lichnoi kollektsii samizdata k obshchestvennoi biblioteke', 35.
57 Ibid., 34.
58 Igrunov, 'Beseda o "Khronike tekushchikh sobytii"'.
59 Poet Lev Losev provides a first-hand account of the workings of the illegal book market, including the behaviour of book sellers and the trajectory by which books reached the market. Losev, 'Samizdat i samogon', esp. 139–41. More recently, this market is portrayed Aleksei German Jr's feature film *Dovlatov* (2018).
60 Irina Roskina, letter to Gennadii Kuzovkin, July 2017. Unfortunately, Roskina could not remember when exactly she bought Mandelshtam's memoirs.

61 Avrutskii, unpublished memoir.
62 Igrunov, 'Odesskaia biblioteka samizdata'.
63 Ibid.
64 Ibid.
65 Ibid.
66 Ibid.
67 Igrunov, 'Beseda o "Khronike tekushchikh sobytii"'.
68 Ibid.
69 Ibid.
70 Igrunov, 'Odesskaia biblioteka samizdata'.
71 Investigation file, cited according to Strukova, 'Delo ob odesskoi biblioteke samizdata', 55.
72 Butov offers a detailed account of his involvement with the library, including the years after Igrunov's arrest when he was responsible, in part 3 of his 'Vospominaniia ob Odesskikh dissidentakh'. On his time as main librarian, see http://igrunov.ru/cv/odessa/dissident_od/samizdat/1110809385.html (accessed 4 April 2019).
73 Igrunov, 'Odesskaia biblioteka samizdata'.
74 Strukova lists some of the confiscated titles in 'Delo ob odesskoi biblioteke samizdata', 56, drawing on Butov's case file from the archive of the SBU for Odessa region, Delo-24444.
75 Igrunov, 'Odesskaia biblioteka samizdata'.
76 Meilakh, 'Kak zhizn' pobedila smert''.
77 Igrunov, 'Beseda o "Khronike tekushchikh sobytii"'.
78 Avrutskii, unpublished memoir.
79 See the personal entry on Sergei Mazlov in Severiukhin et al., *Samizdat Leningrada*, 268.
80 For a reprint of all issues, see A. Vershik, V. Dolinin, E. Maslova and B. Maslov (eds), '*Summa' – za svobodnuiu mysl*' (St Petersburg: Izdatel'stvo zhurnala 'Zvezda', 2002), 40.
81 Vershik et al., '*Summa' za svobodnuiu mysl*'. Additional sources on *Summa* are: A. Vershik, 'Potaennyi daidzhest epokhi zastoia', *Zvezda*, no. 11 (1991); 'Nauka i totalitarizm', *Zvezda*, no. 8 (1998); Sergei Levin, '"Summa" s pozitsii "slagaemogo"', in *Samizdat: Po materialam konferentsii '30 let nezavisimoi pechati; 1950–80 gody*' (St Petersburg: NITs 'Memorial', 1993), 115–19.
82 Vershik, '"Summa" – za svobodnuiu mysl'', 6.
83 Ibid.; emphasis in the original.
84 Anatolii Vershik, interview with the author, 31 July 2015.
85 For example the review of the new Leningrad journal *Obshchina* (1979) and several of its publications in *Summa*, no. 1, republished in Vershik et al., '*Summa' za zvobodnuiu mysl*', 73–5.
86 Inside cover of the first issue, in Vershik et al., '*Summa' za svobodnuiu mysl*'.
87 See Martin and Sveshnikov, 'Between Scholarship and Dissidence', 1018.

88 Vershik, '"Summa" – za svobodnuiu mysl'', 7.
89 Levin, '"Summa" s pozitsii "slagaemogo"', 118. Levin is referring to Vershik, 'Potaennyi daidzhest epokhi zastoia'.
90 Vershik, interview.
91 Vershik, '"Summa" – za svobodnuiu mysl'', 7.
92 Ibid., 8.
93 For Kopelev's opinion on Maslov, see Kopelev and Orlova, *My zhili v Moskve*, 417–21. Kopelev's contributions to *Summa* are listed in Dolinin, 'Summa v kontekste samizdata', 28.
94 Vershik, interview, also Vershik, '"Summa" – za svobodnuiu mysl'', 9.
95 Vershik, '"Summa" – za svobodnuiu mysl'', 17–9; Dolinin, 'Summa v kontekste samizdata', 29.
96 Vershik, '"Summa" – za svobodnuiu mysl'', 19–20.
97 Dolinin, 'Summa v kontekste samizdata', 29.
98 Vershik, interview.
99 On the seminar, called 'Seminar po obshchei teorii sistem' and running from 1968–1982, see Severiukhin et al., *Samizdat Leningrada*, 450–51, and Dolinin, 'Summa v kontekste samizdata'. The names of people involved are given on p. 27.
100 Vershik, '"Summa" – za svobodnuiu mysl'', 8.
101 Ibid., 9. The book to which he is referring is John Barron, *KGB: The Secret Work of Soviet Secret Agents* (New York: Reader's Digest Press, 1974).
102 Vershik, interview.
103 Ibid.

Chapter 5

1 A particularly salient example is the neo-avant-garde journal *Transponans*. Copies are now accessible online, see Project for the Study of Dissidence and Samizdat, 'Zhurnal teorii i praktiki "Transponans": Kommentirovannoe elektronnoe izdanie / Pod red. I. Kukuia – A Work in Progress'. Available online: https://samizdatcollections.library.utoronto.ca/islandora/object/samizdat%3Atransponans (accessed 7 September 2018).
2 A volume exclusively featuring contributions by those involved in Leningrad journals is Viacheslav Dolinin and Boris Ivanov (eds), *Samizdat: Po materialam konferentsii '30 let nezavisimoi pechati; 1950–80 gody'; S.-Peterburg, 25–27 aprelia 1992* (St Petersburg: NITs 'Memorial', 1993). Multiple other sources will be referenced over the course of this chapter and the next.
3 'Map of Soviet Samizdat Periodicals'. Available online: https://utoronto.maps.arcgis.com/apps/webappviewer/index.html?id=2eeb4a7c24254ffe96008429a3d1c6b8 (accessed 4 May 2019).

4 The sources available reflect this perception of Leningrad samizdat as a unified phenomenon. The main reference work is called *Samizdat Leningrada* (eds. Severiukhin et al). Another volume of research that draws on an understanding of Leningrad samizdat, specifically the literary scene, as integrated, is Stanislav Savitskii, *Andegraund: Istoriia i mify leningradskoi neofitsial'noi literatury* (Moscow: Novoe literaturnoe obozrenie, 2002).
5 Kolker, 'Ostrova blazhennykh'.
6 Three respondents mention 'leningradskie zhurnaly' (the Leningrad journals), one calls them 'piterskie zhurnaly' (Petersburg journals), in reply to Question 35: 'Did you read samizdat periodicals?'
7 Kolker, 'Ostrova blazhennykh'. Sergei Stratanovskii confirms this when he points out that 'there [in Moscow] were more official journals, which meant that there were more people who felt sympathy for writers' (Stratanovskii, interview with the author, 14 August 2015).
8 Natalia Rubinshtein, private conversation on the topic of Leningrad in the 1960s.
9 Alongside the already mentioned 1993 conference volume *Samizdat* and Savitskii's study the following works deserve mention and are discussed in more detail in Chapter 6: the encyclopaedia *Samizdat Leningrada* features entries on individuals, publications and groups; also Ivanov and Roginskii, *Istoriia leningradskoi nepodtsenzurnoi literatury*; Dolinin and Severiukhin, *Preodolenie nemoty*; Iuliia Valieva (ed.), *Litsa peterburgskoi poezii 1950–1990-e. Avtobiografii. Avtorskoe chtenie + 5 CD* (St Petersburg: Samizdat, 2011); Boris Ivanov (ed.), *Peterburgskaia poeziia v litsakh.* (Moscow: Novoe literaturnoe obozrenie, 2011); Jean-Philippe Jaccard (ed.), *Vtoraia kul'tura: Neofitsial'naia poeziia Leningrada v 1970-e–1980-e gody* (St Petersburg: Rostok, 2013).
10 Martin and Sveshnikov, 'Between Scholarship and Dissidence', 1010.
11 *Samizdat Leningrada* lists all the main groups. Iuliia Valieva (ed.), *Sumerki 'Saigona'* (St Petersburg: Samizdat, 2009), contains interviews in which many smaller circles are described. Boris Likhtenfel'd reminisces about the groups in which he participated in 'Dlia menia proshloe sushchestvennee nastoiashchego: o leningradskoi "vtoroi kul'ture" i ee geroiakh', Colta, 12 November 2018. Available online: https://www.colta.ru/articles/literature/19696-dlya-menya-proshloe-suschestvennee-nastoyaschego (accessed 19 January 2019). On the literary-artistic salon hosted by Konstantin Kuzminskii in the late 1960s, see Yurii Novikov, 'Stroitel' vavilonskoi bashni (K portretu K. Kuz'minskogo)', *Novoe Literaturnoe Obozrenie* 31 (1998): 328–33. On the Religious-Philosophical Seminar, closely linked to the journal *37*, see von Zitzewitz, *Poetry and the Leningrad Religious-Philosophical Seminar 1976–1980*, ch. 1.
12 For a first-hand account, see Alexander Mironov, 'Malaia Sadovaia: 1960-e. Beseda c Iuliei Valievoi', in Iuliia Valieva (ed.), *Sumerki 'Saigona'* (St Petersburg: Samizdat, 2009), 32–5.

13 The history of the two cafes is extensively documented in Valieva, *Sumerki 'Saigona'*.
14 *Samizdat Leningrada* lists these almanacs in the section on publications. The 1993 volume *Samizdat* features the stories of several editors of these almanacs, in particular Eduard Shneiderman and Vladimir Erl.
15 Stratanovskii, interview.
16 For information on the *Lepta* affair, see Severiukhin et al., *Samizdat Leningrada*, 419. The documentation relating to the *Lepta* case, including the table of contents, the protocols of the editorial committee meetings and the correspondence with Sovetskii pisatel' are published in Kuzminskii and Kovalev, *The Blue Lagoon Anthology of Modern Russian Poetry*, vol. 5B.
17 For a chronological account of the development of Leningrad samizdat, see Boris Ivanov, 'Evoliutsiia literaturnykh v piatidesiatye-vos'midesiatye gody', in Boris Ivanov and Boris Roginskii (eds), *Istoriia leningradskoi nepodtsenzurnoi literatury* (St Petersburg: DEAN, 2000), 17–8; and 'Etapy razvitiia neofitsial'noi literatury 1953-1991', in Severiukhin et al., *Samizdat Leningrada*, 9–51.
18 Tatiana Goricheva, 'Mne nadoeli podval'nost i elitarnost' "Vtoroi kul'tury"', interview with Raisa Orlova, 1985. Available online, in an abbreviated form: http://gefter.ru/archive/17640 (accessed 3 March 2018); Tatiana Goricheva, interview with the author, 4 July 2015; Boris Ostanin, interview with the author, 20 August 2015.
19 Many different accounts confirm this: B. Konstriktor [B. Aksel'rod], 'Dyshala noch' vostorgom samizdata', *Labirint/Ekstsentr* 1 (1991): 35–50; Boris Ivanov, 'V bytnost' Peterburga Leningradom: O leningradskom samizdate', *Novoe Literaturnoe Obozrenie*, 14 (1995): 188–99, 192; 'Po tu storonu ofitsial'nosti', and Viktor Krivulin, '"37", Severnaia pochta', in Viacheslav Dolinin and Boris Ivanov (eds), *Samizdat: Po materialam konferentsii '30 let nezavisimoi pechati; 1950-80 gody'* (St Petersburg: NITs 'Memorial', 1993), 74–81 and 82–9 respectively.
20 Krivulin, '"37", Severnaia pochta', 77.
21 The Research Centre for East European Studies at the University of Bremen has a good - although not full - set; individual copies are in the archive of the Research and Information Centre Memorial in St Petersburg and the Keston Center at Baylor University, Texas. No. 13 is missing from all these collections and might be held in a private archive difficult to access by researchers. For an almost full set of *37*, without no. 13, see Project for the Study of Dissidence and Samizdat, '37 [Tridtsat' Sem', Thirty-Seven]'. Available online: https://samizdatcollections.library.utoronto.ca/islandora/object/samizdat%3A37 (accessed 16 May 2020). It offers full-text search of all materials of the journal.
22 Examples of poets who published in this form include Viktor Krivulin (nos. 1, 14), Viacheslav Kuprianov (no. 3), Elena Shvarts (no. 6), Alexander Mironov (no. 19), Ol'ga Sedakova (no. 10), Lev Rubinshtein (no. 15) and Vsevolod Nekrasov (no. 17).

23 Goricheva, 'Mne nadoeli podval'nost'; also see her autobiography, *Talking about God Is Dangerous: My Experiences in the East and in the West* (London: SCM, 1986).
24 Tatiana Goricheva, 'Zadachi khristianskogo prosveshcheniia: Vystuplenie na vstrechi redaktsii, avtorov i chitatelei dvukh svobodnykh religioznykh zhurnalov; "Obshchina" (Moskva) i zhurnala khristianskoi kul'tury "37" (Leningrad); Leningrad, 22 fevral'ia 1979', in *Khristianskii Seminar*, Vol. 39 (Frankfurt: Posev, 1981), 34–41, 40.
25 The Religious-Philosophical Seminar was one of many unofficial study groups in 1970s Leningrad. For basic information, see Severiukhin et al., *Samizdat Leningrada*, 445–47. For a detailed survey and interpretation, see von Zitzewitz, *Poetry and the Leningrad Religious-Philosophical Seminar 1976–1980*, ch. 1.
26 Confirmed by Viktor Krivulin: 'the journal "37" emerged as a natural continuation of the religious-philosophical and literary seminars with their atmosphere of discussion' (Krivulin, '"37", Severnaia pochta', 77).
27 Goricheva confirmed to me that these exchanges were written explicitly for publication in the journal (Goricheva, interview).
28 Reader no. 7, responding to a questionnaire about reading experience distributed with no. 16, published in no. 17. Almost all respondents complained that part of the journal was conceptually inaccessible to them.
29 Goricheva, interview.
30 Goricheva, 'Mne nadoeli podval'nost''.
31 Severiukhin et al., *Samizdat Leningrada*, 153. *37* no. 20 was dedicated to Goricheva and contained a short text and photographs taken on the eve of her departure.
32 Severiukhin et al., *Samizdat Leningrada*, 458.
33 Krivulin, '"37", Severnaia pochta', 89–90.
34 To give only a few examples, *Chasy* no. 1 included Goricheva's translation of one of Karl Jaspers's lectures from the series *Der philosophische Glaube: Fünf Vorlesungen* (Munich/Zurich, 1948); *Chasy* no. 2 featured a text by Merleau-Ponty on the phenomenology of language; *Chasy* no. 3 featured Albert Camus's *Myth of Sisyphus*.
35 For example: B.I. [Boris Ivanov], 'Na seminare', *Chasy*, no. 12 (1978); Anonymous, 'Na seminare "Religiia i kul'tura"', *Chasy*, no. 15 (1978).
36 For example, *Chasy* no. 9, which includes the first translation of several stories by Jorge Luis Borges, originally published in 37 no 11. Confirmed by Boris Ostanin, interview with the author, 20 August 2015. *Chasy* also published an issue consisting of materials from *Obvodnyi kanal* and another after *Mitin zhurnal*.
37 Ostanin, interview. A full set of *Chasy* can be found in the digital archive of the Andrei Belyi Centre, 'Arkhiv zhurnala "Chasy"', last updated 28 February 2014. Available online: http://samizdat.wiki/%D0%90%D1%80%D1%85%D0%B8%D0%B2_%D0%B6%D1%83%D1%80%D0%BD%D0%B0%D0%BB%D0%B0_%C2%AB%D0%A7%D0%B0%D1%81%D1%8B%C2%BB (accessed 16 May 2020).

38 Ostanin is citing Boris Ivanov almost verbatim, cf. Boris Ivanov, *Istoriia Kluba-81* (St Petersburg: Izdatel'stvo Ivana Limbakha, 2015), 36.
39 Kolker, 'Ostrova blazhennykh'; emphasis in the original.
40 This phenomenon is analysed in Schmidt, 'Postprintium?', 227.
41 Goricheva, 'Mne nadoeli podval'nost'.
42 Two writers who remember being encouraged to submit to *Chasy* are Andrei Ar'ev, who published a prose piece in *Chasy* no. 1, and the poet Boris Likhtenfel'd. Andrei Ar'ev, interview with the author, 16 July 2015; Boris Likhtenfel'd, interview with the author, 25 July 2015.
43 Boris Ostanin, interview.
44 See Natalia Shkaeva, '"Bez redaktsii starykh Bolshevikov andegraunda" ili chto takoe Chasy', Cogita, 12 October 2011. Available online: http://www.cogita.ru/news/sobytiya-i-anonsy-2009-2011/abbez-redakcii-staryh-bolshevikov-andegraundabb-ili-chto-takoe-abchasybb (accessed 8 January 2019).
45 Ostanin, interview. Ivanov himself formulated that *Chasy* had the explicit task to provide structure for the unofficial cultural process (Ivanov, *Istoriia Kluba-81*, 32, 36).
46 Ostanin, interview.
47 Andrei Belyi Prize, 'O premii'. Available online: http://belyprize.ru/index.php?id=3 (accessed 7 October 2019). Ostanin, who serves as the director of the prize-giving committee, is now the director of the Andrei Belyi Centre, a well-known venue for literary events in contemporary St Petersburg.
48 For conference reports and papers, see *37* no. 19 (1979) and *Chasy* nos. 21, 22 (1979), 23, 24 (1980). See also V. Nechaev, 'Nravstvennoe znachenie neofitsial'noi kul'tury v Rossii: Materialy konferentsii v muzee sovremennoi zhivopisi', *Poiski* 1 (1979): 303–14; and Ivanov, *Istoriia Kluba-81*, 20–1.
49 About the second, inter-city conference being secret, see Dolinin and Severiukhin, *Preodolenie nemoty*, 88.
50 Sergei Stratanovskii, interview with the author, 14 August 2015.
51 Krivulin, '"37", Severnaia pochta', 75.
52 Sergei Dediulin, '"Tam byl gorod." "Severnaia pochta": iz vozpominanii o real'nom sotrudnichestve redaktsii s poetami i kritikami', in Jean-Philippe Jaccard (ed.), *Vtoraia kul'tura: Neofitsial'naia poeziia Leningrada v 1970-e–1980-e gody* (St Petersburg: Rostok, 2013), 84–113. See pp. 100–03 for a perceptive if polemical assessment of both journals' shortcomings.
53 Stratanovskii, interview.
54 One of the first theoretical discussions of conceptualism, Boris Groys's now iconic 'Moskovskii romanticheskii kontseptualizm', was first published in *37* no. 15 (1978).
55 Kirill Butyrin, 'U istokov Obvodnogo kanala', in Viacheslav Dolinin and Boris Ivanov (eds), *Samizdat: Po materialam konferentsii '30 let nezavisimoi pechati; 1950–80 gody'; S.-Peterburg, 25–27 aprelia 1992* (St Petersburg: NITs 'Memorial', 1993), 124–29, 126–27.

56 Ibid., 128.
57 Kolker, 'Ostrova blazhennykh'.
58 Evgenii Gollerbakh, 'Table of contents for the journal *Obvodnyi kanal*', unpublished. Shared with me by Sergei Stratanovskii.
59 Stratanovskii, interview.
60 Ibid.
61 Kolker, 'Ostrova blazhennykh'.
62 Butyrin, cited in Severiukhin et al., *Samizdat Leningrada*, 435.
63 Gollerbakh, 'Table of Contents'.
64 The first ten issues of *Obvodnyi kanal* are held in the archive of the Research Centre for East European Studies at the University of Bremen, see Project for the Study of Dissidence and Samizdat, 'Obvodnyi kanal'. Available online: https://samizdatcollections.library.utoronto.ca/islandora/object/samizdat%3Aobvodnyikanal (accessed 4 June 2019).
65 Sergei Dediulin, 'Severnaia pochta: Zhurnal stikhov i kritiki', Bibliograf vypusk 2 (Paris: Russkii institut v Parizhe, 2001). A complete set of *Severnaia pochta* is held in the Research Centre for East European Studies at the University of Bremen. See Project for the Study of Dissidence and Samizdat, 'Severnaia pochta'. Available online: https://samizdatcollections.library.utoronto.ca/islandora/object/samizdat%3Asevernaiapochta (accessed 4 June 2019).
66 Dediulin, '"Tam byl gorod."'. His collaboration with Krivulin is detailed on pp. 103–04.
67 First published in *Severnaia pochta* 1/2 (1979) under the pseudonym A. Kalomirov. The article is based on a paper given at one of the conferences on the significance of unofficial culture in 1979. See Viktor Krivulin, 'Dvadtsat' let noveishei russkoi poezii', Mikhail Gendelev. Available online: http://gendelev.org/kontekst/leningrad/439-viktor-krivulin-dvadtsat-let-novejshej-russkoj-poezii.html (accessed 4 March 2019).
68 Compare Chapter 6. Examples that make extensive use of material prepared by the critics of the 1970s and 1980s include Aleksandr Zhitenev, *Poeziia neomodernizma* (St Petersburg: Inapress, 2012); and Josephine von Zitzewitz, 'Self-Canonisation as a Way into the Canon: the Case of the Leningrad Underground', *Australian and East European Studies* 31 (2017): 197–228.
69 Compare Chapter 3. Dediulin describes in detail how his flat was searched and his personal archive confiscated, how the KGB saw how many samizdat works he was producing and must have concluded that the biggest part of the collection was elsewhere. See Marco Sabbatini, 'K istorii sozdanii "Severnoi pochty"; O Viktore Krivuline; Interv'iu s Sergeem Dediulinym' (Paris: Assotsiatsiia 'Russkii institut v Parizhe', 2004), 5.

70. Ivanov, *Istoriia Kluba-81*, 29, 37; see also Yurii Kolker, 'Leningradskii Klub 81', *Dvadtsat' Dva* 39 (1984). Available online: http://yuri-kolker.com/articles/Club-81.htm (accessed 4 March 2019).
71. Severiukhin et al., *Samizdat Leningrada*, 450.
72. For details on *Transponans*, see Ilya Kukui, 'Laboratoriia avangarda: Zhurnal *Transponans*', *Russian Literature* 59, nos. 2–4 (2006), 225–59. A full set of the journal can be seen online, see Project for the Study of Dissidence and Samizdat, 'Zhurnal teorii i praktiki "Transponans"'.
73. That *Transponans* belongs to the Leningrad tradition is confirmed by its inclusion into the encyclopaedia, Severiukhin et al., *Samizdat Leningrada*, 456.
74. Information on the journals can be found in Severiukhin et al., *Samizdat Leningrada*, 404–06 and 425–26.
75. Severiukhin et al., *Samizdat Leningrada*, 414. Issues of *Krasnyi Shchedrinets* can be found in the archive of the Research and Information Centre Memorial in St Petersburg.
76. Severiukhin et al., *Samizdat Leningrada*, 455–56. The volume O.N. Ansberg and A.D. Margolis (eds), *Obshchestvennaia zhizn' Leningrada v gody perestroiki: Sbornik materialov* (St Petersburg: Serebriannyi vek, 2009) documents the unique spirit of the Perestroika years and is particularly valuable in this context for the many first person accounts describing the many new semi-official journals that sprang up during that period.
77. Email from Dmitrii Volchek to the author, 27 August 2015.
78. Ibid.
79. Severiukhin et al., *Samizdat Leningrada*, 429.
90. Volchek, email. Valentina Parisi's volume features an entire chapter on the ideal versus the real reader: 'Lettore ideale e lettore reale', see Parisi, *Il lettore eccedente*, 81–106.
81. Olga Abramovich, telephone interview with the author, 27 August 2015.
82. Ibid.
83. Ibid.
84. Volchek, email.
85. See Kolonna Publications, 'Magazine'. Available online: http://kolonna.mitin.com/?page=magazine (accessed 16 May 2020).
86. Krivulin, '"37", Severnaia pochta', 81.
87. Il'ia Kukui, Predislovie; "Sokhranit' nit' poeticheskogo avangarda": zhurnal teorii i praktiki "Transponans"', Project for the Study of Dissidence and Samizdat, October 2015. Available online: https://samizdatcollections.library.utoronto.ca/content/%D0%BF%D1%80%D0%B5%D0%B4%D0%B8%D1%81%D0%BB%D0%BE%D0%B2%D0%B8%D0%B5 (accessed 7 September 2018).
88. Ry Nikonova [Anna Tarshis], 'Anketnaia ikra Obvodnogo kanala', *Transponans*, no. 34 (1986).
89. A similar questionnaire had been distributed on the occasion of the anniversary of Alexander Blok in 1980 by *Dialog* and was reprinted in *Severnaia pochta* no. 8.

For a discussion on the phenomenon of such questionnaires, see Josephine von Zitzewitz, 'Reader Questionnaires in Samizdat Journals: Who owns Alexander Blok?', in Juliane Furst and Josie McLellan (eds), *Dropping out of Socialism* (Lanham, MD: Lexington, 2016), 107–27.

90 Liudmila Alekseeva explicitly lists religiosity as one of three categories of dissent in *Istoriia inakomysliia v SSSR*; another scholar who uses the term 'Orthodox dissent' is Jane Ellis, *The Russian Orthodox Church: A Contemporary History*, Keston Book No. 22 (London: Croom Helm, 1986).

91 Materials on issues affecting the neophyte Christians in contemporary society were regularly published in 37. They include 'Christianity and Ethics' in no. 6, 'Christianity and Humanism' in nos. 7 and 8, and 'Contemporary Christianity' in no. 9. Milutin Janjic dedicated his PhD thesis to the question of theology in *37*, published as *Leningrad's Religious-philosophical Seminar: A Place of Encounter Between Text and Mission* (Berkeley, CA: Graduate Theological Union, 2015).

92 Two scholars who offer valuable insight into the resurgence of Russian nationalism in the late Soviet Union are Yitzhak Brudny, *Reinventing Russia: Russian Nationalism and the Soviet State 1953–1991* (Boston: Harvard University Press, 1998); and Nikolai Mitrokhin, *Russkaia partiia: Dvizhenie russkikh natsionalistov v SSSR; 1953–1985* (Moscow: Novoe literaturnoe obozrenie, 2003).

93 The persecution of *Veche* is detailed by Leonid Borodin, one of the journal's editors, in his memoir *Bez vybora* (Moscow: Molodaia gvardiia, 2003), 184. Borodin explicitly identified *Moskovskii sbornik* as a continuation of *Veche* (ibid.).

94 For details, see *Khristianskii Seminar*, vol. 39 (Frankfurt: Posev, 1981). In their manifesto the seminar members voice their 'thirst for a living Christian communication of love', 'the vital need to strengthen the Orthodox worldview' and proclaim the first aim of their group to be 'service of the cause of Russia's Spiritual Renaissance' (*Khristianskii Seminar*, 5–6). The *Christian Seminar*'s journal, called *Obshchina* (Community), was short-lived; leaders managed to produce nineteen copies of a single issue before they were arrested in 1979 and sentenced to long terms in a labour camp, illustrating the heightened risk of persecution run by samizdat activists whose interests might be deemed political. See also the reminiscences of Alexander Ogorodnikov, the Seminar's founder: 'Monolog o seminare – fragment kruglogo stola', *Okhapkinskie chteniia Almanakh No 2*, edited by Tat'iana Koval'kova (St Petersburg: Russkaia kul'tura, 2018), 29–35.

95 Goricheva, 'Mne nadoeli podval'nost''.

96 Butyrin, 'U istokov Obvodnogo kanala', 127.

97 Savitskii, *Andegraund*, 29. The chapter is entitled 'Ugon samoleta s dukhovnymi tseliami'.

98 Goricheva, 'Mne nadoeli podval'nost''.

99 Goricheva, interview.

100 Goricheva, 'Mne nadoeli podval'nost''.
101 Ibid.
102 Severiukhin et al., *Samizdat Leningrada*, 457.
103 See Liudmila Polikovskaia, 'Zhurnal "37"', *Antologiia samizdata*. Available online: http://antology.igrunov.ru/after_75/periodicals/37/ (accessed 16 May 2020); the entry corresponds to Krivulin's words in Krivulin, '"37", Severnaia pochta', 76.
104 Goricheva, 'Mne nadoeli podval'nost''.
105 Severiukhin et al., *Samizdat Leningrada*, 458; Ostanin, interview.
106 The émigré journal *Posev* regularly published new information about the Religious-Philosophical Seminar (see no. 3 [1977], no. 9 [1979], no. 3 [1980]); *Vestnik RKhD* printed disjointed excerpts from *37* (see no. 118 [1976], no. 121 [1977], no. 123 [1977]).
107 Krivulin, '"37", Severnaia pochta', 76.
108 Archive of the Research Centre for East European Studies. Fond No. 75 (Boris Groys Collection).
109 Goricheva, interview.
110 Galina Drozdetskaia, interview with the author, 10 July 2015.
111 Ostanin, interview.
112 Ibid.
113 Kirill Kozyrev, interview with the author, 7 July 2015. Kozyrev also replied to the samizdat reader survey and remembers his reason for typing and circulating samizdat as 'My close acquaintance and friendship with the editors of the journals *Chasy*, *"37"*, *Obvodnyi kanal* and others' (in reply to Question 17/17.1: 'Which samizdat activity were you involved in? You can tick several options. Please give details about your answer.').
114 Ostanin, interview.
115 Natalia Volokhonskaia, interview with the author, 12 July 2015.
116 Ostanin, interview.
117 Kozyrev, interview.
118 Ostanin, interview.
119 Including that of the Andrei Belyi Centre, 'Zhurnal "Chasy"', last updated 25 June 2013. Available online: http://arch.susla.ru/index.php/%D0%96%D1%83%D1%80%D0%BD%D0%B0%D0%BB_%C2%AB%D0%A7%D0%B0%D1%81%D1%8B%C2%BB,_%D0%A2%D0%BE%D0%BC_%E2%84%961 (accessed 16 May 2020).
120 Irina Tsurkova, interview with the author, 13 August 2015. On *Perspektiva* and the persecution of its makers, see 'Delo "levoi oppozitsii" 3 (1979, 4–1)', *Vesti iz SSSR*, no. 4 (16 February 1979). Available online: https://vesti-iz-sssr.com/2016/11/20/delo-levoi-oppositsii-1979-4-1/ (accessed 14 June 2019); Alexander Skobov, '"Perspektiva" – zhurnal novykh levykh', in Viacheslav Dolinin and Boris Ivanov

(eds), *Samizdat: Po materialam konferentsii '30 let nezavisimoi pechati; 1950–80 gody'* (St Petersburg: NITs 'Memorial', 1993), 105–14.
121 Kozyrev, interview. His comments apply specifically to *Chasy*.
122 Previously, Dediulin had made annotated 'literary supplements' of the classics for a samizdat journal entitled *LOB*, which he had produced with his university circle of friends, as well as an anthology on Akhmatova. See Sabbatini, 'K istorii sozdanii "Severnoi pochty"', 3–4.
123 Krivulin, '"37", Severnaia pochta', 80.
124 Kolker, 'Ostrova blazhennykh'.
125 Dediulin, '"Tam byl gorod."', 107.
126 Severiukhin et al., *Samizdat Leningrada,* 450.
127 Kozyrev, interview.
128 Krivulin, '"37", Severnaia pochta', 75.
129 Ibid., 77.
130 Ibid., 80.
131 For example, see A. Kalomirov [Viktor Krivulin], 'Problema sovremennoi russkoi poezii. Stat'ia 1; Iosif Brodsky; Mesto', *37*, no. 9 (1977): 204–14; also see Lev Losev (ed.), *Poetika Brodskogo: Sbornik statei* (Tenafly, NJ: Hermitage, 1986), 219–29. I owe this point to Anna Borovskaya, who raised them on the panel 'In Search of a Light in the Darkness: Cultural Restoration in the Works of Natalya Gorbanevskaia and Victor Krivulin' at the ASEEES Convention in Boston, December 2018. Borovskaya also pointed out that Krivulin claimed to only ever having translated Czesław Miłosz, in an interview with Tatiana Kosinova (see Kosinova, *Polski mit: Polska w oczach sowieckich dysydentów* [Krakow: Instytut Książki-Nowaja Polsza, 2012], 120). Mikhail Sheinker, a close friend of Krivulin, affirmed that Krivulin translated with the help of literal versions done by his friends who were fluent in the respective language. (Mikhail Sheinker, interview with the author, 26 August 2015).
132 Viktor Krivulin, 'Fragment poemy', *37*, no. 9 (1977): 26.
133 Viktor Krivulin, 'Pol'sha kak background', *Novaya Pol'sha* 10 (2011). Available online: http://novpol.org/ru/S16PIuMPi-/POLShA-KAK-BACKGROUND (accessed 10 January 2019).
134 The stories in question are 'Vavilonskaia biblioteka' ('La Biblioteca de Babel', 1941), 'Sad s razdvaivaiushchimisia dorozhkami' ('El jardín de senderos que se bifurcan', 1941), 'P'er Menar – avtor Don Kikhota' ('Pierre Menard, autor del *Quijote*', 1939).
135 Goricheva, interview. On the subject of theological literature, Goricheva remarked: 'We had nothing at all. Tourists would sometimes bring a random book, sometimes Ratzinger, sometimes Rahner, sometimes Balthasar'.
136 I have investigated the *Publichka*'s records on selected Western thinkers and theologians mentioned or published in samizdat journals (Martin Heidegger, Mircea Eliade, Edmund Husserl, Søren Kierkegaard, Martin Buber, Roland

Barthes, Emile Durkheim, Erich Fromm, Jacques Maritain, Dominique Grisoni, George Orwell, Theodor Adorno, Ernst Jung, Max Scheler). Unlike the electronic catalogue, the disused card index retains a record of the date of acquisition. The records show that foreign-language editions (including English translations of German thinkers) that appeared after 1953 were mostly acquired within five years of the publication date, although it is impossible to conclude on the basis of this data that their works were collected systematically. During the 1960s, the *Publichka* acquired a particularly large number of foreign-language works in philosophy and theology. Thus Goricheva is correct when she replied to my question about foreign-language editions in the library 'Everything was in the *Publichka*, but few people would read it' (Goricheva, interview).

137 To give only a few examples, *Chasy* no. 1 included Goricheva's translation of one of Karl Jaspers's lectures from the series *Der philosophische Glaube*.

138 Ostanin, interview. The *Book of the Dead*, *Chasy*, no. 17; Beckett, *Breath*, *Chasy*, no. 10, trilogy of Beckett (*Molloy – Melone dies – The Unnameable*) as a literary supplement in 1979; Robbe-Grillet, *Chasy*, no. 59; Bonhoeffer, 'Letters from Prison', *Chasy*, no. 5; Barth, *Christian Ethics*, *Chasy*, no. 7; Tillich, *The Courage to Be,* chapters in *Chasy*, no. 4, *The Protestant Era*, chapters in *Chasy*, nos. 7, 51, 53, 55, 57, 60, 71, 72. A list of all translations published in *Chasy* can be found in the index to the journal, see Andrei Belyi Centre, 'Index of Authors'.

139 Dolinin and Severiukhin, *Preodolenie nemoty*, 96. Severiukhin et al., *Samizdat Leningrada*, provides a list of translated authors on pp. 443–44.

140 Stratanovskii, interview.

141 Severiukhin et al., *Samizdat Leningrada,* 431.

142 Krivulin, '"37", Severnaia pochta', 75.

143 Boris Likhtenfel'd, interview with the author, 25 August 2015.

144 Stratanovskii, interview.

145 Butyrin, 'U istokov Obvodnogo kanala', 126.

Chapter 6

1 Etienne Wenger, *Communities of Practice* (Cambridge: Cambridge University Press, 1999), further developed by David Barton and Karin Tusting in *Beyond Communities of Practice* (Cambridge: Cambridge University Press, 2005).

2 Pierre Bourdieu, *Outline of a Theory of Practice* (Cambridge: Cambridge University Press), 1979. See also his *Language and Symbolic Power* (Cambridge Polity Press, 1991), 30 ff.

3 Wenger, *Beyond Communities of Practice,* 2.

4 Ibid.

5   For a table with details on the persecution of each editor, see Wikipedia, 'Khronika tekushchikh sobytii', last updated 30 April 2020. Available online: https://ru.wikipedia.org/wiki/%D0%A5%D1%80%D0%BE%D0%BD%D0%B8%D0%BA%D0%B0_%D1%82%D0%B5%D0%BA%D1%83%D1%89%D0%B8%D1%85_%D1%81%D0%BE%D0%B1%D1%8B%D1%82%D0%B8%D0%B9 (accessed 17 May 2020).
6   See Chapter 5, n. 93.
7   See Chapter 5, n. 94.
8   Sergei Oushakine, 'The Terrifying Mimicry of Samizdat', *Public Culture* 13, no. 2 (2001): 191–214, 207–08. For a complication of a view which positions dissenters in the same semantic field as official discourse, see Benjamin Nathans and Kevin M.F. Platt, 'Socialist in Form, Indeterminate in Content: The Ins and Outs of Late Soviet Culture', *Ab Imperio*, no. 2 (2011): 301–24, 316–17.
9   The fundamental openness of many groups in the 1970s, which did not employ conspiracy measures precisely because they did not engage in any activities that could be labelled 'dissident', chimes with the assessment of historian and sociologist Nikolai Mitrokhin. He distinguishes between 'underground' groups (*podpol'nye*), that is, circles of like-minded people that were accessible only to the initiated and abounded until the end of the 1960s, and the 'unofficial' cultural and political groups (*neofitsial'nye*) that replaced them after 1968, which existed openly and were tolerated by the security services. See Mitrokhin, *Russkaia partiia*, 183.
10 The quotation is from Sergei Stratanovskii's obituary of Oleg Okhapkin, see Dmitrii Volchek, 'Tol'ko stikhi. Pamiati Olega Okhapkina', Svoboda, 10 October 2008. Available online: http://www.svoboda.org/content/article/468261.html (accessed 23 October 2019).
11 Boris Ostanin and Alexander Kobak, 'Molniia i raduga. Puti kul'tury 60–89-kh godov', in *Molniia i raduga: literaturno-kriticheskie stat'i 1980-kh godov* (St Petersburg: Izdatel'stvo imeni N.I. Novikova, 2003), 9–38, 33.
12 Ostanin defines these terms, see ibid., 14–16.
13 Kolker, 'Ostrova blazhennykh'; emphasis in the original. '*Discrediting the Soviet social or political order*' was the crime punishable under Article 90 of the Soviet Criminal Code.
14 As told to Marco Sabbatini in 'K istorii sozdanii "Severnoi pochty"', 3.
15 The term belongs to Friederike Kind-Kovacs, *Written Here, Published There: How Underground Literature Crossed the Iron Curtain* (Budapest: Central European University Press, 2014), 426.
16 Natalia Chernykh, 'Kontsert dlia geniia pervonachal'noi nishchety'. Available online: http://nattch.narod.ru/nbmironov.html (accessed 15 May 2020).
17 Popularized by and attributed to Stalin, who used it in 1932 at a meeting with Soviet writers. In fact he was quoting the novelist Yurii Olesha. See 'Inzhenery chelovecheskikh dush'.

18 See Chapter 1, n. 52.
19 Elena Rusakova, interview with the author, 9 August 2015. Poet Elena Pudovkina has written a short memoir on her teachers in Derzanie and literary youth clubs in general: Elena Pudovkina, 'Klub "Derzanie"', *Pchela* nos. 26–7 (2000).
20 Svetlana Boym, *Death in Quotation Marks: Cultural Myths of the Modern Poet* (Cambridge, MA: Harvard University Press, 1991), 120.
21 In their theoretical and critical writings many underground writers made conscious use of this stance. Relevant examples, published in *samizdat*, are Boris Ivanov, 'Kul'turnoe dvizhenie kak tselostnoe iavlenie', 37, no. 19 (1979); 'K materialam 2-oi konferentsii kul'turnogo dvizheniia', *Chasy*, no. 24 (1980): 256–78; and A. Kalomirov [Viktor Krivulin], 'Dvadtsat' let noveishei russkoi poezii'. After the fall of the Soviet Union, the same people developed this direction of research: Viktor Krivulin, 'U istochnikov nezavisimoi kul'tury', *Zvezda*, no. 1 (1990): 184–88; 'Peterburgskaia spiritual'naia lirika vchera i segodnia', in Boris Ivanov and Boris Roginskii (eds), *Istoriia leningradskoi nepodtsenzurnoi literatury* (St Petersburg: DEAN, 2000), 99–110; Ivanov, 'Evoliutsiia literaturnykh dvizhenii v piatidesiatye-vos'midesiatye gody'.
22 The term 'leningradskaia shkola' is found, for example, in Savitskii, *Andegraund*, 20; and Vladimir Kreid, 'Stratanovskii i leningradskaia poeticheskaia shkola', *Novyi zhurnal* 155 (1984): 103–14.
23 Krivulin, 'U istochnikov nezavisimoi kul'tury', 185. For a statement to the contrary, see Lev Losev, *On the Beneficence of Censorship: Aesopian Language in Modern Russian Literature* (Munich: Otto Sagner, 1984). Losev, although himself a poet and member of the literary underground, who emigrated in 1976, maintained that censorship could be beneficial to art because it forces a writer to refine his means of expression.
24 There is no room in this study to trace these rediscoveries and developments with the help of concrete examples. For a linguistically informed study on the poetics of the underground, see Liudmila Zubova, *Sovremennaia russkaia poeziia v kontekste istorii iazyka* (Moscow: Novoe literaturnoe obozrenie, 2000). Stanislav Savitskii observes that the Leningrad underground poets' orientation towards literary heritage afforded them the role of conservative philologists trying to define and 'recreate lost historical reality' (Savitskii, *Andegraund*, 119). I write about the significance of religious imagery in their work in von Zitzewitz, *Poetry and the Leningrad Religious-Philosophical Seminar 1976–1980*.
25 Stanislav Savitskii discusses these terms in his *Andegraund*, 43. At the time, those involved seem to have preferred 'unofficial culture'. Compare: Tat'iana Goricheva, 'O neofitsial'noi kul'ture i tserkvi', *Posev* 9 (1979): 45–7; 'Ekzistentsial'no-religioznoe znachenie neofitsial'noi kul'tury', 37, no. 19 (1979); Tatiana Goricheva, Evgenii Pazukhin and Vladimir Poresh, 'Diskussiia o zhurnale *"37"* i obshchikh zadachakh

neofitsial'noi kul'tury', 37, no. 18 (1979); Nechaev, 'Nravstvennoe znachenie neofitsial'noi kul'tury v Rossii'.

26 Anna Katsman (Krivulina), 'Kofe s limonom – vkus vremeni', in Iuliia Valieva (ed.), *Sumerki 'Saigona'* (St Petersburg: Samizdat, 2009), 261–64, 261.

27 Dragomoshchenko, Arkadii and Nikolai Beliak, 'My govorim ne o meste, a o sud'be pokolenia. Beseda s Tat'ianoi Koval'kovoi', in Iuliia Valieva (ed.), *Sumerki 'Saigona'* (St Petersburg: Samizdat, 2009), 146–48, 147.

28 Kirill Kozyrev, interview with the author, 7 July 2015. The two Palaces of Culture Kozyrev mentioned hosted the first officially permitted exhibitions of unofficial artists, in December 1974 and September 1975. See Anatolii Basin and Larisa Skobkina, *Gazanevshchina* (St Petersburg: P.R.P., Seriia Avangard na Neve, 2004).

29 Stratanovskii, interview with the author, 14 August 2015.

30 To give an example, poet Oleg Okhapkin submitted a collection for publication to *Lenizdat* as late as 1978, but ultimately refused to comply with the request of his reviewers to introduce alterations. He described the editor's suggestions as 'they suggest I maim my poems' (cited in *Khristianskii Seminar*, 92).

31 This is how Evgenii Pazukhin describes the Religious-Philosophical Seminar: 'A significant proportion of those who attended the seminar were bohemians, i.e. the regulars of the famous cafe "Saigon". They came to the sessions in order to "get off". There was an almost complete turnover from session to session.' Evgenii Pazukhin, 'Russkaia religioznaia filosofiia v podpol'e', in S. Gorbunova (ed.), *Preobrazhenie: Khristianskii religiozno-filosofskii almanakh* (St Petersburg: Zvezda, 1992), 19.

32 Butyrin, 'U istokov Obvodnogo kanala', 126.

33 Boris V. Dubin, 'Kruzhkovyi steb i massovye kommunikatsii: K sotsiologii kul'turnogo perekhoda', in *Slovo – pis'mo – literatura: Ocherki po sotsiologii sovremennoi kul'tury* (Moscow: Novoe literaturnoe obozrenie, 2001), 164.

34 'Stiob differed from sarcasm, cynicism, derision or any of the more familiar genres of absurd humour in that it required such a degree of *overidentification* with the object, person or idea at which it was directed that it was often impossible to tell whether it was a form of sincere support, subtle ridicule or a peculiar mixture of the two.' Yurchak, *Everything Was Forever*, 250, emphasis in the original.

35 The names of the laureates in different categories can be found online, see Andrei Belyi Prize, 'O premii'.

36 For details, see von Zitzewitz, *Poetry and the Leningrad Religious-Philosophical Seminar 1976–1980*, ch. 1.

37 Polly McMichael makes a similar observation with regard to Soviet rock singer-songwriters within the rock community in Leningrad. See 'After All, You're a Rock and Roll Star (At Least That's What They Say): Roksi and the Creation of the Soviet

Rock Musician', in *The Slavonic and East European Review* 83, no. 4 (2005): 664–84, esp. 667.

38 The reader can convince themselves of the seriousness of the undertaking by reading the talks as published in *37* no. 12 (1977), with an introduction by Shvarts, and from her talks on Fet and on Kuzmin, published in volume 3 of her *Collected Works*. For details on the 'Shimpozium', see Sarah Clovis-Bishop, 'In Memoriam: Elena Andreevna Shvarts (17 March 1948–11 March 2010)', *Slavonica* 16, no. 2 (2010): 112–30, 115–116, and Evgenii Pazukhin, 'Antisotsium', in Valieva, *Sumerki Saigona*, 163–70, 168–69.

39 Kozyrev, interview.

40 An instructive example of such a section can be seen in *37* no. 11 (1977).

41 As a single example, *Chasy* published works by Arkadii Dragomoshchenko, Viktor Krivulin, Elena Shvarts, Elena Ignatova, Alain Robbe-Grillet, Grigorii Pomerants, Sergei Stratanovskii, et al., in the form of 'literaturnoe prilozhenie'.

42 Discussed in Lovell, *The Russian Reading Revolution*, in particular, 50 ff. I discuss the repercussions in Leningrad unofficial culture in von Zitzewitz, 'Reader Questionnaires in Samizdat Journals'.

43 The importance of distinguishing between informal (i.e. uncensored) publishing and platforms that publish indiscriminately has been discussed in Schmidt, 'Postprintium?', 228. Dmitrii Volchek, distinguishes between 'regulated' and 'free-flow' samizdat, citing journals such as his own *Mitin zhurnal* as examples of the first group. Dmitrii Volchek, 'Skol'ko ostalos' zhit' samizdatu', *Mitin zhurnal*, nos. 9/10 (1986), reproduced in *Chasy*, no. 68 (1987).

44 To give a few high-profile examples: Alexander Pushkin started publishing *Sovremennik* in 1836. The journals of the Silver Age include Valerii Briusov's Symbolist *Vesy* (1906–1909), and the Acmeist *Giperborei*, edited by Sergei Gorodetskii and Nikolai Gumilev (1912–1913). In the early Soviet years, Vladimir Mayakovsky edited LEF (1923–1925) and Novyi LEF (1927–1929); in the post-Stalin years the poet Alexander Tvardovskii served as editor-in-chief of *Novyi mir* from 1950–1954 and 1958–1970.

45 A list of their critical works can be found under their biographical entries in *Samizdat Leningrada*.

46 Shortly before his death in 2015, Boris Ivanov published the entire history of Klub-81, including foundation documents and correspondence with official bodies: *Istoriia Kluba-81*. Originals of a list of members and foundation documents are held in the archive of the Research and Information Centre Memorial, St Petersburg.

47 Ivanov, *Istoriia Kluba-81*, 32.

48 Ibid., 34.

49 Kolker, 'Leningradskii Klub 81'.

50 Klub-81 and *Krug* are described in Severiukhin et al., *Samizdat Leningrada*, 410–13 and 415–16 respectively.
51 For the Solzhenitsyn Foundation, see Chapter 1, n. 27. For the Christian Seminar, see Chapter 5, n. 94.
52 Ivanov, *Istoriia Kluba-81,* 28–9, 37.
53 Ibid., 46.
54 Ivanov's memoir confirms this thesis. Eduard Shneiderman, himself a member of Klub-81, describes this process and provides a list of new tamizdat publications in 'Klub-81 i KGB,' *Zvezda*, no. 8 (2004): 209–17.
55 Severiukhin et al., *Samizdat Leningrada*, 170–71.
56 Kolker, 'Leningradskii Klub 81'.
57 Eduard Shneiderman, 'Chto ia izdaval, v chem ia uchastvoval', in Viacheslav Dolinin and Boris Ivanov (eds), *Samizdat: Po materialam konferentsii '30 let nezavisimoi pechati; 1950–80 gody'* (St Petersburg: NITs 'Memorial', 1993), 46–57, 55. Shneiderman was one of the editors of *Ostrova* and links the anthology to the emergence of Klub-81.
58 Yurii Kolker, 'Ostrovitianki: iz Antologii *Ostrova*', *Strelets* 10 (1987). Available online: http://yuri-kolker.com/articles/Ostrovityanki.htm (accessed 21 September 2018).
59 Shneiderman, 'Chto ia izdaval', 55.
60 Kuzminskii and Kovalev, *The Blue Lagoon Anthology of Modern Russian Poetry*.
61 See Yurii Novikov, 'Stroitel' vavilonskoi bashni (K portretu K. Kuz'minskogo)', *Novoe Literaturnoe Obozrenie* 31 (1998): 328–33.
62 Kolker, 'Ostrovitianki'.
63 For bibliographical information, see Severiukhin et al., *Samizdat Leningrada*, 438–39; and Shneiderman, 'Chto ia izdaval', 56.
64 Some individual writers – Shvarts, Dragomoshchenko, Stratanovskii – have achieved individual fame and are actively studied. There are now several book-length studies on the aesthetics and literary theory of the Leningrad underground, including Savitskii's *Andegraund*; Marco Sabbatini, *'Quel Che Si Metteva In Rima': Cultura E Poesia Underground a Leningrado* (Salerno: Europa Orientalis, 2008); Zhitenev, *Poeziia neomodernizma*; the essay collection *Vtoraia kul'tura: Neofitsial'naia poeziia Leningrada v 1970-e–1980-e gody*, edited by Jean-Philippe Jaccard; von Zitzewitz, *Poetry and the Leningrad Religious-Philosophical Seminar 1974–1980*.
65 Conferences: Vtoraia kul'tura: Neofitsial'naia poeziia Leningrada v 1970-e–1980-e gody (University of Geneva, 2011); 'Poetika i poetologiia iazykovykh poiskov v nepodtsenzurnoi i sovremennoi poezii' (Higher School of Economics, Moscow, organized in collaboration with the University of Trier- DFG-Kolleg-Forschungsgruppe 'Russischsprachige Lyrik in Transition', 2018). See Nikolai

Podosokorskii, 'Konferentsiia "Poetika i poetologiia iazykovykh poiskov v nepodtsenzurnoi i sovremennoi poezii"', *Live Journal*, 25 April 2019. Available online: https://philologist.livejournal.com/10873150.html (accessed 17 May 2020).

66 Two highly frequented groups are: International Samizdat [Research] Association. Facebook community, created 22 October 2012. Available online: https://www.facebook.com/samizdat.community/; and Samizdat. Facebook group. Available online: https://www.facebook.com/groups/353375628083079/ (both accessed 16 May 2020).

67 Mark Lipovetsky, Tomáš Glanc, Maria Engström, Ilja Kukui and Klavdia Smola (eds), *The Oxford Handbook of Soviet Underground Culture* (Oxford: Oxford University Press, forthcoming 2021).

68 Stratanovskii, interview.

69 Kozyrev, interview.

70 Stratanovskii, interview.

71 A review of *Chasy* no. 15, reviewed in *Summa* in 1979, affirms: 'In these publications the Leningrad cultural movement explained itself as a phenomenon and recognized its own issues' (republished in Vershik et al., *"Summa" – za svobodnuiu mysl'*, 86). The author of this review is Sergei Maslov, whose perceptive analysis already emphasizes *Chasy*'s preoccupation with reflecting the situation of unofficial culture. The writer and editor Andrei Ar'ev, who has been editing the prominent literary journal *Zvezda* (Star) since 1990, remarked that 'those underground [writers] which later, beginning in the late 1980s, began to appear in print, had mainly passed through *Chasy*' (Andrei Ar'ev, interview with the author, 16 July 2015).

72 Definitions of canonicity are naturally contingent. Comparatively non-contentious ones include: (1) published book-length collections, (2) inclusion in anthologies not focused on the 'underground', (3) published translations, both single-author collections and anthologized poems, and (4) scholarly interest beyond studies focused on the social aspects of unofficial culture. The 'big names' of Leningrad unofficial poetry – Krivulin, Shvarts, Stratanovskii, Dragomoshchenko and a few others – fulfil every one of them.

73 And they were successful: *Novoe Literaturnoe Obozrenie*, the most prestigious Russian literary and academic journal today, dedicated their central section to 'Leningrad Poetry from the 1950s–1980s' as early as 1995 (no. 14); the editors understood 'Leningrad Poetry' to mean 'unofficial poetry', publishing material relating to the people whose names feature in this and the preceding chapter. No. 115 in 2012 dedicated a section to 'From the Archives of Leningrad Uncensored Poetry', in honour of Elena Shvarts and Alexander Mironov who both died in 2010.

74 Dolinin and Ivanov, *Samizdat*.

75 Dolinin and Severiukhin, *Preodolenie nemoty*. Dolinin also published a miscellaneous collection of stories and memories about his activity: Viacheslav

Dolinin, *Ne stol' otdalennaia kochegarka: Rasskazy, vospominaniia* (St Petersburg: Izdatel'stvo N.I. Novikova, 2005).

76 Compare his work pre-Perestroika: Ivanov, 'Po tu storonu ofitsial'nosti (iz knigi "Chazy kul'tury")'; 'Povtorenie proidennogo', *Chasy*, no. 12 (1978); 'Tserkovnaia vera i vera v miru', *Chasy*, no. 13 (1978): 157–78; 'Kul'turnoe dvizheniie kak tselostnoe iavlenie', *37*, no. 19 (1979); 'K materialam 2-oi konferentsii kul'turnogo dvizheniia', *Chasy*, no. 24 (1980): 256–78. And these are some examples of his publications after the end of the Soviet Union: 'Po tu storonu ofitsial'nosti'; 'V bytnost' Peterburga Leningradom'; 'Evoliutsiia literaturnykh dvizhenii v piatidesiatye-vos'midesiatye gody'.

77 This phenomenon has been analysed in Jens Herlth, '"Chem ty dyshish' i zhivesh' … ": O sootnoshenii istorii i kul'tury v tvorchestve Viktora Krivulina', in Jean-Philippe Jaccard (ed.), *Vtoraia kul'tura: Neofitsial'naia poeziia Leningrada v 1970-e–1980-e gody* (St Petersburg: Rostok, 2013), 309–27, 309–11.

78 Published in *Severnaia pochta* 1/2 (1979), see Kalomirov [Krivulin], 'Dvadtsat' let noveishei russkoi poezii'.

79 Stratanovskii, interview.

80 In their introduction to the *Collected Works* of Leonid Aronzon, editors Petr Kazarnovskii and Ilya Kukui note that Aronzon, who died in 1970, did not get the exposure he deserved even in the literary underground precisely because the mechanisms set in motion by the journals and the groups around them were not in place during his lifetime. Kazarnovskii and Kukui, 'Vmesto predisloviia', 17.

81 Leonid Zhmud's testimony refers to academic humanities rather than literature, but is nevertheless valid here as it illustrates a point that was very specific to the Soviet context: 'In the Soviet Union of the 1970s, the situation was altogether different. Only a Party inspector or director could allow himself to criticize Ivanov, Averintsev, Lotman or Bakhtin, but certainly no decent person who was a member of the academic community. Criticism was interpreted in a Soviet vein, that is, as an element of social struggle and something that would inevitably entail organizational consequences.' Zhmud', 'Studenty-istoriki mezhdu ofitsiozom i "liberal'noi"', 208.

82 Kolker, 'Ostrovitianki'.

83 Wenger, *Communities of Practice*, 58–9.

84 Wenger's concept of reification in relation to language-based interaction is discussed in David Barton and Mary Hamilton, 'Literacy, Reification and the Dynamics of Social Interaction', in *Beyond Communities of Practice* (Cambridge: Cambridge University Press, 2005), 14–35. Journals score high on all four features of reification: succinctness and power to evoke meanings – a typescript journal triggers immediate associations; portability across time, physical space and context – digitization on the one hand and scholarship on the other make this possible; physical durability – the journals explicitly recorded a culture that had

been oral, and many are now digitized; and focusing effect – their ability to draw attention to specific features within social reality (ibid., 27).
85 I discuss this phenomenon in von Zitzewitz, 'Self-Canonisation as a Way into the Canon'.
86 The volume Ansberg and Margolis, *Obshchestvennaia zhizn' Leningrada v gody perestroiki: Sbornik materialov* documents the mushrooming of semi-official (i.e. not linked to a Soviet institution but acting in the open) publishing houses and journals in the 1990s. For a distinction between samizdat and the 'alternative press' that began in 1987, see 'Katalog periodicheskikh i prodolzhaiushchikhsia neformal'nykh izdanii na russkom iazyke v arkhive samizdata', *Materialy samizdata*, no. 8 (1991): iii; Elena Strukova, *Al'ternativnaia periodicheskaia pechat' v istorii rossiiskoi mnogopartiinosti (1987–1996)* (Moscow: Istoricheskaia biblioteka, 2005), 24–5.

Conclusion

1 Harrison C. White, *Identity and Control: A Structural Theory of Social Action* (Princeton, NJ: Princeton University Press, 1992).
2 DeNel Rehberg Sedo, 'An Introduction to Reading Communities: Process and Formations', in DeNel Rehberg Sedo (ed.), *Reading Communities: From Salons to Cyberspace* (Basingstoke: Palgrave Macmillan, 2011), 5. Research into reading communities is a thriving interdisciplinary field, bringing together historians, sociologists, anthropologists and literary scholars. A search on the catalogue of the British Library yields forty-eight entries for book-length studies.
3 Boris Dubin, *Klassika, posle i riadom: Sotsiologicheskie ocherki o literature i kul'ture* (Moscow: Novoe literaturnoe obozrenie, 2010), 121–23.
4 Anatolii Vershik, interview with the author, 31 July 2015.
5 Benedict Anderson, *Imagined Communities: Reflections on the Origin and Spread of Nationalism* (London: Verso, 1991), 224.

Bibliography

Archives used

Archive of the International Memorial Society, Moscow.
Archive of the Research and Information Centre Memorial, St Petersburg.
Archive of the Research Centre for East European Studies (Forschungsstelle Osteuropa, FSO), University of Bremen.

Personal websites of samizdat activists

Igrunov, Viacheslav, 'Dissdenstvo: istoki i smysl'. Available online: http://igrunov.ru/vin/vchk-vin-dissid/smysl/1058065392/ (accessed 15 May 2020).
Smirnov, Aleksei, 'Biografiia'. Available online: http://gendirector1.blogspot.com/p/blog-page.html (accessed 15 May 2020).

Digital repositories of samizdat

Andrei Belyi Centre, 'Index of Authors', last updated 13 December 2013. Available online: http://samizdat.wiki/%D0%97%D0%B0%D0%B3%D0%BB%D0%B0%D0%B2%D0%BD%D0%B0%D1%8F_%D1%81%D1%82%D1%80%D0%B0%D0%BD%D0%B8%D1%86%D0%B0 (accessed 15 May 2020).
Igrunov, V., M. Barbakadze and E. Shvarts, *Antologiia samizdata*. Available online: http://antology.igrunov.ru/ (accessed 15 May 2020).
International Memorial, 'Obzor fondov Archiva istorii inakomysliia'. Available online: https://www.memo.ru/ru-ru/collections/archives/dissidents/guide/ (accessed 15 May 2020).
'Izdatel'stvo "Ekho"'. Available online: http://russianemigrant.ru/tag/izdatelstvo-eho (accessed 7 October 2019).
Keston Center for Religion, Politics and Society. Available online: https://www.baylor.edu/kestoncenter/ (accessed 15 May 2020).
'Map of Soviet Samizdat Periodicals'. Available online: https://utoronto.maps.arcgis.com/apps/webappviewer/index.html?id=2eeb4a7c24254ffe96008429a3d1c6b8 (accessed 4 May 2019).

Neofitsial'naia poeziia: Antologiia: Anthology. Available online: http://rvb.ru/np/ (accessed 15 May 2020).

OSA Catalog, 'Russian'. Available online: http://catalog.osaarchivum.org/?f%5Blanguage_facet%5D%5B%5D=Russian&f%5Brecord_origin_facet%5D%5B%5D=Digital+Repository (accessed 13 May 2020).

Project for the Study of Dissidence and Samizdat. Available online: https://samizdatcollections.library.utoronto.ca/ (accessed 15 May 2020).

Research and Information Centre Memorial St Petersburg, 'Obshchestvennyi archiv po istorii sovetskogo terrora'. Available online: http://iofe.center/elarch (accessed 15 May 2020).

Research Centre for East European Studies at the University of Bremen (Forschungsstelle Osteuropa, FSO), 'Archives and Research News'. Available online: https://www.forschungsstelle.uni-bremen.de/en/9/20110606113229/Archive_Library.html (accessed 15 May 2020).

'Second Literature': Elektronnyi archiv zarubezh'ia imeni Andreia Siniavskogo. Available online: https://vtoraya-literatura.com/ (accessed 15 May 2020).

Soviet Samizdat Periodicals. Available online: https://samizdat.library.utoronto.ca/ (accessed 15 May 2020).

Tamizdat Project. Available online: http://tamizdatproject.org/en (accessed 13 May 2020).

Interviews

Olga Abramovich, 22 August 2015.
Boris Aksel'rod, 18 August 2015.
Andrei Ar'ev, 16 July 2015.
Natalia Dobkina, 11 August 2015.
Galina Drozdetskaia, 10 July 2015.
Nikolai Gol', 20 August 2015.
Tatiana Goricheva, 2 July 2015.
Kirill Kozyrev, 7 July 2015.
Boris Likhtenfel'd, 25 July 2015.
Boris Ostanin, 20 August 2015.
Tatiana Pritykina, 13 July 2015.
Elena Rusakova, 9 August 2015.
Mikhail Sheinker, 26 July 2015.
Sergei Stratanovskii, 14 August 2015.
Irina Tsurkova, 13 July 2015.
Anatolii Vershik, 31 July 2015.
Dmitrii Volchek, 27 August 2015.
Natalia Volokhonskaia, 12 July 2015.
Irina Roskina, letter to Gennadii Kuzovkin, July 2017.

References

Adams, Thomas R. and Nicholas Barker, 'A New Model for the Study of the Book', in *A Potencie of Life: Books in Society* (London: British Library, 1993), 5–44.

Alekseeva, Liudmila, *Istoriia inakomysliia v SSSR* (New York: Khronika Press, 1984; New edition, Moscow: RITs Zatsepa, 2001).

Alekseeva, Liudmila, *Pokolenie ottepeli* (Moscow: Zakharov, 2006).

Alekseeva, Liudmila, *Soviet Dissent: Contemporary Movements for National, Religious, and Human Rights*, translated by Carol Pearce and John Glad (Middletown, CT: Wesleyan University Press, 1985).

Anderson, Benedict, *Imagined Communities: Reflections on the Origin and Spread of Nationalism* (London: Verso, 1991).

Andrei Belyi Centre, 'Arkhiv zhurnala "Chasy"', last updated 28 February 2014. Available online: http://samizdat.wiki/%D0%90%D1%80%D1%85%D0%B8%D0%B2_%D0%B6%D1%83%D1%80%D0%BD%D0%B0%D0%BB%D0%B0_%C2%AB%D0%A7%D0%B0%D1%81%D1%8B%C2%BB (accessed 16 May 2020).

Andrei Belyi Centre, 'Zhurnal "Chasy", Tom No 1', last updated 25 June 2013. Available online: http://arch.susla.ru/index.php/%D0%96%D1%83%D1%80%D0%BD%D0%B0%D0%BB_%C2%AB%D0%A7%D0%B0%D1%81%D1%8B%C2%BB,_%D0%A2%D0%BE%D0%BC_%E2%84%961 (accessed 16 May 2020).

Andrei Belyi Prize, 'O premii'. Available online: http://belyprize.ru/index.php?id=9 (accessed 7 October 2019).

Anonymous, 'Na seminare "Religiia i kul'tura"', *Chasy*, no. 15 (1978).

Ansberg, O.N. and A.D. Margolis (eds), *Obshchestvennaia zhizn' Leningrada v gody perestroiki. Sbornik materialov* (St Petersburg: Serebriannyi vek, 2009).

Aronson, M. and S. Reiser, *Literaturnye kruzhki i salony* (1929; St Petersburg: Akademicheskii proekt, 2001).

Bagno V.E., et al., *Bashnia Viacheslava Ivanova i kul'tura Serebrianogo veka* (St Petersburg: Filologicheskii Fakultet Gosudarstvennogo universiteta, 2006).

Basin, Anatolii and Larisa Skobkina, *Gazanevshchina* (St Petersburg: P.R.P., Seriia Avangard na Neve, 2004).

Barron, John, *KGB: The Secret Work of Soviet Secret Agents* (New York: Reader's Digest Press, 1974).

Barton, David and Mary Hamilton, 'Literacy, Reification and the Dynamics of Social Interaction', in *Beyond Communities of Practice* (Cambridge: Cambridge University Press, 2005).

Barton, David and Karin Tusting, *Beyond Communities of Practice* (Cambridge: Cambridge University Press, 2005).

Belenkin, Boris, '"Rukopisnoe" ili "pechatnoe"? "Pechatnoe" kak "rukopisnoe"? Malotirazhnye izdaniia v kontekste sovremennogo kul'turnogo protsessa', in *Acta Samizdatica: Zapiski o samizdate*, pilot edition (Moscow: GPIB Rossii – Mezhdunarodnyi 'Memorial' – 'Zvenia', 2012), 14–23.

Bel'tser, Larisa, 'Operatsiia "Gutenberg-1984"', *Cogita*, 9 March 2017. Available online: http://www.cogita.ru/a.n.-alekseev/publikacii-a.n.alekseeva/operaciya-gutenberg20131984 (accessed 20 June 2018).

B.I. [Boris Ivanov], 'Na seminare', *Chasy*, no. 12 (1978).

Borodin, Leonid, *Bez vybora* (Moscow: Molodaia gvardiia, 2003).

Bourdieu, Pierre, *Language and Symbolic Power* (Cambridge: Polity Press, 1991).

Bourdieu, Pierre, *Outline of a Theory of Practice* (Cambridge: Cambridge University Press, 1979).

Boym, Svetlana, *Death in Quotation Marks: Cultural Myths of the Modern Poet* (Cambridge, MA: Harvard University Press, 1991).

Brudny, Yitzhak, *Reinventing Russia. Russian Nationalism and the Soviet State 1953–1991* (Cambridge, MA: Harvard University Press, 1998).

Butov, Petr, 'Vospominaniia ob Odesskikh dissidentakh', parts 1 and 2. Available online: http://igrunov.ru/cv/odessa/dissident_od/samizdat/1109017845.html (accessed 14 September 2019).

Butov, Petr, 'Vospominaniia ob Odesskikh dissidentakh', part 3. Available online: http://igrunov.ru/cv/odessa/dissident_od/samizdat/1110809385.html (accessed 4 April 2019).

Butyrin, Kirill, 'U istokov Obvodnogo kanala', in Viacheslav Dolinin and Boris Ivanov (eds), *Samizdat: Po materialam konferentsii '30 let nezavisimoi pechati; 1950–80 gody'; S.-Peterburg, 25–27 aprelia 1992* (St Petersburg: NITs 'Memorial', 1993), 124–29.

Chernykh, Natalia, 'Kontsert dlia geniia pervonachal'noi nishchety'. Available online: http://nattch.narod.ru/nbmironov.html (accessed 15 May 2020).

Clovis-Bishop, Sarah, 'In Memoriam: Elena Andreevna Shvarts (17 March 1948–11 March 2010)', *Slavonica* 16, no. 2 (2010): 112–30.

Daniel', Aleksandr, Ekho Moskvy, 2019. Available online: https://echo.msk.ru/guests/8880/ (accessed 13 May 2020).

Daniel', Aleksandr, 'Istoki i smysl sovetskogo samizdata', in V. Igrunov, M. Barbakadze and E. Shvarts (eds), *Antologiia samizdata: nepodtsenzurnaia literatura v SSSR 1950-e–1980-e* (Moscow: Mezhdunarodnyi institut gumanitarno-politicheskikh issledovanii, 2005), vol. 1, 17–33.

Daniel', Aleksandr, 'Chelovek protiv SSSR' [lecture series], Arzamas. Available online: https://arzamas.academy/courses/40 (accessed 15 June 2018).

Darnton, Robert, 'What Is the History of Books?', *Daedalus* 111, no. 3 (1982): 65–83.

Dediulin, Sergei, 'Severnaia pochta. Zhurnal stikhov i kritiki', Bibliograf vypusk 2 (Paris: Russkii institut v Parizhe, 2001).

Dediulin, Sergei, '"Tam byl gorod." "Severnaia pochta": iz vozpominanii o real'nom sotrudnichestve redaktsii s poetami i kritikami', in Jean-Philippe Jaccard (ed.), *Vtoraia kul'tura: Neofitsial'naia poeziia Leningrada v 1970-e–1980-e gody* (St Petersburg: Rostok, 2013), 84–113.

'Delo "levoi oppozitsii" 3 (1979, 4–1)', *Vesti iz SSSR*, no. 4 (16 February 1979). Available online: https://vesti-iz-sssr.com/2016/11/20/delo-levoi-oppositsii-1979-4-1/ (accessed 14 June 2019).

de Zwart, Melissa and David Lindsay, 'Governance and the Global Metaverse', in Daniel Riha and Anna Maj (eds), *Emerging Practices in Cyberculture and Social Networking* (Amsterdam: Rodopi, 2010), 65–82.

Dolinin, Viacheslav, *Ne stol' otdalennaia kochegarka: Rasskazy, vospominaniia* (St Petersburg: Izdatel'stvo Novikovoi, 2005).

Dolinin, Viacheslav, 'Predislovie', *Akt – Literaturnyi samizdat* 3 (2001): 1.

Dolinin, Viacheslav, 'Summa v kontekste samizdata', in *Summa' – za svobodnuiu mysl'* (St Petersburg: Zvezda, 2009), 21–30.

Dolinin, Viacheslav and Boris Ivanov (eds), *Samizdat: Po materialam konferentsii '30 let nezavisimoi pechati. 1950–80 gody'; S.-Peterburg, 25–27 aprelia 1992* (St Petersburg: NITs 'Memorial', 1993).

Dolinin, Viacheslav and Dmitrii Severiukhin (eds), *Preodolenie nemoty: Leningradskii samizdat v kontekste nezavisimogo kul'turnogo dvizheniia (1953–1991)* (St Petersburg: Izdatel'stvo Novikovoi, 2003).

Dragomoshchenko, Arkadii and Nikolai Beliak, 'My govorim ne o meste, a o sud'be pokoleniia. Beseda s Tat'ianoi Koval'kovoi', in Iuliia Valieva (ed.), *Sumerki 'Saigona'* (St Petersburg: Samizdat, 2009), 146–48.

Dubin, Boris, *Klassika, posle i riadom: Sotsiologicheskie ocherki o literature i kul'ture* (Moscow: Novoe literaturnoe obozrenie, 2010).

Dubin, Boris, 'Kruzhkovyi steb i massovye kommunikatsii: K sotsiologii kul'turnogo perekhoda', in *Slovo – pis'mo – literatura: Ocherki po sotsiologii sovremennoi kul'tury* (Moscow: Novoe literaturnoe obozrenie, 2001).

Dunlop, John (ed.), *VSKhSON: Materialy suda i programma*; Vol'noe slovo; Samizdat. Izbrannoe, vol. 22 (Frankfurt: Posev, 1976).

Eisenstein, Elizabeth, *The Printing Press as an Agent of Change: Communication and Cultural Transformations in Early Modern Europe* (Cambridge: Cambridge University Press, 1979).

Ellis, Jane, *The Russian Orthodox Church: A Contemporary History*, Keston Book No. 22 (London: Croom Helm, 1986).

Etkind, Efim, *Zapiski nezagovorshchika* (London: Overseas Publications Interchange, 1977).

Ezerskaia, Bella, 'Kak eto bylo v Odesse', *Vestnik* no. 11 (348) (2004). Available online: http://www.vestnik.com/issues/2004/0526/win/ezersky.htm (accessed 14 September 2019).

Feldbrugge, F.J., *Samizdat and Political Dissent in the Soviet Union* (Leyden: A.W. Sijthoff, 1975).

Fokin, Maria (ed.), 'Chronicle of Current Events', translated by Julie Draskoczy. Available online: http://www.memo.ru/history/diss/chr/ (accessed 4 September 2019).

Franklin, Simon, 'Mapping the Graphosphere: Cultures of Writing in Early 19th-Century Russia (and Before)', *Kritika* 12, no. 3 (2011): 531–60.

Fraser, Nancy, 'Rethinking the Public Sphere: A Contribution to the Critique of Actually Existing Democracy', in Craig Calhoun (ed.), *Habermas and the Public Sphere* (Cambridge, MA: MIT Press, 1992), 109–42.

Ginzburg, Aleksandr, *Belaia kniga* (Frankfurt: Posev, 1967).

Glotser, V. and E. Chukovskaia (eds), *Slovo probivaet sebe dorogu: Sbornik statei i dokumentov ob A.I. Solzhenitsyne; 1962–1974* (Moscow: Izdatel'stvo Russkii put', 1998).

Golomshtok, Igor', *Zaniatie dlia starogo gorodovogo: Memuary pessimista* (Moscow: AST, 2015).

Gollerbakh, Evgenii, 'Table of contents for the journal *Obvodnyi kanal*' unpublished.

Gorbanevskaia, Natalia, *Polden': Delo o demonstratsii 25 avgusta 1968 goda na Krasnoi ploshchadi* (Moscow: Novoe izdatel'stvo, 2007).

Goricheva, Tat'iana, 'Ekzistentsial'no-religioznoe znachenie neofitsial'noi kul'tury', *37*, no. 19 (1979).

Goricheva, Tat'iana, 'Mne nadoeli podval'nost i elitarnost' "Vtoroi kul'tury"', interview with Raisa Orlova, 1985. Available online, in an abbreviated form: http://gefter.ru/archive/17640 (accessed 3 March 2018).

Goricheva, Tat'iana, 'O neofitsial'noi kul'ture i tserkvi', *Posev* 9 (1979): 45–7.

Goricheva, Tatiana, *Talking About God Is Dangerous: My Experiences in the East and in the West* (London: SCM, 1986).

Goricheva, Tat'iana, 'Zadachi khristianskogo prosveshcheniia: Vystuplenie na vstrechi redaktsii, avtorov i chitatelei dvukh svobodnykh religioznykh zhurnalov, "Obshchina" (Moskva) i zhurnala khristianskoi kul'tury "37" (Leningrad); Leningrad, 22 fevralia 1979', in *Khristianskii Seminar*, vol. 39 (Frankfurt: Posev, 1981), 34–41.

Goricheva, Tat'iana, Evgenii Pazukhin and Vladimir Poresh, 'Diskussiia o zhurnale "37" i obshchikh zadachakh neofitsial'noi kul'tury', *37*, no. 18 (1979).

Gorny, Eugene, *A Creative History of the Russian Internet* (Saarbrücken: VDM Verlag, 2009).

Haigh, Maria, 'Downloading Communism: File Sharing as Samizdat in Ukraine', *Libri* 57 (2007): 165–78.

Hänsgen, Sabine, 'The Media Dimension of Samizdat: The Präprintium Exhibition Project', in Valentina Parisi (ed.), *Samizdat: Between Practices and Representations; Lecture Series at Open Society Archives, Budapest, February–June 2013* (Budapest: Central European University/IAS, 2015), 47–62.

Herlth, Jens, '"Chem ty dyshish' i zhivesh' …": O sootnoshenii istorii i kul'tury v tvorchestve Viktora Krivulina', in Jean-Philippe Jaccard (ed.), *Vtoraia kul'tura: Neofitsial'naia poeziia Leningrada v 1970-e–1980-e gody* (St Petersburg: Rostok, 2013), 309–27.

Hirt, Günter [Georg Witte] and Sascha Wonders [Sabine Hänsgen], *Präprintium: Moskauer Bücher aus dem Samisdat* (Bremen: Edition Temmen, 1998).

Igrunov, Viacheslav, 'Beseda o "Khronike tekushchikh sobytii" i biblioteke samizdata', interview with Gennadii Kuzovkin and Nikolai Kostenko, 31 January 2004. Available online: http://www.igrunov.ru/cv/vchk-cv-memotalks/talks/about-chronika-et-samisd.html (accessed 4 September 2019).

Igrunov, Viacheslav, 'Ia byl dissident v dissidenstve', interview with Gleb Morev, in Gleb Morev (ed.), *Dissidenty: Dvadtsat' razgovorov* (Moscow: Izdatel'stvo AST, 2017), 195–218.

Igrunov, Viacheslav, 'Neofitsial'naia literatura i nekotorye voprosy praktiki' and 'K problematike obshchestvennogo dvizhenia'. Available online: http://igrunov.ru/cv/vchk-cv-chosenpubl/vchk-cv-chosenpubl-ego.html (accessed 1 October 2019).

Igrunov, Viacheslav, 'O biblioteke Samizdata, o Gruppe sodeiztviia kul'turnomu obmenu i o Larise Bogoraz-Brukhman', interview with E.S. Shvarts, 2001. Available online: http://www.igrunov.ru/cv/vchk-cv-memotalks/talks/vchk-cv-memotalks-talks-bogoraz.html (accessed 20 August 2019).

Igrunov, Viacheslav, 'Odesskaia biblioteka samizdata: 1967–1982', interview with Elena Strukova, July–August 2005. Available online: http://igrunov.ru/cv/odessa/dissident_od/samizdat/1123138219.html (accessed 4 September 2019).

Igrunov, Viacheslav, 'Primernaia struktura biblioteki samizdata v Odesse'. Available online: http://igrunov.ru/cv/odessa/dissident_od/samizdat/library-structure.html (accessed 14 September 2019).

Igrunov, Viacheslav, M. Barbakadze and E. Shvarts (eds), *Antologiia samizdata: nepodtsenzurnaia literatura v SSSR 1950-e–1980-e*, 4 vols. (Moscow: Mezhdunarodnyi institut gumanitarno-politicheskikh issledovanii, 2005).

International Memorial Society, 'Chteniia pamiati Arseniia Roginskogo' Roginskogo: Den' vtoroy', YouTube, 30 March 2019. Available online: https://www.youtube.com/watch?v=JwnRcfDkWbk (accessed 17 September 2019).

International Memorial Society, Issledovatel'skaia programma "Istoriia inakomysliia v SSSR. 1954–1987 gg." Available online: https://www.memo.ru/ru-ru/history-of-repressions-and-protest/protest/dissidents/programma-istoriya-inakomysliya-v-sssr-1954-1987-gg/ (accessed 15 June 2018).

'Inzhenery chelovecheskikh dush', in Entsiklopedicheskii slovar' krylatykh slov i vyrazhenii (Moscow: Lokid-Press, 2003). Available online: http://dic.academic.ru/dic.nsf/dic_wingwords/1087/Инженеры (accessed 13 May 2020).

Ishkov, M., I. Akhmet'ev, V. Kulakov and T. Gromova (eds), *Samizdat veka: Neofitsial'naia poeziia; Antologiia* (Minsk: Polifakt, 1998). Available online: http://rvb.ru/np/ (accessed 15 May 2020).

Ivanov, Boris, 'Etapy razvitiia neofitsial'noi literatury 1953–1991', in Dmitrii Severiukhin, Viacheslav Dolinin, Boris Ivanov and Boris Ostanin (eds), *Samizdat Leningrada 1950e–1980e: Literaturnaia entsiklopediia* (Moscow: Novoe literaturnoe obozrenie, 2003), 9–51.

Ivanov, Boris, 'Evoliutsiia literaturnykh dvizhenii v piatidesiatye-vos'midesiatye gody', in Boris Ivanov and Boris Roginskii (eds), *Istoriia leningradskoi nepodtsenzurnoi literatury* (St Petersburg: DEAN, 2000), 17–28.
Ivanov, Boris, *Istoriia Kluba-81* (St Petersburg: Izdatel'stvo Ivana Limbakha, 2015).
Ivanov, Boris, 'K materialam 2-oi konferentsii kul'turnogo dvizheniia', *Chasy*, no. 24 (1980): 256–78.
Ivanov, Boris, 'Kul'turnoe dvizheniie kak tselostnoe iavlenie', 37, no. 19 (1979).
Ivanov, Boris (ed.), *Peterburgskaia poeziia v litsakh* (Moscow: Novoe literaturnoe obozrenie, 2011).
Ivanov, Boris, 'Po tu storonu ofitsial'nosti', in Viacheslav Dolinin and Boris Ivanov (eds), *Samizdat: Po materialam konferentsii '30 let nezavisimoi pechati; 1950–80 gody'* (St Petersburg: NITs 'Memorial', 1993), 82–93.
Ivanov, Boris, 'Povtorenie proidennogo', *Chasy*, no. 12 (1978).
Ivanov, Boris, 'Tserkovnaia vera i vera v miru', *Chasy*, no. 13 (1978): 157–78.
Ivanov, Boris, 'V bytnost' Peterburga Leningradom: O leningradskom samizdate', *Novoe Literaturnoe Obozrenie* 14 (1995): 188–99.
Ivanov, Boris and Iurii Novikov (eds), *Krug: Literaturno-khudozehstvennyi sbornik* (Leningrad: Sovetskii pisatel', 1985).
Ivanov, Boris and Boris Roginskii (eds), *Istoriia leningradskoi nepodtsenzurnoi literatury* (St Petersburg: DEAN, 2000).
Jaccard, Jean-Philippe (ed.), *Vtoraia kul'tura: Neofitsial'naia poeziia Leningrada v 1970-e–1980-e gody* (St Petersburg: Rostok, 2013).
Janjic, Milutin, *Leningrad's Religious-Philosophical Seminar: A Place of Encounter between Text and Mission* (Berkeley, CA: Graduate Theological Union, 2015).
Kalomirov, A. [Viktor Krivulin], 'Dvadtsat' let noveishei russkoi poezii', *Severnaia pochta* 1/2 (1979): 38–59. Available online: http://gendelev.org/kontekst/leningrad/439-viktor-krivulin-dvadtsat-let-novejshej-russkoj-poezii.html (accessed 4 March 2019).
Kalomirov, A. [Viktor Krivulin], 'Problema sovremennoi russkoi poezii: Stat'ia 1; Iosif Brodskii; Mesto', 37, no. 9 (1977): 204–14.
'Katalog periodicheskikh i prodolzhaiushchikhsia neformal'nykh izdanii na russkom iazyke v arkhive samizdata', *Materialy samizdata*, no. 8 (1991): iii.
Katsman (Krivulina), Anna, 'Kofe s limonom – vkus vremeni', in Iuliia Valieva (ed.), *Sumerki 'Saigona'* (St Petersburg: Samizdat, 2009), 261–64.
Kazarnovskii, Petr and Il'ia Kukui, 'Vmesto predisloviia', in Leonid Aronzon, (ed.), *Sobranie proizvedenii*, vol. 1 (St Petersburg: Izdatel'stvo Ivana Limbakha, 2006), 7–20.
Khersonskii, Boris, 'Beseda s Borisom Khersonskim 1. iiunia 2002 g. Odessa', interview with E.S. Shvarts. Available online: http://www.igrunov.ru/cv/vchk-cv-side/vchk-cv-side-stories-herson.html (accessed 14 September 2019).
Khersonskii, Boris, 'Pamiati semidesiatykh', 2 November 2008. Available online: https://magazines.gorky.media/interpoezia/2008/2/pamyati-semidesyatyh.html (accessed 14 September 2019).

Khodorovich, Sergei, 'My nakhodili v sebe sily protivostoiat' idiotskomu bezumiiu', interview with Gleb Morev, in Gleb Morev (ed.), *Dissidenty: Dvadtsat' razgovorov* (Moscow: Izdatel'stvo AST, 2017), 247–75.

Kind-Kovacs, Friederike, 'Radio Free Europe and Radio Liberty as the "Echo Chamber" of Tamizdat', in Friederike Kind-Kovacs and Jessie Labov (eds), *Samizdat, Tamizdat and Beyond: Transnational Media during and after Socialism* (New York: Berghahn, 2013), 70–91.

Kind-Kovacs, Friederike, *Written Here, Published There: How Underground Literature Crossed the Iron Curtain* (Budapest: Central European University Press, 2014).

Kind-Kovacs, Friederike and Jessie Labov, 'Introduction', in Friederike Kind-Kovacs and Jessie Labov (eds), *Samizdat, Tamizdat and Beyond: Transnational Media during and after Socialism* (New York: Berghahn, 2013), 1–23.

Kind-Kovacs, Friederike and Jessie Labov (eds), *Samizdat, Tamizdat and Beyond: Transnational Media during and after Socialism* (New York: Berghahn, 2013).

Khristianskii Seminar, vol. 39 (Frankfurt: Posev, 1981).

Klots, Iakov '"Rekviem" Akhmatovoy v tamizdate: 56 pisem' ('Requiem' Akhmatova in Tamizdat: 56 Letters), Colta, 24 June 2019. Available online: https://www.colta.ru/articles/literature/21637-rekviem-ahmatovoy-v-tamizdate-56-pisem?fbclid=IwAR0CTmzFHK_QlQGB_slVbQkabMytb_KS3QA12aHqgIUz1_PfOjaBw5deimw (accessed 4 August 2019).

Komaromi, Ann, 'Ardis Facsimile and Reprint Editions: Giving Back Russian Literature', in Friederike Kind-Kovacs and Jessie Labov (eds), *Samizdat, Tamizdat and Beyond: Transnational Media during and after Socialism* (New York: Berghahn, 2013), 27–50.

Komaromi, Ann, 'The Material Existence of Samizdat', *Slavic Review* 63, no. 3 (2004): 597–618

Komaromi, Ann, 'Samizdat and Soviet Dissident Publics', *Slavic Review* 71, no. 1 (2012): 70–90.

Komaromi, Ann, 'Samizdat as Extra-Gutenberg Phenomenon', *Poetics Today* 29, no. 4 (2008): 629–67.

Komaromi, Ann, *Uncensored: Samizdat Novels and the Quest for Autonomy in Soviet Dissidence* (Evanston, IL: Northwestern University Press, 2015).

Kolker, Yurii, 'Leningradskii Klub 81', *Dvadtsat' Dva* 39 (1984). Available online: http://yuri-kolker.com/articles/Club-81.htm (accessed 4 March 2019).

Kolker, Yurii, 'Ostrova blazhennykh: Vtoraia literatura i samizdat v Leningrade', *Strana i mir*, nos. 1–2 (1985). Available online: http://yuri-kolker.com/articles/Ostrova_blazhennykh.htm (accessed 21 September 2018).

Kolker, Yurii, 'Ostrovitianki. Iz Antologii "Ostrova"', *Strelets* 10 (1987). Available online: http://yuri-kolker.com/articles/Ostrovityanki.htm (accessed 21 September 2018).

Kolonna Publication, 'Magazine'. Available online: http://kolonna.mitin.com/?page=magazine (accessed 16 May 2020).

Konstriktor, B. [B. Aksel'rod], 'Dyshala noch' vostorgom samizdata', *Labirint/Ekstsentr* 1 (1991): 35–50.

Kopelev, Lev and Raisa Orlova, *My zhili v Moskve 1956–1980* (Moscow: Kniga, 1990).

Korotkov, A.V., S.A. Mel'chin and A.S. Stepanov (eds), *Kremlevskii samosud: Sekretnye dokumenty Politbiuro o pisatele A. Solzhenitsyne* (Moscow: Rodina Edition "Q", 1994).

Kosinova, Tatiana, *Polski mit: Polska w oczach sowieckich dysydentów* (Krakow: Instytut Książki-Nowaja Polsza, 2012).

Kostriukova, Anastasia, 'Chitat' i slyshat' nastoiashchuiu literaturu', in *Acta Samizdatica: Zapiski o samizdate*, pilot edition (Moscow: GPIB Rossii – Mezhdunarodnyi 'Memorial' – 'Zvenia', 2012), 84–94.

Kreid, Vladimir, 'Stratanovskii i leningradskaia poeticheskaia shkola', *Novyi zhurnal* 155 (1984): 103–14.

Krivulin, Viktor, 'Fragment poemy', *37*, no. 9 (1977): 26.

Krivulin, Viktor, 'Peterburgskaia spiritual'naia lirika vchera i segodnia', in Boris Ivanov and Boris Roginskii (eds), *Istoriia leningradskoi nepodtsenzurnoi literatury* (St Petersburg: DEAN, 2000), 99–110.

Krivulin, Viktor, 'Pol'sha kak background', *Novaya Pol'sha* 10 (2011). Available online: http://novpol.org/ru/S16PIuMPi-/POLShA-KAK-BACKGROUND (accessed 10 January 2019).

Krivulin, Viktor, *Stikhi*, 2 vols. (Paris and Leningrad: Beseda, 1988).

Krivulin, Viktor, 'U istochnikov nezavisimoi kul'tury', *Zvezda*, no. 1 (1990): 184–88.

Krivulin, Viktor, '"37", Severnaia pochta', in Viacheslav Dolinin and Boris Ivanov (eds), *Samizdat: Po materialam konferentsii '30 let nezavisimoi pechati; 1950–80 gody'; S.-Peterburg, 25–27 aprelia 1992* (St Petersburg: NITs 'Memorial', 1993), 74–81.

Kukui, Il'ia, 'Predislovie; "Sokhranit' nit' poeticheskogo avangarda": zhurnal teorii i praktiki "Transponans"'. Project for the Study of Dissidence and Samizdat, October 2015. Available online: https://samizdatcollections.library.utoronto.ca/content/%D0%BF%D1%80%D0%B5%D0%B4%D0%B8%D1%81%D0%BB%D0%BE%D0%B2%D0%B8%D0%B5 (accessed 7 September 2018).

Kukui, Il'ia, 'Laboratoriia avangarda: Zhurnal *Transponans*', *Russian Literature* 59, nos. 2–4 (2006): 225–59.

Kukulin, Il'ia, 'Prodistsiplinarnye i antidistsiplinarnye seti v pozdnesovetskom obshchestve', *Sotsiologicheskoe obozrenie* 16, no. 3 (2017): 136–74.

Kuz'minskii, Konstantin, 'O Grigorii Kovaleve', in Konstantin Kuz'minskii and Grigorii Kovalev (eds), *The Blue Lagoon Anthology of Modern Russian Poetry* (Newtonville, MA: Oriental Research Partners, 1980–1986), vol. 1, reprint edition, 2006 (pagination different from original), 18–23.

Kuz'minskii, Konstantin, 'Boris Taigin', in Konstantin Kuz'minskii and Grigorii Kovalev (eds), *The Blue Lagoon Anthology of Modern Russian Poetry* (Newtonville, MA: Oriental Research Partners, 1980–1986), vol. 1, reprint edition, 2006 (pagination different from original), 25–6.

Kuz'minskii, Konstantin and Grigorii Kovalev (eds), *The Blue Lagoon Anthology of Modern Russian Poetry* (Newtonville, MA: Oriental Research Partners, 1980–1986). Available online: http://kkk-bluelagoon.ru/ (accessed 15 June 2018).

Kuzovkin, Gennadii, 'Nauchnoe izdanie "Khroniki tekushchikh sobytii" i novye vozmozhnosti dlia izucheniia samizdata', in *Acta Samizdatica: Zapiski o samizdate*, pilot edition (Moscow: GPIB Rossii – Mezhdunarodnyi 'Memorial' – 'Zvenia', 2012), 36–45.

Kuzovkin, Gennadii (ed.), *Neskol'ko interv'iu o samizdate* (forthcoming). Partial pre-publication available online: https://urokiistorii.ru/article/55967?fbclid=IwAR1JJq ennOLl27L5OONaHeaENVYs0N_bNcR3j3cRP0X_D_Z_rAeDba_eLxs (accessed 15 May 2019).

Kuzovkin, Gennadii, 'Samaia znamenitaia mashinistka samizdata', Uroki istorii: XX vek 22 July 2019. available online: https://urokiistorii.ru/article/55967?fbclid=IwAR1JJ qennOLl27L5OONaHeaENVYs0N_bNcR3j3cRP0X_D_Z_rAeDba_eLxs (accessed 14 May 2020).

Kuzovkin, Gennadii and Josephine von Zitzewitz, 'Neskol'ko voprosov o samizdate' ('A Few Questions About Samizdat') Project for the Study of Dissidence and Samizdat. https://samizdatcollections.library.utoronto.ca/content/survey

Labedz, Leopold and Max Hayward (eds), *On Trial: The Case of Sinyavsky (Tertz) and Daniel (Arzhak)* (London: Collins and Harvill Press, 1967).

Lashchiver, Irina, 'Posleslovie' to Asia Lashchiver, "Dissidentskie vospominaniia"', in *Acta Samizdatica: Zapiski o samizdate*, pilot edition (Moscow: GPIB Rossii – Mezhdunarodnyi 'Memorial' – 'Zvenia', 2012), 107–20.

Lashkova, Vera, 'U nas ne bylo zhelaniia uvidet' zariu svobody', interview with Gleb Morev, in Gleb Morev (ed.), *Dissidenty: Dvadtsat' razgovorov* (Moscow: Izdatel'stvo AST, 2017), 97–113.

Lashkova, Vera, 'Vera Lashkova – zhivoi golos russkoi istorii', interview with Iaroslav Gorbanevskii, 2011. Available online: http://ru.rfi.fr/rossiya/20111113-vera-lashkova-zhivoi-golos-russkoi-istorii (accessed 14 April 2019).

'Lev Mnukhin', interview with Ann Komaromi, Project for the Study of Dissidence and Samizdat, August 2014. Available online: https://samizdatcollections.library. utoronto.ca/interviews/ru/lev-mnukhin (accessed 2 October 2019).

Levin, Sergei, '"Summa" s pozitsii "slagaemogo"', in Viacheslav Dolinin and Boris Ivanov (eds), *Samizdat: Po materialam konferentsii '30 let nezavisimoi pechati; 1950–80 gody'* (St Petersburg: NITs 'Memorial', 1993), 115–19.

Likhtenfel'd, Boris, 'Dlia menia proshloe sushchestvennee nastoiashchego: o leningradskoi "vtoroi kul'ture" I ee geroiakh', interview with Evgenii Kogan, Colta, 12 November 2018. Available online: https://www.colta.ru/articles/literature/19696-dlya-menya-proshloe-suschestvennee-nastoyaschego (accessed 19 January 2019).

Lipovetsky, Mark, Tomáš Glanc, Maria Engström, Ilja Kukuj and Klavdia Smola (eds), *The Oxford Handbook of Soviet Underground Culture* (Oxford: Oxford University Press, forthcoming 2021).

Losev, Lev, *On the Beneficence of Censorship: Aesopian Language in Modern Russian Literature* (Munich: Otto Sagner, 1984).

Losev, Lev (ed.), *Poetika Brodskogo: Sbornik statei* (Tenafly, NJ: Hermitage, 1986).

Losev, Lev, 'Samizdat i samogon', in *Zakrytyi raspredelitel'* (Ann Arbor, MI: Hermitage, 1984) 139–79.

Lovell, Stephen, *The Russian Reading Revolution: Print Culture in the Soviet and Post-Soviet Eras* (Basingstoke: Macmillan, 2000).

Lygo, Emily, *Leningrad Poetry 1853–1975: The Thaw Generation* (Bern: Peter Lang, 2010).

Makarov, Aleksei, 'Ot lichnoi kollektsii samizdata k obshchestvennoi biblioteke. Trudnosti granits i definitsii', in *Acta Samizdatica: Zapiski o samizdate*, pilot edition (Moscow: GPIB Rossii – Mezhdunarodnyi 'Memorial' – 'Zvenia', 2012), 24–35.

Makarov, Aleksei, 'Putevoditel' po vystavke 'Ot tsenzury i samizdata k svobode pechati: 1917–1990', *Acta samizdatica*, no. 3 (2016): 221–39.

Makarov, Aleksei, 'Zhurnal domashnei biblioteki: Kak bylo ustroeno virtual'noe sobranie zapreshchennykh knig', Arzamas. Available online: https://arzamas.academy/materials/1155 (accessed 13 June 2018).

Malakhovskaia, Natalia, 'Feministskii samizdat: zhurnal "Mariia"', *Live Journal*, 24 January 2013. Available online: https://feministki.livejournal.com/2499778.html (accessed 5 May 2018).

Mamonova, Tatiana, 'Introduction', in Tatiana Mamonova (ed.), *Women and Russia: Feminist Writings from the Soviet Union* (Oxford: Blackwell, 1984).

Mandel'shtam, Osip, *Sobranie sochnineniia v trekh tomakh*, introduction by Clarence Brown, G.P. Struve and B.A. Filippov (Washington, DC: Inter-Language Literary Associates/Mezhdunarodnoe Literaturnoe Sodruzhestvo, 1967).

Matthews, John, 'The West's Secret Marshall Plan for the Mind', *International Journal of Intelligence and Counter Intelligence* 16 (2003): 409–27.

Martin, Barbara and Anton Sveshnikov, 'Between Scholarship and Dissidence: The Dissident Historical Collection *Pamiat'*', *Slavic Review* 76, no. 4 (2017): 1003–26.

Martin, Barbara and Anton Sveshnikov, *Istoricheskii sbornik 'Pamiat'': Issledovaniia i materialy* (Moscow: Novoe literaturnoe obozrenie, 2017).

McKenzie, D.F., *Bibliography and the Sociology of Texts* (Cambridge: Cambridge University Press, 1999).

McMichael, Polly, 'After All, You're a Rock and Roll Star (At Least That's What They Say): Roksi and the Creation of the Soviet Rock Musician', *Slavonic and East European Review* 83, no. 4 (2005): 664–84.

McMichael, Polly, '"A Room-Sized Ocean": Apartments in Practice and Mythology of Leningrad's Rock Music', in William Jay Risch (ed.), *Youth and Rock in the Soviet Bloc* (Lanham, MD: Lexington Books, 2015), 183–209.

Meilakh, Mikhail, 'Pervym moim sledovatelem byl Viktor Cherkesov', interview with Gleb Morev, in Gleb Morev (ed.), *Dissidenty: Dvadtsat' razgovorov* (Moscow: Izdatel'stvo AST, 2017), 329–45.

Meilakh, Mikhail, 'Kak zhizn' pobedila smert'', interview with Vitalii Leibin, *Russian Reporter*, no. 16 (455), 11 August 2018. Available online: https://expert.ru/russian_reporter/2018/16/kak-zhizn-pobedila-smert/ (accessed 26 June 2019).

Miklashevskaia, Liudmila *Povtorenie proidennogo* (Sankt-Peterburg: Zvezda, 2012).

Miller, Matthew Lee, *The American YMCA and Russian Culture: The Preservation and Expansion of Orthodox Christianity, 1900–1940* (Lanham, MD: Lexington Books, 2012).

Mironov, Aleksandr, 'Malaia Sadovaia: 1960-e; Beseda s Iuliei Valievoi', in Iuliia Valieva (ed.), *Sumerki 'Saigona'* (St Petersburg: Samizdat, 2009), 32–5.

Mitrokhin, Nikolai, *Russkaia partiia: Dvizhenie russkikh natsionalistov v SSSR; 1953–1985* (Moscow: Novoe literaturnoe obozrenie, 2003).

Morev, Gleb (ed.), *Dissidenty: Dvadtsat' razgovorov* (Dissidents: Twenty Conversations) (Moscow: Izdatel'stvo AST, 2017).

Moscow Helsinki Group. Available online: https://mhg.ru/ (accessed 17 May 2020).

Murav'eva, Irina, *Salony pushkinskoi pory: Ocherki literaturnoi i svetskoi zhizni Sankt-Peterburga* (St Petersburg: Kriga, 2008).

Murray, Andrew D., *The Regulation of Cyberspace: Control in the Online Environment* (Oxford: Routledge, 2006).

Nathans, Benjamin and Kevin M.F. Platt, 'Socialist in Form, Indeterminate in Content: The Ins and Outs of Late Soviet Culture', *Ab Imperio*, no. 2 (2011): 301–24.

Nechaev, V., 'Nravstvennoe znachenie neofitsial'noi kul'tury v Rossii: Materialy konferentsii v muzee sovremennoi zhivopisi', *Poiski* 1 (1979): 303–14.

Nikonova, Ry [Anna Tarshis], 'Anketnaia ikra Obvodnogo kanala', *Transponans*, no. 34 (1986).

Novikov, Iurii, 'Stroitel' vavilonskoi bashni (K portretu K. Kuz'minskogo)', *Novoe Literaturnoe Obozrenie* 31 (1998): 328–33.

NTS: Mysl' i delo; 1930–2000 (Moscow, 2000).

Ogorodnikov, Aleksandr, 'Monolog o seminare – fragment kruglogo stola', *Okhapkinskie chteniia: Almanakh No 2*, edited by Tat'iana Koval'kova (St Petersburg: Russkaia kul'tura, 2018), 29–35.

Okhapkin, Oleg, *Stikhi* (Leningrad: Beseda, 1989).

Ostanin, Boris and Aleksandr Kobak, 'Molniia i raduga: Puti kul'tury 60-89-kh godov', in *Molniia i raduga: literaturno-kriticheskie stat'i 1980-kh godov* (St Petersburg: Izdatel'stvo imeni N.I. Novikova, 2003), 9–38.

Oushakine, Sergei, 'The Terrifying Mimicry of Samizdat', *Public Culture* 13, no. 2 (2001): 191–214.

Parisi, Valentina, *Il lettore eccedente: edizioni periodiche del samizdat sovietico, 1956–1990* (Bologna: Società editrice Il mulino, 2013).

Parisi, Valentina, 'Scribes, Self-Publishers, Artists: Performing the Book in the Samizdat Writing Scene', in Annette Gilbert (ed.), *Publishing as Artistic Practice* (Berlin: Sternberg Press, 2016), 154–69.

Parisi, Valentina, 'The Dispersed Author: The Problem of Literary Authority in Samizdat Textual Production', in Valentina Parisi (ed.), *Samizdat: Between Practices and Representations; Lecture Series at Open Society Archives, Budapest, February–June 2013* (Budapest: Central European University/IAS, 2015), 63–72.

Parta, R. Eugene, *Discovering the Hidden Listener: An Assessment of Radio Liberty and Western Broadcasting to the USSR during the Cold War; A Study Based on Audience Research Findings, 1970–1991* (Stanford, CA: Hoover Institution Press, 2007).

Pazukhin, Evgenii, 'Antisotsium', in Iuliia Valieva (ed.), *Sumerki 'Saigona'* (St Petersburg: Samizdat, 2009), 163–70.

Pazukhin, Evgenii, 'Russkaia religioznaia filosofiia v podpol'e', in S. Gorbunova (ed.), *Preobrazhenie: Khristianskii religiozno-filosofskii almanakh* (St Petersburg: Zvezda, 1992), 16–24.

The Mission of Radio Free Europe and Radio Liberty Broadcast, reprint in A. Buell, 'Radio Free Europe/Radio Liberty in the Mid 1980s', in K.R.M. Short (ed.), *Western Broadcasting over the Iron Curtain* (London: Croom Helm, 1986).

Peskov, N. [V.V. Iofe], 'Delo "Kolokola"', in N. Gorbanevskaia (ed.), *Pamiat', istoricheskii sbornik*, 2 vols. (New York, 1976–1982), vol. 1, 269–84.

Pinder, Julian, 'Online Literary Communities: A Case Study of Library Thing', in Anouk Lang (ed.), *From Codex to Hypertext: Reading at the Turn of the Twenty-First Century* (Amherst: University of Massachusetts Press, 2012), 68–87.

Podosokorskii, Nikolai, 'Konferentsiia "Poetika i poetologiia iazykovykh poiskov v nepodtsenzurnoi i sovremennoi poezii"', *Live Journal*, 25 April 2019. Available online: https://philologist.livejournal.com/10873150.html (accessed 17 May 2020).

Podrabinek, A., '10 dekabria: Moskva; Pushkinskaia ploshchad'; 18 chasov', 6 December 2015. Available online: http://www.cogita.ru/a.n.-alekseev/kontekst/10-dekabrya-moskva-pushkinskaya-ploschad-18-chasov (accessed 15 June 2018).

Polikovskaia, Liudmila, 'Zhurnal "37"', *Antologiia samizdata*. Available online: http://antology.igrunov.ru/after_75/periodicals/37/ (accessed 16 May 2020).

Proffer Teasley, Ellendea, 'How Censorship Leads to Samizdat: Ardis Publishers', keynote lecture, 'Tamizdat: Publishing Russian Literature in the Cold War' conference, Russian and East European Cultures at Hunter College, New York, 10 December 2018. Available online: https://www.reechunter.com/tamizdat-conference.html#Keanote1 (accessed 6 March 2019).

Project for the Study of Dissidence and Samizdat, '37 [Tridtsat' Sem', Thirty-Seven]'. Available online: https://samizdatcollections.library.utoronto.ca/islandora/object/samizdat%3A37 (accessed 16 May 2020).

Project for the Study of Dissidence and Samizdat, 'Interviews'. Available online: https://samizdatcollections.library.utoronto.ca/interviews (accessed 17 May 2020).

Project for the Study of Dissidence and Samizdat, 'Obvodnyi kanal [Obvodnyi Canal]'. Available online: https://samizdatcollections.library.utoronto.ca/islandora/object/samizdat%3Aobvodnyikanal (accessed 4 June 2019).

Project for the Study of Dissidence and Samizdat, 'Severnaia pochta [The Northern Mail]'. Available online: https://samizdatcollections.library.utoronto.ca/islandora/object/samizdat%3Asevernaiapochta (accessed 4 June 2019).

Project for the Study of Dissidence and Samizdat, 'Tridtsat' Sem' [Thirty-Seven] No 03'. Available online: https://samizdatcollections.library.utoronto.ca/islandora/object/samizdat%3A3675 (accessed 17 May 2020).

Project for the Study of Dissidence and Samizdat, 'Zhurnal teorii i praktiki "Transponans": Kommentirovannoye elektronnoye izdaniye / Pod red. I. Kukuia – A Work in Progress'. Available online: https://samizdatcollections.library.utoronto.ca/islandora/object/samizdat%3Atransponans (accessed 7 September 2018).

Pudovkina, Elena, 'Klub "Derzanie"', *Pchela*, nos. 26–7 (2000).

Pushkareva, Natalia, 'Feminism in Russia', in *Encyclopaedia round the World*. Available online: https://www.krugosvet.ru/enc/istoriya/FEMINIZM_V_ROSSII.html (accessed 14 May 2020).

Pushkareva, Natalia L., 'U istokov russkogo feminizma: skhodstva i otlichiia Rossii i Zapada', in Grigorii A. Tishkin (ed.), *Rossiiskie zhenshchiny i evropeiskaia kul'tura* (St Petersburg: Sankt-Peterburgskogo filosofskogo obshchestva, 2001), 79–84.

Reddaway, Peter (ed. and trans.), *Uncensored Russia* (London: Jonathan Cape, 1972).

Rogachevskii, Andrei, 'Novosibirskii samizdat glazami podrostka: (Konets 1970-kh – seredina 1980-kh)', *Solnechnoe spletenie* (Jerusalem), nos. 16–7: 208–12.

Rozhniatovskii, Vsevolod, 'Vlianie Olega Okhapkina na krug pskovskikh poetov: Miroslav Andreev, Evgenii Shesholin, drugie avtory', in Tat'iana Koval'kova (ed.), *Okhapkinskie chtenie: Almanakh No 1* (St Petersburg: Oriental Research Partners, 2015), 17–27.

Russian and East European Cultures at Hunter College, 'Tamizdat: Publishing Russian Literature in the Cold War' conference, New York, 10–11 December 2018. Available online: https://www.reechunter.com/tamizdat-conference.html#Program (accessed 6 March 2019).

Sabbatini, Marco, 'K istorii sozdanii "Severnoi pochty"; O Viktore Krivuline', interview with Sergei Dediulin.' (Paris: Assotsiatsiia 'Russkii institut v Parizhe', 2004).

Sabbatini, Marco, *'Quel Che Si Metteva In Rima': Cultura E Poesia Underground a Leningrado* (Salerno: Europa Orientalis, 2008).

Sapgir, Genrikh, 'Sapgir ob avtorakh i gruppakh', RVB, 21 August 2019. Available online: http://rvb.ru/np/publication/sapgir5.htm#67 (accessed 21 October 2019).

Savitskii, Stanislav, *Andegraund: Istoriia i mify leningradskoi neofitsial'noi literatury* (Moscow: Novoe literaturnoe obozrenie, 2002).

Schmidt, Henrike, 'Postprintium? Digital Literary Samizdat on the Russian Internet', in Friederike Kind-Kovacs and Jessie Labov (eds), *Samizdat, Tamizdat and Beyond: Transnational Media during and after Socialism* (New York: Berghahn, 2013), 221–44.

Schmidt, Henrike, *Russische Literatur im Internet: Zwischen digitaler Folklore und politischer Propaganda* (Bielefeld: Transcript Verlag, 2011).

Sedakova, Olga and Slava I. Yastremski, 'A Dialogue on Poetry', in Olga Sedakova, *Poems and Elegies*, edited by Slava I. Yastremski (Lewisburg, PA: Bucknell University Press, 2003), 11–20.

Sedo, DeNel Rehberg, 'An Introduction to Reading Communities: Process and Formations', in DeNel Rehberg Sedo (ed.), *Reading Communities: From Salons to Cyberspace* (Basingstoke: Palgrave Macmillan, 2011), 1-24.

Sedo, DeNel Rehberg (ed.), *Reading Communities: From Salons to Cyberspace* (Basingstoke: Palgrave Macmillan, 2011).

Semanov, Sergei, *Russkii klub: Pochemu ne pobediat evrei* (Moscow: Litres, 2017, ebook).

Severiukhin, Dmitrii, Viacheslav Dolinin, Boris Ivanov and Boris Ostanin (eds), *Samizdat Leningrada 1950e-1980e: Literaturnaia entsiklopediia* (Moscow: Novoe literaturnoe obozrenie, 2003).

Shkaeva, Natalia, '"Bez redaktsii starykh Bolshevikov andegraunda" ili chto takoe Chasy', Cogita, 12 October 2011. Available online: http://www.cogita.ru/news/sobytiya-i-anonsy-2009-2011/abbez-redakcii-staryh-bolshevikov-andegraundabb-ili-chto-takoe-abchasybb (accessed 8 January 2019).

Shneiderman, Eduard, 'Klub-81 i KGB', *Zvezda*, no. 8 (2004): 209-17.

Shneiderman, Eduard, 'Shto ia izdaval, v chem ia uchastvoval', in Viacheslav Dolinin and Boris Ivanov (eds), *Samizdat: Po materialam konferentsii '30 let nezavisimoi pechati. 1950-80 gody'* (St Petersburg: NITs 'Memorial', 1993), 46-57.

Shvarts, Elena, *Stikhi* (Leningrad: Beseda, 1987).

Skobov, Aleksandr, '"Perspektiva" - zhurnal novykh levykh', in Viacheslav Dolinin and Boris Ivanov (eds), *Samizdat: Po materialam konferentsii '30 let nezavisimoi pechati; 1950-80 gody'* (St Petersburg: NITs 'Memorial', 1993), 105-14.

Solzhenitsyn, Alexandr, *Bodalsia telenok s dubom: Ocherki literaturnoi zhizni* (Moscow: Soglasie, 1996).

Solzhenitsyn, Alexandr, 'Zhit' ne po lzhi!', 13 February 1974. Available online: http://www.solzhenitsyn.ru/proizvedeniya/publizistika/stati_i_rechi/v_sovetskom_soyuze/jzit_ne_po_ljzi.pdf (accessed 8 October 2019).

Starshinina, Elizaveta, 'Iz istorii irkutskogo samizdata', report on a lecture by Vladimir Skrashchuk, 21 March 2014. Available online: http://baikal-info.ru/iz-istorii-irkutskogo-samizdata (accessed 17 May 2020).

Strukova, Elena, *Al'ternativnaia periodicheskaia pechat' v istorii rossiiskoi mnogopartiinosti (1987-1996)* (Moscow: Istoricheskaia biblioteka, 2005).

Strukova, Elena, 'Delo ob odesskoi biblioteke samizdata', *Bibliografiia* 2 (2012): 50-9.

Strukova, Elena, 'Odesskaia biblioteka samizdata Igrunova-Butova i "Masterskaia khudozhestvennykh promyslov" Avraama Shifrina', paper given at the *Chtenie pamiati A.B. Roginskogo*, Moscow, 30 March 2019.

Strukova, Elena, 'Samizdat kak pamiatnik knizhnoi kul'tury vtoroi poloviny XX veka', in *Acta Samizdatica: Zapiski o samizdate*, pilot edition (Moscow: GPIB Rossii - Mezhdunarodnyi 'Memorial' - 'Zvenia', 2012), 7-13.

Struve, Gleb, 'Kak byl vpervye izdan "Rekviem"', in Anna Akhmatova, *Rekviem: 1935-1940*, 2nd edition (New York: Tovarishchestvo zarubezhnykh pisatelei, 1969).

Sukhovei, Dar'ia, 'Krugi komp'iuternogo raia', *Novoe Literaturnoe Obozrenie* 62 (2003).

Talaver, Alexandra, 'Samizdat of the Soviet Dissident Women's Groups, 1979-1982', submitted MA thesis (Central European University Department of Gender Studies, Budapest).
Thevenot, Laurent, 'The Plurality of Cognitive Formats and Engagements: Moving between the Familiar and the Public', *European Journal of Social Theory* 10, no. 3 (2007): 409-23.
Timenchik, Roman, *Istoriia kul'ta Gumileva* (Moscow: Mosty kul'tury, 2018).
Trauberg, Natalia, *Sama zhizn'* (St Petersburg: Izdatel'stvo Ivan Limbakha, 2008).
Trauberg, Natalia, 'Vsegda li pobezhdaet pobezhdennyi?', in *Sama zhizn'* (St Petersburg: Izdatel'stvo Ivan Limbakha, 2008), 409-17.
Troitsky, Artemy, *Tusovka: Who's Who in the New Soviet Rock Culture* (London: Omnibus Press, 1990).
Turchinskii, Lev, 'Kollektsioniruite tekh, kto neizvesten i nedootsenen', Arzamas, 13 June 2018. Available online: https://arzamas.academy/mag/551-turchinsky (accessed 5 March 2019).
Valieva, Iuliia (ed.), *Litsa peterburgskoi poezii 1950-1990-e. Avtobiografii. Avtorskoe chtenie + 5 CD* (St Petersburg: Samizdat, 2011).
Valieva, Iuliia (ed.), *Sumerki 'Saigona'* (St Petersburg: Samizdat, 2009).
Vershik, Anatolii, 'Nauka i totalitarizm', *Zvezda*, no. 8 (1998).
Vershik, Anatolii, 'Potaennyi daidzhest epokhi zastoia', *Zvezda*, no. 11 (1991).
Vershik, Anatolii, '"Summa" za svobodnuiu mysl"', in *"Summa" za zvobodnuiu mysl'* (St Petersburg: Zvezda, 2002), 5-22.
Vershik, Anatolii, V. Dolinin, E. Maslova and B. Maslov (eds), *"Summa" za svobodnuiu mysl'* (St Petersburg: Izdatel'stvo zhurnala 'Zvezda', 2002).
Volchek, Dmitrii, 'Skol'ko ostalos' zhit' samizdatu', *Mitin zhurnal*, nos. 9/10 (1986).
Volchek, Dmitrii, 'Tol'ko stikhi. Pamiati Olega Okhapkina', Svoboda, 10 October 2008. Available online: http://www.svoboda.org/content/article/468261.html (accessed 23 October 2019).
von Zitzewitz, Josephine, 'From Underground to Mainstream: The Case of Elena Shvarts', in Katharine Hodgson and Alexandra Smith (eds), *Reconfiguring the Canon of Twentieth-Century Russian Poetry, 1991-2008* (Cambridge: Open Book Publishers, 2017), 225-64.
von Zitzewitz, Josephine, *Poetry and the Leningrad Religious-Philosophical Seminar 1976-1980: Music for a Deaf Age* (Oxford: Legenda/MHRA and Routledge, 2016).
von Zitzewitz, Josephine, 'Reader Questionnaires in Samizdat Journals: Who owns Alexander Blok?', in Juliane Furst and Josie McLellan (eds), *Dropping out of Socialism* (Lanham, MD: Lexington, 2016), 107-27.
von Zitzewitz, Josephine, 'Self-Canonisation as a Way into the Canon: The Case of the Leningrad Underground', *Australian and East European Studies* 31 (2017): 197-228.
Wenger, Etienne, *Communities of Practice* (Cambridge: Cambridge University Press, 1999).

White, Harrison C., *Identity and Control: A Structural Theory of Social Action* (Princeton, NJ: Princeton University Press, 1992).
Wikipedia, 'Khronika tekushchikh sobytiy', last updated 30 April 2020. Available online: https://ru.wikipedia.org/wiki/%D0%A5%D1%80%D0%BE%D0%BD%D0%B8%D0%BA%D0%B0_%D1%82%D0%B5%D0%BA%D1%83%D1%89%D0%B8%D1%85_%D1%81%D0%BE%D0%B1%D1%8B%D1%82%D0%B8%D0%B9 (accessed 17 May 2020).
Wikipedia, 'List of works by Vladimir Vysotsky', last edited May 12, 2020. Available online: https://ru.wikipedia.org/wiki/%D0%A1%D0%BF%D0%B8%D1%81%D0%BE%D0%BA_%D0%BF%D1%80%D0%BE%D0%B8%D0%B7%D0%B2%D0%B5%D0%B4%D0%B5%D0%BD%D0%B8%D0%B9_%D0%92%D0%BB%D0%B0%D0%B4%D0%B8%D0%BC%D0%B8%D1%80%D0%B0_%D0%92%D1%8B%D1%81%D0%BE%D1%86%D0%BA%D0%BE%D0%B3%D0%BE (accessed 13 May 2020).
Yoo, Hyung-Min, 'Voices of Freedom: Samizdat', *Europe-Asia Studies* 56, no. 4 (2004): 571–94.
Yurchak, Alexei, *Everything Was Forever, until It Was No More: The Last Soviet Generation* (Princeton, NJ: Princeton University Press, 2005).
Zaslavskaya, Olga, 'Samizdat as Social Practice and Alternative "Communication Circuit"', in Valentina Parisi (ed.), *Samizdat: Between Practices and Representations; Lecture Series at Open Society Archives, Budapest, February–June 2013* (Budapest: Central European University/IAS, 2015), 87–99.
Zhitenev, Aleksandr, *Poeziia neomodernizma* (St Petersburg: Inapress, 2012).
Zhmud', Leonid, 'Studenty-istoriki mezhdu ofitsiozom i 'liberal'noi' naukoi', *Zvezda*, no. 8 (1998): 204–09.
Zubarev, D., N. Kostenko, G. Kuzovkin, S. Lukashevskii and A. Papovian (eds), *5 dekabria 1965 goda* (Moscow: Obshchestvo 'Memorial', Izdatel'stvo 'Zvenia', 2005).
Zubova, Liudmila, *Sovremennaia russkaia poeziia v kontekste istorii iazyka* (Moscow: Novoe literaturnoe obozrenie, 2000).

Josephine von Zitzewitz is Marie Skłodowska-Curie Fellow in Russian Literature at UiT – The Arctic University of Norway in Tromsø, having previously held research and teaching appointments at the universities of Cambridge, Oxford and Bristol. A specialist in twentieth-century poetry, she is the author of *Poetry and the Leningrad Religious-Philosophical Seminar 1976–1980: Music for a Deaf Age* (2016) and numerous articles on underground literature in the late Soviet Union.

Index

20th Party Congress 1, 65, 138
37 (samizdat journal) 60, 86, 91, 97,
    117, 122, 125–132, 134, 138–147,
    159–161, 165, 182, 205–214,
    216–219, 221

Abramovich, Olga 70, 88, 122, 136, 137,
    195, 197, 210, 224
Adamatskii, Igor 128
Akhmadulina, Bella 5
Akhmatova, Anna 5, 17, 30, 35, 36, 37, 45,
    49, 53, 134, 183, 189, 213
    and *Requiem* 17, 30, 36, 37, 45, 183,
    189
Aksenov, Vasilii 31
Akvarium (rock music group) 164
Alekseeva, Liudmila 10, 12, 55, 65, 89,
    180, 182, 190, 192, 193, 194, 197,
    198, 200, 211
Alekseev-Popov, V.A. 113
Aleshkovskii, Iuz 83
Alisa (rock music group) 164
alternative public 173
Amalrik, Andrei 40
Andrei Belyi Prize (Premiia Andreia
    Belogo) 129, 158, 160, 162, 171,
    208, 217
Annenkov, Yu 48
Antonov, Viktor 127
Apter, Viktoria 87, 142, 196
archivist 8, 26, 90, 98, 107, 109
Ardis Publishers 46, 47, 50, 183, 190, 191
Aronzon, Leonid 90, 134, 198, 221
Auslender, Elena 45
Averbukh, Igor and Isai 101
Avrutskii, Yurii 12, 75, 101, 104–108, 110,
    111, 115, 116, 181, 196, 200, 202,
    203
Avtorkhanov, Abdurakhman 30, 40, 47,
    50, 108, 110, 188

Balakirev, Valerii 99
Balazs, Sharon 20

Barron, John 119, 204
Barth, Karl 146, 214
Basilova, Alena 90
Beckett, Samuel 146, 214
Begin, M 51
Bel'tser, Larisa 48, 87, 190, 197
Berdiaev, Nikolai 86, 102, 110
Berezhnov A. – see Krivulin, Viktor
Beseda (journal and publishing house) 46,
    50, 164, 168, 181, 189
Bezmenov, Bob 88
Biriulin, Bob 88
Bitov, Andrei 46, 110
blat 22, 174
Blok, Alexander 211
*Blue Lagoon Anthology of Modern Russian
    Poetry, The* 29, 79, 88, 90, 165, 183,
    186, 197, 206, 219
Bobyshev, Dmitrii 88, 134
Bogoraz, Larisa 15, 54, 89, 185, 191, 192
Bolonkin, Alexander 99
Bonch, I. see Ostanin, Boris 160
Bonhoeffer, Dietrich 146, 214
Borge, Jorge Luis 145, 207
Borisov, Vadim 83
Brezhnev, Leonid 1, 151
British Broadcasting Corporation (BBC)
    6, 53, 54, 191, 192
Brodsky, Joseph 6, 9, 29, 31, 35, 46, 53, 59,
    78, 79, 83, 88, 111, 134, 148, 189, 213
Bulgakov, Mikhail 33, 36, 37, 38, 89, 101,
    102
    The Master and Margarita 33, 37, 38,
    186
Butov, Petr 103, 104, 114, 201, 203
Butyrin, Kirill 131, 132, 133, 139, 148, 209,
    211, 214, 217

Camus, Albert 86, 145, 207
Chalidze Publications 46
Chalidze, Valeriin 46
Chasy (samizdat journal) 60, 86, 87, 114,
    122, 125, 127–132, 136–138, 140–146,

148, 151, 152, 155, 158–163, 165–167, 171, 184, 196, 198, 207, 208, 212–214, 216, 218, 220, 221
Chernykh, Boris 29
Chernykh, Natalia 215
Chesterton, G.K. 17
Chronicle of Current Events, The (Khronika tekushchikh sobytii, samizdat bulletin*)* 6, 10, 18, 40, 46, 58, 76, 78, 79, 90, 94, 95, 102, 103, 108, 113, 116–118, 121, 123, 150, 179, 185, 188, 192, 200, 201
Chukovskaia, Elena 73, 188
Chukovskaia, Lidiia 73
community/ communities of practice 149, 150, 157, 168, 169, 170, 171, 175, 214, 221
Conquest, Robert 51

Daniel, Alexander 8, 16, 102, 177, 178, 181, 182, 185
Daniel, Yulii 9, 75, 179, 180
Darnton, Robert 14, 15, 182
Dediulin, Sergei 133, 134, 143, 144, 152, 163, 164, 208, 209, 213
Deutsche Welle 6, 53
Dialog (samizdat journal) 122, 131, 132, 160, 210
Dickinson, Emily 145
dissident/dissidents 1, 6–10, 12, 16, 22, 25, 32, 33, 40, 49, 54, 60, 65, 72, 73, 76, 77, 81, 83, 89, 91, 95, 102, 103, 105, 107, 114, 118, 148, 151, 174, 178, 179–185, 191, 192, 194, 197, 198, 200, 201, 203, 215
Dobkin, Alexander 74, 75, 88, 91
Dobkina, Natalia 66, 88, 90, 196, 198, 224
Dolinin, Viacheslav 43, 71, 128, 146, 167, 181, 188, 195, 203–206, 208, 212, 214, 219–221, 226
Dragomoshchenko, Arkadii 128, 155, 162, 164, 217–220
Drozdetskaia, Galina 91, 141, 198, 212, 224
Dubin, Boris 157, 176, 217, 222
Djilas, Milovan 48, 102

editor/editing (of samizdat) 3, 4, 11, 14, 16, 17, 19, 20, 50, 60, 61, 67, 70, 78, 82, 86–91, 97, 98, 103, 116, 118, 119, 121–123, 125–134, 136–144,

146, 148, 150–154, 155, 158–160, 164, 165, 167, 68, 170, 171, 176, 180, 184, 189, 201, 206, 211, 212, 215, 217, 219, 220, 221
Ekho (journal) 46, 198
El'gort, D.G. 119
Eremin, Mikhail 88
Erika (typewriter brand) 65, 68, 80
Erl (Erl'), Vladimir 89, 191, 206
Erofeev, Venedikt 6, 28, 30, 37, 83
Esenin, Sergei 5, 30, 34
Esenin-Volpin, Alexander 180
Evrei v SSSR (journal) 83, 84, 117, 123, 193
Evtushenko, Evgenii 3, 5, 30
Ezerskaia, Bella 101, 103, 201

Feniks-66 (samizdat almanac) 75, 76
Finkelshtein, Leonid 50
Franklin, Simon 58, 181, 187, 193
Fraser, Nancy 23, 185
Freud, Sigmund 106

Galanskov, Yurii 75
Galich, Alexander 9, 28, 36, 37, 48, 53, 59, 68, 80, 83
Gershuni, Vladimir 83
Ginzburg, Alexander 75, 76, 102, 105, 124, 179
Glants, Anatolii 111
Glavlit 15
Glazkov, Nikolai 6, 63
Gol'denberg, Isidor 101
Goldberg, Anatolii 54, 192
Gollerbakh, Evgenii 132, 209
Golomshtok, Igor 9, 40, 83, 179, 180, 188, 196
Golubev N. see Stratanovskii, Sergei
Gorbachev, Mikhail 27, 33, 35, 50, 175
Gorbanevskaia, Natalia 90, 103, 179, 213
Gorbovskii, Gleb 88
Goricheva, Tatiana 46, 50, 90, 91, 97, 122, 125–127, 135, 139–141, 145, 146, 148, 163, 164, 168, 199, 206–208, 211–214, 216, 217, 224
Gorky, Maksim 83, 102
Gorny, Eugene 19, 184
Gorodetskii, Sergei 218
Grani (journal) 50, 181
Griboedov, Alexander 37
Grigoreva, Galina 135
Grossman, Vasilii 40, 49

Groys, Boris 97, 127, 131, 145, 160, 208, 212
   Inozemtsev, Boris (pseudonym of Boris Groys) 160
   Suitsidov, Igor (pseudonym of Boris Groys) 160
Gubanov, Leonid 90
Gumilev, Nikolai 6, 28, 30, 35, 37, 57, 153, 187, 218
Gutenberg, Johannes 18, 19, 109, 183, 185, 197

human rights 1, 2, 6, 9, 10, 40, 41, 46, 75, 77, 85, 89, 90, 102, 103, 135, 179, 180, 185, 192, 195

Igrunov, Viacheslav 7, 18, 40, 54, 89, 101–109, 111–115, 177, 181, 183, 185, 191, 192, 194, 197, 200–203
Inostrannaia literatura (journal) 146
Inozemtsev, Boris see Groys, Boris
institution/institutions 4, 16, 22, 42, 52, 55, 68, 84, 96, 101, 103, 104, 114, 116, 120, 129, 130, 136, 141, 148, 149, 150, 153, 154, 156–159, 161, 162, 164, 167–169, 171, 174, 176, 188, 200, 222
International Samizdat Association 7, 8, 179, 220
internet 7, 19–21, 25, 67, 103, 115, 184
Ionesco, Eugene 45
Ivanov, Boris 86, 87, 125, 128–131, 135, 137, 141–144, 146, 148, 160–163, 167, 168, 181, 182, 204–210, 212, 216, 218–221

Jung, Carl 60, 106, 214

Kafka, Franz 145
Kalomirov, A. see Krivulin, Viktor
Kaverin, Nikolai 118
Kazarnovskii, Petr 90, 198, 221
KGB 11, 16, 33, 35, 37, 44, 51, 54, 55, 73–75, 79, 83, 84, 96, 114, 119, 127, 130, 133, 134, 139, 162, 163, 169, 179, 200, 204, 209, 219
Kharms, Daniil 29, 50, 89, 191
Khersonskii, Boris 99, 102, 103, 201
Khlebnikov, Velimir 137, 138

Khodorovich, Sergei 9, 179, 185
Khristianskii seminar po problemam religioznogo vozroshdeniia 139, 207, 211, 217
Khronika Press 46, 180
Khronika tekushchikh sobytii, see *Chronicle of Current Events, The*
Khrushchev, Nikita 1, 138
Kim, Yulii 83
Kind-Kovacs, Friederike 8, 52, 178, 183, 184, 191, 192, 215
Kino (rock music group) 164
Kipling, Rudyard 65
Kirichenko, Vladimir 102
Kiselev, Stanek 88
Klub-81 (Leningradskoe professional'noe ob"edinenie literatorov) 130, 132, 134, 146, 156, 160–164, 169, 171, 208, 210, 218, 219
Koestler, Arthur 83
Kolker, Yurii 49, 123, 128, 132, 144, 151–153, 162, 164, 165, 170, 191, 205, 208, 209, 210, 213, 215, 218, 219, 221
Kolokol (samizdat bulletin) 11, 12, 180
Komaromi, Ann 8, 22, 23, 178, 179, 182–185, 190, 191, 196, 199
Kontinent (journal) 51, 117
Kopelev, Lev 3, 12, 25, 45, 53, 118, 177, 180, 182, 189, 192, 193, 204
Kormer, Vladimir 83
Korovin, Sergei 128
Korzhavin, Naum 6
Kotliar, Tatiana 96
Kovalev, Grigorii 29, 88, 165, 183, 186, 196
Kozyrev, Kirill 49, 53, 89, 142–144, 156, 158, 166, 191, 192, 197, 212, 213, 217, 218, 220, 224
Krakhmal'nikova, Zoia 76
Krasnyi Shchedrinets (samizdat journal) 135, 210
Krivulin, Viktor 86, 125, 127, 130–134, 137, 140, 141, 144, 145, 147, 148, 153, 155, 160, 162–164, 168, 169, 189, 206–210, 212–214, 216–218, 220, 221
   Berezhnov A. (pseudonym of Viktor Krivulin) 160
   Kalomirov, A. (pseudonym of Viktor Krivulin) 160, 209, 213, 216, 221

Krug (almanac) 162, 183, 219
Kucheriavkin, Vladimir 146
Kukui, Ilya 90, 198, 204, 210, 220, 221
Kukulin, Ilya 22, 184, 185, 194, 195
Kuzminskii, Konstantin 29, 78, 88, 90, 125, 165, 183, 186, 196, 197, 205, 206, 219
Kuzovkin, Gennadii 26, 177, 179, 181, 186, 188, 191, 193, 194, 197, 200, 202, 224

Labov, Jessie 8, 178, 183, 184, 191
Language Poetry 155
Lapenkov, Vladimir 133
Lashchiver, Asia 54, 192
Lashchiver, Irina 54, 192
Lashkova, Vera 75, 76, 90, 180, 185, 196, 198
Lazareva, Natalia 84, 135
Lem, Stanislaw 9
Leningradskii rabochii (newspaper) 70
Leningradskoe professional'noe ob"edinenie literatorov (Leningrad Professional Association of Writers) see Klub-81
Lepta (samizdat almanac) 124, 125, 162, 206
Levin, Sergei 118, 203, 204
Lewis, C.S. 17
librarian 4, 61, 98–101, 105, 107, 108, 110, 113–115, 173, 203
Likhtenfel'd, Boris 66, 148, 194, 205, 208, 214, 224
Literaturnoe obozrenie (journal) 159
Literaturnye tetradi (samizdat journal) 29
Liubarskii, Kronid 102, 112, 115
Losev, Lev 10, 180, 190, 199, 202, 213, 216
Lur'e, Samuil 70

Maia (samizdat almanac) 29
Makarov, Alexei 99, 100, 106, 182, 186, 199–202
Maksimova Irina 102
Malakhovskaia, Natalia 91, 92, 135, 198, 199
Malraux, Andre 45
Mamonova, Tatiana 91, 135, 199
Mandelshtam, Nadezhda 46, 48, 90, 111, 202
and *Hope Abandoned* 111, 202

Mandelshtam, Osip 5, 9, 28, 35–37, 46–50, 57, 69, 83, 95, 190
Maramzin, Vladimir 46
Mariia (samizdat journal) 84, 91, 135, 198
Markov, Dmitrii 100
Martin, Barbara 88, 197, 203, 205
Martynov, Ivan 35
Maslov, Sergei 115, 116, 118, 119, 204, 220
Maslova, Nina 115, 118
Matizen, Viktor 102
Mayakovsky Square 5
Mayakovsky, Vladimir 218
Meilakh, Mikhail 50, 89, 114, 191, 197, 203
Memorial Society 7, 8, 12, 13, 26, 88, 97–100, 104–106, 143, 167, 178, 181, 185, 194–197, 200, 202, 206, 210, 218, 223
Men', Alexander 83
Miłosz, Czesław 145, 213
Mironov, Alexander 91, 137, 182, 205, 206, 220
Mitin zhurnal (samizdat journal) 77, 88, 122, 135–137, 146, 159, 184, 207, 218
Mnukhin, Lev 97, 199
Molot, Valerii 146
Morev, Gleb 10, 76, 101, 179, 180, 185, 191, 194
Moscow Helsinki Group 9, 89, 179
Moskovskii sbornik (samizdat journal) 139
Moskva (journal) 37, 159, 186
Moskva-Petushki 30, 37, 83
Most (journal) 147

Nabokov, Vladimir 34, 46, 47, 50, 53, 76, 86, 95, 110, 145
Nadezhda (samizdat almanac) 76
Narodno-trudovoi soiuz (NTS) 50
Naumov, Pavel 99
networks 2–5, 9, 10, 12, 13, 19–23, 30, 35, 49, 63, 66, 67, 87, 90, 92–94, 96, 100, 101, 104–106, 113, 118, 120–122, 134, 144, 147, 149, 150, 152, 154, 161, 163, 164, 166, 170, 173, 174, 176, 194
Neva (journal) 70
Nietzsche, Friedrich 106
Nikonova, Ry 135, 137, 138, 210

Novaia Sadovaia (cafe) 124
Novikov, Yurii 128, 205, 219
Novyi mir (journal) 14, 159, 189, 216, 218

Obshchina (samizdat journal) 150, 203, 207, 211
Obvodnyi kanal (samizdat journal) 60, 86, 122, 131–133, 137, 138, 145, 147, 160, 161, 165, 166, 207, 209, 212
Okhapkin, Oleg 29, 137, 168, 186, 189, 215, 217
Okudzhava, Bulat 9
Orlova, Raisa 3, 12, 13, 53, 177, 180, 189, 192–194, 197, 204, 206
Orthodoxy 126, 127, 136, 138, 139, 189, 211
Orwell, George 38, 41, 45, 48, 51, 87, 214
Ostanin, Boris 122, 125, 128–130, 142–144, 146, 148, 151, 160, 167, 181, 184, 196, 206–208, 212, 214, 215, 224
    Bonch, I. (pseudonym of Boris Ostanin) 160
    Vladimirov, O. (pseudonym of Boris Ostanin) 160
Osteuropa (journal) 19, 184
Ostrova (almanac) 164, 165, 219
Ostrovskaia, Sof'ia 114
Ottepel' (Thaw) 1, 32

Pamiat' (almanac) 73, 75, 79, 88, 90, 91, 117, 124, 133, 134, 180, 195, 197
Parisi, Valentina 8, 179, 182, 183, 210
Pasternak, Leonid 14, 28, 45, 95, 102
and *Doctor Zhivago* 14, 28, 45, 89, 101, 102, 111
Pavlovskii, Gleb 102
Pazukhin, Evgenii 125, 127, 163, 217
Perestroika 27, 35, 42, 70, 88, 135, 147, 154, 171, 175, 210
Pervukhina, Natalia 22, 45, 58, 185, 189, 193, 196
philosophical/ philosophy 10, 17, 31, 32, 35, 39, 42, 55, 97, 110, 112, 121, 126, 128, 132, 145–147
photocopying/photocopier 17, 34, 47, 48, 52, 57, 62, 63, 65, 68, 69, 82, 84, 86, 89, 95, 108, 109, 111, 137, 143, 190, 196

photograph/ photography 17, 19, 47, 60, 62, 82, 85, 106–108, 142, 143, 190, 207
Pimenov, Revolt 118, 143
Pinskii, L.E. 96
Platonov, Andrei 9, 17, 40, 47, 71, 76, 95
Poiski (journal), 117, 118, 208
Pomerants, Grigorii 48, 110, 218
Posev (journal and publishing house) 46, 50, 51, 79, 181, 212, 216
Prague Spring 32, 112
Predlog (journal) 146, 147
Prigov, Dmitrii Aleksandrovich 6, 31, 124
Pritykina, Tatiana 66, 70, 73, 77, 79–81, 88–90, 195, 224
Proffer, Carl and Ellendea 46, 190
Project for the Study of Samizdat and Dissidence at the University of Toronto 7, 8, 10, 13, 26, 122, 177, 178, 181, 182, 199, 204, 206, 209, 210, 224
pseudonyms 118, 119, 160
Public Foundation for Political Prisoners and their Families (Solzhenitsyn Foundation) 9, 163, 219, 196
Purishinskaia, Rita 90
Pushkin, Alexander 9, 58, 59, 218

Rabinovich, Alexander 105, 106
Radio Free Europe/Radio Liberty 6, 7, 52, 53, 55, 191, 192, 193
reading community 176, 222
Red Square, demonstration on 26 August 1968 9, 41, 111
Reguliarnye vedomosti (journal) 162
Rein, Evgenii 72
religion/religious 2, 6, 7, 10, 13, 15, 17, 31, 34, 35, 38, 39, 42, 50, 86, 97, 105, 110, 125, 126, 138, 139, 150, 180, 192, 207, 216
Religiozno-filosofskii seminar (Religious-Philosophical Seminar) 126, 128, 132, 138, 139, 143, 187, 205, 207, 211, 212, 216, 217, 219
Repin, Valerii 79, 96
Research Centre for East European Studies (Forschungsstelle Osteuropa) at the University of Bremen 7, 12, 97, 104,

141, 143, 178, 181, 182, 188, 189, 192, 193, 194, 206, 209, 212, 223
Reshetovskaia, Natalia 73
Rezak, Valerii 107, 108
Robbe-Grillet, Alain 146, 214, 218
Rogachevskii, Andrei 28, 29, 181, 186, 188, 190, 199
Roginskii, Arsenii 70, 75, 88, 195
Roginskii, Boris 168, 182, 205, 206, 216
ROKSI (journal) 60, 218
Roskina, Irina 49, 59, 111, 112, 191, 193, 202, 224
Rozhdestvenskii, Robert 5
Rozhniatovskii, Vsevolod 29, 186
Rubinshtein, Lev 31, 124, 206
Rubinshtin, Natalia 205
Rudkevich, Lev 125, 126, 140
Rusakova, Elena 17, 66, 70, 71, 77, 79, 80, 87–89, 153, 183, 194–196, 216, 224
Russian Literature Triquarterly (journal) 47
Russkaia mysl' (journal) 48, 164
Russkoe vozrozhdenie (journal) 117
Rykov, Alexander 107

Saigon, cafe 22, 124, 205, 206, 217
Sartre, Jean Paul 145
Savitskii, Stanislav 124, 134, 205, 211, 216, 219
Scheler, Max 141, 214
Schmidt, Henrike 20, 184
Sedakova, Olga 9, 179, 206
Severiukhin, Dmitrii 167, 181, 187, 188, 195, 197, 203–214, 219, 220
Severnaia pochta (samizdat journal) 131, 133, 134, 140, 143–145, 152, 160, 161, 163, 198, 206–214, 221
Shaklein, Vladimir 99
Shalamov, Varlam 14, 40, 83
Shestov, Lev 106
Shikhanovich, Yurii 102, 107, 112
Shimpozium 158, 218
Shvarts, Elena 6, 90, 158, 168, 189, 198, 206, 218, 219, 220
Sigei, Sergei 135, 138
Sigov, Sergei, see Sigei 135
Silver Age 5, 34–36, 57, 58, 61, 86, 96, 97, 134, 153, 154, 194, 195, 218

Siniavskii, Andrei 9, 25, 46, 53, 75, 86, 178, 180
Sintaksis (samizdat journal) 46, 124
Skrashchuk, Vladimir 29, 180
Smirnov, Alexei 181
Smirnov, Sergei 96
Soboleva, M 145
social media 19–21, 25, 26, 160
Sokolov, Sasha 46, 110
Solzhenitsyn, Alexander 4, 6, 14, 25, 28, 33, 36–38, 40, 50, 51, 53, 95, 99, 179, 190, 191, 195
  and *One Day in the Life of Ivan Denisovich* 6, 14
  and *The Gulag Archipelago* 6, 10, 14, 34, 38, 40, 44, 46, 47, 51–53, 57, 58, 72, 77, 85, 94, 95, 108, 110, 113, 179, 188–190, 193, 197
Solzhenitsyna, Natalia 90
Solzhenitsyn Foundation see Public Foundation for Political Prisoners and their Families
Sosnora, Viktor 88
Stalin, Joseph 1, 3, 5, 30, 32, 34, 65, 182, 187, 215, 218
Starshinina, Elizaveta 11, 180, 186
steb 157, 161, 217
Strana i mir (journal) 48, 191
Stratanovskii, Sergei 54, 74, 86, 122, 125, 126, 130–133, 137, 146–148, 151, 153, 156, 160–162, 166, 169, 193, 196, 197, 205, 206, 208, 209, 214, 216, 217–221, 224
  Golubev N. (pseudonym of Sergei Stratanovskii) 160, 161
Strugatsky brothers 14, 33, 37, 38, 69
Strukova, Elena 8, 13, 104, 178, 181, 183, 197, 201–203, 222
Struve, Gleb 189, 190
Struve, Nikita 46
Suitsidov, Igor see Groys, Boris
Summa (samizdat journal) 93, 115–120, 122, 135, 156, 177, 188, 189, 191, 203, 204, 220
Sveshnikov, Anton 88, 197, 203, 205

Taigin, Boris 79, 88, 197
Takhtadzhian, Suren 127

tamizdat 6, 8, 14, 16, 18, 19, 29–31, 37, 44, 45–52, 55, 57, 62, 85, 86, 94–96, 100, 104, 107, 108, 111, 112, 114, 116–119, 123, 165, 168, 178, 181, 183, 184, 186, 188–191, 199, 219
Tarshis, Anna see Nikonova Ry 135
Tel'nikov Vladimir 102
Ternovskii Leonard 102
theology 31, 126–128, 131, 146, 147, 211, 214
Tillich, Paul 146, 214
Tolstoy, Leo 67
  and *War and Peace* 58, 67
Topka (samizdat journal) 135
translation/translator 11, 17, 34, 38, 45, 46, 51, 58, 81, 97, 99, 121, 122, 126–129, 144–148, 159, 177, 189, 207, 213, 214, 220
Transponans (samizdat journal) 135, 137, 204, 210
Trauberg, Natalia 17, 180, 183
Tsurkov, Arkadii 77, 197
Tsurkova, Irina 16, 23, 66, 68, 69, 72, 77–79, 81, 82, 90, 143, 182, 185, 188, 195–197, 212, 224
Tsvetaeva, Marina 5, 6, 9, 35–38, 53, 57, 69, 97, 177
Turchinskii, Lev 35, 37, 51, 82–84, 96, 187, 191, 196, 199
typewriter 12, 14, 16, 18, 34, 45, 54, 59, 60, 65, 66, 68–70, 72, 73, 75, 76, 78–82, 88, 89, 96, 104, 108, 109, 141–143, 153, 196
typist 3, 11, 16, 17, 30, 58, 65–82, 85–90, 92, 95, 108, 111, 122, 136, 140–143, 153, 173, 196, 197

Uemov, A. 112
Uris, Leon 45

Veche (journal) 139, 150, 211
Vekhi (alamanac) 110

Vershik, Anatolii 43, 51, 116–119, 176, 188, 189, 191, 203, 204, 220, 222
Vestnik RkhD (journal) 48, 212
Vil'liams, Nikolai 90
Vladimirov, O. see Ostanin, Boris 160
Vladimov, Georgii 49, 190
Voice of America 6, 53, 54, 191
Voinovich, Vladimir 9, 47, 57
Volchek, Dmitrii 122, 135–137, 184, 210, 215, 218, 224
Volokhonskaia, Natalia 11, 66, 67–69, 71–73, 76, 78, 80, 81, 85, 86, 88, 142, 180, 195, 196–198, 212, 224
Voloshin, Maksimilian 35, 57, 72
Voronianskaia, Elizaveta 72
Voznesenskaia, Yuliia 91, 125, 135, 163
Voznesenskii, Andrei 5
Vremia i my (journal) 48
VSKhSON (Vserossiiskii sotsial-Khristianskii soiuz osvobozhdeniia naroda), 200
Vvedenskii, Alexander 50, 98, 191
Vysotsky, Vladimir 36, 37, 96, 187

Writers' Union (Union of Soviet Writers, Soiuz sovetskikh pisatelei) 15, 30, 125, 129, 130, 153, 162, 163

Yeats, William Butler 145
YMCA Press 46, 47, 94, 181, 186, 189, 190
Yurchak, Alexei 22, 157, 184, 217

Zastoi (Stagnation) 1
Zhenshchina i Rossiia (samizdat almanac) 91, 134
Zhivlov, Alexander 111
Zhmud', Leonid 9, 21, 76, 179, 184, 196, 197, 199, 221
Zinoviev, Alexander 95, 110, 190
Zuev, Yurii 112
Zvezda (journal) 159, 179, 203, 216, 219, 220

www.ingramcontent.com/pod-product-compliance
Lightning Source LLC
Chambersburg PA
CBHW072139290426
44111CB00012B/1921